AFRICATOWN

AFRICATOWN

AMERICA'S LAST SLAVE SHIP
AND THE COMMUNITY IT CREATED

NICK TABOR

ST. MARTIN'S PRESS
NEW YORK

For everyone who has lived in Plateau, Magazine Point, and the adjacent
neighborhoods—or has been involved with the churches and schools.
And for Fred Tabor, my grandfather.

First published in the United States by St. Martin's Press,
an imprint of St. Martin's Publishing Group

www.stmartins.com

Designed by Omar Chapa

Maps by Emily Langmade

Library of Congress Cataloging-in-Publication Data

Names: Tabor, Nick, author.
Title: Africatown : America's last slave ship and the community it created /
    Nick Tabor.
Description: First edition. | New York : St. Martin's Press, 2023. | Includes
    bibliographical references and index.
Identifiers: LCCN 2022035463 | ISBN 9781250766540 (hardcover) |
    ISBN 9781250766557 (ebook)
Subjects: LCSH: African Americans—Alabama—Mobile—History. |
    Africatown (Ala.)—History. | Clotilda (Ship) | West Africans—Alabama—
    History—19th century. | Slavery—Alabama—History—19th century. |
    Africatown (Ala.)—Social conditions—21st century.
Classification: LCC F334.M6 T22 2023 | DDC 305.896/07376122—
    dc23/eng/20220728
LC record available at https://lccn.loc.gov/2022035463

First Edition: 2023

10 9 8 7 6 5 4 3 2 1

CONTENTS

Prologue: "What Did You Do to Plateau?" 1

Part I: Coast to Coast: 1859–1865

1. The Lion of Lions 11
2. "They'll Hang Nobody" 21
3. Caravan 34
4. Barracoons 46
5. Arrival 57
6. Wartime 72

Part II: African Town: 1865–1935

7. To Have Land 87
8. White Supremacy, by Force and Fraud 108
9. Progressivism for White Men Only 125
10. Renaissance 144

Part III: Preservation and Demolition: 1950–2008

11. King Cotton, King Pulp 167
12. "Relocation Procedures" 181
13. A Threat to Business 195
14. Going Back to Church 213

Part IV: From the Brink: 2012–2022

15. One Mobile 229
16. Houston-East, Charleston-West 242
17. Reconstruction...255

    Acknowledgments 276
    A Note on Sources...280
    Abbreviations...286
    Books Cited in Text..288
    Notes 296
    Index..361

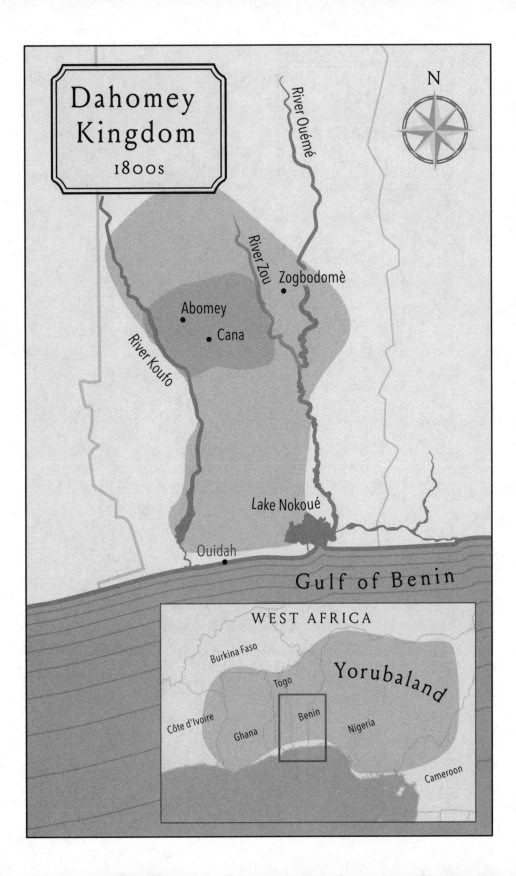

Dahomey Kingdom

1800s

N

River Ouémé

River Zou

Zogbodomè

Abomey

Cana

River Koufo

Lake Nokoué

Ouidah

Gulf of Benin

WEST AFRICA

Burkina Faso

Togo

Yorubaland

Côte d'Ivoire

Ghana

Benin

Nigeria

Cameroon

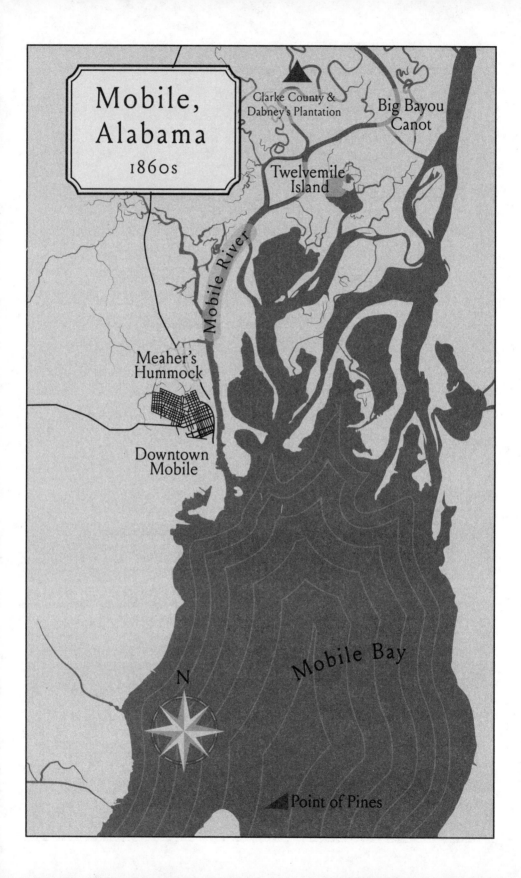

Mobile,
Alabama
1860s

Clarke County &
Dabney's Plantation

Big Bayou
Canot

Twelvemile
Island

Mobile River

Meaher's
Hummock

Downtown
Mobile

Mobile Bay

N

Point of Pines

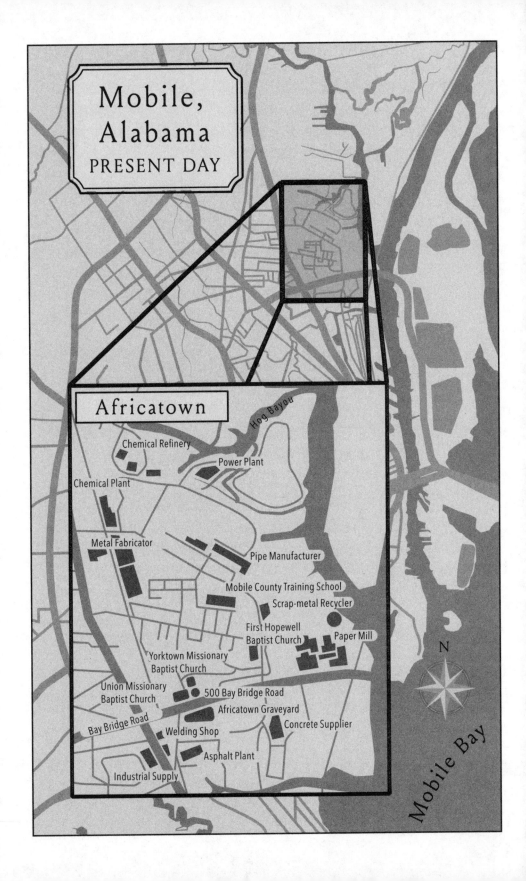

The demands of the slave on the present have everything to do with making good the promise of abolition, and this entails much more than the end of property in slaves. It requires the reconstruction of society, which is the only way to honor our debt to the dead. This is the intimacy of our age with theirs—an unfinished struggle. To what end does one conjure the ghosts of slavery, if not to incite the hopes of transforming the present?

—SAIDIYA HARTMAN, *Lose Your Mother:*
A Journey Along the Atlantic Slave Route

PROLOGUE

"What Did You Do to Plateau?"

Joe Womack was waiting for his turn to speak. He was on a stage in Washington, D.C., in the National Geographic Society's auditorium, facing a crowd of several hundred. He'd flown in the previous night from his home on the Alabama Gulf Coast. The panelists sitting beside him had vaunted pedigrees: one was a famed archaeologist who had spearheaded excavations all over the world; another was a scholar of the African diaspora with a position at Brown University. Womack, for his part, had spent his career as an accountant and truck driver. But in his retirement, he'd found another calling.

They were there to discuss the *Clotilda,* the last slave ship ever brought from West African to American shores. A year earlier, archaeologists had announced that after an exhaustive survey, they had identified the wreckage of the *Clotilda* in the Mobile Delta. The story of the ship's voyage is not widely known and has rarely appeared in history books, but Womack had known about it as long as he could remember. The neighborhood where he grew up, outside the city of Mobile, was settled by the slave ship's survivors.

That story—as it was narrated onstage that night, more or less—goes like this. In the late 1850s, throughout the Deep South, demand for enslaved workers was incredibly high. The federal government had long since made it illegal to import slaves from West Africa. But Timothy Meaher, a business magnate and riverboat captain who lived outside of Mobile, hatched a plan to bring a slave ship in nevertheless. His cargo arrived in 1860, nine months before the Civil War began. The victims were 110 men, women, and children who were brought on the Middle Passage.

Five years later, after the Civil War ended, these West Africans were freed, but they had no way of getting back home. They were marooned in a foreign land. Several dozen of them, making the best of their situation, saved their wages and bought land in a remote region outside of Mobile, where they established a little community of their own. They married among themselves, appointed leaders, and lived according to their own customs. Their settlement came to be known as African Town. Over time, hundreds of American-born Black people moved there, and the shipmates' descendants mixed with the newcomers. All these decades later, the neighborhood still survives, now within Mobile's city limits; and many of the residents can trace their lineage back to the slave ship. The name has been shortened to Africatown.

Womack is not a descendant, at least as far as he knows; but he was born only fifteen years after the last shipmate in Mobile County passed away, and he grew up hearing stories about the West Africans. Traces of their presence were still evident when he was a child. The church the shipmates had built and the cemetery where some of them were buried were each a short walk from his home. Throughout his life, there had also been rumors that the *Clotilda*'s wreckage was still in the Mobile River and could be seen at low tide.

In 2018, archaeologists pinpointed a section of the Mobile Delta that served long ago as a "ship graveyard," where captains had once hauled old vessels and abandoned them. Ultimately, the crew singled out one wreck that matched the *Clotilda*'s dimensions precisely. In 2019, after months' worth of research and peer review, the crew's leader, James Delgado, announced that the slave ship had been identified "beyond reasonable doubt."

The event that evening in early 2020 was billed "Finding the *Clotilda*: America's Final Slave Ship," but Womack and Joycelyn Davis, his travel companion and frequent collaborator, were there to speak about the Africatown community as it still existed. Davis, a teaching assistant in her forties, was asked to speak first. She was a sixth-generation descendant of Oluale, or Charlie Lewis, one of the *Clotilda*'s survivors. Since the identification of the ship, Davis had been helping to run an association for fellow descendants.

"Growing up in Africatown," she said, "I feel like my family—my grandma, my great-grandma—carried on the traditions of Charlie Lewis." She spoke about Lewis Quarters, the section where her ancestor had bought land and built a house in 1870. It was still inhabited by her family, and growing up, Davis had spent her Saturdays there, with an older relative teaching her the family history. When the *Clotilda* news had been announced, Davis said, she had imagined how it must have felt to be stuck in the ship's hold for six weeks. It gave her chills. "Finding the ship has been a great thing," she said, "but it's about the *people*, to me." She hoped the news about the ship would lead to better conditions for the families that remained in the neighborhood.

In the present day, Africatown is no longer bordered directly by rivers and lush forests. Instead, it's hedged in by a chemical plant, a pipe manufacturing plant, a power plant, a tissue mill, a refinery, and a scrap-metal shop, among other industrial businesses. A rock quarry backs up against one section of the neighborhood; and the only way to get in or out of Lewis Quarters is to drive through a lumber mill. Pollution is rampant. Moreover, the business district that Davis and Womack knew as children, which was once lined with the shops of local Black entrepreneurs, has since been replaced with a five-lane highway, designed for trucks carrying hazardous cargo. It is impossible to buy even a bottle of water without leaving the area.

The moderator turned her attention to Womack. She asked him to speak about "some of the concerns and some of the work" happening in Africatown.

"My involvement with the community consists of three things—" he said, "protect, preserve, and prolong." He wore a scarf with an orange and green ankara pattern and a tan sport coat. Behind him, a detailed digital replica of the *Clotilda* was shown on a giant screen. The protection part of his work, he said, was about fending off new incursions by heavy industry. He explained that when he was a child, there had been two enormous paper mills, International Paper and Scott Paper, bookending the residential zone. It was not uncommon in those years for ash to blow from one factory or the other. "Those of you who are over the age of fifty probably remember the old sixteen-ounce Coca-Cola drink," he said. "Ash falls in your drink, and you try to turn it up and turn it out." He made a tilting gesture. "The ashes went this way, and you'd lose all your soda. So how do you get rid of it? You know, you're twelve years old, you got a drink that cost you all of your money, six cents. How do you get rid of that ash? You shake it up. It foams, and you look at it, ain't there, so you drink it." He made a drinking motion. "Most of my friends that were born after 1945 are not living today."

There were gasps throughout the auditorium.

"People talk about statues, about the historic statues," he went on. It seemed to him that while African Americans didn't have many statues honoring their contributions to history, they did have historical sites that were still intact—and Africatown was one of these. "The cemetery, the people, the community—these are the monuments that we have to save," he said, "not only for the sake of the community, but for the sake of the world."

Womack brought up the National Memorial for Peace and Justice, which had opened in Montgomery in 2018. It commemorates the victims of lynching in America. The presentation is stark and unsettling; but within a year of its opening, the memorial had attracted some 400,000 visitors from around the world and had brought nearly $1 billion in economic activity to Montgomery. Womack said its success gave him hope; he and Davis and their allies saw it as a model of what Africatown could become. But there was one major obstacle, he concluded. "Unfortunately, the same people who brought us over are still in charge."

This book began with a phone conversation in 2018. A magazine editor had asked me to track down the descendants of Cudjo Lewis, the most famous survivor of the *Clotilda*'s voyage. His relatives had never made their identities known. After two weeks of reporting, I got in touch with Garry Lumbers, a great-great-grandson who lived near Philadelphia. I was in a hotel room in West Texas, on a separate assignment, when we first spoke by phone. Before I could say much, Lumbers told me forcefully that I shouldn't be writing about the descendants—I ought to concentrate on Plateau, his hometown (which is part of Africatown). He wanted me to write about how it had become so blighted. "What did you do to Plateau?" was how he put it.

When Lumbers was a kid, growing up in the 1960s, he told me, the neighborhood was thriving. Most every block was crammed with houses, and it was normal for a household to have six or seven children. Plateau and its counterpart, Magazine Point, were effectively a town unto themselves (partly on account of segregation). There were grocery stores, gas stations, bars and restaurants, a hotel, and a movie theater. Beyond the neighborhood's bounds, there were forests and rivers, where children could wander unsupervised. But in the present day, Lumbers said, the residential area was dilapidated, on its way toward becoming a ghost town. The population had plummeted, and heavy industry now surrounded the perimeter. I could hear the outrage in his voice. But there was also an earnest question there: he wanted to know what had happened, how it had gotten to be that way.

I visited Africatown later that week. There I met Joe Womack, who gave me a neighborhood tour. Lumbers's words resonated as we drove around in Womack's truck. There were dozens of abandoned houses, with Spanish moss dangling from their gutters and vines winding across their window-panes, as though it were all reverting to forest. And the industrial presence was overwhelming. Everywhere we went, it seemed we were passing through a haze of dust or smoke. I also interviewed a number of residents who believed Africatown was plagued by a cancer epidemic. Each person could rattle off a list of family members who had died from the disease.

Womack's manner, however, was upbeat. He spoke about victories that residents and allies had won in recent years, which included fending off a truck depot and a series of petroleum tanks. He also spoke about concrete plans for the future, including a blueway, which promised to make Africatown's waterways accessible for kayaking, canoeing, and swimming.

I wrote an article based on my visit, but over the following year, Lumbers's question kept resurfacing in my mind. This wasn't like the story of Detroit or Gary or any other Rust Belt town, where factories had closed, eliminating local jobs, and residents had been forced to leave en masse to find work. There was an element of that, but on the whole, instead of deindustrialization, this was a story about hyper-industrialization. And of all the neighborhoods to hand over to factories, to choose this one seemed criminal. No other place in the United States has a story comparable to Africatown's; it was the only community founded by West Africans in the aftermath of the Civil War. So how had this happened? Who was responsible, and what drove the decisions? Equally important, how was it allowed? From both a humanitarian perspective and a preservationist one, Africatown should have been protected. Why hadn't the federal government or a powerful national organization stepped in?

Of course, these questions had ramifications beyond Alabama. The situation in Africatown was a crystalline example of environmental racism, a phenomenon that is widespread in the United States. It's the process where communities of color end up bearing the brunt of an area's pollution, while people who live outside those neighborhoods reap most of the benefits. A glaring example is "Cancer Alley," the corridor of petrochemical plants between New Orleans and Baton Rouge; but there are many other examples, from the chemical plants and refineries in Houston's Harrisburg/Manchester neighborhood, to the contaminated water in Flint, to "Asthma Alley" in the South Bronx. Environmental racism helps explain why African Americans suffer from higher rates of mortality and certain diseases, and were at statistically higher risk during the COVID-19 pandemic.

The question of what happened to Africatown is the question of what drives environmental racism. Unlike Timothy Meaher's actions in 1860, which led to the shipmates being stranded in America, and unlike the white terrorism that spread across the South in the decades after the Civil War (which included three lynchings in Africatown), and unlike George Wallace, upon his inauguration as Alabama governor in 1963, calling for "segregation now, segregation tomorrow, and segregation forever," the industrialization of Africatown was not driven primarily by bigotry. Instead it was a by-product of moneymaking ventures. The residents were at best an afterthought. And yet it was clearly no coincidence that the factories were concentrated where they were. There was a historical through line running from the *Clotilda* to the pollution. So in 2019, in order to trace it, I left New York and moved to Mobile.

To answer Lumbers's question, we must start at the beginning, in nineteenth-century West Africa. Certain forms of slavery had been practiced in African societies for centuries, but it was only the introduction of capitalism, through European traders, that turned it into a profit-making activity of massive scale. It's necessary also to look at antebellum Mobile, where the demand for enslaved workers was acute enough that businessmen like Meaher's associates were becoming desperate. The line has to be followed through the foundation of "African Town" in the Reconstruction era, and through the federal government's failure to provide the shipmates and every other freedperson with forty acres and a mule, or any other means of financial independence.

Narrating the history of these early years is a fraught endeavor. Many of the events were not recorded until decades after the fact, when the story had become part of local mythology. As a result, there are limits to how much the facts can be separated from the folklore. Nevertheless, this book represents a sustained attempt to do that—in part by relying, as much as possible, on documentary sources and firsthand accounts. At the same time, the book also aims to show how the mythology has developed, under changing historical conditions, and has served different interests at different times. As a friend in Mobile told me during the course of my research, "You don't get the history here, so much as the self-fashioning of an identity." He wasn't talking about the *Clotilda* in particular, but it's a case in point. Mobile loves its stories.

The most famous chronicler of the early history is Zora Neale Hurston, the Black writer best known for her 1937 novel *Their Eyes Were Watching God*. In the late 1920s, while she was still an undergraduate student, Hurston visited African Town and spent weeks interviewing Cudjo Lewis. She later wrote a book based on these interviews, called *Barracoon*, which was published posthumously in 2018. I have drawn on it as a major source. As with the other early accounts, there are reasons to doubt Hurston's reliability in some areas; but where these come up, I've flagged them for the reader, and I discuss them at greater length in my Note on Sources. Moreover, Hurston is one of only two writers who recorded Cudjo's memories at length, and of those two, the only one who was African American. Her book is generally free of the Jim Crow mores that dominate the other early accounts. All the quotations from Cudjo in my own book are from *Barracoon*. (Also, wherever white journalists from this period purported to quote the shipmates, I've tended to paraphrase them instead, for fear of amplifying racist tropes.)

Although the last surviving shipmate died in 1940, the neighborhood's story continues on after that. The through line leading to its degradation has to be traced through the 1950s and '60s, the period when Womack was growing up, and when Africatown was annexed into the Mobile city limits. The line runs into the twenty-first century, when Womack became an unlikely fighter for environmental justice. It leads through the identification of the *Clotilda*'s wreckage, up to the present day: a time when the Meaher family, the wealthy descendants of the slave importer, still own a large chunk of Africatown's residential property, as well as much of the surrounding land where the factories are sited.

A similar line runs through every Black neighborhood in Mobile County, and through countless cities across the South. Where the line in Africatown leads from here, however, is impossible to say. The project of reversing the neighborhood's decline, by making it a heritage tourism site, seems viable, especially now that the *Clotilda*'s remains have been identified. Alex Haley, the author of *Roots*, remarked in 1977 that African Americans needed a "Pilgrim's Rock." From a historic point of view, it's hard to imagine a better candidate than Africatown. The neighborhood is not the first place in the United States where enslaved Africans were brought, but it was certainly the last; and the society the shipmates established remains a stark symbol of self-determination. Whether or not it ever achieves this status, it has potential to draw enormous crowds, which could lead to neighborhood jobs, new and restored housing, environmental protections, and local businesses. But for all this to happen, there are still powerful forces that Womack, Davis, and their many allies will have to overcome.

PART I

COAST TO COAST: 1859–1865

1
THE LION OF LIONS

Enslavement was something that happened to other people. It was a punishment for convicted criminals and a fate of war captives. It wasn't a normal condition for people born in Kossola's town, especially not those from affluent families, families connected to the king.

Kossola's grandfather sometimes spoke about the "Portugee," the pale-skinned men who did business on the coast, far away, and were said to traffic in human beings. Once the child of an enslaved person was making too much noise while his grandfather was trying to sleep, so a guard brought him to the old man. "Where is dat Portugee man?" Kossola recalled him saying. He threatened to sell the boy for tobacco. "In de olden days, I walk on yo' skin!" he said, meaning he would have made shoes from the little boy's hide. He said he would have drunk water from the boy's skull.

There were some West Africans who regarded Europeans as mythical creatures. Mahommah Baquaqua, who was born in the same general area a decade or two before Kossola, reported that people in his hometown imagined white men living in the ocean and cooking their food by the sun, which (they believed) sank deep into the water every night. More common was the rumor that white men were cannibals, and that when they bought captives from the traders on the coast, it was to eat them. By all accounts, most West African adults knew better. They had been trading with Europeans for centuries by this point, albeit with middlemen, and European goods, such as umbrellas and carpets, had become common in many of the region's markets. But parents often let the rumors flourish among their children, in hopes of deterring them from wandering too far without supervision. Kidnappings by slave hunters were not, after all, unheard of.

At roughly age seventeen, Kossola was too old to be spooked by children's stories and too young to have kids of his own. He was preoccupied with girls. His favorite pastime was visiting the market and seeing the beautiful young women walk by, with their arms covered from hand to elbow in gold bracelets. "Oh, dey look very fine to Cudjo," he recalled some seventy years later, using a name he'd taken on later in life. Even as an elderly man, he could remember the sound of their bracelets clinking as they slung their arms.

The limited information that survives about Kossola's early biography comes from interviews he gave as an old man, when he was a widower living in the United States. He related anecdotes that show the texture of his day-to-day life in West Africa and the kind of future he anticipated. One of these stories occurred in this market. The setting is easy enough to picture. It would have been in the center of town, facing the house where the king lived with his many wives and servants. Palm trees probably surrounded the square, giving shade to the vendors who sat or stood along the periphery; and there would have been rows of earthen pots, of all shapes and sizes, filled with yam flour, corn flour, bananas, beans, plums, palm wine, and kola nuts. If the town was rural, the market would have been at its busiest in the afternoons, when women streamed in from the narrow, crooked streets, some carrying children. They wore flowing robes, or wide cloths wrapped around their torsos, with their hair done up in elaborate designs. The volume in the market would escalate as they haggled, shouting to be heard over the din and the vendors.

On this day a young woman brushed past Kossola. He didn't recognize her, but he was arrested by her beauty. Perhaps the noises of the market— the rumble of the wagons, the clattering of cowries in the vendors' hands— seemed to go silent for a moment. Perhaps the background behind her blurred. Kossola didn't say anything to the woman; in his culture, it would have been unthinkable. But he couldn't help but trail her for a few moments, hoping to catch another glimpse. Soon she was gone.

This episode might have been forgettable, except that an elderly man, who wielded some influence in the town, witnessed the whole scene. Later he approached the teenager's father. Kossola was reaching adulthood, the elderly man said, and it was time for his initiation ceremony. His father ought to fetch some goats or a cow so they could put on a banquet. Kossola's father agreed.

There is some mystery as to where Kossola grew up. On two occasions, when he was elderly, he drew maps of his home for interviewers, but the markings are too vague to yield answers. The historian Sylviane Diouf, in her 2007 book *Dreams of Africa in Alabama: The Slave Ship* Clotilda *and the Story of the Last Africans Brought to America,* has found ample evidence that he came from Bantè, now a city of around 100,000 people in western Benin, between Togo and Nigeria. Diouf took into account the dialect Kossola and others from his hometown spoke, as well as the information he gave about the geography, economy, architecture, defense systems, and culture. However, Kossola said in 1906 that he came from a place the interviewer wrote down as "Whinney," and this has led another historian, Natalie Robertson, to conclude that he came from Owinni, a town two hundred miles east of Bantè in what is now Nigeria. When Robertson visited in 2004, a local scholar told her the name Kossola sounded like the regional surname Esuola, which has long since fallen out of use.

Either way, it's clear that he hailed from the broader area called Yoruba-land, a network of autonomous kingdoms that spanned fifty-five thousand square miles in present-day Nigeria, Benin, and Togo. The people were united by a common language, a common pantheon of gods and spirits, and a common currency of cowries, which facilitated a massive volume of trade.

Kossola was the second of six children born to his mother, Fondlolu; and she was the second of his father Oluale's three wives. Kossola had twelve more siblings in his extended family. Together they lived in a compound, with his father's dwelling in the center and the other quarters forming a circle around it, each wife occupying a section with her own children. It was likely a modest place: mud walls, low ceilings of mud, and a roof thatched with long blades of grass. Furniture would have been minimal; Yoruba families typically slept on mats and ate their meals sitting on the floor. Kossola remembered later how he and the other kids kept one another entertained: they wrestled, had footraces, climbed palm trees to fetch coconuts, and scoured the woods for bananas and pineapples.

As a rule, people in the town were not overly possessive about land. A Yoruba mantra said "all land belongs to the king," but this was another way of saying it belonged to everyone; the king held it only in trust. Plots that weren't being actively used were treated as communal property. Besides the

tropical fruit that grew freely, the townspeople also raised sheep and hogs
and planted corn, beans, and yams.

The town's main industry was producing palm oil, a labor-intensive process
that typically fell on the shoulders of women. The palm nuts—orange-colored
balls about the size of walnuts, each one full of oil—had to be soaked, stomped
on, and boiled until the oil could be skimmed off. The oil was sent to port cities, where Europeans bought it by the shipload. Across the ocean, it was used
for making soap and candles and railway grease. Yoruba towns also had many
skilled workers, including blacksmiths, coppersmiths, herbalists, and diviners,
all of whom learned their trades as apprentices. The greatest prestige belonged
to musicians and visual artists. A renowned sculptor could spend a lifetime
traveling from city to city, under the patronage of kings, carving elaborate
decorations for palaces and shrines.

On a ceremonial level, the monarchy was an incredibly lofty position.
A Yoruba king was regarded as a god, and couldn't visit private homes and
generally could not be seen in the streets. No one was allowed to call him
by his personal name or to see him eating or drinking. In practice, though,
Yoruba kingdoms were quite democratic. Every king was chosen by a council.
Free speech was broadly protected, and there were certain festival days when
the people paraded through the streets and voiced criticisms of their leaders.
The economy, too, was fairly democratic, with the role of banking filled by
member-owned co-ops.

Criminal defendants in Kossola's town were entitled to due process. Kossola would later recount a time when someone was tried for killing another
man with a spear. The king sat in the town square, surrounded by chiefs
from other towns nearby. He told the killer to explain himself. The defendant claimed the victim had put a curse on him, causing his children to die
and his cows to get sick. In that case, the king asked, why didn't he appeal
to the leaders of his village? "Doan you know we got law for people dat work
juju?" After the chiefs took their turns interrogating, the king announced a
guilty verdict. The man's punishment was to be tied facedown to the victim's
corpse, with their lips touching, and left that way in the town square until
the defendant died, either of thirst or starvation.

Kossola's grandfather loomed large, both in the town's affairs and in
Kossola's life. He traveled all over as a bodyguard for the king, and he was re-
warded, Kossola said, with abundant land, and with cows, goats, and sheep.
His status conferred some small measure of royalty on his grandson as well.
The older man lived separately, with numerous younger wives to care for him

as he aged. The custom was that whenever a man married a new wife, his neighbors would help him stomp the soil down and build a new house for his compound. The bridegroom would slaughter a cow and get wine for a feast. After all the additions, Kossola's grandfather's compound had grown to the point where it was sprawling.

The old man fell ill when Kossola was a little boy, and his father took him to the big compound for one last visit. After he died, the coffin was kept in the house, with the lid open so friends could lay gifts beside him. He was buried beneath the clay floor of his home. The reasoning, Kossola later explained, was that if a man's family lived with him while he was alive, they ought to be able to live with him after he died. He remembered his father crying, saying the ground "eats up de best of everything." The wives threw off their veils and sobbed.

Kossola's training as a warrior started in his early teens. He was thrilled on the day when the chief called for every young man who had lived through fourteen rainy seasons to present themselves for enlistment. He thought it meant he would learn to fight like his older brothers. As it turned out, the training regimen began with hunting instead. Kossola began to go on excursions with the town elders and the other teenage boys, sometimes lasting a single day, sometimes two or three, where the older men showed him how to track animals and stalk them silently, how to mark a path so he could find his way back, how to set up camp. They taught him how to shoot a bow and how to aim a spear. He graduated to combat training, and by his late teens, he had the stamina to run all day in the woods without getting exhausted. But the training was not, he later insisted, for the purpose of making war. The king simply wanted a powerful security force, to deter any would-be attackers.

Defense, in Kossola's town, like most other facets of life there, was imbued with religious meaning. The Yoruba God with a capital G—the transcendent one, the almighty—is known as Olorun. All the lesser gods, the Orishas, are subservient to Olorun. But Olorun is not worshiped by mortals, at least not directly. Instead the people devote themselves to lesser deities, each of whom have specific associations, such as Yemoja, the goddess of brooks and streams; Shango, the god of thunder and lightning; and Ogun, the patron of hunters and blacksmiths. Their shrines were everywhere: at the gates, all around the king's compound, and in the market.

In his town, the society of men who advised the chief and took responsibility for the general security was oriented around a deity named Oro, whose name meant something like "fierceness" or "tempest" or "provocation." On days set aside in his honor, Oro would be represented by someone dressed in a long robe with shells dangling off, wearing a wooden mask, painted white, with the mouth smeared with blood. Oro was understood to haunt the forests around urban centers. In towns throughout Yorubaland, acts of grotesque violence were attributed to him. If a convicted criminal was offered up in Oro's honor, for instance, the person's corpse might be found days later, on the edge of town, with the head removed. Or else the only trace might be the person's clothing, left tangled up in the branches of a high tree. The people would say that Oro must have devoured the body and dropped the clothes as he flew through the air.

After the day when Kossola encountered the girl in the market, he was inducted into Oro society, thanks to the elderly man's intervention with his father. All the women had to go inside and shut their doors; it was said that if a woman heard Oro's voice, she would die. Kossola was led into a house where he waited with some older men for the ritual to start. Soon he heard a roaring noise, like the voice of a lion. They urged him to go see where it came from. As soon as he opened the door, the roaring ceased. When it started again, it seemed to be coming from the woods nearby. He walked toward the tree line, perhaps beginning to shake from nerves. Suddenly the roaring started behind him. He spun. Now it seemed to be coming from all sides, intermittently—but there was no lion, no leopard or tiger or bull, anywhere in sight. Then older men started to emerge from their hiding places in the bushes, laughing.

They led him to the place where the banquet had been prepared, and there they explained how the sound was made. They also took turns pinching his ear, as a reminder never to divulge the Oro secrets. However, many years later, he did reveal one piece of information, which can be confirmed by other sources: the noise came from a bullroarer, a thin strip of wood about a foot long and two or three inches across, tied to a long string. They would have shown him how to swing it in a wide circle, making the wind buzz as it rushed through.

Before the banquet was over, they gave him a peacock feather to wear and made sure he understood his new status. He was still a rung below them, not quite a man yet. "All men are still fathers to you," they told him.

Had the men in Kossola's town known what was happening in Dahomey, the kingdom that bordered Yorubaland to the south and east, they would have prepared differently.

The king, Glèlè, knew he was presiding over a state in crisis. Since its creation in the 1600s, Dahomey had posed a standing threat to its neighbors. It originally survived by sacking cities outside its borders, capturing the residents, and selling them to West Africans who lived closer to the coast, who in turn sold them to Europeans. Over time, Dahomey's military had become more organized and efficient than any other in the region. A British visitor dubbed it a "small black Sparta." Throughout the 1700s, it conquered a great deal of territory, including the port city of Ouidah, which allowed the kingdom to eliminate the middleman and sell captives to the Europeans directly. By one 1851 estimate, the kingdom spanned roughly thirty-six thousand miles, making it roughly the size of Indiana.

It's true that slavery had been practiced in West Africa for centuries before the European traders came. But it's also important to understand the changes the Europeans brought on. Prior to their arrival, seizing captives in war had been less of a profit-making activity; instead, war captives were often incorporated into the society of the victors. Over time, as Europeans came to the African coast and sold the people goods on a system of credit, they wanted to be paid back in slaves (rather than gold, cloths, or other goods). So enslaved people came to be treated as a form of currency—and not only one form among many, but the basis on which other currencies were valued, as the British historian Toby Green has shown in his book *A Fistful of Shells*. As international trade increased, so, too, did the demand for more slaves.

Warmaking, in turn, became an effective means of generating money and securing a range of imports. It also became the basis of Dahomey's rise. The cycle went like this: Dahomey accrued wealth by selling war captives, and it used that wealth to further build up its military and its state apparatus, which allowed it to seize more captives. Warfare was also central to Dahomey's self-identity. "All my subjects are bread [bred] to it," a Dahomean king declared in 1726. The military was the pride of the land. Young people were drafted for training at least as early as age thirteen or fourteen. Most fearsome were the women warriors, known as "Amazons" to generations of European visitors, who were chosen from the villages and from the pool of war captives. The kingdom's calendar year and its traditional songs and dances were inseparable from its military. There was a heavy degree of violence in the religious rituals as well. The kingdom routinely made human sacrifices, sometimes in tribute to deceased kings, other times so the sacrificial victims could deliver messages to them. Dahomean kings collected the skulls of their enemies, especially of enemy kings, and the act of beheading was constantly reenacted in palace rituals.

However, in the mid-nineteenth century, the problem, from Glèlè's perspective, was that the European demand for enslaved people had been on a downward spiral. Increasingly, the white men wanted to buy palm oil instead. Most every country had banned the importing of slaves (though the policy was not enforced in Cuba, which was controlled by Spain, or in Brazil), and the British government had been pressuring Dahomey to stop selling humans altogether. In theory, the transition should have been simple. The forests of Dahomey were an ideal climate for palm trees, and there was no shortage of labor to harvest the oil. But it didn't work out that way in practice. Palm oil wasn't necessarily as lucrative as the slave trade had been in the past. And if the economy was to go agricultural, Glèlè knew, it would be a threat to his authority. Under the slave-trading system, the military—and by extension, the monarchy—was responsible for generating most of the country's revenue. No one else had the necessary firepower. By contrast, any independent farmer could harvest palm oil.

Glèlè had seen what happened when his father, King Ghezo, tried to change the country's ways. Ghezo's kingship lasted for forty years, from 1818 to 1858, and by most measures his reign was successful. Among his celebrated achievements was a massive expansion of the corps of women warriors. But in 1852, Ghezo had given in to pressure from Britain and agreed to suspend the slave trade. He took measures to diversify the economy, declaring the palm a sacred tree that couldn't be cut down, and making an agricultural tax payable in palm oil. There is also some evidence, albeit contested, that Ghezo drastically reduced the volume of human sacrifices in Dahomey, from hundreds each year down to thirty or forty.

By some historical accounts, these reforms were too much too soon. Ghezo faced a backlash from the priests and military leaders. Glèlè, who was known as Badahun at the time, apparently sided with the opposition, and it seems that over the next several years, the conservative faction helped him edge his father out of power. In 1858, Ghezo died. The official story was that he was felled by a battle wound, though there were reports that he'd been poisoned by traitors in his court. In public, Glèlè mourned his father and praised his memory. In private, it seems, he was careful not to repeat the older man's mistakes. He deliberately cultivated an image as a warrior-king. According to one source, the name Glèlè itself, which he chose upon taking the throne, means "ferocious lion of the forest" or "terror in the bush." (Another source says it comes from the aphorism *Glelile ma hnn ze,* or "You cannot take away a farm [*gle*]"—meaning he wouldn't let anyone take the fruits of his labors.)

Accounts from Europeans who met Glèlè in the 1860s and '70s confirm that he was a calculating leader. On a personal level, he could be charming. He was tall, athletic, and broad-shouldered, with a fairly light complexion and smallpox scars on his cheeks. When he smiled, baring straight teeth that had been tanned by tobacco, he could seem generous and carefree. He dressed with an understated elegance; in one encounter with Sir Richard Burton, the famous and widely traveled British diplomat and writer, who spent time in Dahomey in 1863, Glèlè wore a plain white tunic, laced with green silk, and richly embroidered sandals. J. Alfred Skertchly, a British entomologist who went to Dahomey in 1871, thought Glèlè had a "truly kingly dignity." His only fancy accoutrement was a long-stemmed pipe with a silver bowl.

His guests also found he had no personal taste for violence. "I have seen him turn from the execution scene with a shudder," Skertchly wrote, "and in every case the victim's passage to the other world is as speedy as that by hanging or other orthodox mode of punishment." And Burton wrote that it was "no mere lust of blood nor delight in torture and death" that spurred Dahomey's human sacrifices. To hear Glèlè tell it, as Burton said he did, via an interpreter, the king had little choice. If he tried to cease the military campaigns or the human sacrifices, Glèlè said, it would provoke an immediate rebellion. Burton concluded he was right. The people "would deem it impious were he to curtail or omit the performance," he wrote, "and suddenly to suppress it would be as if a European monarch were forcibly to abolish prayers for the dead."

Especially in his earliest years, Glèlè attacked Dahomey's enemies with gusto. In 1859, for the ceremony following his father's death, the *West African Herald* reported that Glèlè planned to sacrifice more than two thousand people, and that in preparation, he had ordered the digging of an immense pit, "which is to contain human blood enough to float a canoe." Even if the story was sensational, and if the numbers were wildly exaggerated (which they were), Glèlè would likely not have minded.

Predawn raids were Dahomey's hallmark. The tactic was said to date back to the 1600s, and by Glèlè's time, the military had perfected it. Often it sent spies in advance, disguised as itinerant traders, to assess the defense systems and sometimes to spread false information about Dahomey. The campaigns themselves usually happened between November and January, when the rains let up and the roads were easiest to travel. The troops moved in great secrecy: advancing mostly at night, avoiding major arteries, sometimes hacking their way through the bush. As they approached a target, a few soldiers would go out ahead, dressed as traders, and seize anyone they found outside the gates, lest they warn the sleeping inhabitants. The rest of the army would wait in silence, communicating only by gestures and finger snaps. Even smoking was forbidden. Before the sun came up, they'd rush inside, uttering what Burton called "hellish cries."

One day in Kossola's town, likely in 1859 or early 1860, three strangers came into the market, wanting to speak with the king. According to the account Kossola later gave, they asked if he knew about the king of Dahomey.

The Yoruba king said he'd heard of him.

In that case, they said, he must realize Glèlè was known as *Kini, kini, kini,* the lion of lions. Glèlè had a message for the Yoruba king: He was demanding half the town's crops as tribute. If the king didn't send them, Dahomey would make war.

According to Kossola, the king was incensed. He told them to go back and ask if Glèlè had ever heard of *him.* He was known as the Mouth of the Leopard, he said. He wanted the men to tell Glèlè that the crops weren't his—they belonged to the people. Glèlè had plenty of land, and the king thought he should cultivate his own crops instead of making war on other peoples.

So the envoys went back home to tell the Lion he'd been insulted.

2

"THEY'LL HANG NOBODY"

The steamer's torchlights were gleaming off the Alabama River, but the captain had sailed this route so many times, he would have been able to picture the surroundings even in pitch-darkness. The trip between his home outside of Mobile and the docks in Montgomery, where he delivered passengers and freight every week, was around 300 miles, and he knew every bend and canebrake. Given his immense workforce back home, more than a hundred strong, and given the abundance of capable maritime pilots around the city, he could have easily sent someone else in his stead. But he preferred being on the river.

Life on these waterways had treated him well. The ship swaying beneath his feet, the *Roger B. Taney*, was the sixth one built at his own shipyard. The Mobile *Weekly Advertiser*, in announcing the *Taney*'s construction two years earlier, had identified him as "the indomitable Timothy Meaher." For this man who had moved to the Gulf Coast in his youth, a world away from his family in Maine, and steadily carved out a small business empire, the description was undeniably accurate.

At the time when Meaher came down, circa 1835, the Deep South was America's frontier. Alabama had only gained its statehood in 1819, and in the 1830s, vast swaths of it remained undeveloped, some of them still belonging to Native Americans. Young northerners were pouring down for the usual reasons, namely promises of money and adventure. James Meaher (who went by Jim), Tim's older brother by two years, came along but didn't stick it out. He returned to New England and went into the grocery business. But Tim Meaher stayed. He found work on the river, as glamorous a profession back then as any young man could want. At first he was only a deckhand on a single-engine vessel. He worked his way up, moving from one ship to another so he could ascend in rank, and saving his money to go into business for himself.

By this late date, some twenty-four years in, he had amassed an enormous lumberyard and a shingle factory, besides the plantation and the shipyard. It was all on a rugged piece of property north of Mobile, separated by Threemile Creek. The place was known around town as Meaher's Hummock, a now-antiquated way of saying it was on elevated land. The property had also become a family outpost. Jim had moved back down in 1850 and become Tim's business partner, overseeing their finances while Tim ran the ships. Their younger brother, Burns, captained one of their steamboats, and their sister, Abby, had also spent time in Mobile before she married a San Francisco banker in Montgomery. Three of Tim Meaher's younger brothers who also made the move had died, one at age eighteen and the others in their twenties.

The most vivid surviving description of Meaher comes from William Howard Russell, an Englishman who rode on one of his ships in 1861. The captain had a "gray eye full of cunning and of some humor," Russell wrote, "strongly marked features, and a very Celtic mouth of the Kerry type." Newspaper stories also suggest he was hard to get along with. In 1854, the *Selma Sentinel* reported that he had a "difficulty" with the clerk of his ship in Montgomery, and that Meaher was "severely injured by a knife." It was the result of some misunderstanding, "in which the Captain, we learn was to blame." And in 1857, he was accused of ramming one of his ships into another vessel, apparently out of spite for the captain. The *Cahaba Gazette*'s editors found it hard to believe he would risk his life and the lives of many others "to gratify a petty feeling of malice or revenge," but if he did, they opined, he should be "scourged from the river."

This evening on the way to Montgomery, the banks on both sides rose as tall as 200 feet, too high to afford glimpses of the little towns beyond, which were marked only by the long chutes, propped up here and there against the dirt, that carried cotton down to ships. Along the slopes grew maples, oaks, mulberries, and magnolias. The trees occasionally fell and blocked parts of the channel. For northern passengers—and at least a few passengers on board this evening were northerners—this scenery could have an exotic appeal at first. Occasionally they'd catch glimpses of alligators sunning themselves atop the mud or water moccasins slipping off the banks. But the novelty tended to wear off. Sleeping on the ship must have been almost impossible, thanks to the creaking beams and the throbbing engines and the screeching whistle. The passengers usually sought other forms of entertainment: news-papers, card games, and alcohol.

Meaher sometimes regaled them with stories about the river. Russell wrote that he told many "wonderful yarns, which I hope he was not foolish enough to think I believed." At one point on Russell's trip, Meaher pointed to a bluff, where he claimed that thirty years earlier, some white men had tricked a group of Native Americans into making a treaty and then had slaughtered them wholesale. "Many hundreds thus perished, and the whole affair was very much approved of" by the captain, Russell wrote.

Passengers also told stories among themselves, and Meaher must have known his own name sometimes came up. The wreck of one of his first ships was a story practically made for river lore. It began in 1847, when Meaher had commissioned a shipyard up near Louisville to build a vessel to his own elaborate specifications: a massive sidewheeler with thirty-eight cabins and a saloon, decked out with expensive furniture and carpet, plus a nursery be-neath the ladies cabin. He named it the *Orline St. John,* after a young woman he was apparently trying to woo. In the spring of 1850, the boat set off for Montgomery, with its first-class cabins filled and the lower deck bustling. Meaher was the captain; his brother Burns was the first mate.

The river was high that week from spring rains, and the wind was blow-ing against the direction of the ship. But Meaher was vying to reach Mont-gomery within five days, so his passengers could catch a train. During a stop on the fourth afternoon, he had the boat stocked with firewood, so the crew could stuff the furnace and draw out more steam to push against the current. But hours later, sparks from the furnace ignited a stack of logs. Soon the entire boat was up in flames. Meaher, like most everyone else on board, was forced to jump into the cold, muddy water. Between those who didn't jump in time and the ones who couldn't swim, the death toll reached about forty.

From Meaher's point of view, the outcome could have been worse. For his reported efforts to save the passengers, the *Mobile Daily Register* called him a "man of great personal courage and sound discretion." The insurance reportedly netted him $16,000, and he used the capital to open his shipyard. But ultimately his reputation was tarnished. On nights like these, a rumor was sometimes passed around that one of the passengers, a Navy officer, had been carrying a quarter of a million dollars' worth of gold. The gold had never been recovered, and the story went that Meaher had brought divers up from the Caribbean to fish it out of the silt. There was speculation that the gold had funded his later enterprises.

Standing on the deck, Meaher would have been able to hear the passengers' voices rising in agitation from the forecabin. Had he wandered in,
his nostrils would have filled with the smoke of cheap cigars. According to
an interview he gave in 1890, his passengers that night were talking about
the slave trade. Alabama and its neighbors, as the captain well knew, were
desperate for more chattel labor. As of 1859, cotton was arguably the most
coveted commodity in the world. Worldwide consumption of the fabric had
grown from 1.5 billion pounds a year to 2.5 billion since 1850, and a vast
share of the world's cotton came from this expanse between Texas and the
Carolinas, of which Mobile was in the center. The region couldn't keep up
with demand; no matter how much the plantations turned out, it wasn't
enough. The price kept on climbing.

Prior to the introduction of the cotton gin, before Meaher was born,
the most labor-intensive part of the process had been separating the seeds
from the lint. But the appearance of that machine in 1794 had changed
everything. If the average worker could produce a pound a day by hand,
the horse-powered and steam-powered cotton gins available in the 1850s
could handle at least 150 times that amount. Because of those developments, there was now a different bottleneck in the process: getting raw
cotton off the plants. Over time, enslaved people had learned to work faster
and faster—driven by various combinations of rewards and punishments,
not least the threat of savage whipping if they failed to meet their daily
quotas—and some could now pick cotton with extraordinary speed and
skill. But still there were limits. To keep increasing productivity, southern
planters needed more enslaved people, and at the moment, those, too, were
in limited supply.

Since 1808, it had been illegal to bring Africans to the United States in
the transatlantic slave trade. The burden was on the 300,000 enslaved people
already in the United States to keep the labor supply stocked by reproducing.
Humans had become a major export for states in the Upper South, especially Virginia, North Carolina, and Maryland. But the advent of cotton was
making this arrangement unsustainable. More plantations kept opening, and
they all needed laborers. As of that evening when Meaher was riding up the
Alabama River, healthy adult slaves were selling for around $1,500 each in
Richmond; and the men and women at the barracks in downtown Mobile,
a three-story brick building on Royal Street with bars on its windows, went
for as much as $2,400, the equivalent of nearly $70,000 now. At that rate,
Meaher was better off hiring field hands. Lately some of Mobile's hotels had

been staffing their servant positions with Irish immigrants instead, making southern guests uncomfortable.

However, word had been spreading around Mobile that in Africa, enslaved people could be bought for a tiny fraction of the price. The *Mobile Daily Register* had announced it in late 1858: "From the West coast of Africa we have advices dated the 21st of September," a notice in the paper read. "The quarreling of the tribes on Sierra Leone river rendered the aspect of affairs very unsatisfactory. The King of Dahomey was driving a brisk trade in slaves, at from $50 to $60 each, at Whydah. Immense numbers of negroes were collected along the coast for export." The notice did not identify King Ghezo by name. It didn't explain that there had been an uptick in slave raids that year, owing to the pressure Ghezo was facing from his own chiefs, nor did it say where exactly the captives came from. Readers in Mobile wouldn't have known that within two months after the notice was published, the king had died and been succeeded by his son Glèlè. But none of that mattered to an Alabama businessman. The important takeaway was that Dahomey was selling extremely cheap workers.

The obvious solution, in the eyes of more and more cotton planters, was to make the transatlantic slave trade legal again. In the spring of 1859, businessmen from all over the South had gathered in Vicksburg for the annual Southern Commercial Convention, and by a vast majority had approved a resolution calling for a repeal of all restrictions on the slave trade. Then over the summer, the *Register* published an editorial where it brought the debate home. "Now is it consistent," the paper had asked, "with the self-respect, the dignity, the honor of the southern people, to rest satisfied under the degrading stigma upon their most essential institution, which these statutes against the Slave-trade imply?" It continued: "We chafe with a scarcely repressible impatience under the degrading reflection which these Slave-trade statutes cast upon our institutions and our people."

Mobile had been built up almost solely for the purpose of shipping out cotton. "They buy cotton, sell cotton, think cotton, eat cotton, drink cotton, and dream cotton," one British visitor wrote during an 1858 trip. "They marry cotton wives, and unto them are born cotton children." Throughout the 1850s, Alabama's plantations were collectively the most productive in the union, and nearly all the cotton from the southern half of the state went through Mobile. It was a town where most every white person's fortunes rose and fell with the value of the crop. The editorial was a hit—so much so that the *Register*'s editor, John Forsyth, was elected a few weeks after its publication to represent the city in Alabama's state legislature.

Meaher was a zealous advocate for reopening the slave trade. He and his brothers, between the three of them, owned several dozen slaves, and their labor helped power the family's ever-expanding enterprises, including the work of fueling the *Taney*. But his feeling about the subject rose above the level of self-interest. His biography shows that if there was one cause he believed in, beyond his own enrichment, it was the defense of slavery. He expressed this publicly through the names of his ships. A few years earlier he had dubbed one the *Southern Republic,* and later, after the Civil War broke out, he would name another the *Gray Jacket,* a clear nod to the Confederate military. The *Roger B. Taney* itself had been completed in 1857, just four months after the U.S. Supreme Court announced its *Dred Scott* decision, establishing that slaves counted as property, not people, in the eyes of the law, and that Congress could not ban slavery in the territories. The ship was named in honor of the judge who wrote the opinion.

Meaher had also lent resources to the cause. He had recently been involved with a group of men who were trying to establish an American colony in Nicaragua. Their leader was William Walker, an eccentric attorney born in Nashville who had been living in Nicaragua for several years. He had seized the presidency in 1856, during a civil war. Walker had quickly set about making the country a beachhead for Black slavery in Latin America. Given the short supply of enslaved people in the United States, Walker had made it clear he planned to import them from Africa; and southern planters, when they heard about it, rallied to support him. Meaher was among their ranks. In late 1858, he provided one of his ships, the *Susan,* for the transportation of 112 men who planned to go support Walker.

The *Susan* had successfully sneaked out of Mobile Bay in the middle of a December night, narrowly getting past federal authorities who knew what the crew was up to. The plan was to sail to the Honduran coast, where the crew would rendezvous with Walker. But while most of the men were sleeping, a heavy head wind pushed the ship off course, and it crashed into a jagged coral reef, splitting in two. The men built a raft out of water casks, and a British ship later carried them back to Mobile.

Meaher was evidently not too discouraged. Perhaps the expedition's failure only made him eager to sponsor another one. He knew Africans were still being imported to the U.S., albeit in small numbers. Lately the newspapers had been replete with stories about successful slave expeditions where the culprits got off scot-free. In the spring, a Texas paper had published an ad for 400 "likely AFRICAN NEGROES" newly arrived on the Gulf Coast, and in August, there had been accounts of another 600 Africans landing near Tampa. The slave ship most discussed around Mobile's wharves was likely the *Wanderer,* which had left from New York in July of 1858. On a four-month voyage, it had sailed to what is now the Democratic Republic of the Congo, and then returned to Jekyll Island, Georgia, where the crew unloaded 400 African slaves.

President James Buchanan, a Pennsylvania Democrat halfway through his first term, had been threatening to crack down on these voyages. The planters voted for Buchanan overwhelmingly, and for the most part they had found him a reliable ally. He had always maintained that slavery laws should be the domain of the states, and he voiced support for the *Dred Scott* decision. In 1857 and 1858, during the debates over the status of Kansas—whether it should be admitted as a slave state or a free state—Buchanan had joined with the proslavery faction. His vision, however, was only to maintain the status quo. Legally reopening the slave trade was not an option in his mind.

The real question, as of 1859, was whether a de facto reopening might happen. *The New York Times* opined in the spring that there were "plenty of desperate, reckless adventurers, both at the North and South," who would undertake illegal slave voyages if they believed they could get away with it. Unless they were punished sufficiently, "their violation will become a matter of course on our Southern Coasts," the paper predicted. This was apparently just what Meaher had in mind.

According to Gulf lore, some of Meaher's passengers that night were arguing that it would never happen. The Buchanan administration wouldn't allow it.

"Hanging the worst of them will scare the rest off," Meaher heard one person say. At this, the captain reportedly spoke up. "Nonsense!"

They all turned to face him.

"They'll hang nobody. They'll scare nobody."

The men wondered how he could be so sure. Meaher's response is not recorded, but the case would have been easy to make. To begin with, what southern jury would convict a man for importing Africans? White southerners, even poor ones, had come to associate the expansion of slavery with general economic growth and prosperity. Many hoped to own slaves someday themselves. Even for those who didn't, it was a matter of dignity. No matter how low a white southerner's social and economic status, as long as there was a separate laboring class considered to be subhuman, he would never be at the bottom.

But it wasn't just the South that depended on slavery. The textile mills crowding New England, Delaware, and Pennsylvania owed their whole existence to southern cotton and the cheap labor that produced it. The South made up a huge share of their consumer market as well. Northern foundries supplied the South with farming equipment—not just its plows and wagons, but also its cotton gins—and most cotton-hauling steamers were built in Providence and other New England port towns. New York bankers supplied the credit that allowed men like Meaher to purchase more land and more slaves. Cotton also gave the United States more power on the international political stage. A large swath of the workforce in Britain, the most powerful country in the world at that time, depended on American cotton for employment, via the textile industry. Cotton was to America what oil would be to Venezuela and the Persian Gulf a century and a half later.

Meaher might have cited the long history of presidential pardons for slave traders; they had been doled out by Thomas Jefferson, James Madison, James Monroe, John Quincy Adams, and Andrew Jackson. It wasn't hard to imagine Buchanan following suit. But most often, pardons weren't necessary anyway. The captain and crew of the *Wanderer*, in fact, had been caught and prosecuted, but a local jury had found them not guilty.

Granted, abolitionist sentiment was prevalent in the North. After the 1859 elections, the abolitionists' party, the Republicans, would control the House and hold fifteen seats in the Senate; and their presidential candidate, Abraham Lincoln, would run in 1860 on an antislavery platform. At least a few southern leaders believed the institution of slavery was in real jeopardy. Jefferson Davis, a U.S. senator from Mississippi, suggested to his state's legislature in 1858 that secession might be in their future. But this was a minority viewpoint. Many planters were convinced history was on their side, and Meaher was clearly among them. So no, he did not believe the illegal slave trade was going to be quashed.

Still, the passengers had trouble believing that anyone would take the risk when the federal government was threatening execution.

To prove he was right, or so the story goes, Meaher announced that he would do it himself. He vowed to bring a shipful of slaves into Mobile Bay—and predicted that no one would be hanged.

Late on the night of March 3, 1860, William Foster left his home alone, with a bag of gold slung over his shoulder. He walked to the woods, where moonlight glowed through the canopy of oak and maple leaves. He was following a familiar path to Meaher's shipyard, at the mouth of Chickasabogue, where his ship, the *Clotilda,* was anchored.

The boardinghouse where he'd been living belonged to a ship carpenter named Jacob Vanderslice. Vanderslice and his large family all lived there—including Martha Adalaide, Vanderslice's daughter, whom Foster would soon marry. There were also seven more bachelors around Foster's age. (Foster was about thirty-five—census records are inconsistent on his exact date of birth.) Foster had lived in this town for sixteen years, and still there wasn't enough housing for everyone. The population was growing too fast.

As a city, Mobile was only about as old as Foster himself. Spanish conquistadors had come through in the early 1500s, and French explorers had planted a flag there in 1702. The earliest colonists were Pierre Le Moyne d'Iberville and his younger brother Jean-Baptiste Le Moyne de Bienville, Frenchmen who hailed from Montreal. Bienville would go on to establish the city of New Orleans sixteen years later. But for two more centuries after they claimed it for Louis XIV, Mobile remained mostly wilderness, inhabited by Muscogee natives and only small bands of settlers from France, then Spain, then Britain. Serious development had begun only after Americans seized it, in 1813, from what was then Spanish Florida. Then it became a boomtown. The population shot up from 300 in 1813 to 3,000 in 1830. In Foster's day, it was the third-largest port city in the United States, with a population near 30,000.

It had also become quite cosmopolitan. At the main port, where Mobile Bay opened up to the Gulf of Mexico, ships were usually lined up by the dozen, bearing the flags of Sweden, Denmark, Great Britain, Ireland, Germany, France, Italy, and Spain, awaiting loads of cotton. There was a world-class hotel, the Battle House, in the center of downtown, and a reading room for subscribing merchants that stocked newspapers and magazines from all over the globe.

At the same time, the economy could not have been less diverse. Rarely had a city depended so heavily on a single crop. Mobile manufactured little on its own; even locally made clothing was scarce. There were so few tailors and dressmakers, affluent people found it cheaper to have their clothes made in northern cities—using southern cotton, no doubt—and shipped down.

Among the thousands of young bachelors who had rushed down to make their fortunes, Foster was one of the few who had come knowing a rarefied trade. He was a skilled ship carpenter, descended from a line of ship carpenters and mariners. He had grown up in Nova Scotia. Halifax was still a British territory at the time, and his parents were English loyalists who had migrated there after the American Revolution. His father owned a shipyard and a steamboat that he used to shuttle passengers between the local islands. It's unclear exactly why Foster strayed so far from home, though there are records of his family relocating to Rhode Island about the same time he left for the Gulf Coast. However, Mobile had one of the richest lumber supplies south of the Mason-Dixon, and no shipbuilding industry to speak of, at least not when Foster arrived. It would have seemed like a place where he could make a name for himself. At some point his younger brother, Walter, also a ship carpenter, had come down to join him.

Career opportunities aside, Mobile could be a thrilling place for a bachelor. The city consciously competed with New Orleans for its theaters and its nightlife; the impresarios wanted to keep sailors in town when they went on leave, instead of traveling the extra 150 miles to the Crescent City. The downtown area was stacked with brothels, bars, dance halls, and liquor stores. In the gambling district, Shakespeare's Row, there was a courtyard lined with casino rooms on all sides, three stories high, where faro chips clacked and roulette wheels spun every night until the morning hours. Bands of sailors were always stumbling down the streets in the dark, wailing their obscene songs in chorus, looking to pick up women or get into brawls. Often it turned dangerous. "Every person, nearly, secretly carried weapons upon their persons," one of Foster's contemporaries later wrote, "which they used on upon the smallest provocation, and sometimes with none at all; and even sailors, longshoreman, and boat-hands, whipped out their sheath-knives and slashed away at each other, whenever the force of anger or alcohol prevailed over reason."

But Mobile was also a city of more civilized charms. Away from the business district, there were streets lined with villas and palatial mansions belonging to cotton merchants. Octavia Levert, the wife of a prominent physician, held a weekly salon, modeled after the ones she'd witnessed in France, attracting artists, actors, writers, and politicians. In winter, the busy season, Mobile's temperature was often balmy, and by February, the flowers were usually in bloom, filling the city air with a perfume that mingled with the scent of magnolias. In the summertime, everyone who could afford it— around two-thirds of the population—left for places with cooler weather. The city slept during the hottest months, then roused itself again each September.

Amid the distractions, Bill Foster had found the time to finish building the *Clotilda* in 1855. It was his finest achievement to date, the product of a lifetime's training and years' worth of saving and planning. The two-masted schooner had ribs of oak and planks made of southern yellow pine. The design was novel; unlike ordinary Gulf schooners, which were tailored for the shallow coastal bays and rivers, the *Clotilda* had a deep hull, tall enough from top to bottom for a short person to stand upright, spacious enough to hold 120 tons of cargo. Foster had managed to build it this way without sacrificing agility. The first time he rigged it, a reporter from the *Mobile Daily Advertiser* had described it as "light and commodious," and said its design was "of that graceful turn which confers assurance that she will prove a fast sailer." Until recently, the boat had also been a dependable source of income. Foster had hired a captain to take it on freight voyages, shuttling local lumber and grain as far as Texas, Louisiana, and Cuba. For several years, it had averaged a trip every two months.

Did the *Clotilda* secretly traffic in human beings as well? There's no telling for sure. For years, however, local legend held that some of the ships built at Timothy Meaher's shipyard (as the *Clotilda* reportedly was) had been involved in the illegal slave trade in the 1850s. It was fairly common for an American ship to pick up several captives in Cuba and drop them off near the mouth of the Mississippi River, or near Galveston, Texas, and quietly unload them in a bayou. Every port where the *Clotilda* stopped between 1855 and 1859 was involved in the slave trade. In particular, records show that on a January 1857 stop in New Orleans, the *Clotilda* arrived with unlisted cargo, and was consigned to a local firm with proven ties to the illegal slave trade. A year later, members of this same firm were unindicted co-conspirators in the case involving the *Echo*, which was captured on a trip from Angola to Cuba, carrying several hundred captives.

The *Clotilda*'s final voyage in the Gulf of Mexico ended in catastrophe. On a Sunday morning in October of 1859, it was on its way up Mobile Bay, back from a trip to Brazos de Santiago, on the southern tip of Texas. The wind was at its rear. Foster was not present, but the captain who was on board later recounted seeing, off in the distance, a speck on the river. The *Clotilda* was moving at a fast clip, three or four miles an hour. Soon the speck came into focus: it was a skiff holding two fishermen, one Black and one white. For some reason, as the schooner got closer, the skiff wasn't moving out of its way. The *Clotilda* crew, according to the captain, began pulling down the sails, since they were preparing to dock anyway. When they were thirty yards off, the pilot yelled out, "Boat ahead!" and the *Clotilda*'s mate gave the order to veer toward the opposite bank. But the ship couldn't turn fast enough, and it ran into a chain that connected the little boat to a log in the river. The skiff jerked and flipped over.

As the captain later told Foster, when the crew lowered a boat down to search for the fishermen, they found the white man clinging to the *Clotilda*'s anchor, gasping for air. But the Black passenger was nowhere in sight, so they continued on their way.

Weeks later, Foster was summoned to court. It turned out the Black man, an enslaved person named Alfred, had drowned. His owner, W.D.F. Holly, was demanding compensation. A local jury found the crew guilty of negligence and ordered Foster to pay $1,500. Foster must have been hard-pressed to afford it; the *Clotilda* was practically all he owned.

By all appearances, this was around the time when Timothy Meaher approached him about a longer voyage, the most daring one of his life. He wanted to commission Foster to sail to Dahomey, on the African coast, where he was to fetch at least a hundred slaves and sneak them through Mobile Bay. Meaher would cover all expenses, and he would pay Foster with a cut of the proceeds: about half a dozen slaves, who could fetch thousands of dollars on the market.

It seems Foster had no personal investment in the question of slavery. Politically, he was still a subject of the English crown; and on the business front, neither he nor his family had ever owned slaves—but there's no evidence that they were hard-charging abolitionists, either. Foster clearly didn't object to the voyage on moral grounds. As for his ship, it was perfect for Meaher's purposes. The first priority on this voyage would be speed. Besides the navy patrols along the Gulf, there would be international law enforcement to contend with once the ship reached the Atlantic: Portuguese, Spanish, and most worryingly, the British Royal Navy, which averaged dozens of slave-ship seizures each year. There were plenty of fast schooners around Mobile Bay, but most did not have holds large enough to fit a hundred or more people inside. With room enough for about 190, the *Clotilda* was only a fraction of the size of an ordinary slave ship, some of which carried more than a thousand people, but most any other ship of the *Clotilda*'s capacity would have been too slow.

Whatever his reasons, whether he had notions of grandeur or just needed the money, Foster agreed to the voyage.

Meaher, or more likely his fleet of shipyard workers, helped Foster prepare the ship for a longer journey than it had ever taken. They re-rigged it with broad sails, the kind used on racing yachts, and loaded it with provisions: 125 barrels of water, several dozen barrels of beef, pork, rice, and flour, and casks of bread, sugar, and molasses. They also loaded eighty casks of cachaça, a spirit distilled from sugarcane, thinking the Dahomean king might want to trade for it. Knowing this trove would be a dead giveaway if the boat ever happened to be searched, they stacked lumber on top of the hold.

On the night of March 3, 1860, the ship was waiting at Meaher's private port. Docking it there must have been highly preferable to the wharves downtown, which were notorious for their filth—floating, as they were, with driftwood, junk, and wreckage, where dead fish and crabs and river muck piled up, making a horrible stink in the Mobile heat. Foster had recruited two northerners to serve as his mates: John M. Simonton, of Portland, Maine, and James M. Smith, of Boston. The official registry of his crew also lists Joseph DeFlow, James Small, and William Copeland, who all lived in Mobile, and James Welch, another Bostonian. Foster may have found it difficult to recruit them. Sailors generally knew that slave voyages were among the worst assignments in the maritime industry. In the best-case scenario, it would be filthy, smelling of shit and piss that wafted up from the hold. Worst case was a slave revolt. They would also face the risk of imprisonment once they returned to the US. Back in the eighteenth century, a common method of recruitment was to get sailors drunk and trap them in gambling debts, then force them to go on slave errands so they could pay off what they owed. Foster's own methods are not documented.

Once Foster reached the harbor that night, he stepped onto his boat and pulled out part of the cabin wall and stuffed the bag filled with gold inside. He planned to pick up his crew before daybreak. They would sail down the winding Chickasaw Creek, into the delta where it met the Mobile River, down the chute into Mobile Bay, past the wooded Dauphin Island, and into the Gulf of Mexico. After that, it would be unfamiliar territory. According to one version of the story, their papers said they were hauling lumber to St. Thomas, in the Danish Virgin Islands. But the ultimate route on Foster's maps was for Africa.

3

CARAVAN

Kossola woke to the sound of shrieking. He heard terrified voices outside his compound, and in a lower register, the rumble of hundreds of feet pounding the dirt. The young man leapt out of bed and looked outside. It was still dark, but he could make out huge hordes of soldiers, dressed in matching tunics and shorts, wielding muskets and machetes. They had somehow broken through the town gates and were flooding into the village. Already some of Kossola's neighbors had stepped out of their huts, and the soldiers were seizing them at their doors before they could run away. He could see the soldiers sawing at people's necks and removing their heads. All over the ground was pooling with blood.

Kossola knew he had to make a run for it, but from inside the hut he couldn't tell how many warriors there were or where they were positioned. He stepped out, looking around cautiously. He saw neighbors on the ground with their clothes stained red, some with their faces reduced to bloody stumps. Soldiers had hacked off their jawbones, likely wanting them as trophies. Other young people were heading for the gates, but soldiers were catching them, grabbing them by the wrists and rounding them up. Off in the distance, he noticed one gate that looked unguarded. On the other side was a tree line; if he could make it to the woods, he would have a chance. He sprinted toward it, his heart pounding as he got closer. He made it through.

But on the other side, he felt someone's hands clutching his body. Enemy warriors had been waiting there. While one person held him and another tied up his wrists, he probably got his first clear glimpse of the soldiers. Many were women. From a distance, with their shaven heads and matching uniforms, flecked with blood and dirt, they'd been indistinguishable from the men.

In that moment, all Kossola could think about was his mother. He didn't know where she was or whether she was still alive. He pleaded with the soldiers to let him find her, but they wouldn't hear it. They marched him to a place where they had corralled the other young people from the town.

While Kossola was being held, he would later recount, the local king was also being tied up outside the gate. The king was brought to the wooded area outside, the "bush," where a tall, muscular man—who Kossola would later find out was Glèlè, the Dahomean ruler—was waiting.

Glèlè told someone to bring him the interpreter, according to Kossola. When he'd arrived, Glèlè told him to ask the man why he'd dared to stand up against the Lion of Dahomey.

In return, the Yoruba king asked why Glèlè and his soldiers didn't fight like men. They ought to have come in the daytime and met his own military face-to-face.

Glèlè ignored the question. He told the chief to go get in line. He was eager to parade him around as a prisoner.

The defeated leader said he wasn't going to Dahomey. His fathers before him had been kings, he said, and he wouldn't suffer the humiliation of being sold. He'd rather die a king than become a slave.

Glèlè asked the king once more, confirming he wouldn't travel to Dahomey. Then he nodded at his soldiers and pointed at his enemy. Without a word, a woman soldier stepped up, gripping her machete, and swung it in a wide arc, lopping off the Yoruba king's head. She picked it up from the ground and handed it to Glèlè.

When Kossola saw the king lying dead, he broke away from the soldiers and ran toward the woods. They overtook him before he got there. He called out his mother's name; he had no idea where she was. "I no see none my family." Again he begged the soldiers to let him find them, but they weren't sympathetic. As they bound him in a chain with the other captives, it became clear what was happening. The invaders were killing off elderly people but making prisoners of the younger ones. The king of Dahomey had come to hunt slaves, they said.

The whole attack was over within a half hour. When the Dahomeans were finished, their coup de grâce was usually to gather up every goat, chicken, and duck they could, and to raze the whole town. They set out for Dahomey as the sun was coming up.

*   *   *

The stress of the voyage was getting to Bill Foster. The captain lay awake in his bunk, puzzling over what had gone wrong. The first few days had been smooth. They had sailed out of Mobile Bay without serious trouble; no one had stopped them to inspect the cargo. Once the mainland was well out of sight, they slipped into the Gulf Stream. The warm water would have propelled the schooner like a headwind, boosting its speed as it passed the straits of Florida. By the middle of the third day, Foster and the crew had found themselves cutting between Cuba and the Florida Keys, according to a twelve-page handwritten memoir that Foster penned three decades later. Their destination, apparently inspired by that newspaper clip about the "brisk trade" in cheap human commodities, was the port city of Ouidah (or Whydah), deep in the Gulf of Guinea. They'd been on track to reach it within ten weeks.

By 1860 ocean travel had evolved to a kind of science. Where sailors in the Age of Exploration had had to rely on guesswork, Foster's situation was quite the opposite. For journeys like his, mariners brought along journals that gave detailed data on wind patterns and ocean currents. Their maps depicted water depths and navigational hazards, like reefs, rocks, and islands. To pinpoint their location, they had a sophisticated instrument, the sextant, which relied on mirrors to measure their angle from the sun.

But out here on the ocean's depths, there wasn't much to orient the captain or confirm he was on the right course. In every direction there was only sky. Ultimately the stars had tipped him off. Observing them on the deck one night, he realized the ship had been drifting in the wrong direction. He tried to correct it, but as the days and nights went on, he found the problem was persisting. With all that was riding on this voyage, including a massive amount of capital—and with all his other concerns, not least of all the threats of disastrous weather and mutiny by the crew—this navigational problem was becoming a cause for panic.

As he tossed and turned, he had a sudden revelation: the culprit was that bag of gold. He had stowed it away behind the cabin bulkhead, beside the compass. He climbed out of bed and went up onto the deck. With the breeze in his hair, he removed the wooden plank and pulled out the sack. The needle on his compass bounced sideways. The gold had been throwing off the magnetic field.

*   *   *

Two weeks into the voyage, the *Clotilda* passed Bermuda. The surrounding zone was not yet known as the Bermuda Triangle, but spooky stories had already been told about it for centuries. Christopher Columbus found that his compass acted strangely as he crossed the strait in 1492. Columbus also saw a "marvellous flame of fire" fall there "from heaven into the sea"—evidently a meteor—and he later noticed a light on the horizon, which he thought looked like a "wax candle rising and falling." And around the turn of the nineteenth century, a U.S. Navy ship, the USS *Pickering*, disappeared near Bermuda, not leaving any trace. For the most part, the legends can be explained by the extreme weather. The area is prone to hurricanes and tropical storms, and in some parts the water is shallow, making it hard for ships to steer through. The sharks and barracuda that infest those waters are probably responsible for the disappearances of sailors' bodies.

The *Clotilda* nearly became another casualty. It was sixty miles north of Bermuda, just outside the triangle proper, when the heavy winds picked up. For the next nine days the ship was battered. It was pitched from side to side, tilting at such angles that the crew had to hold on for their lives. Everything on deck was swept away, save for two lifeboats that were fastened down, one to the midship house and the other to a cabin. The rudder head was broken into three pieces.

Foster's memoir describes another episode that occurred in the middle of the storm, an episode that strains credulity. Around eight A.M. one day, he wrote, the crew spotted a Portuguese warship approaching. Foster worried the men on board would try to search the *Clotilda* for illegal cargo. He gave the order to flee. All morning and afternoon, the Portuguese ship chased them, he said, with the squall never letting up. The *Clotilda* finally broke free around six P.M. When the sun was setting, the men found that their foresail was falling apart. The captain later remembered it as "the most exciting race I ever saw."

No doubt patrol ships posed a serious concern for Foster. But the ships most likely to stop the *Clotilda* were British, not Portuguese. By mid-century, Britain's West Africa Squadron, a division of the Royal Navy, had more than 4,000 men and 36 ships in its charge. Its sailors were intensely devoted to their work, motivated by the promise of prize money that was doled out by the crown. By 1867, when the squadron was absorbed into another division, it had captured more than 1,600 slave vessels containing some 160,000 captives.

Other nations had patrol ships circling the waters too. As of 1860, France,

Spain, Portugal, and the United States were all nominally lending support to the suppression effort. But the Portuguese squadron was extremely meager. Amid the wind and rain and sleet, perhaps Foster mistook the flag for the wrong nationality. Otherwise he may have added the detail to heighten the drama.

On April 14, according to Foster's memoir, following a second chase by a Portuguese warship, the *Clotilda* arrived at the small city of Praia. Praia is on the southern tip of Santiago, one of the ten islands of Cape Verde, which Portugal colonized in the fifteenth century. For many decades, the islands had served as a trading post in the slave market; but since slave trading had been on the wane, they had been forced to reinvent themselves as ports of call for whalers and merchants. It was a convenient spot for Foster to have repairs done on the *Clotilda*.

Once they were on land, the crew mutinied. By one later account, the men believed Foster was at risk of being found out by the local authorities and arrested, and they seized the opportunity to demand an increase in their wages. He was lucky this was all they did. Sailors, especially those who wound up on slave ships, tended to come from the bottom rungs of society. Financially, they lived voyage to voyage; some had histories of violence; and many of them had little to lose if something went wrong at sea. In the bleak conditions that dominated these trips, it was easy for a mob mentality to take over and for the captain to become the scapegoat, deservingly or not. More than a few slave-ship captains had been murdered by their crews. They could all too easily be tossed overboard, never to be seen or heard from again. As for sailors' pay, the rates varied widely, mostly according to skill sets; but as a rule, the work was not lucrative. Whether the *Clotilda* crew were being paid decently, considering their conditions, is unclear.

Foster instantly agreed to give them a raise, figuring a promise cost him nothing. "Promises are like pie crust," he would later say whenever he told the story, "made to be broken." With the disagreement settled, he wrote, the crew "went to work cheerfully to repair the vessel." Meanwhile, Foster introduced himself to the Portuguese officials and the U.S. consul. He brought gifts of shawls and jewelry for the officials' wives. He may also have given a cash bribe, which was common protocol on Praia, though his memoir doesn't mention it. The American consul quickly ascertained that Foster was on a secret slave voyage, but he let the Clotilda pass through nevertheless. He also offered a tip: he suggested Foster take his business to the island of Guinea, which was suffering from a famine. There the captain might get more in exchange for his wares.

The *Clotilda* sailed out after eight days in the port. As it was leaving, it crashed into a warship, knocking off the warship's boom and its rail. Foster wrote that he was sure the crew would shoot at the *Clotilda* to stop it. But no shots were ever fired, and soon a breeze helped the schooner speed away. Foster felt relieved when his ship was beyond the reach of the guns.

The *Clotilda*'s route during the final three weeks dipped southeast, beyond the French colony of Senegal, beyond Guinea and Sierra Leone. It tacked along the coast, passing each of the regions Europeans had named centuries earlier according to the main commodities they obtained there: the Pepper Coast (Liberia), the Ivory Coast, the Gold Coast (Ghana), and, deep into the Gulf of Guinea, the Slave Coast. On May 15, seventy-two days after its departure, the *Clotilda* reached Ouidah. As it approached the shore, huge waves were crashing in the surf. There was no way to reach the land, so the crew dropped the anchor a mile and a half from shore and waited.

The sun was beating down on the caravan. Since daybreak they'd been marching, all of the captives in a line, chained together so they couldn't escape. Glèlè and his officers rode in hammocks. Each one was supported by bamboo poles that lay parallel to the rider's body, with a man on each end to bear the weight. Relievers walked alongside them to swap places periodically. Kossola looked at the hammocks with longing. All day they hadn't eaten, though he'd barely noticed; he was preoccupied thinking about his family members, none of whom were here on the road.

He probably puzzled over how the Dahomeans had managed to invade his town so easily. Later in life he would blame it on a former resident who had been convicted of a crime and exiled. He claimed the man had gone to Dahomey and told Glèlè's officers all about the town's defense system, helping them strategize. The theory is plausible, given that Dahomey often relied on spies and defectors, but it can't be confirmed.

The Dahomean army, in the full light of day, made an extraordinary spectacle. They typically marched several thousand strong, divided into regiments. Almost all the soldiers wore loose tunics of striped cotton, tied at the waist with cartridge belts, and bright-colored shorts that extended to their knees. Many shaved their heads entirely; others kept only a patch of hair on the top of their skulls. Across their backs they carried giant machetes, some reportedly as long as thirty inches and weighing more than twenty pounds.

It was said that they'd been designed by Ghezo's brother with the aim of making beheadings more efficient.

To anyone seeing the army for the first time, the women warriors stood out the most—despite, or maybe because of, the Dahomean tradition of assimilating them to the men. They were recruited from villages throughout Dahomey for their physique and athleticism. Such was the "size of the female skeleton," wrote Richard Burton, "and the muscular development of the frame," that some of the women warriors' sex could be "detected only by the bosom." Frederick Forbes, a British naval officer who encountered them in 1849 and 1850, said the gender-bending went further. "'We are men,' say they, 'not women,'" Forbes wrote. "All dress alike, diet alike, and male and female emulate each other: what the males do, the amazons [sic] will endeavour to surpass." At the same time, they were nominally the "king's wives." They were expected to live in celibacy, and yet many became pregnant, whether by choice or not.

On the march from Kossola's town, the warriors clutched the heads of several of his old neighbors, carrying them as battle trophies. Some soldiers carried two or three. Despite the heat, which averages about 80 degrees during the region's dry season, it was too early for the rotting to have begun; but the faces must have been stiffening with rigor mortis, their eyes locking into eerie stares.

Before sunset, they reached a town where a red flag was hoisted near the road. Glèlè sent in some warriors, along with his interpreter, while the caravan waited. Soon the local chief came out, riding in a hammock. Kossola couldn't hear his conversation with Glèlè, but soon he was watching the red flag come down and a white one going up. The chief brought the Dahomean soldiers a gift of yams and corn, which they cooked over an open fire. Once the warriors were sated, the march went on.

That night, likely after ten or eleven hours of marching, they set up camp. Glèlè always slept in a spacious enclosure, set apart from the others and surrounded by women warriors, where he'd be protected in case of an ambush. The men pitched their little huts wherever they pleased. Kossola and the other captives had to sleep on the ground. He couldn't get comfortable. "I thinkee too 'bout my folks and I cry," he recalled years later. "All night I cry."

After the sun came up, the march continued. At most every town they passed, the same pattern was repeated: Glèlè would send in a messenger, and the chief would come out to meet him. Sometimes red flags were exchanged for white ones. Kossola pieced together the meanings: a red flag was a symbol of defiance, a sign that the town wouldn't pay Glèlè tribute and was ready to fight instead. A white flag meant they were prepared to pay. When a black flag was flying, the army didn't bother stopping; it meant the king was dead and his son wasn't old enough to replace him.

Before long, the severed heads began to stink, making Kossola queasy. It was clearly bothering the soldiers as well. On the third day, they stopped to set up camp, where they mounted the heads on sticks. Kossola and the other captives watched in disbelief as the Dahomeans held the sticks over the fire and smoked the heads, to stop the rotting. When Kossola recounted the sight some seventy years later, the interviewer wrote that he was overcome with horror and couldn't speak. They stayed at this camp for nine days.

The next stop was one of Glèlè's palaces. Diouf believes it was the one in Abomey, Dahomey's longtime capital city. Kossola recalled that Glèlè's house was made of skulls, or at least appeared to be. An Italian missionary who came to Abomey the following year also described an adobe wall outside the palace where human skulls were set every five meters, held in place by iron picks. Or it may have been Cana, where the king had his secondary home. The historian Robin Law, one of the foremost authorities on Dahomey's history, thinks this is most likely, because the first celebration following the annual war campaigns was always held in Cana. Either way, the war party was greeted with an elaborate procession. Men came to meet them with bleached human skulls mounted on long sticks. They beat the drums so much, Kossola remembered, "lookee lak de whole world is de drum dey beat on."

The procession was undoubtedly similar to the parade Burton witnessed in Abomey in 1864, if a little less extravagant. Burton wrote that the first marchers carried flags and umbrellas, accompanied by trumpet blasts and drumbeats. Glèlè's officials followed, in an order determined by their rank, and then the king himself made no fewer than ten passes through. He rode in a carriage, surrounded by brilliantly colored parasols. "When he passed before us, exchanging salutes," Burton wrote, there was "a frantic rush, filling the air with red dust," and "a swarming of men around him." So thick was the dust, in fact, that Glèlè had to cover his mouth with a handkerchief to avoid breathing it in. After the third pass, Glèlè exchanged his carriage for a rolling chaise that had been gifted to him by previous English visitors. He was followed by a band, "whose thirty rattles, thirty cymbals, and dozens of drums, added their din to the wildness of the spectacle." A group of war captives were paraded before the crowds as well.

As part of the procession, Kossola and the other captives from his town were led through the royal compound. The place must have been dazzling to the provincial teenager. The compound at Abomey, in particular, was a small city within a city, spanning roughly a hundred acres and housing several thousand people. There were six palaces, each built by a former king, plus the one Glèlè had constructed; and every one was connected to the next by a door, symbolizing the generational connections. The buildings were made of red clay, glazed with palm oil to make them waterproof, and some were two stories high.

There are no records of where Kossola and the others were confined, but Burton described a long shed in Glèlè's Abomey compound where the king kept some of his captives. Prisoners there were given white gowns to wear and made to straddle wooden posts, lashed down by their shins and wrists, freed only to sleep overnight. Kossola and the others from his town felt their stomachs rumbling; their daily food rations were scarce. The men and women wept and pleaded to be released, promising they'd give up their yams—as their king had refused to do before. Dahomean warriors beat them and showed them the heads of their mothers and fathers.

On Kossola's fourth day there, the Dahomeans had a feast and a ceremony where they feted their king for another successful conquest. Glèlè reveled in these moments. He would don bead necklaces and carry a short staff, with a colorful silk kerchief dangling from one end. "After singing for a while," Burton wrote, "to the great delight of the listeners, he danced, first to the men's, then to the women's band. He is, unlike his father, a notable performer."

In the spring, there was a festival that had been dubbed the "annual customs" by Europeans, but was known locally as *huetanu*—meaning "yearly head business." The estimated deaths at these ceremonies ranged from forty or fifty up to three hundred, the victims a combination of war prisoners and convicted criminals. Kossola apparently did not witness such a ritual. But the scenes he was exposed to must have been traumatic enough. Even joyful ceremonies in Dahomey were imbued with violence. As the warriors danced, they would pantomime what they had done in battle. In one of the most common steps, a warrior would hold her left arm up, and with a machete or stick in her right hand, as a prop, she would make quick cutting motions. In another dance Burton watched in 1864, the dancers "stamped, wriggled, kicked the dust with one foot, sang, shuffled, and wrung their hands." There was always, in his perception, "a suspicion of beheading in these performances." Still, Burton had to admit that even in these dances, Glèlè's movements were "comparatively kingly and dignified."

If the level of violence in Glèlè's kingdom, from the way he deployed his military to the soldiers' individual practices on the battlefield to the macabre palace rituals, seems hard to comprehend, it makes a little more sense in context. Some of the country's battle rituals were relatively common on the Slave Coast at least as early as the seventeenth century. The soldiers in Allada, the country that Dahomey grew out of, were known to decapitate and castrate their enemies in battle. Dahomey's only real innovation had been to increase the scale. For one Dahomean royal funeral in 1789, some 1,500 people were reportedly killed.

On one level, the beheadings were about domination. From the early days, Dahomean kings had collected the skulls of their defeated enemies. Skulls were routinely mounted on stands or set in earthen pots, and were used in the palaces as drinking cups, all as reminders of the greatness of Dahomey's military. But there were also spiritual and political dimensions to the practice, which sometimes intertwined. Dahomeans separated their enemies' heads from their bodes to ensure that the deceased people would not be venerated after death—an honor the Dahomeans preferred be restricted to former kings. In the case of enemy kings, in particular, seizing the skull was seen as a way of disrupting the dynasty and preventing the community from receiving supernatural help from the deceased person.

As for human sacrifices, Dahomeans viewed them as the greatest gift that could be offered to the royal ancestors. There was an earnest belief that the sacrifices kept the dead happy. Tradition held that Ghezo's predecessor was deposed because he failed to "water the graves" of prior kings. Four years into Glèlè's reign, there would be an earthquake in the kingdom, and Glèlè would be blamed for not making enough sacrifices in his father's honor. To make up for it, three prisoners, all chiefs from a Yoruba town Glèlè had conquered, would be brought out and given a message they were to convey to Ghezo as soon as they reached the next world: that from then on, the annual customs would be better than ever.

Many European visitors to Dahomey were understandably put off by all this violence. But for the most part, they failed to recognize that European slave traders, and the capitalist system they had introduced, were largely responsible for it. Capitalism in West Africa had spurred more than an increase in slaving activity and a series of economic changes; it had also transformed the geopolitical map. Dahomey itself had been spawned by the slave trade. Throughout the eighteenth and nineteenth centuries, even as its culture and political structure had evolved, its drive to expand its borders had always been linked to its involvement with the European market. Some scholars have gone so far as to argue that Dahomean "wars" were nothing but a moneymaking racket, a way of supplying the country's clients with the product that was in such high demand. Whether or not this was true—and Glèlè insisted to Burton that it wasn't, that Dahomey had its own reasons for warmaking, unconnected from the white men—the profits were clearly still a factor.

European influence had also played a role in shaping Dahomey's internal culture. When the traders had begun paying Dahomey in muskets, in the eighteenth century, it had spurred the country to become more disciplined and systematic in the way it used its military. Though white men did not introduce the rituals of beheading and human sacrifice, they certainly abetted Dahomey in taking these practices to a new scale. The king's elaborate parades and palace buildings, too, were funded by profits from the slave economy.

Kossola may have also witnessed the ceremony where Glèlè purchased his soldiers' war trophies, a process the people loved to watch. When Burton was there, "shouts and trills" accompanied the start of the exchange. It seems Dahomean soldiers were allowed to keep the teeth of the people they had killed in battle (which they strung onto necklaces), but they were obligated to sell the skulls. For each one, a soldier received a head of cowries, two thousand of them. When it came to war prisoners, prices were determined on a scale. The minimum was a head of cowries and a six-foot strip of cloth.

Following the sale, the king typically sorted out his new prisoners. Men were separated from women, and then each person was questioned about their skills and occupations. If they were deemed valuable enough, they could be spared. Some were subsumed into the Dahomean military, where they were given the full rights of any soldier. The most capable could rise to high ranks. Tailors, pottery makers, hatmakers, shoemakers, and musicians were incorporated into the craft guilds and given new names. Spiritual leaders were employed, in hopes that the kingdom could acquire the occult powers of their homelands. Certain farmers and hunters would also be retained. The rest, who had no specialized skills, were again divided: some to be sacrificed in the customs, others to be sold off. This last category was the one Kossola found himself in.

There was one more ritual to be carried out before they could leave:

every captive had to throw a stone onto a pile. The significance is not clear. One explanation is that the pile helped the authorities keep track of their trafficking numbers, with each stone representing a captive who had passed through and been taken to Ouidah. Another is that it was a symbolic gesture: it affirmed that the captives were leaving their old lives behind and starting new ones. Once they had added their own rocks, the captives would circle the pile three times.

After Abomey, there were several more stops along the route, though Glèlè evidently did not join for the remainder of the journey. Typically Dahomey's prisoners would go to Zogbodomè, roughly a fifteen-mile walk from the palace, where they would receive medical exams and get treatment if they needed any. From there, they marched the rest of the way to Ouidah—at least sixty miles, depending on their route.

At the coast, the captives were all divided up by their place of origin and locked up in barracoons, the kinds of earthy jails they might have seen along their path. The term *barracoon* is the Spanish word for barracks and comes from *barraca,* meaning hut. Often these structures looked like hybrids of cages and sheds. They were made of heavy poles, driven deep into the earth and lashed with bamboo. The poles were sometimes spaced apart just widely enough to let air in without giving captives room to squeeze through; in other cases, air came in through a space between the wall and the roof. Some had chains along the walls to secure the captives' necks.

Through his bars, Kossola could see ships drifting near the shore. It was almost certainly his first time seeing the ocean, a common experience for captives at Ouidah. Another captive held at that port fifteen years earlier, Mahommah Baquaqua, eventually described the experience in a memoir. "I had never seen a ship before," he wrote, "and my idea of it was, that it was some object of worship of the white man. I imagined that we were all to be slaughtered, and were being led there for that purpose. I felt alarmed for my safety, and despondency had almost taken sole possession of me."

4

BARRACOONS

Ouidah was one of the most heavily trafficked slave ports on the African coast. Between the 1670s and the day in May of 1860 when William Foster steered his ship into the nearby harbor, hundreds of slave ships came and went from the city, carrying more than one million captives. Together those prisoners made up 51 percent of the enslaved people who departed from the Bight of Benin, in the Gulf of Guinea. Only Luanda, a city down the coast in Angola, shipped out more. Statistically, one in every ten enslaved people who were sent to the United States started their transatlantic journey in this port.

For Glèlè, the city was a critical source of cash. Europeans had been trading there since the sixteenth century, and over time the Portuguese, French, and English had each set up their own quarter, installing forts. The Hueda, the Indigenous people who occupied the historic center of town, acted as middlemen between the Europeans and the slave raiders from farther north, including the Dahomeans; but when Dahomey decided to invade in the 1720s, the Hueda were almost powerless to stop them. Even with support from the Europeans and the people of Oyo, they were overwhelmed by Dahomey's superior military. By the early 1740s, Dahomey's king had persuaded the Europeans to do business with his government instead.

Decades later, as the international demand for enslaved people had fallen off, the port itself had remained profitable. The European forts were transformed into palm-oil warehouses. The Dahomean government, besides making money from its own trading activities, imposed taxes on most everything that happened in the region. As of 1850, Europeans had to pay what they considered a "very heavy King's duty" of $800 per ship—equal to the value of ten enslaved people at the going rate.

At the same time, the coastal town was never incorporated into Dahomey culture. No Dahomean king ever set foot there, except perhaps the king who sacked it in 1727. From what Europeans could ascertain, there was a religious taboo against kings seeing the ocean. Besides that, Ouidah had a long-standing culture of independent entrepreneurs. Between the Indigenous people who remained there, the Europeans, and the temporary workers who came and went from other parts of the coast, the city was deeply—maybe hopelessly, from the perspective of the kings—cosmopolitan. A traveler in the 1780s noted that it was common, in passing through the town, to be saluted in several languages, though Portuguese ultimately became the lingua franca.

On the afternoon when Foster arrived, a large canoe came out to meet him. The captain managed to convey that he'd come to trade and needed to speak with the authorities. As he was ferried to the shore, he was impressed at how the men steering the canoe—about twenty natives, by his estimate—"darted through the waves like fish." Most likely these men were professionals, not natives at all but instead migrants from the Gold Coast. Their job was extraordinarily dangerous. Besides the roiling sea, they had to contend with sharks, who often trailed behind their boats and sometimes chomped off the tips of their oars. From onshore, it was so common to hear the screams of capsized canoe handlers and their passengers that another visitor in 1871 would call it a "belt of death."

Once on land, Foster was taken to some interpreters, who congratulated him on his safe passage. They ordered three workers to carry him into the city. In the strictest sense, Ouidah itself is not a port; its borders end a couple miles from the ocean, across from a lagoon. The captain climbed into a hammock, and the men began wading through the slimy black mud. The water was unusually high that month, so high that the hammock bearers practically had to swim through the deepest parts. The authorities could have built a bridge, but instead they did without one, perhaps so they could better control the traffic coming from the coast.

Foster may have seen enormous alligators lying on the banks. The men carried him through a line of towering palm trees and into the town. The crooked streets there were often thick with mud in the springtime. On account of its colonial history, Ouidah had a strange layout: sprawling, more like an assemblage of villages with a centralized government than a conventional West African city. There were big open stretches that had been converted to urban farms, where yams and maize were grown. The buildings, composed of mud and strengthened with oyster shells, tended to crumble and dissolve during the rainy season and required constant repairs. They were clustered in compounds, but were spread out enough to stop their roofs, made of palm branches and thick grass mounted upon bamboo, from collectively catching fire in the drier months. On the ground, deep holes had been dug all over, to supply the mud for walls, and had been left uncovered to fill up with stagnant water.

But if the streets of Ouidah were dirty, parts of Mobile were just as bad; and after months at sea, Foster was no doubt happy just to be on solid ground. When he was dropped off at a hotel for traders, the Merchant's Exchange, he was impressed; years later he recalled his "splendid accommodations."

The next morning, after breakfast, he was taken to see Adoke, Glèlè's nephew and representative. When Adoke entered the room where they were to meet, the fifty officials present all fell to their knees. Richard Burton, who met Adoke four years later, described him as "tall and well made, of coal complexion," and found him wearing a green silk tunic and smoking a Brazilian cigar. Foster estimated that he weighed 250 pounds. Burton found him amiable, and he noted that Adoke had developed a reputation as "cunning" and curious, well versed in "the habits of white men." Foster and Adoke shared a drink—European liquor was easy to obtain in the city—and then Foster explained his business. He wanted to buy 125 enslaved people, and he was willing to pay as much as $100 a head. He had $9,000 in gold, and he could cover the rest with merchandise.

Foster assumed he could simply conduct the transaction and be on his way. But this wasn't how business was done in Ouidah, or anywhere in Dahomey, for that matter. It was common for European travelers to complain about how long they had to wait before they could wrap up their business with Glèlè or his officials. They found it infuriating that Dahomeans did not treat time as a commodity. When the meeting ended, Foster had no clear idea of what was supposed to happen next, or whether Adoke was even accepting his proposal.

While he waited, Foster's guide showed him around the town. The main feature was a well-stocked market, likely one of the best to be found in West Africa. Besides local goods, it had merchandise carried from deep in the country's interior and from Europe. John Duncan, a Scotsman who spent time in Dahomey in 1845 and 1846, found the market stocked with all manner of exotic products: *elu* ("a composition to destroy mosquitoes"), *kootataffue* ("a root resembling onion, but very bitter"), *bodya* ("a root used as a decoction to expedite labour in child-birth"), and stones for grinding corn, brought all the way from Abomey—plus skins of alligators, deer, bushpigs, and cats. Above all, there was a bounty of fish, the cornerstone of Ouidah's cuisine, available smoked, cooked, and raw. According to Burton, workers would catch meals there when they could, wolfing down food in the alley, and "swarms of people" would fill the streets in the late afternoon to "buy and sell, 'swap' and barter." There was a constant rattle of cowries, which vendors hung from their wrists on strings of twisted grass. As he browsed the huts, Foster would have found turkey vultures crowding the walkway like pigeons. They feasted on the rest of the city's fowl, protected as a sacred species. But if Foster had any thought of buying enslaved people there, instead of waiting on Adoke, he was out of luck. Captives were not sold out of the market.

As he continued his tour, the captain was most intrigued by the religious sites. Ouidah was home to a vast cross section of spiritual traditions, resulting from the Dahomean government's habit of trying to gain support from the gods of the peoples it conquered. The religion of the Hueda, in particular, had been allowed to go on flourishing after Dahomey seized political control in the eighteenth century. Everywhere Foster went, he would have seen wooden or clay figures of Legba, the god thought to be responsible for misfortune. The figures were supposed to provide insurance against evil magic.

Foster was taken to a temple dedicated to Dangbe, who was the most popular god in the city, if not the highest ranking. Dangbe was understood to be incarnated in individual snakes—specifically pythons, which commonly grow ten feet or longer. Foster described the place as a square structure with ten-foot walls "covered with snakes." There were trees inside, "loaded with the repulsive things, revelling in their deified elation." Burton estimated that Dangbe had a thousand devotees in the city. The worshipers who were present during Foster's visit were clutching the snakes, letting the animals' brown and olive bodies glide around their necks and waists.

Foster was glad for the chance to explore. "I thought it not waste," he later wrote, "as I was storing up my knowledge of the many things it takes to make up the world." The days there were breezy, and frog calls filled the air during the cool nights. But as time went on, he started getting nervous. After a week, he was convinced he was being held hostage. He may have also begun fretting for his health, if not the health of his crew. It was widely known that the atmosphere on the African coast could be deadly to white men. Sailors heard tell about Guinea worm, an enormous parasite that would bulge beneath the skin of men's legs and feet, and of a contagious skin disease called the yaws. In Ouidah, the biggest threats were malaria (owing to the lagoon), dysentery and cholera (owing to the poor sanitation), and smallpox (owing to the cramped conditions). But Foster evidently managed to stave off any serious illness. And on the eighth day, he was summoned to meet Adoke again.

Kossola's conditions in Ouidah were a little more tolerable than they'd been while he was traveling. He had been in the barracoon a couple of weeks, long enough for his muscles to un-cramp after the long journey and for him to get past the initial shock of his kidnapping. He and the others in his barracoon, including those from his town, took turns climbing up the side of the barracoon to glimpse what was happening outside. There was a big white house between them and the harbor. Since arriving there, Kossola had also gotten his first look at a white man, the fabled species he had heard about.

It's uncertain exactly where in Ouidah enslaved people were kept as of 1860, after the European forts had been converted to palm-oil warehouses. Some locals now believe there were barracoons west of town, in the area called Zomai. The name means "light prohibited" or "fire prohibited," which is widely understood as a description of the prisoners' conditions: it is said that they were brought there by night and kept in the dark, as a means of control. But it's more likely the name referred to a ban on open fire, because gunpowder was evidently stored at the site. Others say the barracoons were in the village of Zoungbodji ("little plateau"), halfway between Ouidah and the beach. There are no records confirming this, and the historian Robin Law suspects it's a recent invention in the "quest for 'sites of memory' connected to the slave trade." However, it seems to sync up with Kossola's description. From this village, he would have been able to see the ocean, and the white house he described may well have been the customhouse, where an inspector doled out permits for people leaving the city, as part of the effort to stop smuggling.

John Duncan, the Scotsman who visited Ouidah in the 1840s, reported that captives in the barracoons were fed every morning and evening, their main dish being ground yuca, and were brought outside every day—though he said they were chained and "driven like cattle," not allowed to roam freely. But another observer from the same period said being in a barracoon was an experience of "filth, disease, and famine." In the middle of the nineteenth century, captives were being held for longer periods than ever, due to the

British Royal Navy's suppression efforts, and the longer they were held, the greater the danger to their health. During a British blockade in 1864, some 800 captives out of 2,000 would die from a combination of smallpox and starvation. But when Kossola looked back on the period, what he highlighted was the sense of community.

There were other barracoons surrounding Kossola's, holding a total of 4,000 people (by Foster's later estimate), with the captives divided up according to where they came from. "Sometime we holler back and forth," from pen to pen, telling one another where they came from, Kossola recalled later. They apparently didn't have much trouble communicating. Language barriers between regions of West Africa had been worn down over time, through trade. Most anyone who came from Yorubaland could understand other people from the region, even if their homes were hundreds of miles apart and they spoke different dialects. To the extent that barriers persisted, there were likely enough captives who were bilingual, or multilingual, to handle the task of translating. Some of the people held in the compound, both in Kossola's own barracoon and elsewhere, soon became his makeshift family. Their exact origins have been lost to memory, but twenty-first-century scholarship has established some likely possibilities.

One young woman confined there would eventually become known as Zuma. At age twenty-three, she would certainly have been married and probably had children. She'd already been sold twice. The historian Sylviane Diouf has argued that her name may have actually been Arzuma, taken from the Arabic word for Friday, which is sometimes used among the Nupe, a predominantly Muslim group that now occupies Nigeria and northern Benin. Diouf suggests Zuma might have attended Qur'anic school, starting around age seven, and learned to recite the Qur'an and write in Arabic. Or her name may instead be linked to Zuma Rock, in Nigeria's Middle Belt. Natalie Robertson, who visited the village surrounding Zuma Rock, found that facial marks common in the area's dominant cultural group, including a line running from the bridge of the nose across the cheek, matched later descriptions of Zuma's scars.

Another woman in the barracoons, who would become known as Lottie in America, was seventeen at the time. Her original name, which would be recorded as Kanko, may—as Diouf believes—have originated from the Yoruba name Kehounco, a Yoruba name indicating her parents had been infertile for a long time before her birth. However, Robertson believes it came from the name Kaninkon, which refers to a people in northwestern Nigeria.

Kanko herself later said she was from Dahomey, but Diouf believes she and her family may only have been refugees there. Regardless, the circumstances of her capture are more clear. She later told her grandchildren she had been sent on an errand by her mother, with a warning not to take a certain path, because it was rumored that slave catchers were lingering there. Curiosity got the better of her. She was kidnapped and never saw her parents again.

Among the voices Kossola heard through the bars, many others could have belonged to captives who would soon wind up on the *Clotilda*. Jaba—or Jabbar, Jaybee, J.B., or Jabez—would become the group's de facto doctor and herbalist. There is evidence that Ossa Keeby, or Osia (as he is remembered by his descendants), was a fisherman in Africa; it's clear that he liked to fish in his spare time, in Mobile. His name, according to Diouf, could have come from either the Osse River or the Kebbi River, both in Nigeria, or from the word Hausa, the name of a large ethnic group. Kuppollee, who would shorten his name to Pollee, came to America wearing earrings that indicated he was a priest in the orisha religion. He would have completed months' worth of spiritual training, learned a new language, and received tattoos or scarification on his face and body, indicating which god he was devoted to.

After three weeks, a white man came to the barracoons, accompanied by two Dahomeans, one an interpreter and the other clearly some kind of chief. Kossola and the others were ordered to stand in circles of about ten each, divided by gender. By the time they finished spreading out, there were hundreds of clusters. The white man started making his way through, standing in the center of each circle, inspecting the other prisoners. Whenever someone seemed to catch his eye, he inspected the person's body all over. When he pointed to one, the captive would be taken off to the side. For every man he selected, he also picked a woman. Eventually he came to Kossola's circle. He stopped in front of the young man, staring. Kossola would have been able to feel the eyes upon him: on his knees, his bare stomach and chest, his wiry arms, his face.

Back when the Ouidah slave trade was booming, local traders had been known to rub palm oil on the captives' skin to make them look healthier, and they had often shaved the heads of older men to get rid of any gray hairs. A German visitor in the 1780s saw the women captives all dressed up in multiple waistcloths, "as if they were going to a dance." But in this case they wore very little, and what clothes they had were surely soiled and tattered.

The buyers were given broad leeway. Portuguese buyers were at one time so insistent upon buying adolescent men that they would lick captives' faces to check for stubble. Larger ships also brought along their own doctors, whose inspections were humiliating for prisoners. The doctors would pry their jaws open, peering over their teeth to estimate the captives' age, and would look over their genitalia for signs of venereal disease. This buyer, however, had come alone.

"He lookee and lookee," Kossola later recalled. He examined their skin, their feet and legs and mouths. Eventually the white man indicated that Kossola had made the cut.

By the time he was finished, he'd selected well over 100 prisoners. Foster later put the number at 125, while Kossola thought it was 130: 65 men and 65 women. Then he climbed into a hammock and was carried off, headed, from what Kossola could see, toward the big white house.

Afterwards Dahomeans came with generous portions of food, saying the prisoners should eat up because they were about to leave. "We eatee de big feast," Kossola later said. Then they cried, already missing the friends they had made in the barracoons. Clueless as they were about what was coming next, the only comfort they had found lately was in being together. Kossola's homesickness again washed over him.

Early the next morning, well before sunrise, Foster was back on board the *Clotilda*. He had four hours until Adoke's men were due to meet his first mate on the beach, with the new cargo in tow. In the meantime he had to make space by unloading the beads, rum, and other merchandise he was using as payment. All told, his stay in Ouidah had gone more or less the way he'd pictured. Besides the captives he had chosen at what he called the "warehouse," he had picked up one extra man. Adoke had wanted to give the captain a gift, as a sign of goodwill, and had invited him to choose one person from a selection of prisoners native to Dahomey. It was rare for natives to be sold; according to oral tradition, it had been forbidden since the earliest days of the kingdom to traffic in native prisoners, on punishment of death. This law was so strict that captive women who had become pregnant while traveling through Dahomey were barred from being sold. Exceptions were made only for Dahomeans who had committed serious crimes.

Adoke, flattering Foster for his supposedly "superior wisdom and exalted taste," had urged him to pick the best specimen in the lot. Foster chose one named Gumpa, who was said to be related to Adoke himself.

Later, after Foster had made all his selections, the interpreter had asked if he wanted the captives branded. For professional dealers, this was a matter of routine, so much so that each one brought an iron bearing his own symbol. The process was usually done on the beach, before the captives were loaded. The branding iron would be held over a fire, then dipped in palm oil so it wouldn't stick to the flesh. It would be pressed against each prisoner's ribs or hip, or sometimes to the chest, for long enough to sear the skin thoroughly. Baquaqua recalled that when he experienced it, a man stood waiting with a whip, lest anyone refused to submit. Foster indignantly declined the offer.

As the sun came up, Foster and his men prepared for their return trip. They tossed watertight casks off the deck, loaded with the cargo they had brought from Alabama. Local workers, who had floated out to meet them, began carrying the barrels back toward the shore, cutting back through the treacherous surf.

Once again Kossola found himself bound up in a line with other captives, being marched to the shore. Duncan, who witnessed a similar caravan, noted that the captives clearly had no awareness of what they were about to experience. Baquaqua described it the same way: "All I knew was, that I was a slave, chained by the neck, and that I must readily and willingly submit, come what would, which I considered was as much as I had any right to know." Kossola, for his part, was well aware that he was about to leave Ouidah. But the concept of leaving the whole continent of Africa was likely not even intelligible to him and his companions.

Since the 1990s, two supposedly historical landmarks have been recognized near this beach in Ouidah. One is a Tree of Forgetting, on the southern edge of the city, which captives supposedly had to circle repeatedly—nine times for men, seven for women—so that their spirits would not harass the people who had enslaved them. The other was a Tree of Return, which they circled three times, supposedly so their spirits would eventually return to Africa. But there is no contemporaneous record of these rituals, and the historian Robin Law has made a persuasive case that they were invented recently.

However, captives went through another ritual that must have been equally demoralizing: their heads were shaved, to avoid the risk of lice. Given the importance of hairstyles in nineteenth-century Africa—they could convey a person's ethnicity, family, social status, or profession—this was almost tantamount to erasing their identity, Diouf has written. After Baquaqua was captured, an old acquaintance once recognized him by his hair, which was shaven on the sides and across the top but long in three spots. And a shaved head could mark someone as a slave. It signified "the cutting off of past affiliations," according to Diouf, and "a sort of virtual death."

Kossola later gave two discordant accounts of what happened next. In one, he was "stolen" by a Dahomean, for reasons unclear, and hidden under the customhouse. From there he heard the waves crashing on the beach—a completely novel sound to him—and wanted to get a closer look. He crept out from his hiding place and climbed up the stockade fence. He saw some of the other captives in a little boat and called out to them. Then Foster noticed him, and he was forced to go along.

In the second version, as the chain gang moved away from the barracoons, they saw white men standing all around speaking with Dahomeans. Then Kossola spotted Foster, whom he recognized from the day before. When Foster noticed the captives were ready, he ended his conversation and got into his hammock to be carried across the lagoon. Kossola and the others followed, wading deeper and deeper until the water was up to their necks. Kossola didn't swim well; for a moment, he panicked, thinking he was going to drown. But everyone made it safely across.

On the other side, Foster was already getting into a canoe. As he sailed off, the Dahomeans started unchaining the captives and shoving them into boats. They sat on the bottom, packed together as tightly as possible. There weren't enough spaces for everyone to fit; it took several trips. Kossola waited for his turn, but before he knew it, the last boat was leaving without him. He was almost left onshore. Then he saw his friend Ossa Keeby in a boat and felt the urge to go with him. "So I holler and day turn round and takee me." In the first version of the story, there is no mention of Ossa Keeby, but in both cases Kossola was one of the last to set out on a canoe.

On board the *Clotilda*, Foster's men were counting the captives as they were loaded on board. They were up to 75 when the situation went haywire. The man surveying the coast with a spyglass called out: "Sail ho! Steamer leeward ten miles!"

Foster looked toward the coast and saw black and white flags, "signals of distress," mounted all along the shore. Two steamers, he wrote, "hove in sight for purpose of capture." His memoir is ambiguous about whom the ships belonged to. According to a later account by the Mobilian writer Emma Langdon Roche, which was based partly on interviews with Foster's widow, Foster thought the Dahomeans "dealt also in piracy" and wanted to seize the *Clotilda*. But it's doubtful they would have gone to all this trouble of loading the captives onto the ship if they had planned to capture it. A better explanation comes from Henry Romeyn, who wrote about the *Clotilda* in 1894. He believed they were vessels of the British Royal Navy. Either way, though, Foster is clear on the point that his crew began to panic. They wanted to take the boats off the ship and paddle to the shore. Foster discouraged them, saying they would never make it through the surf.

While they argued, two more canoes drifted up, carrying a total of 35 more captives. The crew quickly loaded them onto the ship. They were up to 110 people, 15 short of the figure Foster had planned on, but it would have to do.

Kossola and the others in his canoe prepared to climb over the gunwales, onto the waiting vessel. Before they could leave, the Dahomeans grabbed what scraps of clothing they had left, yanking them from their bodies. They said the captives would have plenty of clothes where they were going. He held on, but the cloth was quickly torn away. "Oh Lor', I so shame!" he recalled later.

The captives stepped on board and were shown to a hole. They climbed down, getting out of the breeze and finding themselves in a dim space. Scores of other Africans were already huddled inside. The ceiling was just high enough for them to stand while they found places on the wooden floor to lie. It was so tight, they were practically on top of one another. Then the hole was covered, and everything was dark.

5

ARRIVAL

West Africans were susceptible to violent nausea at sea. That was the conclusion drawn by Alexander Falconbridge, a British doctor who worked on four transatlantic slave voyages during the 1780s. "The hardships and inconveniences suffered by the Negroes are scarcely to be enumerated or conceived," he wrote in 1788, after he had joined the abolitionist movement. "They are far more violently affected by seasickness than the Europeans. It frequently terminates in death, especially among the young women." To be sure, these comments reflect a view, dominant in the doctor's era, that there were major biological differences between Black and white people. This was part of the theoretical infrastructure that had been developed to justify slavery, but it could be hard for even white abolitionists to get beyond it. At the same time, there's no reason to doubt that in general, African captives were more prone to seasickness than their white overseers, if only because they weren't accustomed to maritime life.

During the years when Falconbridge was crisscrossing the ocean, slave trafficking was a highly professionalized industry. For three centuries, Europeans had been perfecting their methods through trial and error. In terms of ship construction, they had learned to install racks for captives to sleep on, so they could be packed in even more tightly, but had also begun cutting slots below deck, to help with ventilation. Cooks on slave vessels tended to serve the same dishes, often involving yams, corn, and rice, which were cheap and filling, but also had the benefit of being easy on captives' stomachs. Crews developed work routines tailored to the unique demands of these voyages, which on some ships included fumigating the captives' living space and scrubbing the deck with sand to remove vomit and refuse. Of course, the point of all this was not to make the conditions more tolerable for the captives. It was about maximizing efficiency in the name of profits. Slave-ship captains and their backers wanted to keep the captives alive, and relatively healthy, for the sake of the bottom line. For centuries before the *Dred Scott* ruling, in 1857, the assumption that enslaved people were mere commodities had already been integral to what happened on the Middle Passage.

By 1860, however, in the days of illegal voyages, the industry had reverted to the ragtag nature of its early years, in some ways for better, in others for worse. The *Clotilda* was a typical slave ship for its period, both in the sense that it wasn't built to carry human cargo, and that its captain and crew were not deeply experienced in the ways of slaving. Foster and his men would have had to figure everything out as they went along. (Even if the *Clotilda* did sometimes ferry enslaved people around the West Indies, it would hardly have prepared Foster for a transatlantic voyage.)

The captives spent their first thirteen days locked below deck, in the ship's hold. They were confined in groups of six and eight. The ceiling was higher than in a typical slave ship, high enough for even the taller captives to stand if they bent over, but on average each captive had only a few square feet of personal space. With no room to move around, captives found that their muscles quickly started to cramp. Sunlight would have briefly beamed in twice each day, when sailors opened the hole to bring the captives food; but otherwise it must have been too dark to even make out the contours of their own naked bodies. Baquaqua recalled that "day and night were the same" to him and his shipmates, "sleep being denied as from the confined position of our bodies," and conditions aboard the *Clotilda* were similar.

Just as bad was the endless rocking of the boat, which sometimes must have been violent enough to send them lurching into one another. Their skin constantly chafed against the coarse wooden planks. Falconbridge wrote that in his experience, the floors where enslaved people sat became so filthy, so thick with "the blood and mucus which had proceeded from them in consequence of the flux" of the ship, "that it resembled a slaughter-house." "It is not in the power of the human imagination," he added, "to picture itself a situation more dreadful or disgusting." The odor that wafted out of these quarters was "noxious" to everyone, including the crew, sometimes strong enough to make captives pass out.

And there was another cause of nausea for the *Clotilda* shipmates: the psychological terror they felt, especially in those first thirteen days. To people who had never seen an ocean, the waves alone were chilling. "I so skeered on de sea!" Kossola recalled years later. The wind and the waves were so loud, he said, they sounded like "de thousand beastes in de bush."

Perhaps it wasn't only the threat of a shipwreck that scared them. They came from a culture where spiritual forces were understood to be at work in nature. Olaudah Equiano, a West African native who made the same journey roughly a century earlier, later wrote that he'd assumed from the waves that the "Ruler of the seas was angry," and that he himself would be "offered up to appease him." Another day on his trip, Equiano spotted some dolphins and thought they were manifestations of the sea god. The wind calmed after they passed, confirming his sense of their power.

Besides the seasickness, the captives were tormented by thirst. They were given water only twice each day. When Kossola remembered this period of the trip more than seventy years later, the dehydration was his starkest memory. "Oh Lor', Lor', we so thirst!" Water kegs took up a lot of space, and captains, bent on using every inch they could for profitable cargo, typically brought as few as they could get away with, keeping rations to "the extreme of existence," as one sailor put it. On Baquaqua's ship, thirst drove another captive to such desperation that he once tried to snatch the knife of the man who brought them water. "I never knew what became of him," Baquaqua reflected; "I supposed he was thrown overboard." Crew members became desperate for water as well. On a voyage in the 1770s, the sailor James Field Stanfield eagerly licked the dew off his ship's hen coops every morning, until the rest of the crew discovered his "delicious secret," after which he was resigned to licking up his own sweat.

While the captives were suffering belowdecks, Foster was focused on getting back without further troubles, whether from the Royal Navy or his own crew. The incident with the two steamers at Ouidah had been a close call, but the winds had been favorable, and within four hours the ships were well out of sight. On day twelve, as Foster was rounding Cape Palmas, on the Liberian coast, he saw another man-of-war. Once again, "We thought we were captured," he wrote; but the *Clotilda* blew by it, thanks to heavy winds. The captives would never know how close they had come to salvation.

When this last patrol ship was far out of sight, Foster decided it was safe to bring the captives up into the sunlight. By then their muscles were so atrophied, their bodies so numb, that they couldn't walk. The crew members had to hoist up their arms and support them as they limped along the swaying deck. Though they were glad for the fresh air, finding themselves on the open sea was frightening in its own way. In every direction, all they could see was water. They hadn't the faintest idea where they were going.

From this point onward, their conditions improved somewhat. They spent much of their remaining time on deck, likely being rotated out of the hold in groups. They would lean over the gunwales, mesmerized by the water coursing beneath them: sometimes blue, sometimes green, occasionally blood red. Whenever it rained, they leaned back, faces to the sky, trying to catch drops on their tongues, and cupped their hands to pool the water up. It's likely they also sang: songs about bereavement, songs that reminded them of home. They may, like captives on other slave ships, have even used singing to communicate among themselves covertly.

Force-feeding was common on these voyages. When captives refused to eat, Falconbridge wrote, he had seen "coals of fire, glowing hot, put on a shovel, and placed so near their lips, as to scorch and burn them," with the threat of the embers being forced into their mouths. Judging from the Africans' later accounts, though, it seems Foster never resorted to these kinds of measures. Abile, one of the captives from Kossola's town, refused food because she still worried the white people were cannibals, trying to fatten her up. When she recounted this later in life, she didn't mention being force-fed. In a separate conversation, Kossola said Foster was a good man. In his telling, Foster didn't beat them or go out of his way to abuse them.

Most of what the shipmates experienced has been lost to memory. For instance, they never spoke about rape or sexual abuse, but these were common on slave ships in general. Death, too, was a near-daily occurrence on the larger vessels. A ship doctor on his morning rounds, Falconbridge said, "frequently finds several dead; and among the men, sometimes a dead and living negroe fastened by their chains together." In such situations they would both be brought on deck and unshackled, so the deceased captive could be tossed overboard. Kossola reportedly said in one interview that no one on the *Clotilda* died, but in another he said two captives passed away on board. Another survivor recalled in 1932 that two passengers, a girl and a man, became ill and were thrown overboard. It's likely that at least one person, and perhaps as many as three, died in transit. Regardless, the survival rate was surprisingly high, especially since Foster didn't bring along a doctor. The mortality rate on slave ships disembarking from Africa, as of 1860, was 6.4 percent, and on the *Clotilda* this would have translated to seven deaths.

After six or seven weeks on board, Foster had his crew stop at the Dry Tortugas, some seventy miles beyond Key West, and down-rig the ship, making it look like a "common coaster" instead of a slaver on a cross-continental voyage. About this time, Foster also sent the captives back belowdecks, knowing patrol ships might be near. The next day a sailor came down, bearing a green branch, to signal that they were near land and the trip was nearly over. While the captives were hidden, the ship passed two more men-of-war, but this time there was no pursuit. The ships "took no notice of us," Foster wrote, thanks to the precautions he'd taken.

On the return voyage, instead of sailing parallel to the Florida coast, the *Clotilda* swung out deep into the Gulf of Mexico, to deter any suspicion that it was coming from Africa. It went west, beyond Alabama, and curved north when it was well out of sight from Mobile Bay. The crew dropped the anchor in Grand Bay, Mississippi. It was a Sunday or Monday in early July. Kossola would be convinced, for the rest of his life, that it had been a seventy-day journey. In fact the days had numbered around forty-five.

The map of the Mobile Bay delta resembles nothing so much as an intricate paper stencil cut from paper. It splits into dozens of rivers and streams, dividing the land into an archipelago. Some of the islands are minuscule; others sprawl for several miles north to south, in curving and twisting oblong shapes. It's easy enough there, without being more than a few miles from civilization, to wind up in deep wilderness. There are endless places to get lost or to hide.

The delta would be the *Clotilda*'s destination, but Foster wasn't planning it that way when he first dropped anchor near the Mississippi coast. He and Meaher had agreed there would be sentinels around the mouth of Mobile Bay and the Mississippi Sound, keeping watch for the ship so they could quietly alert Meaher about the arrival. Meaher was supposed to come with money to pay the crew, who would then help unload the captives onto a tugboat. They would then scrub the hold where the slaves had been living, clearing out all traces of the recent voyage. They would change the masts and the sails and the boom, and they'd sail across the Gulf to the Mexican port city of Tampico, a place the *Clotilda* had anchored several times before on cargo runs. To make the ship's transformation complete, in Tampico they would also change its name and get clearance papers for a trip to New Orleans. It's hard to imagine this would have fooled anyone in Mobile. More likely the point was simply to shield Foster, Meaher, and their cohorts from prosecution.

No part of the *Clotilda*'s journey is more storied than this last stretch. There are at least eight accounts, all written decades after the fact. They contradict one another on many details and in some parts contradict themselves. The sources that are likely the most reliable—Foster's memoir and a newspaper story based on an 1890 interview with Tim Meaher—can mostly be synthesized. But there are several mysteries about the affair that will never be resolved.

Foster wrote that when he arrived in the Mississippi Sound, there was no sentinel there to notice him. When he realized he was on his own, he reluctantly told the crew he'd have to leave for a while and go onshore.

Not so fast, the sailors replied. They were eager to get their money and didn't trust the captain. If he tried to unload the captives without paying them first, they promised they would kill him.

Foster reasoned with them. He didn't have the money on hand, especially since he'd agreed back in Cape Verde to raise their wages. The captives would stay on board, but he himself had to leave for a while; there was no way around it. The crew gave in and helped take down one of the boats.

Once on land, Foster said, he flagged down someone in a horse and buggy. He offered the owner $25 to drive him the forty-odd miles to Mobile, the equivalent of more than $700 now. He couldn't brook any delay, because the longer the *Clotilda* sat near the coastline, the greater the risk of its being seen.

Foster wrote that he found a tugboat and brought it back to the *Clotilda*. He explained to the crew that time had been so tight, he hadn't been able to get their money. The men, perhaps surprised by his gall, gave him an ultimatum: either he come back with the payment or they wouldn't relinquish the ship.

Foster took the tugboat back into Mobile and obtained $8,000 in cash, presumably from Meaher. He also recruited five men to accompany him, evidently for backup. When he got back, he paid the workers what he had originally promised, reneging on his promise to double their wages.

Meaher said he learned from a messenger that the *Clotilda* had arrived. An enslaved man who worked for him, named Noah, remembered it this way, too. He said Meaher was sitting on his porch, with his legs propped up on the banister, and was smoking his pipe. Meaher said he tensed up when he heard the pounding of a horse's hooves in the distance. When the horse and its rider came into sight, kicking up a haze of dust, the animal's body was flecked with foam. Meaher put down his pipe and bounded down the stairs. Between heavy breaths, the messenger whispered to him, "The n—ers have come!"

The next part is difficult to square with Foster's account. Meaher said *he* was responsible for getting the tugboat. He claimed he dispatched someone to find his friend James Hollingsworth, a tugboat captain, who happened to be in church. In his version, the envoy explained that Meaher needed his fastest tugboat and that Hollingsworth was to ask no questions. Once Hollingsworth had it ready, Meaher supposedly took it to the Mississippi Sound as fast as he could. Meanwhile, his younger brother, Burns, was instructed to take his steamship the *Czar* to the mouth of the Spanish River and wait there.

Foster and Meaher agree that the *Clotilda* was towed along the coastline, up through Mobile Bay, and deep into the delta. Below deck, on the slave ship, the captives were startled at the unfamiliar sound of the tugboat's engine, unlike anything they had heard in these many days at sea. They speculated that it was a massive swarm of bees.

Downriver from Twelvemile Island, a remote piece of land shaped like a diamond, the captives were transferred to another steamship (the *Czar*, according to Meaher). Foster said the mates and crew were put on a steamer and sent to Montgomery. Meaher said the crew rode along with the captives up to the plantation of John Dabney, a merchant of food and dry goods, who already owned several dozen enslaved people. Dabney shared Meaher's views on slavery and race. (A few years after the Civil War, the bodies of two Black men would be found in a river near his property, one with handcuffs on his wrists, and Dabney would be charged in their murder.) At the edge of Dabney's property, Kossola and his shipmates were ushered off, and they stepped for the first time onto American soil.

According to Meaher, the *Czar* went back down the river, where he and the *Clotilda*'s crew waited for another steamship, the *Roger B. Taney*, which was headed to Montgomery on its weekly trip. When the ship arrived, they boarded under cover of night. The crew members were put belowdecks and given cards and whiskey. Meaher had asked for supper to be delayed until he got on board. The meal was announced at 9:30 P.M., and when Meaher took his seat at the head of the table, "his face wore a most nonchalant appearance," the newspaper reporter wrote in 1890. "He was plied with all manner of questions as to his whereabouts during the earlier hours of the trip, but to all of these interrogations he made evasive replies and was wholly noncommittal."

Meanwhile, Foster took his ship—his finest achievement as a carpenter—into a bayou, where he stacked it with firewood. He was evidently afraid it had been spotted. According to a much later account, he used seven cords, amounting to a pile twenty-eight feet high and fifty-six feet across, and set them alight. At the same time, he also caused the ship to sink, likely by opening a toilet pipe or boring a hole in the side, so it would flood with water. As the ship went down, it must have given off as much steam as smoke.

Meaher said that when the *Taney* reached Montgomery, he didn't want a single member of the crew to be "turned adrift" there, lest they start talking about their voyage to Africa. So they were put on a train to New York City, "where they were paid off and discharged."

A few questions remain. If Hollingsworth, the tugboat captain, really was in church that morning, then the *Clotilda* must have arrived on a Sunday. But Foster claimed in his memoir that it was July 9, a Monday. There's reason to believe Foster had it right. Newspaper advertisements from 1860 show that the *Taney* made its weekly trip on Mondays, starting at four P.M. Alternatively, it's possible the whole affair happened over a forty-eight-hour period. Foster and Meaher were both vague about the timing.

It's also hard to say where the events diverged from Meaher's original plan. When Foster had arrived in Mississippi that morning, he still planned to take the *Clotilda* to Mexico and change its name. Perhaps he thought Meaher was going to bring a full-size steamship to the Mississippi Sound, so the captives could be transferred there, rather than in the delta. If Meaher had done this, it wouldn't have been necessary to take the *Clotilda* up Mobile Bay, where it was likely to be spotted—and in turn, Foster wouldn't have been forced to torch the ship. Why did the day have to end with the *Clotilda* sinking to the riverbed, half incinerated, rather than sailing to Tampico?

And who actually owned the *Clotilda* at that point? Meaher claimed he had bought it for $35,000. But according to Emma Langdon Roche, who spoke with Foster's widow, the captain regretted for the rest of his life that he had burned the ship. He counted it as a financial loss for him, because it had been worth more, in terms of sheer dollar value, than the enslaved people he received as payment for the expedition.

Somehow the press learned about the ship's arrival immediately. It's possible Meaher tipped a reporter off. In the heated political climate of 1860, where the future of slavery in the United States was a matter of violent debate, this breach of the slave-trading ban was deemed newsworthy everywhere. On

Tuesday, July 10, a brief syndicated report ran in at least ten newspapers, from New Orleans to Wisconsin—eliciting vastly different reactions, no doubt, between readers in the North and South. It was dated July 9. "The schooner *Clotilda*, having on board a cargo of Africans, amounting in all to 103, crossed the bar to-day and anchored in the bay, where she was met by a steamboat, which took the negroes on board and proceeded up the river to some unknown point," it read (though in some cases the ship's name was misspelled *Clotilde*). The next day the news was published in Mississippi, Georgia, Virginia, Maryland, Washington, D.C., New York, Massachusetts, Vermont, and Iowa, and throughout the week it would continue to spread, eventually reaching the European press.

The local authorities were likely reluctant to bring charges. Part of the responsibility fell to Thaddeus Sanford, who presided over the U.S. customs office. Sanford had deep connections to the local business community. He had been elected president of the bank of Mobile in 1833, and for twenty-six years he had owned and edited the *Mobile Register*, which, under his leadership, had become one of the city's chief venues for discussions of slavery. Its editorials had argued that slavery was a local and state matter, while also claiming slave owners' rights should be protected by the federal government no matter where in the country they traveled. Sanford had sold the paper in 1854, the year after he was chosen by President Franklin Pierce to oversee the customs office.

The U.S. marshal, Cade Godbold, who was appointed to his post the same year, was also a sometime business owner and state legislator. Godbold was a loyal member of the pro slavery Democratic Party and would soon become an officer in the Confederate military. Both he and Sanford owned slaves.

But as federal workers, under a president who had repeatedly promised to stamp out the illegal slave trade, they couldn't ignore the *Clotilda*'s arrival, not in the midst of all this national press. On that Thursday, three days after the ship's arrival, Sanford wrote a letter to the U.S. secretary of the treasury, informing him about the voyage. He followed up with a telegraph the next day, saying there was "increased reason" to believe "a vessel with Africans on board" had entered into local waters. Sanford said he had telegraphed the customs office in New Orleans and asked it to send a boat from the Revenue Cutter Service (a forerunner to the Coast Guard) to help investigate.

The day after Sanford sent his telegraph, his old newspaper, the *Register*, published an editorial praising the culprits: "Whoever conducted the affair has our congratulations on his or their success, as the case may be," it read, "whether the Africans came from the Gold Coast via Key West, or whether they made a straight-out trip by the shortest route from their native land." The paper took the voyage's success as evidence that the slave trade was effectively back open—which the editors considered a cause for celebration. "Why should not those who are in want of negro labor import it at a low cost, when they are civilizing and Christianizing a set of barbarians by the same course which redounds to their interest?"

Sanford dispatched Godbold, the U.S. marshal, to go snooping around the delta, an area Godbold knew well. Sanford believed the *Clotilda* was "secreted [*sic*] in some one of these by-places," he wrote to Cobb: unless, as rumor had it, the ship had been destroyed. Godbold set out on the evening of July 16, a week after the ship's arrival.

For Kossola, Keeby, Zuma, and the others, conditions had barely improved since they left the ship. Now they had a little more freedom to move around and had scraps of clothing to cover themselves; but they had been divided up into smaller groups, the better to stay hidden, and warned not to speak above a whisper, lest anyone hear them while passing on the river. Instead of Dabney's house or even his storage barns, they were forced to crouch down in the "canebrake country," the thickets of grass and bamboo that rose high out of the marsh. There they were tormented by mosquitoes; as Kossola said later, they felt they were going to be eaten. But they were lucky if they didn't have worse problems. The delta is infested with dangerous animals: bears, bobcats, feral hogs, alligators, sharks, and several kinds of venomous snakes (including diamondback rattlers, which grow as long as seven feet, and aggressive cottonmouths). The shipmates' crude tents, fashioned from the *Clotilda*'s sails, didn't afford much protection.

On top of the mosquitoes, they probably had skin infections, diarrhea, constipation, and dysentery. And it was still impossible for them to get a decent night's sleep. James Dennison, Meaher's enslaved riverboat pilot, was assigned to move them to a different part of the canebrake every day. They had no idea what would happen next or when they'd be rescued from the marsh. "In this strange land," Emma Langdon Roche wrote many years later, after interviewing them, "among strange faces and an unknown tongue, the Tarkars" (as she called them) "say that at first they almost grieved themselves to death."

It was later reported that they stayed for eleven days, successfully evading federal investigators. In 1890, Meaher claimed there had been one extremely close call, but he boasted that he escaped it with a ruse. Someone got word to him that the authorities had found out where the captives were being held and had chartered a steamboat, the *Eclipse,* to find them. Meaher said he gave $50 in gold to a "trusted employee." "The *Eclipse* is going after the negroes this evening," he reportedly said. "Take this and fix the crew with liquor." Legend has it that when federal officials realized the *Eclipse* men were in no shape to operate a ship, they rounded up another crew, but by the time they arrived at Dabney's, it was too late. The captives had been moved to another canebrake farther up the river. The officials supposedly searched for days and never found them.

The second hiding place was Burns Meaher's property, up in Clarke County. There the Africans were introduced to plantation life. For people who had lived their entire lives in freedom and who still did not see themselves as slaves, the shock was extreme. Cotton was just coming into season, and they were ordered to help with the picking. They spoke no English, but every time they failed to say, "Yes, sir," "Thank you, sir," or "Please, mistress," they explained years later, they were taken out and whipped until they pleaded for mercy. Ultimately an enslaved person who had grown up in America gathered them together at night and covertly taught them the languages of courtesies that their overseers expected.

However, federal records reveal an episode that oral tradition has glossed over. Thaddeus Sanford, the customs official, wrote to the U.S. treasurer that Godbold *had* in fact found the captives at Dabney's plantation: more than a hundred, by the marshal's count. "He did not discover the schooner which brought them here," Sanford wrote on July 18, "but gained information that appears to be conclusive that she had been scuttled and sunk somewhere up the river."

Godbold sought out the acting district attorney. He wanted authorization to take the captives with him, but the district attorney shot down his request. "He says there is 'no warrant in the statutes authorizing a process for taking possession of the negroes' in the absence of a Judge," Sanford explained in his letter. It's unclear why the federal judge, William Jones, couldn't be reached, but he might have been intentionally ducking any involvement. In any event, Jones would not have been sympathetic to the investigation. At least twice before, he had gone out of his way to absolve defendants who had brought African-born slaves into Alabama. And in this case, he had a personal connection: he and Tim Meaher were close enough that Meaher had named a ship after him.

The district attorney had forwarded the case to the U.S. attorney general, to see whether he wanted to intervene. As of the eighteenth, when Godbold wrote this letter, everyone was still waiting for the response. Sanford worried that soon the captives would all be sold, "and so distributed and mingled with our slave population that they can never be identified." Despite their political loyalties, it's possible Sanford and Godbold felt that Meaher was outflanking them and genuinely wanted to catch him. Either that, or Sanford was only feigning concern so that he and the marshal wouldn't be accused of shirking their responsibilities. "Mr. Godbold is much chagrined at this aspect of the case," Sanford wrote, "and proposed if I would stand by him to take the negroes at once into his possession. I told him he had better ask authority directly from the Government."

Sanford's prediction quickly came true. Within days after the U.S. marshal visited Dabney's plantation, Meaher started rounding up the men who had committed to buying captives. Some of the would-be buyers, jittery because of the criminal investigation and the press coverage, backed out of their agreements. The rest made arrangements to board one of Meaher's riverboats. Dennison ferried each buyer up to the hiding spot, and there the Africans were brought out and made to stand in two long rows: men on one side, women on the other.

They must have been somewhat worse for the wear. Burns had a volatile temper and was known as an especially callous master. He had been making them sleep under a wagon shed. Each white man would walk between the rows, carefully examining them, the way Foster had done two months earlier. Some looked closely at the captives' teeth, and they may have gotten more invasive still, though the Africans never mentioned it later. Those who were picked were ushered to one side. When a buyer was finished, he would wave his hand around the group he had picked out, then draw his palm to his chest.

Kossola, Zuma, Abile, Keeby, Gumpa, and the others who stayed took the separations hard. After weeks together on the ship, they had developed deep attachments. "We cain help but cry," Kossola said later.

In the end, the Meahers took more than half the captives themselves. Thirty-two of them, split evenly between men and women, went to Tim

Meaher; twenty went to Burns; and the others, including Kossola, went to Tim's older brother, Jim. Foster took at least ten.

At the national level, it seems the *Clotilda* news was quickly forgotten. Most papers never followed up on the brief announcement of its arrival. But the regional press continued covering the saga. On July 23, the *Mobile Mercury* reported on the sale, saying that "some negroes who never learned to talk English went up the railroad the other day." It said there were twenty-five, "apparently all of the pure, unadulterated African stock."

On or before July 25, the federal prosecutor, A. J. Requier, filed paperwork for the captives to be seized. He asked that both Dabney's plantation and Burns Meaher's property be searched. Judge Jones waited until July 27 to issue the order for Godbold to carry out the search. He also ordered Burns Meaher and Foster to appear in court. Foster's charge was failing to report the *Clotilda*'s arrival to the customs department, a violation carrying a $1,000 fine.

It's hard to say whether Tim Meaher was ever charged. Years later, he claimed he had been arrested immediately after the *Clotilda*'s arrival and let out on bail. Noah, the enslaved man on his plantation, confirmed this independently in 1893. According to a report by a local writer, Mary McNeil Scott, Noah said he remembered Meaher leaving the plantation to intercept the *Clotilda* and being gone for a week. When he came back, riding a horse, his wife was deeply relieved. Noah remembered Meaher saying he'd "done fooled 'em now," and adding that the authorities were looking for the captives on the other side of Montgomery, while in reality they were still hiding in a canebrake nearby. However, the court records have no mention of Meaher being charged or released.

As the investigation went on, the local press turned scornful. "We have no idea that any vessel by the name of the *Clotilde* ever did bring any Africans inside of Mobile Bay," said a July 28 editorial in the *Mobile Mercury*, the same paper that had just reported several days earlier on the sale. That "such a one did is all a mere fabrication," it went on, "and so Federal officers have been on the qui vive for ever so long a time, all without making any discovery."

To no one's surprise, by the time Godbold went back to Dabney and Burns Meaher's plantations, with the authority to seize the captives, they were long gone. Sanford wrote to the treasurer again on August 10, filling him in. "So much time elapsed" since the day Godbold found them there, he wrote, "that the opportunity was afforded to run them off." There were rumors that some of the captives had been sent to Mississippi. Sanford also worried the case against Foster would fall apart. Two "respectable persons" had spotted his ship near Grand Bay in July, Sanford explained, and they "saw the negroes and conversed with the man having them in charge," but they didn't see Foster, who they were told had gone ashore for a steamer. And since they didn't see the ship's name painted anywhere, they couldn't swear under oath that it was the *Clotilda*. Still, he believed the circumstantial evidence was strong enough to make up for the lack of witnesses.

Meanwhile, Sanford continued, everyone knew that two other steamers were involved in towing the *Clotilda* up the river. He presumably meant *Czar* and the *Taney*, though he didn't name them. But there was not enough evidence to indict the captains or their crews. "What everybody seems to know, no one individual has as yet been found who will testify to it in terms." Requier, the district attorney, who would later write poems praising the Confederacy, argued that there was no need to rush, because the steamers traveled constantly on local waters and could be seized anytime.

In early September, Bill Foster got married. His bride was Martha Adalaide Vanderslice, the daughter of his landlord. At age twenty, she was roughly fifteen years his junior. It's unclear whether they had been romantically involved before Foster's trip to Africa in the spring, but an obituary published many years later implies that he wooed her over that summer, after he returned. The couple said their vows at the Exchange Hotel in Montgomery, the same hotel where Jefferson Davis would be introduced to the public in 1861 as the president of the Confederate States. The newlyweds traveled to Talladega Springs, a tiny town some sixty miles north, for their honeymoon, hoping to keep a low profile; but Foster's reputation preceded him, and the town was abuzz about his presence.

All the while, tensions between northern and southern states had been building. In April and May of 1860, during the middle of the *Clotilda*'s voyage, the Democratic Party had a convention in Charleston, where the delegates sought to choose a nominee. Stephen A. Douglas, a U.S. senator from Illinois, was the front-runner; but the southern faction refused to support him because of his moderateness on the question of slavery. (Douglas thought settlers in new territories ought to decide for themselves whether slavery would be allowed, whereas southerners, following the Supreme Court's ruling in *Dred Scott*, wanted slavery protected in all territories.) The convention ended in a stalemate after a number of southerners walked out, leaving the group without the two-thirds majority needed for a vote. Later that year, in

Baltimore, the party successfully made Douglas its nominee—but by then its ranks were split. Some southern Democrats ran their own candidate, and others decamped for a new party.

In the November presidential election, Abraham Lincoln won almost every northern state but none in the South. His party's official platform was anathema to southern planters. It called the recent acts of slave importation in the United States "a crime against humanity" and a "burning shame" to the country, and demanded that slavery not be extended into new states or territories. That December, South Carolina voted to secede from the Union.

Mobile's power elites felt a growing sense of a divide from the federal government. And accordingly, the will to prosecute Foster, the Meahers, and their accomplices—whatever will there had been in the summer—died out. An order was issued for Foster, Burns Meaher, and Dabney to appear in court on December 10. Burns Meaher and Dabney, however, did not receive their summonses until the seventeenth. At a hearing in January 1861, Requier asked to have their cases dismissed. A newspaper reporter wrote in 1890, after interviewing Tim Meaher, that Meaher had been put on trial. He had only gotten off, the paper reported, by showing that he'd traveled on the *Taney* every single week in 1860. Meaher claimed the affair had cost him $100,000, which comes out to nearly $3 million now. But again, there is no mention of such a trial in the official records. As for Foster, his case was continued after a January 10, 1861, hearing; but the next day, it became moot, when Alabama became the fourth state to secede from the United States. The following month, leaders from six other states would convene in Montgomery to form the Confederate States of America.

6

WARTIME

Tim and Jim Meaher together owned a vast amount of property north of Mobile proper. Their manufacturing base, Meaher's Hummock, was separated from the city by a dense forest and an impassable swamp and could be reached only by circuitous detours. As of the early 1860s, by at least one account, Native Americans still inhabited the woods, in homes crafted from pine bark; and there also were legends of buried treasure, said to be guarded by the ghosts of bandits and pirates. In this rugged setting, the brothers had built a formidable operation. Their lumber mill was on a high embankment made of oyster shells and hard-packed clay, and looked out on a broad bayou forty feet deep. A fawning correspondent for the *Mobile Evening News*, who visited in 1853, described it as "one of the most romantic spots that nature ever, in her gayest mood, endowed." But there was a near-constant industrial ruckus, from the clanking of hammers, the ringing of anvils, and the buzzing of saws. Powering the operation were a hundred or so workers who lived on-site, sleeping in what Meaher called his "barracts" and taking their meals in a mess hall, at a single table long enough to seat them all. As of the late 1850s, the Meahers were producing some two million feet of sawed lumber and 1.2 million shingles a year. All told, at least half a dozen ships were also built at the adjacent shipyard.

The shipmates who were not sold to other buyers spent the Civil War years on the brothers' plantations, evidently not far from the mill. Census and tax records show that as of 1860, Jim Meaher owned twenty-two other slaves, eighteen of whom were men between the ages of eighteen and fifty-five. Burns

Meaher also owned nineteen people as of that summer—eight adults, two teenagers, and nine children. There are no public records showing how many were on Tim Meaher's estate. It's clear, however, that from the moment they arrived, the shipmates stuck out. Noah later recalled that the ones who came to Tim Meaher's plantation were initially dressed in rags and pieces of corn sacks. Mary Meaher, the owner's wife, had pants and shirts and petticoats fashioned for them, and she told Noah to deliver the clothing. He dropped some off at each cabin. More than thirty years later, when he told the story, the memory of them stepping out in their new attire made Noah laugh so hard he cried. They were wearing the garments inside out, upside down, and backward. The women had tied the dresses around their bodies with the sleeves, and the skirts were dragging behind them in the sand. The men had their legs in the sleeves of shirts, with the cuffs buttoned around their shins.

Diouf has suggested the shipmates deliberately put on the clothing in the ways they would have worn garments back home. After all, they had been around Americans long enough by then to know how the clothes were usually worn. Whether it was intentional or not, the episode speaks to their collective status as outsiders. Their appearance and speech also set them apart. From Noah's perspective, they seemed physically larger, with darker skin and straighter posture than their American counterparts. Their speech was quick and smooth; he said it flowed along like the deep parts of Chickasabogue Creek. It seemed to him that they never argued among themselves. There's an unmistakable note of fondness in his descriptions. But when Kossola looked back on the period later, what stood out to him was the sense of alienation. Everyone gave them strange looks. They wanted to talk with the other enslaved people, but no one understood their speech. "Some makee de fun at us."

Kossola and the others at Jim Meaher's plantation were forced to sleep under the house, in a cellar-like space where the owner had set up quarters. Blankets were in short supply, and the shipmates spent many winter nights shivering in bed. Still, by the Meaher family's standards, Jim qualified as humane. He wasn't like his brother, Tim, Kossola said later. He didn't have them whipped by overseers; and once, when he noticed Kossola's shoes were wearing through, he got the young man a better pair. Whenever one of Jim's brothers (Kossola didn't say which one) lost his temper with the shipmates, Jim would try to calm him down, reminding him that they were still adjusting.

The shipmates were not put to work right away; first the native-born Black people had to teach them American farming methods. The shipmates had never seen a mule dragging a plow. Back home, Roche reported, "they had but to scratch the top soil and whatever they planted grew." The Alabama soil, by comparison, was so much less fertile that they thought it must be cursed. But they adapted, and over time they came to be seen as dependable workers—as peaceful as lambs, as Noah put it.

But there were limits to what they would put up with. At least twice the men ganged up on Americans who tried to use violence against the African women. The first time, a field hand made the mistake of trying to whip someone in their group. The other shipmates reportedly seized the lash and started whipping the field hand instead. After that, Kossola said later, the man never tried whipping African women again. The second instance involved a young woman to whom Mary Meaher had taken a liking. The girl was gentle and pretty, Noah remembered. Mary Meaher had assigned her to household duties like dusting and sweeping. The girl apparently had trouble learning the technique. One day Aunt Polly, the household cook, lost her patience and smacked the girl on the head. The girl put a hand to her face and stood still, looking like she'd "lost her senses." From Noah's description, it seems there was a pregnant silence. Polly started backing toward the door. Then the girl threw back her head and screamed.

Never in his life, Noah said, had he heard a sound like the one she made. The noise gave him goose bumps. Most every African on the plantation heard it. From the cotton fields, the creek, and the rice fields they came, carrying rakes, spades, and sticks, letting out a fearsome noise themselves. When Polly saw them coming, she bolted up the stairs, yelling out prayers for God's protection. The Africans pounded on the door outside, looking so ferocious that Noah thought they were going to kill everyone. Noah followed Mary Meaher outside and tried to calm them down. Before long the shipmates were marching back to the fields, carrying their rakes and hoes. In the weeks that followed, Noah said, Polly left the plantation and found work in Mobile, and no one tried to hurt any of the shipmates again.

The Civil War began on April 12, 1861, with the shelling of Fort Sumter, the U.S. Army garrison in Charleston. Combat started in earnest that July, at the First Battle of Bull Run, near Washington, D.C. White Mobilians had mixed feelings about the conflict. Two-thirds of their state delegates had voted for Alabama to secede. Some of the city's business leaders predicted that once the South gained its independence, Mobile would truly come into its own as an international metropolis. Much like Tim Meaher, they envisioned a future southern republic that would annex Mexico and the West Indies. Mobile would be in the geographic center. With this picture in mind, the editors of the *Mobile Daily Advertiser* argued that the city ought to be made the capital of the Confederacy.

At the same time, it was clear that among Alabama's cities, Mobile had the most to lose if the war went poorly. Given its position on the coast, the city was vulnerable to attacks. It had three military posts: Fort Morgan, Fort Gaines, and Mount Vernon; but none were well equipped to fend off Union soldiers. That first summer was "long, dreary, and anxious," wrote Kate Cumming, a local nurse who kept a diary during the war years. "Everything was arranged for sudden flight to the woods. In case of an attack, none of the women and children would have been permitted to remain in the city. The signal was to be the ringing of the town bell, and if it happened to give an extra clang, we were on the alert in a moment."

For the shipmates, not much information about the war trickled through. They didn't hear about its commencement, and at first they couldn't tell what was getting the white people so flustered. Eventually someone told them people in the North were fighting to free them from slavery. The news brightened their spirits. They started to wonder if their freedom might be imminent. But as the months went on, nothing happened, so "we think maybe dey fight 'bout something else."

As of July 1861, Mobile had only a modest turnout for the military, with about 20 percent of the men between eighteen and fifty signing up, many for single-year commitments. Those who stayed home were reluctant to help build up the defenses. City authorities proposed a tax of $50,000 to improve the forts, but there was such an outcry, the issue was dropped before it came up for a vote. Later, when the mayor tried to recruit white laborers, offering $2.50 a day (now the equivalent of about $65), plus meals, again Mobilians demurred. It was difficult and often dirty work. Instead the authorities drafted slave labor, paying the masters $1 a day plus expenses for the help of each able-bodied man.

Multitudes of enslaved men, on periods of sixty-day leave from their owners, joined this workforce. "They are in such numbers," wrote one Mobilian who saw them at work, "that they look like ants on the side of an ant hill. Just as we passed, the signal to 'knock off' work was given, & they obeyed the summons with alacrity, forming at once into companies, to march into the city, where they are quartered." The jobs included strengthening the existing forts, constructing a new garrison, planting makeshift mines in the waterways, building barriers at the mouths of the rivers, and digging earth-works where soldiers would be stationed with heavy artillery. Early on, the living conditions were unimaginably poor. The workers were housed near a swamp, amid vast swarms of mosquitoes, and were constantly catching fevers, measles, and pneumonia. Later on, new quarters were built, mostly to drive down the mortality rate.

However, based on a report from 1922, it seems the shipmates were likely spared this particular assignment. Kossola told an interviewer that when-ever Confederate officers came near the plantation where he was living, the planter, evidently Jim Meaher, would yell, "Run to the swamp." There they'd hide until it was safe to come back out.

Kossola spent the war years on the Alabama River, riding on the Mea-hers' ships. At each stop he carried on wood for the engine and helped load the freight. The diary of William Howard Russell, who rode one of the Meahers' ships in the spring of 1861, gives an idea of what the atmo-sphere must have been like. The ship Russell was on, the *Southern Republic*, was "nothing more than a vast wooden house," he wrote, "of three sepa-rate stories, floating on a pontoon which upheld the engine." There was a dining hall at one end, surrounded by dormitories, and a cluster of small rooms upstairs. Passengers would sit at their tables, in hazes of cigar smoke, talking about the war. They claimed they would "burn every bale of cotton, and fire every house, and lay waste every field and homestead," before they would give in to the Yankees, Russell reported. The tune of "Dixie" played constantly, like an ice-cream-truck jingle, from a calliope (a shrill, steam-powered organ) on the roof.

In Russell's description, workers like Kossola wore little clothing—perhaps by choice, given the heat they labored in—and at every stop, they raced toward the shore to gather firewood. The overseer would stand at the end of the gangplank, holding his whip, berating them. When Kossola rem-inisced about it as an old man, he could still hear the overseer's voice, telling him to run faster, scolding him for not carrying large enough loads. He found himself perpetually exhausted. At night, the workers all slept on the floor, with the ship's wooden beams creaking loudly and its engine roaring. There were evenings when Kossola stood on the deck, seeing the fireflies flash above the water, feeling so worn out he could barely stand. Sometimes it was all he could do not to tumble overboard.

From Russell's account, it's clear that the *Clotilda*'s voyage had already achieved the status of legend by 1861. It's also clear that Meaher gloried in his notoriety, though he continued to deny the incident had actually happened. When a passenger narrated the tale that spring, "It was worth while to see the leer with which [Meaher] listened to this story about himself," Russell wrote.

"Wall now!" the captain said. "You think them n—ers I've abord came from Africa! I'll show you. Jist come up here, Bully!" A boy of about twelve approached. His skin was "jet black," Russell noted, and his teeth had been partly filed down.

"Where were you born?" Meaher asked.

The boy said he was from South Carolina.

"There, you see he wasn't taken from Africa," Meaher told the passengers.

Someone asked about the parallel scars on the boy's face, which seemed to confirm he was an African native.

"Oh, them?" Meaher said. "Wall, it's a way them n—er women has of marking their children to know them; isn't it, Bully?"

What about the tattoos on his chest? a passenger asked.

"Wall, r'ally I do b'leve them's marks agin the smallpox."

"Why are his teeth filed?"

"Ah, there now! You'd never have guessed it; Bully done that himself, for the greater ease of biting his vittels."

Russell made it clear in his travelogue that he didn't trust a word Meaher said.

One evening on the *Southern Republic*, Russell said, the passengers were treated to a performance by a fiddler and a banjo player. The enslaved men danced a dance of "overwhelming solemnity," until "the rum-bottle warmed them up to the lighter graces of the dance." Meaher told everyone they were the "happiest people on the face of the airth."

Trade in Mobile was throttled during wartime. As early as the spring of 1861, Abraham Lincoln imposed a blockade on all the ports of the Confederacy between Texas and Virginia. Soon there was a federal ship stationed at Mobile Bay, controlling which vessels could enter and leave. For a place where virtually nothing was produced locally, where every item from food to clothes to candles had to be imported—and where the whole economy was based on cotton exports—this was a catastrophe, especially for the lower economic classes. The price of butter increased from 50 cents a pound to $5, and flour went from $45 a barrel to $400. In September 1863, the scarcity was so severe that several hundred poor women started a "bread riot." They marched downtown, wielding axes, hammers, and brooms and waving banners that said "Bread or Blood." They smashed store windows and pillaged the merchandise, mostly targeting Jewish-owned establishments. The women dispersed only when the mayor promised to supply them with food and clothing.

Kossola and the other shipmates suffered from the shortage as well. In place of coffee, they parched rice and drank the water; and since there was no sugar, they sweetened it with molasses. They didn't like the taste, but it was the best they could do. Jim Meaher sent word that he didn't want the enslaved workers to starve, so they were to kill one of his hogs anytime they ran out of food.

The affluent, however, found ways to keep up their prewar routines. It became evident after the first summer that Mobile wouldn't be attacked anytime soon. Balls and parties went on as usual, if anything becoming grander and more frequent. For much of the war, it was regarded as "the Paris of the Confederacy." Russell's travelogue describes an 1861 evening in wartime Mobile. "After dinner," he wrote, "we walked through the city, which abounds in oyster saloons, drinking-houses, lager-bier and wine shops, and gambling and dancing places. The market was well worthy of a visit—something like St. John's at Liverpool on a Saturday night, crowded with negroes, mulattoes, quadroons, and mestizos of all sorts, Spanish, Italian, and French, speaking their own tongues, or a quaint lingua franca, and dressed in very striking and pretty costumes." Russell found people gorging themselves on oysters, raw, roasted, stewed, deviled, broiled, fried, and mixed in puddings, "as if there was no blockade, and as though oysters were a specific for political indigestions and civil wars."

Scenes like the one Russell witnessed were possible, in part, because many of Mobile's sea captains moonlighted as blockade runners. The practice started as a way of helping the Confederate military. Mariners would set out for Havana, roughly a three-day journey if the weather was right. There they would trade cotton for military supplies. Over time, they also opened their services to civilians. Mobile's housewives learned to negotiate with sea captains along the wharves, handing over shopping lists for needles, buttons, thread, fabric, and sometimes hard candy for their children. Between 1861, when the blockade was imposed, and the end of the war, it's estimated that there were 208 successful runs, out of 220 recorded attempts. "Little wonder that today nearly every Old Mobile family worth its salt can point to a daring blockade runner somewhere in the family tree," the Mobile historian John Sledge has written.

Tim Meaher was known as the most daring of the bunch. He was responsible for at least two failed runs. In the first instance, a steamer called the *Gipsy*, which he and Foster both owned shares in, was seized by the U.S. Navy—either on the Mississippi coast in 1861, or near Pensacola, in 1863 (records show the Union seized two ships with the same name). The ship and its cargo were worth the equivalent of $360,000, which Meaher and the other co-owners never recovered. The second instance involved the ship known as the *Gray Jacket*. It left Mobile Bay on the night of December 30, 1863, carrying 513 bales of cotton—much of which came from the Meahers' own plantations. Half belonged to the brothers, and the rest they planned to trade on behalf of the Confederate government. A Union commander working the blockade spotted the *Gray Jacket*'s sails and gave chase. But a heavy storm set in, and amid the wind and the high waves, Meaher's ship slipped into the darkness.

The commander caught up with it the next morning, finding it damaged by the squall. He fired a gun across the bow, as a warning shot, and the steamer surrendered. Around ten A.M., the commander sent a boat over. The twenty or so crew members and three passengers were put onto another ship, and Meaher and his chief engineer were sent to New Orleans on the *Gray Jacket*. There the government impounded the vessel. One Navy official, Lieutenant Commander William P. McCann, described it as "one of the most perfect sea boats he ever saw." He was eager to convert it to a Union gunboat.

Two months later, Meaher fought in court to get the ship back. He claimed he hadn't been working for the Confederacy. In fact, he said, he'd been trying to leave Alabama altogether, because of his loyalty to the Union. His wife and children were going to meet him in Havana, and from there they would all relocate to Maine, where his mother still lived.

The prosecutors must have been amused at his audacity. They may have pointed out that the ship itself was clearly named for the uniforms of the Confederate military. They presented a document found on board the ship: it was an agreement between Meaher and a Confederate officer, saying the purpose of the trip was to sell cotton for the Confederacy. Meaher had an explanation—he said the Confederates had forced him to sign it, threatening to seize his ship if he refused.

The federal judge was not persuaded that Meaher had meant to leave Alabama. "We are satisfied that at the time of the capture, no such intention existed," he wrote. Meaher's appeals dragged on well after the war was over, until the U.S. Supreme Court ruled in 1866 that he was not entitled to any compensation.

* * *

Back on the Meahers' plantations, the war years also marked the beginning of the shipmates' adjustment to American culture. This was a process of negotiation that would go on for the rest of their lives. One aspect was the taking of new names. Kossola's name in America would logically have been Oluale Kossola, but Jim Meaher struggled to pronounce it, so the young man made it easier on him. "Well, I yo' property?" he asked. He said Jim Meaher could call him Cudjo. For some ethnic groups in West Africa, Kodjo is the name given to boys born on a Monday. Oluale, his father's name, was converted to Lewis, so Kossola was known thereafter as Cudjo Lewis. Several of the others took on common American names. The man named Oluale became Charlie Lewis (though he and Cudjo were not related). Kanko became known as Lottie; Gumpa took on the name Peter Lee; Omolabi became Katie; Abile became Celia; and Abache became known as Clara. Zuma may have shortened her name from Arzuma, and Kupollee began going by Pollee.

The shipmates also adapted to some American customs, like observing the Christian Sabbath. When they first arrived, they were glad to have Sundays off, Cudjo said, so they danced like they'd always done back home. He remembered that the American-born enslaved people would call them savages and laugh at them. But a Black man known as Free George came to the plantation and introduced himself. George's wife had a job cooking for a Creole man, a free person of mixed race. She had saved enough money to buy George's freedom. George wanted the West Africans to know they weren't supposed to dance on a Sunday. He explained the meaning of the Christian Sabbath, which was foreign to them. "Nobody in Afficky soil doan tell us 'bout no Sunday," Cudjo recalled. They heeded George's words. This is not to say, however, that they were changing their religion—at least not yet. Noah mentioned that whenever there was thunder and lightning, the shipmates would run outside and throw themselves onto the ground, offering prayers. Once the Americans and the Africans had learned enough of each other's language to converse, the shipmates told the others they associated God with the sun and moon.

The shipmates also continued practicing rituals from back home, apparently unconcerned with what Americans might think. When there was a new moon, Noah said, the Africans would collect bay leaves in the woods and fashion crowns for themselves. Once, he remembered, a baby was born on the night of a new moon, and it was given a tattoo of a snake eating its own tail, with a moon in the center. Noah noticed that the child was treated specially. According to Diouf, the child was likely born to Gumpa, the Dahomean, and another shipmate named Josephine. The rainbow snake is a sacred symbol in Dahomey's culture, and the image of it biting its own tail represents the continuity of the kingdom. If it was indeed Gumpa's child, the tattoo indicated that even though the child was born in America, his parents saw him as a member of Dahomean society.

Generally, when an African child was born, Noah claimed, the mother would take her to a creek and toss her in. If the child would kick and try to stay afloat, the mother would jump in and save her. But if the infant passively let herself sink, the mother would turn away and leave her to drown. Diouf has concluded that Noah could have been describing one of two customs from Benin. There was a time when abnormal babies were said to be deities that belonged in the water, according to Diouf, and the idea was that they had to be returned. This was the reason they were left to drown. In another custom, which is still practiced, male babies are put in the water so the mother can assess their virility. If the boy's penis does not move, he's typically given a treatment.

It was Noah's understanding that the shipmates had a similar ritual for the elderly. Once, he said, an elderly enslaved man named Mose had intense pain in his leg, "so bad he couldn't even hobble." The *Clotilda* group pointed at him and said something in Yoruba, which Noah took to mean that Mose should be drowned. Noah was appalled; he accused them of being "wicked." But they explained that back home, at the third new moon of each year, everyone in the town had to swim to an island off the coast. Adults who were too sick or too old to make it simply drowned—or at least that was how Noah understood it.

However, he found the group's funeral practices strangely moving. Whenever someone from their ranks died, the shipmates would pick a spot at the top of a hill, where they'd dig a deep grave—about fifteen feet down, in his estimation. They would fill it halfway with tree bark. They also put bark around the corpse, binding it with switches of sapling, and put the body on the mound. Once the grave was filled to the top, they would stand around it, with each person crossing her arms and linking hands with those on either side. They would move slowly in a ring, swinging their legs in synchronicity. As they danced, they sang a mournful song, with tears running down their cheeks.

This description is entirely plausible, according to Diouf, but it suggests several departures from the way these funerals are typically done in West Africa. Most important, the ritual is usually reserved for people over sixty years old. Since no one in the group had reached that age, Diouf believes the shipmates conferred the status of elders on their oldest members. "The funerals show that the shipmates maintained the fundamental structures of their communities by sliding the building block, the age group, forward," she has written. "In other words, they did not eliminate certain rituals because the people they were geared to did not exist among them; they simply shifted the attributes and prerogatives of the elders to the eldest among them, thus assuring the continuity of their culture."

By July of 1864, Major General William Tecumseh Sherman was well into his crusade through the South, which would ultimately cripple the Confederacy and hasten the end of the Civil War. Sherman began his attacks in North Georgia, with three Union armies under his command. After defeating Rebels in the town of Resaca and at Kennesaw Mountain, he set out for Atlanta. With its factories and its railroad connections, the city played a critical role in supplying the Confederate military. Sherman cared less about seizing its resources than cutting off the enemy's access.

Mobile played into the general's strategy. He wanted the Port City attacked—partly to divert Rebel troops that might otherwise get in his way, and partly because he knew Mobile, with its own railroad connections and its waterways, could be valuable to the North. David Farragut, a Union Navy commander, had led the charge against New Orleans in 1862 and was well positioned to make an advance on Mobile. Early on the morning of August 5, Farragut sent a line of battleships into Mobile Bay. Working in coordination with troops on land, he laid siege to the garrisons. Fort Powell was abandoned by the Rebels within hours. By August 8, there was a Union flag above Fort Gaines as well. The shelling of Fort Morgan lasted for weeks, until the garrison was reduced to a "mass of debris," in the words of its Confederate commander. It formally surrendered on the afternoon of August 23, 1864.

The Union's victory likely did not change the day-to-day lives of the *Clotilda* shipmates much. The Confederacy still occupied Mobile itself, plus several more garrisons nearby, and skirmishes would continue for another eight months. But at some point—likely in this period, while the northern soldiers were stationed at the mouth of the bay—James Dennison, the Meahers' riverboat pilot, tried to escape. A band of other enslaved people, including Kanko, went along with him. Kanko had spent the war years at

Burns Meaher's plantation, where she was assigned to domestic duties, such as cooking, cleaning, and gardening. The owners forced James and her to marry, in hopes that they would procreate, as she would later tell her grandchildren. But Kanko considered the ceremony a sham, and at first she refused to be intimate with her new partner.

According to an account later written by their granddaughter, Dennison made plans to board one of the Meahers' ships late at night and escape, presumably to where the Yankees were stationed. He hoped he and his companions would all be emancipated. At the last minute before the trip, however, he realized someone had informed on him. He had to act fast, so he rounded up some of his siblings and cousins, along with Kanko. They sailed down the Tombigbee River, in deep darkness, while their owners rode along the shore on horseback, hoping to intercept them. When the refugees reached Twelve-mile Island, it looked like they were in the clear. The land there was swampy, and their owners' horses couldn't trudge any farther. But before they reached the end of the bay, some other white men caught them. Burns had put the word out to other slave owners in the area.

Elsewhere in the Confederate states, during the second half of 1864, Sherman was continuing his march to the southern coast. Atlanta surrendered on September 2. Before Sherman's troops departed that November, they laid the city to waste, destroying every railroad, factory, and commercial building that might be of value to their enemies. From there, they marched the rest of the way through Georgia, reaching Savannah on December 10. The soldiers tore up some 300 miles of railroads along the way, seized more than 20,000 horses, mules, and cows, confiscated nearly ten million pounds of corn, and destroyed cotton mills, bridges, and telegraph lines. The campaign devastated southern morale at the same time that it cut off supply lines.

In the spring of 1865, between the losses the Confederacy had sustained in battles in Virginia and the damage Sherman was by then inflicting in the Carolinas, Robert E. Lee decided the war had to end. He surrendered in Virginia on April 9, 1865. As it happened, on that same day, the Union soldiers near Mobile were waging a final attack on the last Confederate garrison in the area. Three days later, in the early evening on a Wednesday, thousands of Union soldiers marched into the city itself. As the sun went down, the place was "resonant with every patriotic refrain," one resident wrote, "from the Star Spangled Banner to John Brown's Soul is Marching On. Every one realized for the first time, as he listened to the 'tramp, tramp' of the orderly files, that 'the boys' had come."

For most white Mobilians, the spectacle was galling and humiliating, but Black residents were gleeful. Many rushed down to the wharf and greeted the soldiers. Kate Cumming, the young nurse, wrote in her diary that she was out of town when the soldiers arrived. When she came back, some days later, she was scandalized at how the formerly enslaved people were behaving. In the daytime, they were "gaily dressed," and some refused to get off the sidewalks to let Cumming pass. At night, she could hear Black Union troops serenading freedwomen who lived nearby. "The songs consisted chiefly of what was to be done with the white people, when the negroes got into power," she wrote. "One of their favorites seemed to be that *lovely* refrain, 'The hanging of Jeff Davis on a sour apple tree.'"

Cudjo was on one of the Meahers' ships when he heard the joyous news. The ship was preparing to set out for Montgomery, but for some reason Jim Meaher had not shown up. Cudjo thought it was odd. Then he saw some Yankee soldiers picking berries off of mulberry trees. The soldiers told Cudjo and the other enslaved men they were free; they no longer belonged to anyone. The workers didn't understand. In that case, where were they going? The soldiers said they didn't know. "Dey told us to go where we feel lak goin'," Cudjo remembered. "They say we ain' no mo' slave."

The shipmates on Burns Meaher's plantation came down to celebrate with the others. They fashioned a drum and played it like they would have done back home.

PART II

AFRICAN TOWN: 1865–1935

7

TO HAVE LAND

On July 4, 1865, three months after the Union army entered Mobile, the freedpeople in town threw a celebration. They clustered in the parks and listened to speeches by Black leaders, who urged them to work hard and be patient. The main event was a parade, where 6,000 men and women marched in columns through the downtown streets, wearing their finest clothing. It's possible no civilian in Mobile, Black or white, had ever seen so many African Americans gathered in one place. To Ann Quigley, the principal of a white secondary school, seeing this gorgeous city, this very monument to the cotton trade, overtaken by freedpeople seemed "a sight calculated to strike horror into every Southern heart." But with two regiments of Black troops flanking the crowd, carrying bayonets and rifles, there was nothing resentful whites could do to stop it.

For nearly all the freedpeople within a wide radius of the city, Mobile had become the default place to go after leaving a plantation: a place of relative safety, a place for gleeful reunions. "Almost the entire negro population of South Alabama and a large portion of Mississippi is looking to Mobile as the *Ultima Thule* of its hope," wrote one Mobilian later that year. By 1870, the city would record more than a 50 percent increase in its Black population, from 8,400 in 1860 up to 13,900, while the white population dropped by more than a third. But already, in this ecstatic moment, the challenges that would define the Reconstruction era were becoming manifest. To begin with, Mobile had a dire housing shortage. Freedpeople who couldn't find rooms in the city were staying on the outskirts, in deserted houses, in huts they built with rejected lumber, under sheds and bridges, and along riverbanks. The Union general overseeing Mobile had issued an advisory on April 22, saying that if freedpeople could stay on with their former masters—being paid for their labor and having their newfound rights respected—they ought to stay in place. The government did not want to "disturb abruptly the connections now existing," he wrote.

And out in the countryside, well removed from the Black Union troops, whites were taking it upon themselves to enforce the directive. They began patrolling the rivers in southern Alabama, looking for boats of African Americans who were trying to leave plantations, to "hang, shoot, or drown the victims they may find on them," an official with the Freedmen's Bureau wrote on July 29. Other bands of whites roamed the highways, chasing freedpeople with their hounds. That summer, Black travelers were "almost invariably murdered" no matter which route they took, the official wrote. Angry whites were also threatening to burn down the local schoolhouses and churches where Blacks assembled, and one Black preacher had to be put under special guard by the Union Army.

There is no record of exactly where the *Clotilda* shipmates went in these early months, but Cudjo mentioned that someone invited them to come sleep in a "section house." The Meahers apparently wouldn't let them stay on the plantations, even for a little while. Cudjo recalled later that they were at a loss about where they'd live next.

At some point the African men had a meeting, as their elders would have done, to discuss the long-term future. They agreed they wanted to go back home. It was obvious to them that Foster and and Meaher had a moral obligation to take them, if only because they'd given the Meahers five years' worth of unpaid labor. At the same time, they knew the white men wouldn't agree and saw no point in trying to persuade them. So they decided instead to save up and pay their own fares. The men told the women they'd have to help save money. If they saw fine clothes, they shouldn't desire them. The women turned the admonition back on the men, saying they shouldn't wish for fine clothing or new hats, either. They'd all work together.

They felt a sense of urgency. They had heard that slavery was still practiced in places not so far away from Mobile—including Cuba, a relatively short boat ride away—and they worried that if they didn't leave soon, they might be taken to work there. This fear was in fact well founded. Besides all the violence that summer, there were credible reports of men in Clarke County, where Burns Meaher's plantation was located, coaxing freedpeople into contracts to go work near the coast, then selling them into slavery in Brazil and Cuba. The Freedmen's Bureau received reports that these men were also buying African Americans from their former owners at $50 to $100 a head.

As Diouf has pointed out, there was an organization that would have been eager to help the shipmates leave the United States, had it known about their situation: the American Colonization Society. It had been created in 1816 by white southerners who wanted to rid the country of free Black men and women by sending them to the colony that became Liberia. The abolitionist William Lloyd Garrison worked with the group briefly as a young man, but he soon became convinced it was undermining the cause of emancipation. "My warfare is against the American Colonization Society," he wrote in 1832. The more he examined the colonization project, he said, "the stronger is my conviction of its sinfulness." But throughout the years of its existence, the group had powerful backers, including James Madison, who served as one of its early presidents, and Thomas Jefferson.

Up until the Civil War, fewer than 11,000 Blacks had taken the ACS up on its offer, but it became more popular after emancipation. In 1867, several families from Mobile participated. They appealed to the Freedmen's Bureau for help leaving the country, and ultimately the federal government paid for their transportation to Savannah. From there the ACS sent them across the Atlantic, along with hundreds of other freedpeople. Once in Liberia, each household received thirty acres and six months' worth of support. Had the *Clotilda* shipmates learned about the ACS, it could have presented a singular opportunity. From Liberia, they could have taken a boat along the coast and found their homes, as other Africans had done successfully. But between the language barrier they were still dealing with and their physical isolation from downtown Mobile, they never learned about the program.

There were already several industrial firms in the northern part of Mobile County. Some of the men took jobs at powder mills, and others made bricks or worked for the railroad. The Meahers hired several, including Cudjo, to cut lumber at their sawmill. The men left for work at dawn every morning, and those at the Meahers' mill were forced to work an extra hour each evening for free, on threat of firing—lest they develop any notions of equality. The group apparently settled on a savings target of $1,000, guessing this was roughly what chartering a ship would cost. Their wages were $1 a day (about $17 now) at the lumber mills and 75 cents at the masonry. But apart from the rent, they had virtually no expenses. They subsisted on bread and molasses and whatever they could grow in their gardens. Once the violence subsided, the women started making trips into Mobile, carrying produce on their heads, in baskets they fashioned from strips of oak, and selling it door to door. When the baskets were empty, they sold those, too.

While they bided their time, the shipmates decided they needed a leader—a king or a chief, like they would have had back home. Gumpa, who came from nobility, was the obvious choice. No matter that he was from Dahomey, the country of their captors; he had been imprisoned and sold and enslaved just like the rest. Besides, as Cudjo said, he hadn't done anything to hurt them.

What sustained them during these anxious months was the increasingly tangible hope of returning home. As their savings grew, perhaps their minds fastened on specifics. How would they know where to go once they arrived on the continent? They couldn't even point to their homes on a map. Would they be able to find any relatives or friends?

When they reached their $1,000 target, they approached Bill Foster and asked if he'd take them back for that sum. That amount wouldn't even cover the basic expenses, he said—let alone turn a profit; and he had brought them over as a business venture, nothing more, nothing less.

So any hopes they had for an imminent return were quashed. In the best-case scenario, they were looking at an entirely different cost scale than they had realized, and it would take them years, not months, to save up enough. And the worst-case scenario, that they would never see their home country again, was looking more and more probable. Either way, it meant they had to start making lives for themselves in Alabama. As they talked it over, a different kind of vision emerged. They could build a kind of replica of their hometowns, at least for the short term: a place where they could speak Yoruba, cook familiar foods, raise children, and appoint a council of elders, where no one would mock their foreign ways. They would "makee de Affica where dey fetch us," as Cudjo put it.

Some weeks or months later, Cudjo was at work, cutting down trees at the Meahers' mill. His eyebrows were probably saturated with sweat, his arms and shoulders sore from swinging the axe. But when he saw Tim Meaher coming, he must have felt a jolt of adrenaline. He kept on chopping, mentally bracing himself.

The community had decided to ask Meaher for some land. Not a lot— not even enough to farm, necessarily—just enough to build houses on. This seemed like truly the least he could do. The group had agreed that Cudjo, because he was well spoken, ought to be the one to approach Meaher and present their case. This was an intimidating task. Meaher was mean-spirited even in normal circumstances and had a notorious temper. But the request was coming at an especially bad time. The Meahers had taken a severe financial blow after the war, losing nearly $1 million worth of assets when their enslaved people were freed. Business had also been bad since the war, with Mobile's wharf jammed with sunken ships and pilings, and with the nearby railroads largely destroyed. It was not inconceivable that Meaher would attack Cudjo or even try to kill him. The risk of prosecution would have been nil.

Meaher sat down on a tree Cudjo had just felled. He pulled out a pocket-knife and started whittling at the bark. After a moment, the young man stopped swinging the axe and stared at his boss. Apart from birds chirping in the trees or perhaps the sounds of wood being chopped and sawed in the distance, the scene would have been silent. Meaher noticed and looked up. He asked why Cudjo seemed so sad.

"Cap'n Tim," Cudjo said, "I grieve for my home."

Meaher replied that Cudjo had a good home where he was.

"Cap'n Tim, how big is de Mobile?"

Meaher said he didn't know—he'd never been to all four corners.

Cudjo said that if he were given all of Mobile, including the railroad and all the banks, he wouldn't want it, because it wasn't his home. "Cap'n Tim," he said, "you brought us from our country where we had lan'." He made them slaves. Now they weren't enslaved, but they were destitute, with no country and no land of their own. In all likelihood the shipmates had been rehearsing these arguments for weeks. Why didn't Meaher give them a piece of the land they were on so they could build homes?

Meaher was incensed. It's easy to imagine his eyes widening as he listened, a vein rising on his neck. He jumped to his feet. "Fool, do you think I goin' give you property on top of property?" he shouted. He had taken good care of his enslaved workers until emancipation, he said, and therefore he owed them nothing. They didn't belong to him anymore, so why should he give them his land?

Cudjo's reaction is not recorded, but there's little doubt that he was rattled. He may have felt he'd let the community down. Later he asked Gumpa to call an assembly where they could fill the others in. When they were all together, the shipmates agreed to resort to plan C: they would keep saving and buy land with their earnings. Their plan to charter a ship would have to wait indefinitely.

Cudjo's request probably cut deeper for Meaher than the young man realized. At the time of their conversation, it was a genuine possibility that southern tycoons like Meaher would have parts of their land seized by the federal government and divvied up among the people they had once enslaved. This was the famed prospect of "forty acres and a mule" that never came to fruition. In the century and a half since Reconstruction, the phrase has become a familiar shorthand for the country's abandonment of southern Blacks after emancipation; but the story of how that failure happened is rarely told, and it's critical to understand in order to grasp what happened to the shipmates and their descendants.

When the war ended, the federal government had no consensus or plan for what Reconstruction should look like. Lincoln had issued one possible blueprint in December 1863 that came to be known as the Ten Percent Plan: he offered to pardon any Confederates, except those in high-ranking positions, who would pledge allegiance to the Union and accept the abolition of slavery; and when 10 percent of any state's voters took the deal, that state could form a new government and be readmitted—with almost no regulation of how they treated Blacks, as long as they didn't officially reinstate slavery. The proposal showed that Lincoln did not "understand emancipation as a social revolution," the historian Eric Foner has written. However, Foner considers the Ten Percent Plan more of a "device to shorten the war" and to persuade whites to support emancipation—not a "hard and fast policy from which Lincoln was determined never to deviate."

As far as the freedpeople themselves were concerned, there were two main issues at play in Reconstruction. The first was the question of land. In this area, the precedent came not from Lincoln but from General Sherman. In January 1865, Sherman called together twenty Black leaders in Savannah to discuss the future of Georgia's Black population. The group's spokesman, a Baptist minister named Garrison Frazier, was clear about what they wanted: "to have land" and to "till it by our own labor." By any reasonable standard, they had already more than earned their stake in the plantations; and anyway, federal land giveaways to white families were an established part of the American tradition. But Frazier clarified that Georgia's African Americans weren't even asking for a giveaway. "We want to be placed on land until we are able to buy it," he said, "and make it our own."[487] Four days later, Sherman issued an order setting aside a portion of the Atlantic coast for the exclusive settlement of the Black population. It was to be divided up in plots as large as forty acres, and Sherman later said the army could lend mules to families.

As the word spread, freedpeople converged on the coast, hoping to claim their own plots—and the concrete idea of getting "forty acres and a mule" took hold throughout the South. In the summer, the commissioner of the Freedmen's Bureau ordered that the southern land under its control, some 850,000 acres, be distributed to Black families, in parcels of forty acres. The plan was to let freedpeople lease it at minimal cost and then buy it with their earnings. There wasn't enough land under federal control yet to give every freedman a sizable plot, but the policy was seen as a step in that direction. For the shipmates living in Mobile County, receiving forty acres each would have changed everything. They would have been entitled to more than a thousand acres altogether, which they could have farmed or potentially sold for cash. It also would have transformed the entire southern economy, breaking up the plantation system and creating a broad class of Black entrepreneurs. In the long term, that economic independence might have translated to political equality.

The second concern for freedpeople was getting the ballot. It was hardly a foregone conclusion that they'd be enfranchised; before the Civil War, in fact, only five New England states allowed Blacks to vote on the same conditions as whites. But throughout the war, the prospect of Black suffrage had started to gain traction, thanks to the influence of abolitionists like Frederick Douglass. Lincoln himself slowly came around. On April 11, 1865, two days after the formal end of the war, the president announced, in a speech at the White House, his qualified support for nationwide Black suffrage. "I would myself prefer that [the vote] were now conferred on the very intelligent, and on those who serve our cause as soldiers," he said. But three days later, on April 14, Lincoln was assassinated.

For the Radicals in the Republican Party, who wanted to see an aggressive intervention in the South, his death was a major setback. Andrew Johnson, Lincoln's vice president, assumed the White House on April 15—and he was no friend to the Radicals' cause. As a Tennessean, Johnson sympathized only with poor southern whites, who he thought were economically harmed by slavery. He sometimes displayed "a morbid distress and feeling against the negroes," his personal secretary later wrote. He did not share the Radicals' expansive view of federal power, nor their commitment to political equality for freedpeople. "This is a country for white men," he reportedly wrote to

Missouri's governor in 1866, "and by God, as long as I am President, it shall be a government for white men."

Johnson was prepared to welcome the southern states back into the Union on the most generous terms he could get away with. Under his Presidential Reconstruction plan, which he announced in May 1865, southern states could be readmitted to the Union once they passed new constitutions that banned slavery. He offered to pardon all Confederates who took oaths of loyalty and to restore their property rights, apart from their rights to own slaves (though the wealthiest property owners and the Confederacy's former officers had to apply for pardons individually). Johnson also annulled the order to give forty-acre tracts to freedpeople that summer, shortly after it was issued. The question of Black citizenship would be left up to the southern states. At first his plan was popular among white leaders on both sides of the Mason-Dixon. Bringing back the cotton industry promised to be a boon to the North's economy. Northern members of Johnson's party, the Democrats, thought the return of southern legislators would help their political fortunes, and moderate Republicans didn't want to spend their political capital securing Black rights. Only the Radicals were dismayed at Johnson's terms.

That fall, as the southern states started writing new constitutions that would satisfy the president—Alabama's was written in September—they also tested the limits of what the federal government would allow. They passed a series of "Black Codes," to reinstate the old order as nearly as they could. One representative law in Alabama allowed local judges to seize children from their parents and make them "apprentices," compelling each child to work for a "master" until adulthood. Another said that anyone deemed a "vagrant"—a legal category covering not just the unemployed, but also any "laborer or servant who loiters away his time"—could be forced to work without pay on a chain gang. (The governor vetoed some of these Black Codes to avoid a backlash from the North.) And in Mobile, a local tax of $5 was imposed on every Black man. Those who didn't pay were also consigned to chain gangs, according to the local Black newspaper. The *Clotilda* shipmates were likely exempt from this tax, since they were outside the city limits, but they may have been subject to other onerous taxes because of their race.

Over the summer and fall, the Radicals were discouraged, but they weren't giving up. They began laying out specific alternatives to Johnson's policies. In a speech that September, Thaddeus Stevens, a Congressman from Pennsylvania, called for the government to seize 400 million acres from the wealthiest 10 percent of southerners—a group that would have included Tim and Jim Meaher, as well as other white entrepreneurs who owned property in the area where the shipmates were staying. Under Stevens's proposal, each freedman would receive forty acres, and the rest of the land would be auctioned off in relatively small plots, with the proceeds largely going to Union army veterans. "It is impossible that any practical equality of rights can exist where a few thousand men monopolize the whole landed property," Stevens declared. "If the South is ever to be made a safe republic, let her lands be cultivated by the toil of the owners, or the free labor of intelligent citizens. This must be done even though it drive her nobility into exile. It they go, all the better." Even most Radicals were not ready to go as far as Stevens, but they all favored aggressive federal measures.

Johnson's response was to double down. By December, the southern states had all submitted their new constitutions and ratified the Thirteenth Amendment, which formally outlawed slavery. Johnson declared the Reconstruction process complete and withdrew almost all the Union troops from the South. As of January, all but 223,600 acres of southern land had been disbursed from the Freedmen's Bureau, back to white owners. But the Black Codes had cost the southern states the support of many moderate Republicans. These legislators wanted the South to accept that it had lost the war and to show some remorse—not to reinstate slavery under a different legal framework.

At the same time, the Radicals were gaining support from an unlikely source: big business. There was a clash here between the moneyed interests in the North and those in the South. If the leaders of the old Confederacy had their way, it was clear that they'd lower tariffs, nullify the national banks, and impose tighter corporate regulations at the state level—all measures meant to benefit planters, at the expense of the finance and manufacturing industries. Northern businessmen, therefore, started to find common cause with the likes of Thaddeus Stevens. Black suffrage, in particular, became a priority for these capitalists. After the Thirteenth Amendment was passed, the South gained twenty-nine U.S. representatives, because representation was based on the free population. Unless the freedpeople were given the ballot, the only effect would be to empower white southern Democrats. It was under these circumstances that Congress rejected the new southern state constitutions and refused to let the South rejoin the United States. "In a selfish point of view free suffrage to the blacks is desirable," a Rhode Island businessman wrote to Charles Sumner, a leading Radical legislator. "Without their support, Southerners will certainly again unite."

If Presidential Reconstruction was over, the second phase, Congressional Reconstruction, was about to begin. In early 1866, legislators passed a Civil Rights Act that granted citizenship to most freedpeople, along with certain kinds of legal equality: the rights to sue and be sued, to make and enforce contracts, and to buy and sell real estate. It annulled large parts of the Black Codes. When the bill came to Johnson's desk, he vetoed it. But the Republicans had enough votes—a two-thirds majority in each chamber—to override him.

The Radicals were also gaining popularity with the voters. At the elections in the fall of 1866, their party consolidated its hold on the legislature. They used the opportunity to pass four laws known as the Reconstruction Acts. These laid out new terms for southern states to reenter the Union: namely, they had to draft new constitutions once again, this time recognizing freedpeople's rights, including the right to vote. The Republicans also divided the South into five military districts, each overseen by a general. Only Black men and white men who took oaths of loyalty to the Union would be allowed to pick delegates for the constitutional convention, and the military would oversee the process.

Alabama's constitutional convention met in November 1867. Among the one hundred delegates, ninety-six were Republicans and eighteen were Black. The constitution that emerged was the most progressive governing document in Alabamian history. It established Black suffrage and the property rights of women, and allotted money for public education, created a state agricultural school, and made it easier for Black men to run for the legislature.

But neither the moderate Republican legislators nor northern capitalists supported a land-redistribution program. Legislators like Thaddeus Stevens thought it was sound political strategy, on top of being morally right. Stevens, in particular, hoped it would promote an alliance between African Americans and poor white voters. By this line of thinking, Reconstruction was principally a question "of labor, and not of race," as one Radical newspaper put it in 1867. But such an alliance would have been detrimental to the business class. The moderate Republicans, for their part, saw their party as representing business interests first, and freedpeople second at best. The elections that fall tilted the balance of power toward the moderates. Democrats, campaigning on the notion that the Reconstruction party was out of control, snatched seats in

Maine, California, New York, and Ohio; and at the same time, referendums on Black suffrage were defeated in Minnesota, Ohio, and Kansas. "It would be vain to deny," *The Nation* opined, "that the fidelity of the Republican party to the cause of equal rights" had been "one of the chief causes of its heavy losses." Afterward, Stevens's group could no longer command as much influence. Instead of pushing for further reforms, Republicans began to focus on protecting the gains they had already made. By the time Alabama reentered the Union in the summer of 1868, the prospect of any land-redistribution policy already seemed unrealistic.

So the shipmates went on working and saving, all for a prize much humbler than forty-acre plots. Whatever land acquired they would have to buy at full price, and their budgets were small. At least a few graduated to semiskilled labor. Cudjo learned to make shingles and bricks, Pollee Allen stacked lumber, and Ossa Keeby became a carpenter.

By this time Cudjo was one of the only single people left in the group. Most everyone else had paired off: Kanko with James, Pollee with Rose, Charlie with Maggie, Ossa with Annie, Gumpa with Josephine. Cudjo couldn't very well remain single. In his home culture, there was no such thing as a bachelor or a spinster. Fortunately there was one Yoruba woman roughly his age who didn't have a husband: Abile. The more he considered it, the easier it was to picture a life with her.

Back home, Cudjo would have told his parents he was interested, and they would have approached Abile's family. But as the situation stood, the responsibility fell to him alone. Approaching her directly violated every rule he had grown up with, but there was no other choice. So one day he told her what was on his mind.

"I likee you to be my wife," he said. He was tired of being alone.

She seemed receptive. But if she were to marry him, she asked, would he be able to provide for her?

He promised he could work for her, and added that he wouldn't beat her. As a husband in Yoruba culture, he would have been considered within his rights to do this, and the same was true for an American husband at the time. But given that Abile had lived on a plantation for five years, where beating would have been commonplace—and given all the other trauma she'd experienced in her young life—she would have been especially sensitive about it. For Abile, Cudjo's promises were enough. A month later, they started living together as husband and wife. Their first child was born on July 4, 1867. They gave him an American name, Aleck; but in their community, he was known as Iyadjemi, meaning "I suffered too much." It was probably a nod to Abile's difficult pregnancy.

The shipmates began to explore the wilderness around them. According to neighborhood lore, this was a time of bonding for the Africans and the American-born freedpeople, as the Africans taught their new friends how to be independent. Joe Womack learned about it from his grandfather, who was born in the early 1900s and grew up while some of the shipmates were still living. Womack tells the story well.

When they brought the last ship of slaves over, the overseer said, "Okay, y'all come on now, y'all be slaves." So the oldest one was twenty-four. We'll call him Joe. Joe raised his hand and said, "Look, man, I don't know how to be no slave. I've never been a slave in my life. What's a slave?" So the overseer looked back there and saw a slave named Jim. He said, "Jim, come here." He said, "Y'all follow Jim. Do everything Jim do and y'all be all right."

At the end of the day, Joe went, "I don't like being no slave. Ain't no fun. You work and work and work. They won't give us nothing. They won't let us stop. If you stop, they beat you." Jim said, "You gotta slave, man. See that food over there? If you don't slave, they ain't gonna give you no food. They won't let you take a bath, they won't let you stay in that place. You got to be a slave."

Five years later, the Civil War is over. Overseer come back and say, "Okay, y'all free. Y'all gonna be free." Jim said, "Look, if I don't slave, I don't know how to feed my family, man. They don't give me food, they don't give me no free bath, don't give me no free housing. How'm I gonna survive?" Joe said, "Y'all got that place there, Hog Bayou, right?" He said, "Yeah." Said, "Y'all got all sorts of food. Y'all got deers over there. When I was a kid, they gave me a spear and told me to kill a lion. I went out there and the lion tried to eat me. And I killed it. You think a deer gonna scare me? Y'all got deer, y'all got hogs, turtles, y'all got fish, y'all got coons, y'all got squirrels. We gonna catch 'em! We gon kill 'em! And we gon eat 'em all!"

And Jim said, "Yeah, man, but out there on Hog Bayou, they got these big ol' alligators." Joe said, "Yeah, you right. We gonna eat them suckers, too."

The influence continued to go both ways. The American-born freedpeople acquired citizenship in July of 1868, when the Fourteenth Amendment was ratified. For the shipmates, it wasn't automatic, but they must have been coached on how to apply, because on October 24, Charlie, Gumpa, Pollee, Ossa, and Cudjo went to the courthouse downtown and took citizenship oaths, where they renounced allegiance to "every foreign prince, potentate, state, or sovereignty." In all likelihood, they didn't see it as a severing of ties with their homeland, but only as a pragmatic measure. It gave them the right to vote, ensured they couldn't be deported against their will, and gave them recourse to the courts, should they ever have disputes with neighbors or employers.

One person who visited them often was Free George, their American-born friend from the plantation days. Over time George persuaded them they needed to "gittee de religion," as Cudjo put it, and join the Christian church. The majority started attending a little Methodist church in the town of Toulminville, several miles west of their settlement. As far as they were concerned, they were not abandoning the faith of their homeland. They believed the Bible revealed more about the same God they had always worshiped—and it bothered them when visitors suggested otherwise. Cudjo explained later that back home, they'd always known there was a god, but "we doan know God got a son," because no one had told them. And in 1887, a writer for *Harper's Weekly* suggested to Abile that if she were to return home, she'd have to give up her religion. She paused for a moment, then replied solemnly—almost like she felt sorry for this ignorant journalist—"White man, yo' no t'ink God in my country same like here?"

The religion they encountered at Free George's church was not the staid Protestantism of most white Alabamians, nor the Catholicism of the Meaher family. It was a version of Christianity developed by generations of enslaved people, meaning it was tailored to the shipmates' experiences. The worship, for one thing, was far more expressive. When Mobile's white churches had opened their galleries to their members' servants, before the Civil War, "often the fervent singing of the black people excelled that of their white masters on the floor below," a white local historian wrote in 1913. And after emancipation, when they had established their own churches, the "singing was melodious" there, "and the responses to the preacher took the form of shouting, especially among the Methodists." The themes of Black Christianity, too, spoke directly to Africans' lives. Only the Black church would have produced a spiritual like "Go Down, Moses," which describes the Israelites' escape from Egypt, with the refrain "Let my people go."

In 1869, the shipmates were baptized at Stone Street Baptist Church, where there had been an all-Black congregation since well before the Civil War. But they were still uncomfortable being surrounded by American-born Blacks, some of whom continued making fun of them. They began hosting prayer meetings in their homes.

There was an auction in 1869 for the land of Thomas Buford, a farmer and entrepreneur who had owned several of the shipmates. His holdings amounted to well over a thousand acres. In 1870, Charlie and Maggie Lewis, and Jaba and Polly Shade, all of whom had lived on Buford's plantation, went in with some American-born Blacks and bought seven acres of the property from the new owners—making them the first shipmates to possess their own land. They paid $200, about $4,000 now. Their plots were a mile southwest of where the other shipmates would settle, bordering Three-Mile Creek and a railroad track but otherwise surrounded by forest. This area became known as Lewis Quarters.

Then in the fall of 1872, the group bought several more acres in what would become the neighborhood of Plateau. The first plot belonged to one of Mobile's most distinguished couples: Colonel Lorenzo Wilson, a local railroad magnate active in city politics, and his wife, Augusta Evans Wilson, a novelist of international fame. This one went to Cudjo and Abile, who by then had a second son, a toddler named Ahnonotoe (or Jimmy, as he'd be known to outsiders). With help from the others, Cudjo built a four-room cabin. He cut the logs himself and secured them together with a mortar of sand and lime, and he made his own shingles for the roof. "No wind or nothing could go in," his grandson recalled years later. Not having any glass panes, he used wooden shutters for the windows. The group also bought four acres from the Meaher family, where Pollee and Rose Allen and Ossa and Annie Keeby erected similar houses.

With their dwellings complete, and their families growing, they started working on the church. They constructed a small wooden building beside Cudjo and Abile's property, calling it the Old Landmark Baptist Church. The first minister who agreed to oversee the place was a twenty-six-year-old from Mississippi named Henry McGray. Pollee Allen served as a minister as well, according to one of his daughters. The shipmates also arranged for their children to receive formal education. Most of them had not been exposed to anything like classroom teaching back home, but they wanted to help their children acclimate to the local culture. As it was, the kids were being picked on relentlessly by the children of other settlers in the area, most of whom evidently worked at the mills. They called Cudjo's children ignorant savages and compared them to monkeys. Neighborhood tradition holds that the first classes in the shipmates' settlement were held at the church, during the summer of 1880. The first teacher was sent over by the county.

In this period, the shipmates also codified their leadership structure. Never mind that they had sworn loyalty to the American government; they still identified themselves with their homelands. So they appointed Jaba and Ossa Keeby to serve as judges with Gumpa, who remained their chief. Anytime someone committed a serious transgression, they would call a meeting, perhaps at one of the three leaders' houses, where the person would have to answer questions before the whole community. Since they worked all day, these meetings happened at night, which led to rumors that they were practicing some kind of "barbaric rites." But it was quite the opposite. They had strict laws against stealing and fighting, and they didn't want anyone getting drunk, if only because it would bring shame on the rest of the community. First-time offenders got off with a warning. For subsequent violations, the penalty was whipping.

In or around 1871, Cudjo turned thirty. He had lived nearly half his life, and all of his adult years, in Alabama. It wasn't the life he had pictured, but it did bear certain resemblances. He was a respected patriarch like his father and grandfather. His family with Abile was still growing. Ultimately they had six children, most of whom had two names—one to connect them to their African heritage, and another that would be easy for Americans to pronounce. Their son Adeniah went by David; Fëichitan, the youngest boy, went by Cudjo; and Ebeossi, their only girl, was called Celia, like her mother. Pollee Dahoo, their third child, was the only one who evidently didn't have an American name. All of this made it easier for Cudjo to accept that he was in America to stay. The name the group gave to its settlement, African Town, was a nod to their collective fate. "We say dat 'cause we want to go back in de Affica soil and we see we cain go."

These improvements mirrored what was happening throughout Alabama and across the South. By the summer recess of 1867, the Freedmen's Bureau was operating 175 schools in Alabama, with nearly 10,000 students enrolled. Parents were teaching themselves to read by borrowing their children's textbooks, and teachers counseled the adults on labor contracts and legal matters.

Democracy was flourishing among the freedpeople. Local chapters of the Union League, an auxiliary of the Republican Party, were burgeoning; in Mobile, it was reported that 2,500 men, over half of those in the city, signed up as soon as the chapter was launched in 1867. They met wherever they could find space, in Black churches and schools, in members' homes, sometimes even in fields and forests. At meetings, they read Republican newspapers out loud, debated political questions, nominated candidates for local offices, and planned rallies, parades, and barbecues. In 1872, the state senate had five Black members, and the house of representatives had another thirty.

At the same time, Black southerners were nowhere close to achieving real political or social equality with whites, because their economic situation had not significantly changed. A small number of white men owned nearly all of the land and the industrial equipment, including railcars, steamers, and cotton gins, that was needed to make it profitable, while millions of Black men and women owned barely anything but their bodies and perhaps their meager homes. The shell of the old plantation system, in other words, was still intact. Black men still railed in Union League meetings about the need for radical reform, for a federal "forty acres and a mule" program, but in the halls of Congress those proposals were becoming a distant memory. A land-redistribution bill submitted to Congress by Benjamin Turner, a Black representative from Alabama, in 1872, failed to even come up for a vote.

By the early 1870s, these conditions were giving rise to the sharecropping system. The shipmates in the Mobile County settlement never resorted to sharecropping work, but millions of other freedpeople did. Under this arrangement, laborers would harvest crops—typically cotton, in Alabama—on land they didn't own, and in exchange be allowed to take home a third to a half of the profits. The workers typically lived in primitive log cabins or small clapboard houses on the landowner's property. For some, it seemed at first to be a step in the right direction, a middle ground between wage labor and entrepreneurialism. A sharecropper didn't have to be at his employer's mercy for the duration of a shift. His schedule was his own, and in theory, the amount he earned depended on what he put in. But in practice, it was more often a step back toward slavery. Sharecroppers were all too easy to cheat at harvest time. By the 1890s, when tenant farming dominated Alabama agriculture, sharecroppers produced more cotton per acre than wage workers—but they were lucky to break even after the crops were sold, and some ended up owing huge amounts of money to their landlords. They could be trapped in debt cycles for decades.

Another grim development in these years was the rise of a distinct southern network of white terrorist groups. By most estimates, the Ku Klux Klan
had more than a thousand members in Alabama at its Reconstruction peak,
including many members of the Democratic Party's leadership, and it was
only the largest of several like-minded groups. Klansmen would surround
freedpeople's houses at night, set the buildings on fire, and drag the occu-
pants into the yard to beat them and sometimes rape the women. Often the
beatings were accompanied by warnings not to vote, lest the Black families
be murdered. Between 1868 and 1871, Klansmen killed more than a hundred
people and committed thousands of other acts of violence and intimidation
in Alabama alone. Under Ulysses S. Grant, who assumed the presidency in
1869, a series of laws were enacted that ultimately stamped out the group's
power. But the racial violence would continue in different forms.

The Reconstruction effort had mostly petered out by 1874. But the event
that would end it decisively was an economic collapse. Given the poor shape
of the southern economy, by the early 1870s, the Reconstruction governments,
including those of Alabama and of Mobile, were taking on enormous debt to
provide basic services and invest in their futures. Then in 1873 the entire country spiraled into a depression. It began with the collapse of a northern bank,
which sent the broader credit system into panic. Factories laid off workers by
the hundreds. Farmers saw drop-offs in the value of their land and the prices
they could fetch for crops. Over time, financiers who still had capital to invest
would buy up struggling companies, and the ownership of industry would
become increasingly concentrated in fewer hands. There were also political
ramifications. As the midterm elections in 1874 approached, the Republicans
were more vulnerable than they'd been in at least a decade.

On a Tuesday in November 1874, Cudjo, Pollee, and Charlie were trudging
up the dirt road to a polling place in Whistler, a few miles west of their settlement. They were on their way to cast votes in the day's election. It was a
monumental one for Alabama. The state Republican Party was in crisis, split
between a largely Black coalition (the Black-and-Tans) who wanted to keep
pushing for civil rights, and the Lily-Whites, who were afraid of losing moderate voters. So the Democrats had a chance of seizing both the statehouse
and the governor's mansion—and if they did, Alabama's freedpeople would
be in dire straits. The federal government had already withdrawn much of
its support.

The Democrats' strategy was simple: to win over as many white voters as they could, through an openly racist campaign, and to suppress the Black vote with violence, fraud, and intimidation. Though they attacked the incumbent Republican governor for his handling of the economy, they didn't pretend the election was about policies. "The struggle going on around us is not a mere contest for the triumph of this, or that, platform of party principles," the *Montgomery Advertiser* had declared nine months earlier. "It is a contest between antagonistic races and for that which is held dearer than life by the white race." The *Mobile Daily Tribune*, a Democratic-friendly paper, articulated the Democratic Party's specific aim: "Let us plant the banner of white supremacy upon the dome of the capitol, and defy the world to take it down," it declared on election day. "Let us shake off the leeches who are sucking our life blood" and "preserve our temples from African contamination—our sanctuaries from pollution."

Tim Meaher had recently stopped by the shipmates' settlement for a visit. He had explained how American elections worked and what it meant to cast a ballot, and he'd tried to persuade the shipmates to vote for the Democratic ticket. He may have used the party's talking points for Black voters, telling them the Radicals had been making grand promises to freedpeople for years but had never delivered, blaming the Republicans for the high price of pork, and saying they'd encouraged lazy Black people to steal what industrious freedpeople like the shipmates had earned. In characteristic fashion, he may have also tried intimidation. He could have described how during the summer, two Republican leaders had been assassinated in Sumter County, 160 miles due north of Mobile, and how white mobs had destroyed other Republicans' homes and crops. There was no need to remind the shipmates that Meaher himself still paid some of their wages.

Sometime after Meaher's visit, a group of Republicans, likely Black members of the Union League, had also come by to canvass. Their case was easier to make. The choice was between one party with a mixed record on civil rights and another that was consistently, openly hostile toward freedpeople. Black Republicans were fighting for equal access to schools, churches, railroads, cemeteries, hotels, and theaters; and if they hadn't succeeded—even if white Republicans had resisted their attempts—this was still more than the Democrats could say. To make the process as easy as possible, the visitors may have brought printed ballots, resembling train tickets, with their party's candidates listed. The Africans would only have needed to sign their names and submit the ballots.

The shipmates had discussed the matter as a community and agreed to support the Republicans. So Cudjo, Pollee, and Charlie were voting not only for their households but on behalf of everyone.

In that morning's edition of the *Mobile Daily Tribune*, the editors had issued a call to arms for local whites. They reported that the previous day, "the darkey cohorts of Radical misrule" had filled the municipal buildings and courts, instructing the masses on how to steal the election. They warned that Black people would likely try voting twice, and that hundreds more Blacks were being brought in from Mississippi to cast fraudulent ballots. "Men of Mobile! Behold the insolent foe are at hand," they admonished. "Let us rise in our majesty and hurl them back, broken and discomfited." The editorial urged white Democrats to go to the polls early and stay there all day, keeping watch.

Meaher clearly felt a personal stake in this election. He had such spite toward Black people that he'd "quit the river" in 1870 because the "colored citizens demanded cabin passage," as he told a journalist years later. He welcomed the apartheid policies the Democrats were promising. There was also the matter of his personal finances. Alabama's property taxes were at an all-time high, just as they were in other Southern states. The tax base before the Civil War had been predicated on slavery, and there were no other ways to make up for the lost revenue. The Democrats were eager to reduce the burden on the wealthy. So on election day, Meaher did exactly what the *Daily Tribune* suggested.

When Cudjo and the other shipmates arrived at the polling place, the mogul was already there. "See those Africans?" he said to the clerk, pointing. "Don't let them vote—they are not of this country." The clerk didn't need to be told twice; everyone knew Meaher's reputation. So even though the shipmates had been legal citizens for six years, the clerk sent them away.

They took it in stride and went to another polling place. But Meaher had beaten them there on his horse. Again they were sent away. Then it happened a third time, at a polling location on St. Stephen's Road, a major artery that runs north and south from downtown. As they were arriving, they saw Meaher dismounting his horse. "Don't let those Africans vote," they heard him say. "They have no right—they are not of this country."

If anything, the setbacks only intensified their desire to cast ballots. So out on the road, the three men linked their hands and raised them toward the sky. They prayed that God would let them vote.

With sundown drawing closer, they started walking all the way to downtown Mobile. When they arrived, their shoes must have been coated with dust, their leg muscles starting to ache. Meaher was nowhere in sight. A clerk told them they had to pay $1 each—no small amount at their income level. But they paid, then they proudly cast their ballots for the Republicans.

They could have had it worse. Many Black voters in other parts of the state did. Earlier that same day, hundreds of Blacks had come to Eufaula, a town roughly halfway between Mobile and Atlanta, planning to vote. To minimize any chance of violence, their leaders had urged them to come unarmed. As the Black voters cast their ballots one by one, their leaders tried to keep the peace, knowing they'd be far outmatched in a fight. But an argument erupted when a Black Republican saw some Democrats trying to coerce a young Black man into voting for their party. Then the shooting began. Either seven or eight Black men were killed, and another seventy to eighty men were wounded, fewer than a dozen of them white.

Some seventeen miles northwest of Eufaula, in a rural community called Spring Hill, roughly fifty Democrats paraded around the polls that afternoon, trying to scare away Black voters. In the evening, Judge Elias Keils, a Republican, and his sixteen-year-old son locked the doors of the building and prepared to wait there all night, protecting the ballots that had made it through. But at six P.M., a Democratic election official unbolted the door. Armed men rushed inside and started shooting. Keils and his son hid behind a counter, but the teen was hit with four bullets. When the judge left to find a doctor, the ballot box, containing more than seven hundred tickets, was taken and burned. The sixteen-year-old died two days later.

And blood was also spilled in Mobile. The day had begun with whites hanging an effigy of Benjamin Butler, the Union major general turned Radical legislator. Throughout the day, whites arrested scores of voters on accusations of fraud, killing one supposed offender. In the afternoon, Democrats blocked the Seventh Ward poll, so Allen Alexander, a local freedman and politician, led several hundred Blacks on a march toward another ward. The sheriff and some Democratic deputies blocked Alexander in the street, then shoved him into a carriage. Someone, likely a deputy, fired a shot, then the crowd broke into a melee. One or two Black men were killed and several more were wounded. Alexander was "jerked out of his vehicle" while "begging for his life," the *Daily Tribune* reported, and one policeman heard cries of "Shoot him; kill him; the damn son of a bitch." He survived long enough to be arrested and taken to jail, where he stayed that night instead of posting bail, reasoning that it was safer.

When the ballots were counted, to no one's surprise, the Democrats had won in a landslide, seizing both the governor's office and control of the legislature. "White supremacy sustained," the *Mobile Daily Register* declared in a headline. The *Register* also reported "glorious" news from elsewhere in the country, including "great gains for the Democratic party" in Massachusetts, South Carolina, New York, Florida, Louisiana, Pennsylvania, Virginia, and Georgia. It was the greatest turnover between parties in the entire nineteenth century. The Republicans went from holding a 110-vote majority in the House to having 60 fewer votes than the Democrats, and among the 107 new House members elected from southern or border states, 80 had served in the Confederate military. In the Senate, the Democrats cut the Republican majority in half. They also took nineteen gubernatorial races. The Republicans' loss certainly owed more to the depression than it did to Reconstruction policies being unpopular. But for freedpeople, the effects were the same.

The last gasp of Reconstruction came in 1875. It was a federal Civil Rights Act that outlawed racial discrimination in public venues like hotels and restaurants. But there was no enforcement to speak of, and the Supreme Court declared the law unconstitutional in 1883. Apart from that bill, the Republicans in the nation's capital could barely agree on anything dealing with race relations. They shifted their focus to economics, reaffirming their commitment to manufacturing and fiscal responsibility. In the spring of 1875, as the Democrats prepared to take over the House of Representatives, *The Nation* remarked that the country had passed "out of the region of the Civil War."

And in Alabama, in 1875, the new Democrats called a constitutional convention. Presiding over it was LeRoy Pope Walker, formerly the Confederacy's secretary of war. The purpose was to repeal the 1868 constitution, which had secured rights for Blacks, and adopt a new one more favorable to planters and big business. The document slashed property taxes, eliminated the state board of education, cut education funding, segregated schools, and imposed a new poll tax meant to exclude both Blacks and poor whites from voting. It also replaced a line from the 1868 constitution declaring that "all men are created equal" with the statement "all men are equally free and independent"—which would be rendered increasingly false as the constitution itself took effect.

Cudjo, Charlie Lewis, and Pollee Allen would never vote again. But they kept their voting receipts from 1874 until the papers were yellowed and brittle.

8

WHITE SUPREMACY, BY FORCE AND FRAUD

Near the end of 1890, Richard Hines Jr., a thirty-five-year-old reporter for the *Mobile Register*, went to visit Timothy Meaher at his home near Mobile. The house was a two-story structure atop a red clay hill, surrounded by a picket fence. Hines found Meaher on the porch, basking in the sunshine. At age seventy-seven, he was partly paralyzed, and had not been into the city since 1886, the year after his brother Jim died. His other brother in Mobile, Burns, had also died in 1889. Meaher was living in isolation, forced to rely on newspapers to keep up with events. He must have been glad to have a visitor.

Over the summer, the magazine *Scribner's* had published the short memoir of George Howe, a doctor living in Massachusetts. It described Howe's experiences working on a slave ship, called the *Rebecca*, that docked in Trinidad in 1859. The article was titled "The Last Slave-Ship." Ely Creek, a man living across the bay from Mobile, wrote to a newspaper to point out the error. Howe could not have been on the last slave ship, Creek said, because he wasn't on the *Clotilda*. The designation belonged instead to Bill Foster and his crew. This exchange may have been what inspired Foster, who still lived in Mobile County, to set his own memories down in writing. That September, ten weeks after the *Scribner's* article came out, Foster sent a twelve-page handwritten document to a friend, chronicling his experiences at sea and in Ouidah. It never appeared in print, but it would be preserved by Foster's relatives.

On this November day, it was Meaher's turn. For the first time, the elderly man agreed to go public with his crimes. As a warm breeze blew across the porch, he narrated the whole affair from his perspective: how some northern passengers had dared him to charter a slave ship, and he had agreed; how he'd bought the *Clotilda* for $35,000 and retrofitted it; how he'd waited weeks for the ship's return, and then conspired with his brother Burns and with Foster to hide the captives and destroy the evidence. Later he was put on trial in federal court, he said, and he dodged execution only by persuading the jury of a false alibi. The article Hines later wrote was the first to render the story in any detail—and this was thirty years after the fact. If Meaher was embellishing, it's likely he had a willing collaborator in Hines, who was keen to present him as a hero. "His life is full of thrilling incidents," the journalist wrote, "and many stories are extant of his personal prowess." The story was published on November 30 in New Orleans's *Daily Picayune*, and in the *Pittsburgh Dispatch* and the *St. Louis Globe-Democrat*, perhaps among other major newspapers.

Throughout the South, nostalgia for the Confederacy was on the rise. The United Confederate Veterans, the first group of its kind spanning the entire South, had been organized a year earlier in New Orleans. More than ten thousand veterans would attend the reunion in 1896, some of them sleeping in parks, in yards, and in the streets. Thousands of southerners were taking an interest in genealogy, and the fabled aristocracy of the Old South, "long on its last legs, was refurbished," as the historian C. Vann Woodward has written, "its fancied virtues and vices, airs and attitudes exhumed and admired."

Hines's article cemented Meaher's reputation as a hero of the Lost Cause. To southern audiences, no doubt, the illegal voyage he'd arranged in 1860 was seen as a courageous act of rebellion against northern tyranny. He was no longer just a retired entrepreneur; he was now elevated to the status of a national symbol. He died at his home two years later, "of old age," as an obituary put it. His funeral had a large turnout, and he was interred at Mobile's main Catholic cemetery. The obituary identified him as "the venerable steamboatman" and declared that among his many achievements, the *Clotilda* escapade had brought him the most fame. Much like the news of the *Clotilda*'s arrival, three decades earlier, a report of Meaher's death was syndicated in dozens of newspapers across the country, including *The Monroeville Breeze* in Indiana and the *Griggs Courier* in North Dakota. His death was also covered in *The New York Times*, in a short dispatch riddled with errors, under the headline "Last of the Slave Traders."

By this time, the shipmates also had occasional visitors from the press. The resulting articles give a picture of the community's evolution and its changing relationship to white Mobile. Kirk Munroe, a correspondent from *Harper's Weekly*, who came in 1887, appears to have been the first. When he traveled there, the area was still remote and still separated from the city by swamps; but traveling back and forth had become easier. There were make-shift roads ("slabs," Munroe said) coated with sawdust from the shingle mills, which made for a smooth wagon ride. For the journalist, this only added to the mystique. "The sensations produced by this muffled riding," he wrote, "amid the impressive silence of the densely wooded swamps, are peculiar, but strictly in accord with the funereal environment of the scene." The shipmates' settlement—or "African Village," as he referred to it—was a "unique cluster of cabins," housing thirty or forty families of shipmates. This included a few *Clotilda* survivors who had been sold to buyers up the Alabama River and had found their way back after the war. Many of the residents, Munroe found, barely understood a word of English. Most of the men worked in the shingle mills, and the families made extra money by selling produce from the garden patches surrounding their homes. Munroe was fascinated with Cudjo, who had become the senior deacon of the shipmates' church. He struck the reporter as the smartest man in the group. At this late date, Munroe noted, twenty-seven years after the shipmates' arrival in the United States, it was still their "ever-present day-dream and hope" that they could earn enough money to go back home.

The second report was written by a local writer, Mary NcNeil Scott, who would later become a popular novelist and poet. Circa 1893, Scott had a cousin visiting from New York City who was eager to see the "African Village" that she had heard "spoken of so often." At first Scott didn't know what her cousin was talking about, but then she remembered: "I believe I have heard the servants say something about 'Affika Town.'" It had never occurred to her to visit. "Well," her cousin replied, "you are equal to those horrid people who live within sound of Niagara and have never taken the trouble to go and look at it." Scott asked a "house boy" how she could get there, and he advised her to hire a Black driver, Uncle Noah, who he promised would know the way.

Noah's carriage pulled up that afternoon. Before the women climbed in, Scott asked him whether the African settlement was safe. He assured her it was. On the long ride up, Noah spoke about his personal history with the shipmates, going back to the days when he himself was enslaved at Tim Meaher's plantation. He described their habits and rituals as he had observed them. When the carriage arrived in the village, no one was out and about, except an elderly woman hoeing a melon patch. Noah called out, but she didn't answer. Scott seems to have found the place unimpressive. Apart from the shipmates' gardens, all she saw were "dilapidated fences and unattractive cabins." But from Noah's narration alone, she had enough material for an article. Her piece was published in the August 1893 issue of *Fetter's Southern Magazine*. It contained a detail that would become a fixed part of the lore: that the idea for the voyage started not only with a boast (as Meaher himself said in his 1890 interview) but with a wager. Scott claimed her cousin had read this in a New Orleans newspaper. Stories about this fabled bet would become more elaborate in later accounts, with chroniclers claiming the amount was $1,000—the equivalent of almost $30,000 now—and the parties were drunk.

A third visitor, Henry Romeyn, was more thorough in his research. Romeyn was a U.S. Army captain who had commanded a Black regiment in the Civil War. He paid at least one visit to Mobile as he was winding down his military career. On a muggy Sunday afternoon in June 1893, Augustine Meaher, Timothy Meaher's son and heir, who was in his mid-thirties, took Romeyn out to where the shipmates lived. Their village spanned forty to fifty acres on a "high, broken ground"—a plateau—and was surrounded by a pine forest, inset with ditches and hills. Romeyn recognized these as earthworks, dug to block off Yankee intruders during the Civil War. Unlike Scott, he thought the thirty or so houses looked "quite comfortable" for rural dwellings. He also reported that the shipmates were not alone. On the adjacent land, there were houses that Augustine Meaher rented out to American-born Blacks who worked in the area. The neighborhood was coming to be known as Plateau (emphasis on the first syllable—*PLA-teau*). Romeyn noted that among white Mobilians, who tended to resent freedpeople, the shipmates were thought to be unusually honest and hardworking.

Per usual, Cudjo and Gumpa, who was still recognized as the leader, did most of the talking. Romeyn thought them both "shrewd," if "somewhat comical." When Romeyn asked Gumpa whether he'd rather be in America or back home, Gumpa answered abruptly: "Dah-ho-mah," and repeated the word three or four times. A woman chimed in, saying that back home, no one was possessive about land; it wasn't necessary to purchase or pay taxes on it. But then something Romeyn said caught them off guard. At the 1893 World's Fair, in Chicago, there had been a "Dahomey Village" exhibit, where dozens of Gumpa's countrymen were put on display as captives. Gumpa couldn't believe it. Dahomey could never have been subdued by a foreign power, he said; the military was too powerful. In fact Dahomey had been partially conquered by France in 1890, the year after King Glèlè's death. It would become a French protectorate in 1894. This encounter must have left Gumpa perplexed.

Romeyn came back to African Town the following week, hoping to catch more of the villagers at church. He arrived while the sermon was still in progress. The preacher, he noted dryly, "was not weak-lunged nor troubled with any bronchial affliction." For nearly an hour Romeyn waited, while the pastor "dwelt upon the heinousness of disrespect to the Holy Spirit." Romeyn noticed the congregants were dressed exceptionally well for wage workers and were more cool-mannered than he'd expected. No one shouted out responses to the pastor's words. At the end, the parishioners said the Lord's Prayer in unison, making a sound "really fine and touching in its soft melody." Afterward it was raining, so most everyone stayed at the chapel. Some of the shipmates described their journey across the ocean and their years of enslavement. The pastor informed Romeyn that all told, thirty to forty of the shipmates still survived, and roughly sixty children attended the Sunday school. By then there was a second church in the neighborhood as well: Yorktown Missionary Baptist Church, which had opened in 1888.

Romeyn assessed, quite rightly, that the community was going through a transition. He heard the shipmates had abandoned their traditional burial practices. In town, it was rumored that they still practiced some kind of "fetich" or "vodou" rites, but he found no evidence for this, either. At the same time, it was clear that their children and grandchildren were becoming Americanized. The shipmates funded a school where a young Black woman from the city taught classes on weekdays. During Romeyn's visit, a girl of eleven acted as interpreter whenever the adults' English failed, and she showed a command of both American and African geography. It seems Romeyn was impressed with how they'd adapted, but he also recognized that African Town, as he was encountering it, couldn't last much longer. Any "romance" the place held (for outsiders, presumably) was quickly fading—"and with the passing of the original members of the colony from the scenes of action, it will have ceased to exist." Their descendants, he assumed, would merge with the surrounding community. His story was published in New Orleans's *Times-Democrat* in 1894 and was reprinted elsewhere throughout the 1890s.

If these articles give a panoply of outsiders' views on African Town, the memories of Pollee Allen's youngest daughter, which were recorded by several different researchers throughout the 1980s, give a perspective from the inside. Allen's daughter was named Clara Eva Allen Jones, but when she was elderly, everyone knew her as Mama Eva. She was born in 1894.

Social life, when she was growing up, revolved around the shipmates' church. "I don't know any other place they went for enjoyment except the house of prayer," she told a graduate student from the University of Wisconsin. On Saturday nights, everyone took baths, then went to bed early. Sundays began with a "sunrise meeting" around four A.M., when the sky was still "black dark." Oil lamps helped the parishioners find their way to the pews. Once it was bright outside, families went home for breakfast, then returned for Sunday school at nine and a service at eleven. There was a midday meal, then a service at three, then supper. "At seven o'clock, we was right back in the church," Jones told the interviewer. "You'd better believe it!" There were also services on Wednesday and Friday evenings. When Jones was a preteen, she had a spiritual awakening. "It come a time when I couldn't hold my feet sturdy and I was wiggling on the bench and trying to hold my feet to the floor," she told the graduate student. Suddenly she felt herself walking down the aisle, "and I was saying 'Thank you, Jesus, thank you, thank you, thank you.' And when I found myself, I couldn't control myself no longer." She was baptized in Threemile Creek, according to the church's custom, in 1906.

The shipmates still grew much of their own food. Pollee Allen kept a big garden, spanning two or three acres, and gave away as much produce as he harvested for his family. "Anybody didn't have, and you had, they'd come and get it," Jones recalled. "That's what they raised it for—to feed the community." Ossa Keeby ran a vegetable wagon, and she remembered a time when her father's cow wandered toward Keeby's house and gobbled up his plants. Her father was broken up. The shipmates met in someone's house to pray and sing hymns. The way Jones remembered it, Keeby's vegetables grew back within a couple of weeks.

Jones watched with fascination whenever her father cooked at their fireplace. He'd roast corn over the coals and bury potatoes beneath the ashes. When he dusted them off, "They'd be just like you baked 'em in the stove." He cooked peanuts the same way. As a remedy for colds, the shipmates made "life-everlasting tea" with a leaf they fetched from the woods. "All of 'em knew about it, and if one of 'em give out, they'd go to the other'n house. 'You got any more of that tea?'" They'd sweeten it with honey from the bees Jones's father kept.

When the adults were together, they always spoke their native tongue—"this mumba, mumba, mumba that we children couldn't understand," she told a reporter in 1985. "We'd just laugh because we thought they were talking about us." She picked up only a few words, including her Yoruba name, which was Jo-Ko ("I understand that it means love"). Later in life, she often lamented never learning to speak Yoruba. "They didn't try to shove it down our throat. It would've been all right if we'd have took it up and we'd asked 'em to teach it to us—I know they would have." But she and others in her generation felt conflicted about their heritage. When she reached school age, classes were being held at a union hall, and the shipmates' children were mixed in with other kids. They were constantly singled out because of their background. "They say 'There comes some o' them little Black Africans,'" she recalled. "That's what they would call us then." Often it was enough to make them cry.

In 1891, Cudjo and Celia's twenty-four-year-old son, Aleck, their oldest, married a young woman named Mary Woods. She was sixteen, a second-generation Alabamian whose parents had been enslaved. Her mother, Martha, was a laundress, and her father, Sandy Woods, was a farm laborer. In 1892, Cudjo and Celia became grandparents. Mary gave birth that year to Zanna. Zanna was followed by a younger brother, Motley, in 1895, then by Emmett in 1897 and Angeline around 1901. The young family lived in a compound with Cudjo and Celia, following Yoruba custom.

But for Cudjo and Celia, middle age brought more sorrow than joy. A new round of tragedies began for them in 1893, when their youngest child and only daughter, who was also named Celia, took ill. A doctor examined her and prescribed some medicine, but she didn't get better. Cudjo prayed, telling the Lord he'd do anything to save his child's life. Celia died that August. She was buried in the cemetery beside the shipmates' church. At the funeral, their friends and neighbors gathered around them and sang the American hymn "Shall We Meet Beyond the River?" "Shall we meet there many a loved one," they intoned together, "that was torn from our embrace?"

As much as Cudjo was steeped in Christianity, on that day the lyrics didn't resonate. Internally, he recited a hymn from back home, with a phrase found in every Yoruba funeral hymn: *a wa n'lo,* "we are going away." He urged his wife not to cry, but he couldn't hold back tears himself. In the weeks that followed, it distressed him to think about their daughter's coffin lying out there alone in the family plot, so he built a fence around her grave for protection.

As for the couple's five sons—Aleck, James, Pollee, David, and Cudjo Jr.—they had always had violent tempers, quite unlike their father. Because they were part of the first generation born in America, growing up some twenty years before Clara Eva Allen Jones, their conflicts with American-born Black children had been much more intense. Their peers had claimed Africans were cannibals and compared the boys to monkeys. They knew the insults hurt their parents, and they wanted to defend the family's honor. Cudjo didn't blame them for getting into fights all the time. Eventually they partnered with the sheriff's department and helped with arrests around the neighborhood, which did not help their popularity. Neighbors warned Cudjo that the situation might get out of hand and that someone might get killed. Cudjo was dubious; whenever his sons were blamed for something, it seemed the accusers told only half the story. He invariably took the boys' side. Provoking them, he said, was like provoking a rattlesnake in the woods. "If you know de snake killee you, why you bother wid him?"

Then in 1899, the neighbors' predictions were borne out.

NEGRO KILLED LAST NIGHT AT PLATEAU read the *Mobile Daily Item* headline on July 10. At a party the previous night, sponsored by African Americans at a hall in Plateau, "several fights occurred," the paper said, "fists, knives and pistols being used." A twenty-six-year-old man, Gilbert Thomas, died at the scene after being shot in the head and abdomen. Cudjo Lewis Jr. was charged with his murder. The sheriff was called at home, and Cudjo Jr. was booked around four in the morning. The newspaper couldn't determine what had sparked the conflict, but it was clear there had been a melee. Another partygoer, Charlie Bradley, tried twice to shoot a Willie Giles, then had beaten Giles over the head with his pistol; and a woman named Alice Bradley was cut severely on her head by a Malissa Taylor. However, it's also possible that Cudjo Jr. and Gilbert Thomas had some kind of ongoing feud. Thomas shared the last name of Cudjo Jr.'s new bride, Louisa Thomas, suggesting they could have been brothers-in-law; and Thomas's father was a shingle-maker, so it's possible he worked alongside Cudjo Sr.

Cudjo Jr. couldn't make bail, so he was locked up while awaiting trial. His court date was in January 1900. He was fortunate to have a skilled attorney, Edward M. Robinson. Robinson was only twenty-six, but he had already served five years in the state legislature. In 1907 he would become the youngest president of the Mobile Bar Association in the organization's history. Little record survives of the proceedings, apart from the jurors' names;

but court records filed later give clues about Robinson's argument. The killing was not technically self-defense, he later wrote, but it wasn't far off. Robinson considered Thomas a "most desperate character" and thought "his taking off was really a riddance to the county." In his opinion, Cudjo Jr. had not committed any moral transgression. The jury, which was predominantly white, convicted the defendant of manslaughter on January 23, 1900. Eleven days later, he was brought back to court for his sentencing. The judge gave him five years in the state penitentiary. He was also billed for the cost of his own prosecution, though he would be excused from this charge because he was too poor to pay.

And with that, Cudjo Jr. was plunged into the cruelest institution of the Jim Crow South: the convict-leasing system.

Alabama had been forcing criminal convicts to do unpaid work since before the Civil War. When the state built its first penitentiary, in 1841, in the town of Wetumpka, legislators believed it would pay for its own operating costs. The inmates manufactured wagons, saddles, ropes, and other products for the state to sell. But by 1846, the prison was operating at a net loss. The state began contracting the place out to private-sector wardens. In these antebellum years, virtually all the prisoners were white, because planters themselves handled the discipline and punishment of enslaved people.

Two decades later, after the Civil War, white Alabamians looked to the penal system to bring back some semblance of the old social order. They passed laws that made it possible to arrest freedpeople on the thinnest of pretexts. Inmates were forced to build a railroad through Alabama's mineral region, and they were later leased to mine iron and coal, to haul timber, and to harvest turpentine. Corporations were happy to have the cheap labor, and the supply rose along with the demand. Between 1874 and 1877 alone, the prison population almost tripled, and it continued growing from there. Revenue from convict leasing jumped from $14,000 in 1877 to $109,000 in 1890, helping to compensate for the state's low taxes.

After Cudjo's conviction, he was taken to Wetumpka, where a physician looked him over. His intake report details his appearance: he was just under five and a half feet tall and weighed 160 pounds; and he had a scar on the right side of his forehead, another scar on his left thumb, and a dark birthmark on his shoulder. His demeanor was described as "intemperate." According to his paperwork, his release date would be between December 1903 and February 1905. It was almost a foregone conclusion where he would serve out his sentence. By this time a single corporation, the Tennessee Coal and Iron Company, was renting nearly all of Alabama's prisoners to work at its Pratt Mines, near Birmingham. TCI supplied fuel to every railroad in the South, and it powered southern cotton mills, oil mills, foundries, and other factories. Huge batches of its coke were also dispatched to Mexico.

Cudjo would have found the living quarters dismal at best. Ventilation was poor. One prison had no sewer system, and the latrines were emptied only once a day, so the air was always putrid. Diseases thrived in this atmosphere. Between 1898 and 1900, roughly thirty inmates died from some form of tuberculosis, more than ten of pneumonia, and others from typhoid, smallpox, septicemia, and heart disease. The year Cudjo arrived, there was a flu epidemic, followed by an outbreak of dysentery. Violence, from both guards and fellow prisoners, was also a perpetual threat, especially for Black inmates.

The mines operated around the clock, in two twelve-hour shifts. Workers had to walk or crawl, sometimes as far as a mile, to the "rooms" where they were assigned. Skilled inmates, who worked as "cutters," would lie on their backs or sides, making undercuts in the rocks several feet deep, then blowing them apart with dynamite. Cudjo was expected to load three tons of coal per day; but this number on its own doesn't convey the scope of his duties, nor how hard it was to carry them out. According to an 1891 estimate, a new prisoner typically shoveled 15,000 to 20,000 pounds of "dead weight" each day, mostly while on his knees. "The cramped position that he must assume is entirely new to him," a physician wrote to the governor that year. Besides that, "the constant fear of being killed is an obstacle, and the presence of smoke both from the lamps and the powder used in blasting the coal makes him sick." Inmates also faced the perpetual threat of being flogged for their job performance. They could be whipped for failing to meet their quotas (even if the mines were open for only half a day), for including rock with their coal, and for failing to "show interest" in their work. Nearly every inmate who testified before a legislative committee in 1889 said he had been whipped or had witnessed a whipping.

In other words, Cudjo's conditions were likely even worse than those his parents had experienced during enslavement, apart from their time on the *Clotilda*. At best, four or five years in the Pratt Mines could cause permanent physical and psychological harm; at worst, they could be a death sentence. In Cudjo's case, however, there was hope. Back home, his attorney, Edward Robinson, was working to bring him home early. For reasons that aren't entirely clear, Robinson was going to rather extraordinary lengths.

By the late summer, the attorney had successfully tracked down ten of the twelve jurors who served in the trial (the other two had left Mobile). They all agreed to sign a statement saying that Cudjo had "always been a man of most excellent character," and that based on the situation, they doubted he was truly guilty of manslaughter (let alone murder). The statement urged the governor, Joseph F. Johnston, to grant a pardon or early parole. Robinson also gathered the signatures of twenty-two other Mobilians. The first and most prominent name on the paper was Augustine Meaher's. Four sheriff's deputies also added their names.

To his packet, Robinson added letters from people of considerable influence. Jabez J. Parker, a former Alabama secretary of state, wrote a note about the circumstances of the killing. Cudjo Jr. was unpopular with people of his own race, Parker said, because he often helped law enforcement by "ferreting out crime" and arresting other African Americans. Gilbert Thomas, on the other hand, had been nothing but a "dangerous, turbulent and blood-thirsty scoundrel" and a "perambulating arsenal of homicidal fury and destruction." Cudjo Jr. deserved no blame for Thomas's death, Parker said, because he'd done only what he had to do. Samuel Barnett Browne, another attorney, who would later become a judge, cosigned Parker's letter. And in a third statement, the county sheriff, Charles McLean, agreed that Cudjo Jr. was "one of the very best negroes in Mobile County," and that Mobile was better off with Thomas gone. Robinson sent the packet to Governor Johnston on July 25.

Johnston knew the convict-leasing system well. Before he went into politics, he had been president of the Sloss Iron and Steel Company, which leased state prisoners for its mine in Coalburg. But he was no uncritical defender of convict leasing; on the contrary, he had called for an investigation of the leasing system upon taking office. He was also fairly generous with pardons; in the period between September 1998 and August 1900, he issued a total of 175, along with 44 commutations. In Cudjo Jr.'s case, there was no serious risk of political blowback, because the young man had not harmed any white people, and because white law enforcement were vouching for him. When the governor received the application, he was evidently won over. On August 7, he approved the request for early parole.

Cudjo Jr. would have received a ticket home and a new set of clothes. By the end of August, after roughly seven months of hell, he was back home.

* * *

In the political sphere, the 1890s brought more turbulence than Alabama had seen since Reconstruction. For years, the Democratic Party had ruled the state uncontested. But that all changed in 1891, when a group called the Populists, who had first organized in Kansas, started holding rallies throughout the Deep South. Their message was that major corporations, especially banks, railroads, and factories, had seized full control of the economy and were ruthlessly exploiting farmers and laborers. The Democratic Party, they said, had been bought off and converted into an instrument of big business. In most states, Populists ran on a third-party ticket called the People's Party. They promised that if they were elected, they would raise corporate taxes, abolish price-fixing, and regulate commerce. In their best moments, they tried to unite Black and white voters on the basis of these shared interests. The Georgia politician Tom Watson laid out this rhetorical strategy in an 1892 speech. Watson asked his audience to picture a Black and white tenant living side by side. "Now the People's Party says to these two men, 'You are kept apart that you may be separately fleeced of your earnings. You are made to hate each other because upon that hatred is rested the keystone of the arch of financial despotism which enslaves you both.'" As Watson saw it, these men would be bound to recognize that any political change that benefited the white worker benefited the Black one as well, because "their every material interest is identical."

In Alabama, a Confederate veteran, Reuben Kolb, rose up to lead the Populist push. Kolb was perhaps the state's most successful farmer in his day. He had tried running for governor in 1890, on the Democratic ticket, but was forced out by party leadership. In 1892, propelled by the new Populist movement, he challenged the sitting governor, Thomas Goode Jones, crusading against what he called the "unholy cliques and combinations now forming of plutocrats against the people." When the votes were tallied up that August, Jones won by a 5.5 percent margin, but it was an open secret that the election had been stolen. Ballot boxes from Populist precincts were thrown out, and bribery and corruption were rampant. By one estimate, nine out of ten Alabamians believed Jones's victory was fraudulent. This pattern was repeated in 1894, when Kolb lost a second bid by some 26,000 votes. In December 1894, his supporters marched on Montgomery and nearly started a riot. Kolb himself prevented it by mounting a wagon and asking the crowd to be "peaceable."

By the decade's end, the Populist movement had died down, both statewide and nationally. But Alabama's power brokers wanted to avoid future risks. They resolved to strip poor and uneducated Alabamians, who formed the basis of the Populists' support, of their voting rights. Mississippi had already shown how this could be done. In 1890, it ratified a new constitution that included a poll tax and a literacy test for would-be voters. The point was to end Black suffrage, and loopholes were added for poor whites; but over time, a vast number of white sharecroppers were also purged from the voter rolls. In the aftermath of the Populist uprising, other states took up Mississippi's example: South Carolina in 1895, Louisiana in 1898, and North Carolina in 1900. In 1901, Alabama followed suit, holding a referendum on whether a new constitution should be drafted. It's clear Alabamians were skeptical, because twenty-five predominantly white counties voted against it. The referendum passed with a 60 percent majority, but a great share of the votes in favor came from majority-Black counties—making it safe to conclude that election fraud had carried the day once again. Plans were made for a convention that spring.

On May 21, 1901, 155 legislators, judges, attorneys, and mayors gathered at the state capitol in Montgomery. It was a sea of white faces; not one African American was among the delegates. Several dozen of the men were Confederate veterans. Presiding over them was John B. Knox, a forty-four-year-old corporate lawyer from Anniston. Knox was the perfect man for the job. He came from an old Alabama family, and two of his brothers had died fighting for the Confederacy. But he also represented new trends in the southern economy. His client list no doubt included banks, railroads, and factories. As of 1894, before the state income tax was scrapped, Knox had the largest professional income of any Alabamian. Shortly after eleven A.M. on the convention's second day, Knox addressed the crowd. Never had the state been confronted with a more important situation, he said, except perhaps when it seceded from the Union in 1861. "Then, as now," he said, "the negro was the prominent factor in the issue." He acknowledged frankly that his party had been stealing elections. In the short term, he said, these actions had been justified by "the menace of negro domination." But if the state were to let the practice go on for decades, he predicted corruption and dishonesty would seep into every part of public life. "If we would have white supremacy, we must establish it by law—not by force or fraud."

Apart from Knox, the delegates could be divided into four sects. A handful were remnants of the Populist movement. Another small group were Progressives; they favored funding for schools, expanded public services, antilynching laws, and prison reforms. But the two groups dominating the convention were the Planters and the Big Mules. The Planters were large landowners, concentrated in the Black Belt (so named for its rich dark soil); and the Big Mules represented banks, railroads, and the state's growing industries, including lumber and textiles and steel.

Much of the spring and summer were spent in committee hearings. By the end of July, the suffrage committee, which was chaired by another corporate attorney, had prepared a new set of voting restrictions. These were more sweeping than the rules in any other state. The committee wanted a poll tax of $1.50 a year (the equivalent of around $50 now), accumulating every year it wasn't paid. In a state where the average sharecropping family made less than $100 a year (which would be $3,200 now), this alone promised to disqualify a vast share of the population. The committee also called for a literacy test, though it wrote in an exemption for anyone who owned at least forty acres' worth of land or $300 worth of personal property. And it wanted to exclude anyone convicted of certain crimes, ranging from murder and treason to vagrancy and adultery. As a concession to poor white voters, it was proposing a one-year window, where military veterans and their descendants, and anyone else who the authorities thought was of "good character," could register without taking the literacy test.

Throughout the summer debates, the differences among the delegates' agendas became more pronounced. Some delegates were truly fixated on ensuring "white supremacy," and their hope was to eliminate the Black vote while protecting poor whites. For others, racial questions were largely beside the point. "What are we here for?" the delegate Robert Lowe asked on June 24. "Not to preserve white supremacy. White supremacy is secure in Alabama." For Lowe and his cohort, the point was to establish what they called "fair elections," and that meant the same rules had to apply to Blacks and whites alike; any exceptions made for poor farmers would be hypocritical. But for the most powerful camp, the main objective was to disfranchise the "ignorant and vicious voter," regardless of his race. These delegates championed the rhetoric of white supremacy, both because they were genuinely bigoted and because it was politically popular; but in practice, wealthy whites were the only ones they held up as supreme. They intended to trample down poor white Alabamians, who they regarded as a threat to their power. They wanted a poll tax that would "pile up so high" that poor residents would "never be able to vote again," as one delegate said. After weeks' worth of discussion, the voting restrictions passed by a vote of 95–19.

Although voting issues dominated the proceedings, the Planters and Big

Mules also used subtler measures to tighten their grip on the state's politics—and these would endure longer than the suffrage restrictions. Delegates were concerned that if counties and cities were left to their own devices, they might hike taxes on the wealthy or try to regulate corporate affairs. So they stripped local governments of most decision-making power. Under the new rules, local officials would have to seek a constitutional amendment before they could accomplish any major change. This way business leaders wouldn't have to worry about local elections; all of their lobbying resources could be concentrated on the governor, the lieutenant governor, and the 140 legislators. "Control more than half those 142 offices," the Alabama historian Wayne Flynt has written, "and they controlled every town and county in the state."

The delegates also reduced the already minimal tax burden on the wealthy. County and city taxes were capped at 0.5 percent. Local governments were restricted in their rights to take on debt, and school districts were banned from raising taxes for education. As a result, schools could get money only by selling bonds (which meant paying high interest rates) or through sales or income taxes. The constitution also stopped communities from raising taxes to build infrastructure. With all these provisions in place, the delegates adjourned on September 3.

It would be up to voters that November to approve or reject the new constitution. The Democrats' strategy was to win over the white masses by appealing to their racial pride and distorting the document's true contents. They tried to sell it as a "clean white man's document," as one newspaper put it. Knox himself canvassed the state three times, making speeches where he couched racial bigotry in lofty moral rhetoric. "The demand for a new constitution, I regard as the re-awakening of the moral sense of our people," he said in a lengthy speech near Tuscaloosa, two days before the election. He told the crowd they were about to make history. "It is as if we are going to build a great house—a house in which we are all to live—not for a few years, but perhaps as long as we do live—and not only those of us that are here, but our children and our children's children." He promised the new constitution would place control of the government "where God Almighty intended it should be—with the Anglo-Saxon race."

Black leaders fought the new constitution in the limited ways they could. More than a hundred prominent Black men gathered in Birmingham on September 25, with A. N. Johnson, the editor of the *Mobile Weekly Press,* a Black newspaper, presiding. They called for poor whites to vote no, warning that they were "being used as instruments to effect their own political destruc-tion." They also vowed that if the oppressive new document were ratified, they would fight it in the U.S. Supreme Court; and if that failed, they said, Blacks would migrate en masse to friendlier states. In the meantime, they agreed to boycott the polls on election day, knowing their votes would be thrown out or changed if they participated.

The election was on November 11. All told, it seems, the Democrats' campaign failed to win over as many white voters as party leaders had hoped. Outside the twelve counties of the Black Belt, the tally was 76,263 against ratification and 72,389 in favor. But the white leadership of the Black Belt counties, where the population was more than two-thirds African American, held off on submitting their returns. When the Black Belt's results finally came in, the numbers were 36,224 in favor, 5,471 against. The proportion of yes votes decreased from county to county as the Black proportion of resi-dents went down. Reports from elsewhere in the state suggested that Black residents had voted overwhelmingly against ratification. So the constitution passed, but it was clear that election theft had occurred once again.

The result was that a massive share of Alabamians were banned from participating in the state's affairs. Before the constitution passed, roughly 181,000 Black residents were eligible to vote. By January 1, 1903, only 2,980 had been allowed to register under the new rules. The effects on white voters were more gradual. In 1900, the state had 232,800 eligible white voters. Three years later, that figure was down to 191,500, though the population was increasing. And several decades on, the Alabama Policy Institute would find that roughly 600,000 whites and 520,000 Blacks had been disfranchised by the constitution. In most counties, more white residents were disfran-chised than were registered.

True to their promise, Black Alabamians challenged the new constitu-tion in federal court. Booker T. Washington personally recruited a New York attorney to handle the case. (Washington had by then formed an alliance with southern planters and industrialists himself—"against the poorer class of whites," as his biographer Louis Harlan has written—and his public per-sona was largely based on acquiescence to white supremacy. Washington kept his involvement in this case a secret, going so far as to use code names in his personal correspondence, lest any letter be intercepted. His involvement was not discovered until decades later.) The suit was dismissed by a federal judge in Alabama. The U.S. Supreme Court took up the appeal in the spring of 1903. In a 6–3 opinion, Oliver Wendell Holmes declared that the Alabama judge had been right to throw it out. If Black Alabamians had a problem with their state government, Holmes reasoned, they had to take it up with the state. It was not the federal government's place to intervene.

The ramifications would not immediately reach Cudjo Lewis or the other shipmates. After all, by one account they had not voted since 1874, and they had never received much in the way of government services. But true to John B. Knox's promise, the new constitution would profoundly affect their children and grandchildren.

One day in the spring of 1902, Cudjo was riding his wagon back home from the city, hoping to beat the rain. It had been a good morning. Celia had made him breakfast; then he'd prevailed on her to come help him in the garden. He asked her to drop beans in the soil while he planted them. Before long, though, she had grown impatient. He didn't need her dropping the beans, she said; he'd brought her there just for company. "You cain work 'thout no woman 'round you." After more than thirty years together, she knew him too well. He went on planting alone, but before he was finished, he'd run out of beans. The market near Plateau had none in stock—thus this trip into the city.

Cudjo was several blocks west of downtown, on Government Street, a beautiful promenade lined with gigantic oak trees. As he approached the railroad track, another horse-drawn wagon was coming slowly from the opposite direction, occupying the middle of the road. Cudjo spurred his horse on; but as he passed, he saw a train bearing down on his wagon. It's likely the other vehicle had blocked his view. He yelled for the conductor to stop, but there wasn't enough time. The train slammed into his buggy, knocking Cudjo to the ground. His horse panicked and fled.

Cudjo lay there on the street for a moment. Pain shot through the left side of his body. Someone helped him up and carried him to a doctor's office. A stranger, a white woman, who had been on the street, saw him hurting and made sure he was taken care of. The doctor prescribed him some morphine.

Once he made it back home, he was laid up for fourteen days. Three of his ribs were broken. His son David, fortunately, found the horse a day after the wreck. The nice white lady sent him a basket, as a get-well gift, and later visited him at home. She had witnessed the collision, she said, and the train company needed to be held responsible. The operator had failed to ring the bell or blow the whistle, warning Cudjo that it was coming. She said she was going to speak with someone at the Louisville and Nashville Railroad Company.

9

PROGRESSIVISM
FOR WHITE MEN ONLY

There was a popular idea for years that Progressivism—the movement in the early 1900s for cleaner government, cleaner cities, better schools, and improved public health—never touched down in the Deep South. Southern culture was too conservative to foster the spirit of reform that took hold in the North—or so the story went. This wasn't true. Southern cities, from Dallas to Atlanta, did give rise to a Progressive movement of their own. But it was simply restricted to one side of the color line. It was Progressivism, as C. Vann Woodward wrote in 1951, "for white men only." Once African Americans had been stripped of voting eligibility, there was no effective way for them to stand up for their rights. Nowhere was this more true than in Mobile.

Mobile never regained its status as one of America's top port towns. A national railroad network, running east and west, beneath the Ohio River, was in place by then, and much of the cotton that had once passed through Mobile was now being diverted to other ports. The 1850s city of Mobilians who used to "live in cotton houses and ride in cotton carriages" was by this time a distant memory. And as Mobile was outpaced in industrial growth, it also lost its prominence in other ways. As of 1900, its population was dwarfed by that of New Orleans, which had 287,000 residents, compared to Mobile's 38,500. Atlanta, Savannah, Charleston, Richmond, Nashville, and Memphis had also surpassed Mobile in size. Erwin Craighead, the editor of the *Mobile Register*, who was the period's most prominent city booster, admitted in 1902 that Mobile had "fallen behind in the race to the front rank of Southern cities." He predicted it would soon catch up; and it became his refrain that Mobile was on the verge of "greatness." Reading his editorials now, however, it's easy to see the origins of Mobile's derisive nickname, which is passed around among locals: the City of Perpetual Potential.

It's true that Mobile was modernizing. Electricity was introduced by a private company between 1893 and 1906. Craighead boasted in 1902 that sewers had been installed "with a completeness not found elsewhere," and the city assigned twenty men to clean streets, gutters, and drains on a daily basis. It also purchased one waterworks system and built another, so that for the first time, the majority of residents dependably had clean water. Its public parks were improved and expanded, and in 1896, the first ballpark was established, along with a professional team that competed in the Southern Baseball League. By 1915, roughly forty miles' worth of roads had been paved. Most important for the city's growth was the expansion of electric streetcars. As commuting became easier, new homes were built on Government Street, Dauphin Street, Spring Hill Road, and Old Shell Road, all to the west of the city. On the south side, a streetcar suburb called Oakdale was developed; and on the north side, a network of small neighborhoods flourished, with Plateau and its counterpart, Magazine Point, among them. According to one record from this period, which may or may not be accurate, Plateau's population mushroomed to 1,500, making it one of the largest Black settlements in the country.

But all this growth hewed to a Jim Crow framework. By custom, Black Mobilians had long been confined to separate spaces when they rode in carriages, stayed in hotels, and frequented restaurants and theaters. In the early twentieth century, Mobile, like countless other cities in the South, codified this practice into law. It started with an ordinance segregating the streetcars in 1902. Racial distinctions were also being sharpened at the neighborhood level. The expansion of plumbing, sewage, and paved roads generally stopped at the color line, so that even within city limits, Black wards were effectively left in the nineteenth century. In 1915, Dr. Charles Mohr, the city health officer, described the Black wards as "the least desirable" in Mobile, "far removed from the better residential districts" and "unfrequented except by those who, from choice or necessity, have their homes there." It was evident to Mohr, if not to his peers, that this planning strategy could be disastrous for public health everywhere. Diseases like tuberculosis, malaria, diphtheria, and typhoid fever were still rampant in Black communities after they'd been quelled in the rest of the city. Mohr warned that they posed a "constant menace to the white community." Ultimately the city did extend sewage and other services to the city's Black wards. But even then, Plateau, Magazine Point, and the neighboring districts were left out, because they were beyond the city limits. (When an annexation bill passed in 1915, after years' worth of debate, it covered only the new western suburbs.)

There was a vicious cycle at work. The more thoroughly white Mobilians were separated from Blacks, the less they knew them—and the larger the void for their imaginations to fill. Popular media was a toxic influence. Thomas W. Dixon's novel *The Clansman*, which dealt with Reconstruction from the southern aristocracy's point of view, was published in 1905 and rapidly sold more than a million copies. The novel blamed the federal government for turning freedpeople against southern whites, depicted Black characters as murderers and rapists, and cast the Ku Klux Klan as the white South's salvation. The film adaptation, *The Birth of a Nation*, which was released in theaters in 1915, became the most profitable film of its time and was the first to be screened at the White House. In white communities everywhere, North and South, the film stoked fears of Black men and the threats they allegedly posed.

A similar tone was also struck in the white press of Mobile. In 1902, Mobile's *Daily Herald* described Magazine Point as "the stamping ground for all kinds of negro desperadoes" who made enough money in the nearby sawmills to gamble and buy whiskey. In the area's dance halls and saloons, it claimed, "pandemonium frequently reigns where the two sexes gather for their weekly orgies." More broadly, Erwin Craighead and other white journalists described Black Mobilians as prone to violence, drug addiction, and alcoholism. Craighead said in 1906 that relations between the races had become "severely strained everywhere." However, he blamed this not on segregation, but on African Americans themselves, who had grown less dependent on white people—which, to his mind, represented a "failure to be guided by the better judgment of the superior race."

There was one more change in this era that would have enduring consequences for Black political prospects. The electoral districts were already gerrymandered to make sure Black residents didn't make up a voting majority in any given ward. Craighead was frank about this in a 1907 editorial: "It is a well-known historical fact," he wrote, that when the districts were drawn in 1879, the point was to "preserve white supremacy" in government. However, in 1910, there was a push to do away with electoral districts altogether. Businessmen, represented by the chamber of commerce, wanted to restructure the city government, eliminating the board of aldermen and the city council and re-placing them with a city commission. Instead of twenty-plus elected leaders, there would be only three. In all likelihood these commissioners would be businessmen or attorneys. They would also be invested with more executive power. Cities across the nation were making this switch. The idea was to re-fashion administrations in the image of corporate America, so they'd be less prone to patronage and more concerned with their bottom lines. Craighead championed the proposal, saying Mobile needed a "business administration." The "city with the best government," he predicted, "will attract the most new people." Montgomery and Birmingham had already made the conversion.

After a lobbying campaign in the state legislature, the change was made in 1911. Under the new system, the city elected its commissioners at large, not on a ward-by-ward basis. For city leaders, this was an insurance policy. There was always the chance that the voting restrictions in the state consti-tution would be knocked down by a court; but this way, Black Mobilians would remain relatively powerless at the local level. As long as conservative whites made up more than 50 percent of the city's total vote share, no Black candidate would ever be elected to the commission.

If Plateau and Magazine Point were coming to be seen as dangerous and crime-ridden, this was not necessarily just a bigoted projection by white Mo-bilians. The poor conditions there, which resulted from the deep inequities in Mobile society, were bound to spur increases in violence. Taken together with the communicable diseases that were still ravaging the area, the mortality rate must have been staggering. The Lewis family's experiences bear this out. Their daughter was only the first casualty; more deaths in the family were to follow.

As of 1901, Cudjo and Celia's five sons were running their own business, Lewis Bros. Grocery Dealers. It was one of the first retail shops in Plateau. Ahnonotoe, or Jimmy, the second oldest, was the manager. The store also served as the brothers' base of operations as they worked with the sheriff's de-partment to keep the peace in Plateau and Magazine Point. At a meeting there in 1901, they dubbed their little auxiliary unit the Hickory Club. There were at least a couple of members from outside the family. According to one news story, they saw it as their mission to police other African Americans within the community. A few of their deeds are recorded. In the fall of 1901, a man named Peyton Alexander tried to kill his wife and in-laws; and when a Black mob came after him, Hickory Club members held him until the sheriff arrived to arrest him. Another time they helped sheriff's deputies find two white hunters who were lost in a nearby swamp. In March 1902, a Hickory Club member named Bella Jones was knifed while arresting a woman for assault and battery. And in May of that year, a man named Will Jones sought a warrant for the arrest of two other Hickory Club members, claiming they had robbed him at gunpoint. The *Mobile Register* noted in its coverage that the Hickory Club had done "good work in capturing criminals in the section around Plateau." The sheriff recognized their contributions by installing a telephone at the Lewis brothers' grocery store, for use in emergencies. In the judgment of David Alsobrook, a historian of Mobile's Progressive Era, the Hickory Club represented "a stop-gap measure against the swelling tide of racism in Mobile."

But as the brothers' ties with law enforcement became stronger, it seems, they continued making enemies with other locals. It's rumored that there was a fight on July 28, 1902, where at least two or three men ganged up on Cudjo Jr. The young man reportedly shot one of the attackers to death and seriously wounded another with a knife. Whether or not this actually happened is impossible to say; the only source is Zora Neale Hurston's account, which was written more than twenty-five years after the fact and was based on hearsay. It seems no such killing was reported in the local press in 1902, and Hurston may have been confusing it with the bout in 1900 that led to Cudjo Jr.'s arrest. Nevertheless, the story goes that a Black sheriff's deputy, Samuel Powe, set out to arrest him that summer in 1902. Powe was reportedly afraid to confront Cudjo Jr. head-on—so he kept looking for a chance to catch him off guard.

One day roughly three weeks after the fight, some neighbors came to Cudjo Sr. and told him one of his sons had been hurt at the grocery store. He rushed over, no doubt hobbling from his train injury. The site he saw there was a brutal shock. Cudjo Jr. was lying in a pool of blood; he had been shot in the throat.

This is the story that was later told: The butcher had come to the store that day, in his wagon, and Cudjo Jr. stepped out to meet him and discuss business. Powe, who was hiding in the back of the vehicle, leapt out and killed him.

As the family looked at his wounded body, the clothes surely drenched in blood, it must have been clear that he wouldn't survive. There was nothing to do but bring him home. They laid him down in bed and made him as comfortable as they could. "He try so hard to ketchee breath," Cudjo recalled years later. "Oh, Lor'! It hurtee me see my baby boy lak dat." Almost as bad was watching Celia's reaction. It made Cudjo cry to see her in such pain.

All night and the next day the couple kept vigil at their son's bed. Celia wouldn't step away. She stood over her son, staring into his face. "Cudjo, Cudjo, Cudjo, baby, put whip to yo' horse!" she urged him. Summoning all his energy, he'd whisper that he was already trying.

All three of them prayed. Cudjo pleaded with God to spare his child's life. But after two days and two nights, the young man succumbed to his injuries. It had been only nine years since the death of their daughter. The bell that had tolled for her, he said, was still ringing in his ears when it tolled again for his son. It grieved him to think the young man had never set foot in West Africa.

Cudjo said later that he doubted whether Powe, the killer, was a sheriff's deputy at all. It seems he was right to be suspicious; the story doesn't add up. If Cudjo Jr. did kill someone and badly wound another, it's hard to believe the sheriff would have left it up to some lone deputy to arrest him, especially since Cudjo Jr. was known to fight back. Moreover, it's not clear that there were any Black sheriff's deputies in this period. Hurston described Powe, decades after the fact, as a Black deputy sheriff, but if he was in fact working for the sheriff's department, he may have been what was known in Mobile as a "Creole of color." (The 1900 census has a Sam Poe who was African American and lived in Whistler, near Plateau, but it lists his occupation as "Raftsman.") Perhaps, as Sylviane Diouf has suggested, if Powe truly was a sheriff's deputy, he thought the sheriff would be reluctant to arrest Cudjo Jr., given that he saw the Lewis brothers as valuable allies. If that's true, maybe Powe took the matter into his own hands. There are no other surviving records to clear up the mystery.

Cudjo hoped to see Powe arrested. But in the weeks that followed, there was no arrest, nor any repercussion as far as he could see.

In January 1903, nearly a year after the train incident, Cudjo and his son David were in a courtroom downtown. The railroad company had refused to compensate him, so the white woman had urged him to get a lawyer. One of Mobile's preeminent attorneys, Richard Clarke, agreed to take the case on a contingency fee: half the compensation if they won, nothing if they lost. Given Clarke's credentials, the offer wasn't unreasonable. The sixty-year-old attorney had been a U.S. congressman until 1897 and then a state legislator in 1900 and 1901. He had also fought for the Confederacy and worked as a prosecutor. Since the lawsuit was against a railroad, one of America's biggest and most powerful corporations, Cudjo needed someone of Clarke's skill and stature on his side. There was no doubt the defense would come prepared.

Cudjo had more than one cause for a grudge against the rail industry. In September, Gumpa, one of his oldest friends, had also been hit by a train. Gumpa, too, had initiated a lawsuit. But less than two weeks after the accident, he died. He was seventy. (He had been raising his two granddaughters alone—it appears his wife and children may have all died before him—and a judge declared the girls were entitled to $500, in compensation for the Mobile and Bay Shore Railroad Company's negligence.)

On this day in court, the judge, William Strudwick Anderson, announced that the first case on the docket would be *Cudjo Lewis v. The Louisville and Nashville Railroad Company*—involving a claim for $5,000, the equivalent of more than $140,000 now. Cudjo was taken by surprise. He had not asked for that much.

The attorney representing the railroad addressed the jurors first. Cudjo was entitled to nothing, he said. The wreck occurred in the daylight, when the train was perfectly visible. It was the plaintiff's fault if he hadn't seen it coming.

When Clarke's turn came, he called a doctor as a witness. Cudjo was asked to remove his shirt. After examining at the left side of his torso, where the ribs had been broken and the skin bruised, the doctor confirmed that Cudjo wouldn't be able to work again. Later Clarke addressed the jury. The train had a bell, he said, but the operators hadn't rung it. It had a whistle, but it hadn't been blown. And Cudjo had simply been using a public roadway. How could the city let a company run its tracks directly across the road and then not hold it accountable when its trains injured people? Clearly, the attorney said, the railroad had a duty to take care of Cudjo from this point on.

In his instructions to the jury, it seems, Judge Anderson did his best to influence the outcome in the company's favor. Train workers had no obligation to stop for someone crossing, the instructions said; and if jurors believed all the evidence and believed Cudjo had time to get off the track, they were obligated to deny him any award.

Court recessed, and everyone went to eat dinner. Cudjo was tired. He decided he'd stop by the market to pick up some meat. But while he was there, David came running up. The judge had awarded Cudjo $650 from the company, he said—a verdict worth nearly $19,000 now. The attorney said he could come the next day and get his money.

However, in the weeks that followed, Clarke, the attorney, repeatedly told him to wait. Then, in 1904, the verdict was overturned by the Alabama Supreme Court. The train's brakeman and flagman both testified that they'd warned Cudjo and given him ample time to get out of the way. Cudjo was ordered to pay the cost of the appeal, though it's unlikely he ever did.

One evening two years after the trial, Cudjo and Celia heard someone laughing outside. It was the Saturday before Easter. Springtime in Mobile is a season when the days start running long and the temperature is balmy—before the summer's unbearable heat sets in. After a dinner of baked fish, David had set out for the city, saying he'd run out of clean undershirts and had to go pick up the laundry. Hearing the unfamiliar voice outside, the couple figured he must have come back with a friend.

Cudjo looked out to see who it was. Two men were there, and neither was their son.

"Uncle Cudjo," they told him, "yo' boy dead in Plateau."

They were mistaken, Cudjo said—David was in Mobile.

The men insisted: a train had killed him in Plateau. Cudjo kept trying to explain, but Celia piped up, saying he should go see who the victim was.

The men led Cudjo down the road. As they approached the railroad track, a crowd was blocking their view. Cudjo made his way to the front. He saw a man's body, near the telegraph pole, with the head taken off. One bystander told him it was his boy. "Cudjo," another asked, "which son of yours is dis?" He brushed it off, telling himself David was in Mobile.

As he tried to slip out of the crowd, others kept approaching him. A voice asked if someone should toll the church bell on his son's behalf. Usually it was Cudjo's duty to toll it for other families. Possibly trembling at this point, Cudjo walked back home, wishing desperately David would show up so these people would leave him alone.

The crowd was following him. One of the shipmates was present—in the account he gave later, Cudjo didn't say which one—and this person had arranged for the body to be taken to the Lewises' house. Carrying it on a window shutter, they lifted it over the gate and set it on the porch.

Celia saw it and screamed.

Cudjo, steadying his nerves, said he wouldn't believe it was David unless he saw the head. Someone brought him a cracker box, and when he looked in, he saw his son's lifeless face.

"Git off my porch!" he yelled at the onlookers. "Git out my yard!"

When they had cleared out, he fell down upon the body. He opened the shirt and put his hand on the chest. Until he felt the marks, he later said, it didn't seem real. When Celia watched his expression change, she understood that it was David. She screamed and screamed; then she fell down, sobbing.

Cudjo started running. He went to a pine grove nearby, where he fell on his face. There he caught his breath. He couldn't stand to hear Celia cry; in the moment, her shrieks hurt him more than the news itself. He lay there until some of the other shipmates came and found him. Celia wanted him, they said.

Back at the house, he asked a friend to put David's head back on his body, so that when mourners came the next day, they wouldn't know it had been separated. Cudjo conceded that it was time to toll the bell.

Cudjo and Celia's third son, Pollee, was enraged about David's death. All his life, he said, other kids from the area had picked on him and his brothers, calling them savages. A sheriff's deputy had murdered his younger brother. A railroad company owned by white men was responsible for practically maiming his father. And now another train had killed his brother. He wanted his father to sue the company.

What good would it do? Cudjo asked. He understood his son's position. Pollee hated feeling powerless; and at least filing a lawsuit would mean doing something. For his own part, as a devout Christian, Cudjo was struggling to let go of his bitterness. But there was more tragedy still to come.

One day not long after that conversation, Pollee went fishing—someone said they saw him headed toward Twelvemile Creek—and he never came back. Cudjo suspected he was murdered. Many people in the area resented Pollee, Cudjo later said, because he was like his brothers; he didn't stand for people abusing and insulting him. A friend suggested he might be in Africa, and Cudjo found this thought comforting. This loss was especially painful because there wasn't even a burial. Pollee was not included in the family plot.

Cudjo and Celia's sorrows put a strain on their marriage. They had only one son, James, still living in their house, since Aleck lived separately with his wife and children. Cudjo tried to make Celia happy, in whatever small ways he could, but he found it hard to look at her; it always seemed like she wanted to cry.

In November 1905, only seven months after David's death, Cudjo noticed that Jimmy, who was thirty-five, wasn't feeling well. He was lying around the house, sapped of his energy. "Son, you gittee sick?" Cudjo asked. He thought Jimmy shouldn't go to work if he didn't feel well. "Papa, tain nothin' wrong wid me," he replied. But the next day, he came home looking worse, so his parents put him in bed. They realized the illness was more serious than they'd thought. A doctor came to examine him. Repeating the pattern they'd experienced with their daughter, Cudjo and Celia followed the doctor's instructions, but Jimmy did not get better. On November 17, their fourth son died, while Cudjo held his hand. The coroner's report listed the cause of death as paralysis. Diouf believes the symptoms point to diphtheria, one of the diseases that was always lurking in the area, thanks to the unsanitary conditions.

It seemed to Cudjo as if his children were lonesome for one another—"So dey hurry go sleep together in de graveyard."

While the family grieved, racial lynchings were reaching a historic peak throughout the South. Murders by mobs were nothing new in the region, and before the Civil War, the victims had frequently been white. But with the onset of Reconstruction, lynchings became principally a form of racial terrorism. For years, Mobile mostly staved off the phenomenon. One Black man was lynched in the county in 1891, and police broke up another would-be lynch mob in 1902. But in 1906, the year after David and Jimmy Lewis died, local lynchings began to surge. Three of them occurred in or beside Plateau.

The first victim was a twenty-year-old Black waiter named Will Thompson. He was accused of raping several white and Creole women during the summer of 1906. At his preliminary hearing that August, two ten-year-old girls testified that Thompson had lured them into a vacant house on Dauphin Street, where they were "inhumanely treated." According to a letter the county solicitor wrote to the governor, Thompson "strenuously denied touching either of the girls," and a doctor who examined them testified that they hadn't had intercourse. But it seems the public was grossly misled. The *Daily Item* claimed the testimony at the hearing had been "too revolting to put into print," and the *Register* reported that Thompson had confessed to the crime. The sheriff, anticipating trouble, transferred Thompson to the jail in Birmingham. On two consecutive nights, huge mobs stormed the Mobile County jail, not knowing the prisoner was gone.

A month later, on October 2, a mob came looking for another Black defendant: Cornelius Robinson, a seventeen-year-old unemployed laborer, known to his friends as Dick. He was accused of raping an eleven-year-old girl on her way home from school. Again the sheriff, John F. Powers, transferred Robinson to Birmingham. When the mob rushed the Mobile jail, it found an empty cell.

Thompson and Robinson had hearings scheduled in Mobile that October, and Sheriff Powers and a deputy went to Birmingham to retrieve them. As the group rode back down on the train, stopping at various stations on the way, they kept hearing that a mob was waiting for them near the city. When they were roughly thirty miles north of Mobile, eight men in white masks reportedly stepped onto the train, brandishing revolvers. They disarmed Powers and his deputy, then told the conductor to move the first-class passengers to the back. Closer to town, a few dozen more masked men came on board. According to one news report, a mob leader announced that the newcomers were all "leading business men of Mobile" who had decided to join "only after careful consideration."

When the train reached Plateau, they exited en masse. A state legislator was on the scene, and he reportedly urged the mob to let the men stand trial, so they could be "legally hanged." One of the leaders replied that they were going to deal with the matter outside the city limits, to avoid a race riot. Thompson and Robinson were marched east of the railroad tracks, down a dirt road, toward Magazine Point. Ropes were slung over the limbs of a tall tree, and the men were tied up. Accounts differ on who was killed first. In one telling, Robinson was jerked up about fifteen feet, then lowered and given a chance to confess. An Associated Press reporter was called over to listen. The young man screamed that he was innocent. Within a few minutes both defendants were dead.

Later in the afternoon, a huge crowd, possibly more than three thousand people, came to see the bodies. They took away souvenirs, including pieces of the victims' clothing, bark from the tree, and bits of the rope. The men were buried in a potter's field. The following day, *The Birmingham News* reported that an effort had been made to protect Thompson and Robinson. The bar association in Mobile had sent the governor a telegram, asking for a military escort; and the governor in turn sent a message to Powers, in Birmingham, telling him to come through Montgomery first, where armed guards would join him for the rest of the trip. According to the paper, Powers didn't get the message in time. But in all likelihood, this whole report was fiction. It looked better for the governor, and for Mobile's professional class, if they could claim they had tried to stop the violence.

Another lynching occurred a year later in the same spot—on what reporters claimed was the same tree. The chain of events began when someone broke into the home of a ninety-year-old white woman, a few miles west of Plateau. She screamed for help, and the intruder fled. Based on her description, a sheriff's deputy suspected a man named Mose Dorsett, who was portrayed in the white press as a well-known troublemaker. Within a few hours, Dorsett had been arrested. By one account, Dorsett insisted he knew nothing about the crime, but the elderly woman said his clothes were the same as the intruder's. However, the *Mobile Daily Register* said Dorsett admitted to entering the woman's home but told officials he had only wanted a match. He reportedly admitted that he'd grabbed the woman when she tried to scream. ("This confession, to my mind, was conclusive," a sheriff's deputy said.) Meanwhile, as word about the incident spread, a mob started gathering. As the deputy took Dorsett to jail, he opted for a circuitous route—hewing to Telegraph Road, which skirts Plateau—in hopes of avoiding the crowd.

Around 12:40 A.M., several miles north of the city, Dorsett's wagon was stopped and surrounded by men with revolvers and shotguns. Dorsett was marched to the woods. In language that was typical in these reports, journalists claimed the murder was done in an orderly, almost elegant manner. "So quiet were the proceedings," one wrote, "that persons living less than a hundred feet away from the scene did not know of the affair until early this morning when they saw the body of the negro swinging to and fro in a drenching rain."

Why were all three of these spectacle-murders committed in Plateau? The killers could have pulled Thompson and Robinson off anywhere along the train line or surrounded Dorsett's wagon elsewhere along the way to the jail. Clearly the mobs wanted to send a message by doing the deeds in a Black neighborhood, and the significance of Plateau being the home of African Town likely wasn't lost on most Mobilians, either. Another factor was the neighborhood's being located outside the city limits. For a lynching to be committed inside Mobile, even in a Black ward, would have undermined the image of elegance and sophistication that the power elites were trying to cultivate. Across that border, however, anything went.

Over the days that followed Dorsett's lynching, rumors began circulating that Black residents around Plateau and Magazine Point were holding secret meetings to plan revenge for his killing. There were reports that they had a stockpile of guns. On September 27, at the behest of white residents, the sheriff and the militia director ordered a search of the neighborhood. They did not find any weapon stash, but they did arrest several people of both races who were carrying concealed weapons. Whether or not the secret armory existed is a mystery. Many decades later, one Black resident who lived through it claimed there had been guns hidden in a boxcar near the railyard, and said he'd personally brought home a shotgun. But either way, the rumor that African Americans were secretly plotting an insurrection was another trope in southern society, one that dated back to the antebellum period. "This was just a topic that white officials loved to talk about," said Alsobrook, the Mobile historian. "Whether or not there was a grain of truth to it, it didn't matter." Reports like this could be used to justify all manner of violence by whites. The same day the search was ordered, a note was found on the nearby gates of the Mobile and Ohio Railroad station, warning Plateau residents that there were "plenty of ropes and trees left."

On a chilly November night in 1908, Celia awakened Cudjo in bed. She was reeling from a bad dream: she had pictured their children shivering in the cold. Cudjo said she was thinking too much and urged her to go back to sleep. But her description pained him, too; he remembered how she used to check up on the kids while they slept, making sure they had enough quilts.

The next day, Celia wanted to go visit the graves. Cudjo agreed, but he was reluctant—he worried it would only make her more anxious. He went over to the church, trying to look busy, hoping she would forget. When he came back outside, Celia was nowhere in sight. He walked up the hill and saw her standing in the cemetery, in their family's plot. She was walking from one stone to the next, as if she were covering them up with more quilts.

The following week, according to Cudjo, she died. Her cause of death was a mystery; she hadn't been sick. His explanation was that she went to be with her children. "She cry 'cause she doan want me be lonesome," he said.

His last remaining child, Aleck, died the following month. Virtually no information survives about the circumstances. Both Aleck and Celia may have been victims of the extremely poor public health conditions. Cudjo was in the same situation he'd been in almost fifty years earlier, when he had first arrived in America: bereft of his family, the only one left standing. Only Mary, his daughter-in-law, and his grandchildren were left.

In the early 1910s, there was a development in Plateau that seems to have transformed its reputation: a school was built that had no equal in the region. The driving force was Isaiah J. Whitley, a young man who arrived in 1910 with a newly minted degree from Selma University. Whitley had grown up on a farm in Washington County, which borders Mobile County on the north.

At the same time that Whitley was settling in Plateau, Booker T. Washington was starting a campaign to build similar schools in rural Black communities throughout the South. He had fundraising connections with northern philanthropists and a ready supply of trained teachers coming out of the college he'd founded upstate, the Tuskegee Normal and Industrial Institute. Though Whitley did not attend Tuskegee, he was every bit a Washington disciple. "Dr. Washington is our spokesman," he wrote in a 1915 letter to the Tuskegee-aligned *New York Age*. "He has never advised the race wrong, neither has he betrayed the trust committed to him by whites and blacks alike." Whitley took cues from Washington's educational philosophy, which held that curricula, at least in Black schools, ought to be geared toward the job market. Whitley believed in education for the masses, Black and white alike, he said in a 1916 speech; but he also believed no education could be complete with "book learning" alone. It was no less important to "have the hands trained to work" than for "the mouth to eat and the body to wear clothes."

In his early months in Plateau, Whitley commenced classes in a log cabin, with two teachers and a hundred students; and at the same time, he organized a committee to help him erect a proper building. Reverend Joyful Keeby, Ossa Keeby's son, helped spearhead the effort. (Joyful Keeby was the rector of the church started by the shipmates, which had changed its name to the Union Missionary Baptist Church.) By February 1911 they had raised $600 toward their goal. The following year, the burgeoning little school was brought into the Mobile County school system. It was named the Plateau Normal and Industrial Institute. (The designation "normal school" meant it trained teachers; this name came from the French term *école normale*, suggesting the classroom would be a model that students could replicate in their own teaching careers.)

As of 1915, the Plateau school had two buildings, three hundred students, and eight teachers, who had degrees from Tuskegee, Selma University, and other Black colleges. It had also evolved into a resource hub for Black adults throughout southern Alabama. It started hosting an agricultural conference every summer (another idea Whitley must have borrowed from Tuskegee), where farmers could study the newest agricultural techniques. It had a night school, where adults could learn to read and write, and workshops where they could learn to can food. There was a Mothers Club, a Law and Order Club, and a Business League. Later Whitley also arranged classes for boys in blacksmithing and carpentry, and taught them agriculture on a small hog farm someone donated to the school, while girls studied sewing, mat making, and cooking.

On a personal level, it seems Washington and Whitley had a chilly relationship. Washington was familiar with Plateau. He had friends in Mobile, and he visited the African settlement at least once. There is a tender passage in his 1909 book *The Story of the Negro* where he describes an exchange he had with Ossa Keeby. "When I asked this old man if he ever thought of returning to Africa, he replied: 'Yes, I goes back to Africa every night, in my dreams.'" It made Washington feel as if he'd "discovered the link by which the old life in Africa was connected with the new life in America." However, Washington was steeped in the social Darwinist philosophy that dominated American discourse at the turn of the century, and in the end, he believed in a hierarchy that placed Plateau's uneducated shipmates on the bottom. He said this explicitly in a *New York Times* op-ed that year. If the shipmates were compared to Black doctors, lawyers, and educators who had risen up in recent years, he suggested, it showed how far the race had progressed. In other words, he was claiming the shipmates represented Blacks in their most inferior state.

This callous side of Washington is on display in his correspondence with Whitley. Between 1912 and 1914, the younger man invited Washington to Plateau several times, saying the people there were "more than anxious" to hear him speak. Whitley also told Washington's confidant, Emmett Jay Scott, that he was personally eager to take Washington on a tour of the region. Washington's responses, which are found in his vast trove of personal papers at the Library of Congress, were brusque. "My dear sir," one began. "The trips that I have made through various states have been under the general direction of the Local or State Negro Business Leagues." In another, he addressed his response to the white superintendent of the Mobile County school system, rather than Whitley himself, saying he couldn't come but would try to send an envoy. However, he added that he'd "heard the most encouraging reports of Prof. Whitley's work," and was glad Whitley had gained the confidence of the superintendent and other local whites.

Plateau, in these years, was dangerously unprepared for emergencies. This became clear in 1913, when a fire destroyed part of the neighborhood. Not only was there no fire service; the absence of any water source besides wells and natural springs also meant there wasn't much Black residents themselves could do to put out the flames. The school was spared on that occasion. When another fire tore through in 1915, the community was not so fortunate. This blaze started on the afternoon of March 25, when sparks from a residence's chimney apparently spread to the roof. It was pushed along by a heavy wind, and one house after another caught fire. Soon everyone in town was filling buckets, bowls, pitchers, and wash basins, trying to douse the flames, but it wasn't much use. The people were all "hushed in breathless suspense," according to one correspondent, when the fire spread to the school grounds. By the evening, all that was left of the two school buildings were their brick pillars. More than 40 of the town's 150 houses were also destroyed. Whether any of these belonged to the shipmates or their descendants is not recorded.

In the aftermath of the fire, Whitley went north on a fundraising tour, apparently taking cues from Washington, who was a master at persuading northern philanthropists to give him money. In the summer of 1915, Whitley stopped to see a journalist named Cleveland G. Allen, at Allen's West 53rd Street office in New York City. Allen wrote a profile that was published the following week in *The Freeman,* a national Black newspaper that was based in Indianapolis and had ties to Tuskegee. It was hyperbolic in its praise. "There are some stories that read like fiction," it began, "and if it were not for the living evidences that bear out their realities one would hardly believe them to be other than novels of romance or fiction." It went on to describe Whitley's journey to Plateau, "a dark and forsaken section of Alabama," and the teacher's heroic efforts over the previous five years, which it said had transformed the community from "a lawless one to one of order and thrift." Allen was referring to Plateau's reputation for crime, but his words also reflected the hierarchical vision that he and Whitley both apparently shared with Booker T. Washington.

The flattering press must have helped Whitley's efforts, but Washington's connections would also make a difference in the campaign. For several years, Washington had been working with Julius Rosenwald, the president of the Sears corporation, to establish a construction fund for Black rural schools throughout the South. Washington died in late 1915, but ultimately Rosenwald's money would fund nearly five thousand schools, filling a void that had largely been created by southern state and local governments. The Plateau community became one of the early beneficiaries. In January 1918, a new school building opened there. The name had been changed to the Mobile County Training School (MCTS). The facility had a dedicated principal's office and individual desks for the students, improvements that seemed cutting-edge at the time. All of Mobile County's Black elites came out for the opening ceremony. The superintendent of the county school system gave an address, and a Black student orchestra from the city performed. "The school is the pride of Southwest Alabama," *The Birmingham Reporter* declared, "and its mission is to teach the training of the hand, head and heart and give to our teaching force better trained teachers."

* * *

Cudjo's life as a widower centered on his church, Union Baptist. To support him after his train accident, the congregation had created a job for him as the sexton. He cleaned the building before every service, sometimes with help from neighborhood children, who all knew him as Uncle Cudjo. "I'd get down on my little knees with a bucket and somebody else's children, and we would scrub that church," Clara Eva Allen Jones (Mama Eva) recalled years later. Cudjo "would fix them lamps and wash them benches off and have them beautiful." For years, it was also Cudjo's singular honor to ring the church bell when services were starting.

The church community also kept him company. The parishioners often put on picnics, where the men would barbecue cows, hogs, and goats in backyard pits, and the women would serve food on a long table. Families from the city could come up and eat their fill for a flat rate of $1.20. Mama Eva remembered one New Year's Day party when the deacons stayed up all night, cooking half a cow. Since there was no electricity, it took two or three hundred pounds of ice to chill all the fruit punch.

Twice a month, on the first and third Sundays, Cudjo would catch a streetcar after the morning service and share a meal with Kanko and James's family in Mobile. He and Kanko would teach the children how to pronounce words in Yoruba, and they'd tell folktales they had learned as kids. Sometimes everyone would go walking along the streetcar tracks, taking in the sights of the city. The children struggled to keep up—because "the oldsters were fast walkers, fast talkers, and hard workers," as Kanko and James's granddaughter, Mable Dennison, wrote later. Cudjo always left in time to prepare the church for the evening service. His other consolation in old age was watching his grandchildren grow up. When Motley, his oldest grandson, was fourteen, he started coming over to Cudjo's house to read the Bible out loud. Cudjo's favorite book was the Psalms. "There would be some words I couldn't pronounce," Motley told a researcher in the 1980s. "I would skip that and go on and he'd notice. He would say, 'You're skipping something there.'"

When he was alone, his garden kept him busy. Visitors could often find him there, barefoot, with his pants rolled up above his knees. His clothes and derby hat were so full of patches they almost looked like quilts. Tending to his garments was one of the old man's pleasures; when Celia had been alive, she had typically set them aside after washing so he could mend the holes in the evenings.

Whatever comforts Cudjo found, though, it's hard to fathom the sorrow he must have felt in these years. Mama Eva sometimes saw her father, Pollee Allen, and Cudjo sitting together and crying for their home. To hear them tell it, the weather there was always warm, the planting was easier, and the fruit and vegetables were more abundant. "I heard them say many times they did *not want to leave their home,*" Mama Eva recalled when she was elderly. Cudjo also revealed to an interviewer that the sunrise services at the church were a source of pain for him. Every week, as the morning light dawned, he was reminded of the attack on his town when he was a much younger man.

About this time, a local writer, Emma Langdon Roche, gave the *Clotilda* saga its first book-length treatment. Roche was a Mobile native, but she had studied at the Art Students League in New York City, where she'd almost overlapped with Georgia O'Keeffe. She evidently spent a fair amount of time in Plateau, getting to know the surviving shipmates and eliciting their memories of their homeland and their early years in America. By this time, it seems, only nine were left: Cudjo, Pollee Allen and his wife Abache (who also went by Clara Turner), Ossa Keeby, Charlie Lewis, Kanko, Zuma, a woman named Omolabi (or Katie Cooper), and another woman named Shamba (who had taken the last name Wigfall). Roche supplemented these interviews by speaking with Martha Adalaide Foster, the widow of Bill Foster (who had died in 1901). Roche's book, *Historic Sketches of the South,* was released in 1914 by the New York–based publisher Knickerbocker Press. Though her tone in the manuscript is sometimes paternalistic, it's never vicious, unlike the writing of Erwin Craighead and other white Mobilians of her era. On the whole, Cudjo and the others are presented as intelligent, thoughtful people with rich inner lives. Their time in America, in Roche's words, was characterized by "hard work, cooperation, self-sacrifice, and a deep longing for home"—not by superstition, as many outsiders believed. Following the shipmates' request, Roche used their Yoruba names, in hopes that word about what had become of them might reach their homeland. The manuscript also included photographs of the shipmates and portraits drawn by Roche herself.

Some of her descriptions are touching. After Celia's death, she wrote, Kossola still saw traces of her throughout his house. "Everything reminds him of her." Even so, Roche found him to be "cheerful—even merry" during most of her visits. She noticed that Pollee Allen, who had apparently learned to read with help from the neighborhood children, carried a small, well-thumbed copy of the New Testament everywhere he went. All of the shipmates were rigorous about personal hygiene and kept their homes in perfect order. Kossola and Abache's moods were easy to detect, because their countenances were "intensely emotional and capable of expressing very deep feeling," she wrote. Whenever their capture and voyage came up, "unspeakable and indescribable anguish" came over their faces. Pollee, on the other hand, always maintained a blank expression. Only his eyes, which Roche described as "small, deep-set, watchful," hinted at how he was feeling.

At the time of the book's publication, the Meaher family was no less prominent than it had been during Tim Meaher's heyday. Only two of his children survived, and the older one, James, had long since moved to Cleveland, where he worked as an attorney. But the younger son, Augustine, was following in his father's footsteps as a business magnate. He was wealthy enough that when he remarried, after the death of his first wife, Annie, the society pages of the national press took notice. POOR STENOGRAPHER BECOMES BRIDE OF MILLIONAIRE read the headline in the *San Francisco Examiner*. According to the gossip columns, Augustine Meaher had plans to marry an heiress in New York; but while he was in Manhattan, he had some business to conduct at a brokerage firm on Wall Street, and he was so taken with a nineteen-year-old stenographer there that he immediately began courting her instead. Her name was Helen Van Nimwegen, and she was the daughter of a baker. They were wed in Paterson, New Jersey, in October 1905. There were reports that the groom's gift to the bride was a $100,000 check, and that she wore a piece of diamond jewelry worth $10,000 in the ceremony. Two weeks later, when the couple had returned to Mobile, the *Montgomery Advertiser* reported that Augustine Meaher was furious about these "sensational statements," including the reports about his gifts, and was preparing to sue the newspapers.

There's no telling how he felt about Roche's book. He may have been ashamed of his father's deeds, or he may have been proud of them. But either way, his lot in life had been determined by his father's actions, just as much as the lot of the shipmates and their children and grandchildren had been. Some of Augustine's income still came from renting out properties in Plateau. In 1909, a white rent collector who worked for him was shot by the Black keeper of a boardinghouse there.

Over the next several years, most of the remaining shipmates passed away. Kanko died in 1917, Omolabi in 1919, and Pollee Allen in 1922. By 1923, only Cudjo and Ossa Keeby were left. Then Keeby died early that year, at the reported age of ninety-seven. Practically everyone in Plateau turned out for his funeral. When the crowd dispersed, Cudjo was left alone.

10
RENAISSANCE

In the mid-1920s, whether or not Cudjo knew it, his name was starting to travel around New York City. These were the years of the Harlem Renaissance, that famous flowering of art, literature, and scholarship that dealt with the African American experience. Its cornerstone text, a 1925 anthology called *The New Negro: An Interpretation*, summed up the movement best. Harlem had by then "brought together the Negro of the North and the Negro of the South," the introductory essay read, "the man from the city and the man from the town and village; the peasant, the student, the business man, the professional man, artist, poet, musician, adventurer and worker." As a result, it argued, there was a unique opportunity in Harlem for African Americans to define and articulate their collective culture.

The author of this essay was Alain Locke, a philosophy professor at Howard University in Washington, D.C., who had also edited the volume. Locke was widely seen as the leader of the Harlem Renaissance (or the New Negro movement, as it was known at the time, thanks to the book's influence). *The New Negro* also contained poetry by Claude McKay and Langston Hughes and essays by W. E. B. Du Bois, Arturo Schomburg, and James Weldon Johnson, among other Black luminaries.

Two other notable names also appeared in its pages. One was Cudjo's. He'd been visited in August 1925 by a former student of Locke's, and he told the young man an African folktale about a turtle and an eagle. The interviewer transcribed it as closely as he could. It was printed in the book verbatim, under the title "T'appin (Terrapin)". The byline read: "Told by

Cugo Lewis, Plateau, Alabama. Brought to America from West Coast Africa, 1859." As the interviewer explained in a separate piece, the members of the Harlem Renaissance felt an urgent need to collect stories like these while Cudjo and others from his generation were still living.

The other important name in the anthology was Zora Neale Hurston's. It would be another twelve years before the publication of her masterpiece, the novel *Their Eyes Were Watching God*, and several decades longer before she would be recognized as one of her generation's greatest literary talents—and as the aunt "of all black people," a title bestowed by the novelist Alice Walker. At the time, Hurston was a thirty-four-year-old undergrad at Barnard, the women's college affiliated with Columbia. She was also a social fixture among Harlem intellectuals. Her contribution to the anthology was a short story called "Spunk." Hurston's path and Cudjo's would soon converge.

In the course of her studies, Hurston fell in love with the discipline of anthropology. She was studying under Franz Boas, a revered pioneer of modern anthropology. The two of them had an easy rapport. Like other students, she referred to Boas as "Papa Franz," and he joked that Hurston was his long-lost daughter. Her first class project was to measure the skulls of men and women around Harlem. "Almost nobody else could stop the average Harlemite on Lenox Avenue and measure his head with a strange-looking, anthropological device and not get bawled out for the attempt," her close friend Langston Hughes wrote—"except Zora, who used to stop anyone whose head looked interesting, and measure it." Her playful, disarming manner made her a natural interviewer. Though her main interest was writing fiction and plays, she immediately saw how anthropology could be useful to her. Boas's curriculum was "as full of things a writer could use as a dog is of fleas," she wrote to a friend during her second semester.

In the fall of 1926, as her graduation approached, Boas went looking for fieldwork on her behalf. He wrote a letter to the historian Carter G. Woodson, recommending her for a fellowship. Woodson's organization was able to give her $700, and she received a matching grant from the American Folklore Society. Altogether it was enough to let her spend much of 1927, February through August, collecting Black folklore in the Deep South. "I was extremely proud that Papa Franz felt like sending me," she wrote later.

Her first stop was her hometown of Eatonville, Florida, on the northern border of Orlando. It was the first incorporated all-Black town in the United States. She needed a car, so on her brother's advice, she bought something cheap but reliable: a $300 Nash coupe. She named it Sassy Susie. From Eatonville she bobbed along through other Florida towns, trying to persuade strangers to sing her old songs and tell her old stories. Knowing about the dangers of traveling alone on those country roads—not only as a woman, but also as an African American, in the Deep South, at a time when lynchings were still relatively common—she carried a chrome-plated pistol for protection.

In those early months, Hurston didn't have the success she had been hoping for. The research turned out to be harder than she'd expected. The trouble, she wrote later, was in the way she was approaching people. "I went about asking, in carefully accented Barnardese, 'Pardon me, but do you know any folk tales or songs?' The men and women who had whole treasuries of material just seeping through their pores, looked at me and shook their heads. No, they had never heard of anything like that around there. Maybe it was over in the next county. Why didn't I try over there? I did, and got the self-same answer." She was getting the "feather-bed resistance" that African Americans often put up for outsiders, where unwelcome questions are deflected with "a lot of laughter and pleasantries," as she put it in her 1935 book *Mules and Men*.

In the summer of 1927, several months into her travels, she pulled into Plateau. Boas had specifically told her to go find the place. He evidently knew about Cudjo from *The New Negro,* and he wanted her to go deeper than the young man who had interviewed Cudjo for the anthology. He hoped Hurston would produce a fuller account of Cudjo's personal story.

So Hurston went up to the gate of African Town's last surviving founder and introduced herself. There is no record of this historic encounter, apart from some quotations Hurston later used in an article, but it must not have gone the way she wanted. It seems Cudjo answered some of her questions but didn't open up. It also took time to understand his accent, even for a Black native southerner. So to supplement her findings, she also visited a local library or an archive, seeking more information. She was in luck; there was a copy there of Roche's book *Historic Sketches of the South.* Hurston took extensive notes, copying down large blocks word for word.

Around September, when she was back in New York, Hurston wove her research on Cudjo and the *Clotilda* into a sixteen-page essay and sent it off to Woodson. He published it in the October issue of the *Journal of Negro History,* which he edited, with the title "Cudjo's Own Story of the Last African Slaver." Hurston's original material accounted for only a small fraction of the piece; the rest came directly out of Roche's book. Out of sixty-seven paragraphs she wrote, only eighteen are entirely her own prose, and the last seven pages were lifted almost verbatim. The footnote gave a small nod to the source: "She made a special trip to Mobile to interview Cudjo Lewis, the only survivor of this last cargo," it read. "She made some use, too, of the Voyage of Clotilde and other records of the Mobile Historical Society." But it didn't credit Roche by name, let alone acknowledge how much Hurston had borrowed.

This was an incredibly reckless move on Hurston's part. Roche was still alive, and was herself connected to literary and artistic circles in New York. There was a significant chance that she would see Hurston's article, and if she did, she could have called attention to the plagiarism. No doubt Hurston's prospects for an anthropology career would have been torpedoed. It would have also caused professional embarrassment to Boas, who had used his fame to help her. Her biographers have struggled to make sense of her actions. Perhaps she thought the report was only for Woodson's files and didn't expect him to publish it. Perhaps on some level Hurston wanted to get caught, because she sensed that she didn't belong in academia and was looking for a way out. There's no question that she felt stifled by the rigid, scientific rules of formal anthropology. Or perhaps she didn't want to deal with the shame of telling Woodson about her failure and was instead taking a calculated risk. If this was the case, it paid off, because the plagiarism was never discovered during her lifetime.

She was open with Boas, however, about her general difficulties out in the field. She stood before him and "cried salty tears," she wrote in her 1942 memoir, *Dust Tracks on a Road*. "He gave me a good going over," letting her think he was more disappointed than he really was. "He knew I was green and feeling my oats, and that only bitter disappointment was going to purge me. It did."

Hurston and Cudjo had not seen the last of each other. There was another development in the young writer's life that fall that would soon lead her back to Plateau. In September, she was introduced to Charlotte Osgood Mason. Mason was one of the most influential figures connected with the Harlem Renaissance, even though she was neither an artist nor a writer nor a scholar. She was a seventy-three-year-old heiress living in a Park Avenue penthouse, a self-proclaimed "Black God" whose ancestry was Dutch.

Mason had been infatuated with Africa for decades. She believed West African cultures, or as she put it, "the creative impulse throbbing in the African race," could cure the ills of modern American society, which she believed was stifled by commercialism and industry. Starting in her early thirties, she had experienced dreams in which she pictured the African continent as a "flaming pathway" to some kind of glorious future. In the mid-1880s, she had found a kindred spirit in Rufus Osgood Mason, a physician who specialized in parapsychological phenomena, like telepathy and clairvoyance. He held séances for New York aristocrats who wanted to reconnect with departed relatives. During the years of their marriage, the doctor had encouraged his wife's instincts, telling her she belonged to a rarefied class of people who could understand the "divine energy permeating the universe."

He died in 1903, leaving Mason an immense fortune. As a widow, she pursued her quirky vision with great focus. At first she dabbled in anthropology herself. She traveled around the Southwest, accompanied by an ethnomusicologist, documenting the songs and folktales of Native Americans. In 1907 the pair compiled their work into an anthology, titled *The Indians' Book: Songs and Legends of the American Indians.* But that pursuit was short-lived. By the time she met Hurston, Mason was suffering from severe arthritis and was using her money to support younger artists and scholars instead.

Mason's involvement with the Harlem Renaissance evidently began in February 1927, when she saw Alain Locke give a lecture on African art. She approached him afterward, saying she wanted to support this burgeoning creative movement and wanted Locke to be her adviser. The professor was happy to oblige. Over the months that followed, he brought her into Harlem's cultural scene, introducing her to all the prominent people. To the ones she favored most, Mason started giving monthly stipends of $150 to $200, on top of expensive gifts, including fine suits and luggage. For a starving young poet, this was like receiving a Guggenheim or MacArthur fellowship. In most cases, the only formal condition was that recipients had to keep her identity a secret and refer to her simply as "Godmother."

Either Locke or Hughes was responsible for putting her in touch with Hurston. On September 20, 1927, Hurston was invited up to the twelve-room penthouse Mason occupied in Midtown, below 54th Street. With its high ceilings, wood paneling, and fireplaces, it may have been the most opulent home Hurston had ever seen. Mason usually sat in a flower-patterned armchair, wrapped in a shawl, while servants bustled around her. Finger sandwiches, lemonade, and cookies were served on bone china and fine crystal. The decor, however, was unusual for Park Avenue. Mason liked to display African artifacts from her collection, including totem masks and headdresses. On the side tables, instead of *Time* and *The Literary Digest*—or maybe alongside them—she left copies of *Opportunity* and *The Crisis,* the journals associated with the Harlem Renaissance.

Hurston had an immediate rapport with the white-haired heiress. She could tell Mason's interest in African American culture was genuine; she belonged to that group Hurston called the "Negrotarians," white humanitarians who wanted to boost the Black race. Hurston invited her to the Harlem church she and Langston Hughes liked to attend. "I think that we got on famously," she later wrote to Hughes, who was already one of Mason's protégés. "God, I hope so!" Hurston would also write that Mason was "just as pagan as I" and would claim there was a "psychic bond" between them. Even if she was exaggerating, for the sake of flattery, her biographers agree their connection was genuine. And in Hurston, the older woman, who fancied herself an anthropologist and an honorary African American, may have seen an idealized version of herself.

Later in the year, Mason offered the young writer a stipend of $200 a month, the equivalent of roughly $3,000 now, to collect folklore in the South. Hurston would also receive a motion picture camera and a new car. For the most part, she could roam wherever she wanted, but Mason had one specific assignment in mind: she wanted to see Hurston's article on Cudjo developed into a book. Hurston would have to go back and interview Cudjo as thoroughly as possible. As Mason had told Locke, she wanted "to see the same thing done by the Negroes as I did with the Indians."

These terms were not as generous as Hurston might have wanted. Langston Hughes was receiving monthly checks from Park Avenue that he could spend however he liked. By contrast, her own arrangement with Mason was a form of wage work. When Hurston returned to the penthouse on December 8 to sign a contract, the document underscored this, saying she would be an "independent agent," conducting research Mason was physically incapable of doing herself. Whatever Hurston collected or wrote would belong to her patron and would be kept in a safe-deposit box to which Hurston would not have a key. The contract said Hurston couldn't share drafts with anyone else unless Mason gave permission. Hurston's other creative projects, including a Black folk opera she and Hughes wanted to write together, would have to be put on hold.

Six days after the contract was signed, Hurston left New York from Penn Station. She planned to roam all over the South, but her first stop would be Mobile—because Cudjo was elderly, and she feared he "may die before I get to him otherwise," as she wrote to Hughes.

* * *

In the book manuscript where Hurston later rendered her interviews with Cudjo, she started with the disclaimer that the manuscript was not a "scientific document." The idea, she said, was to "set down essential truth rather than fact of detail, which is so often misleading." She gently implied that Cudjo was responsible for any factual errors. "If he is a little hazy as to detail after sixty-seven years, he is certainly to be pardoned." But it appears Hurston reported at least a few details incorrectly herself. She wrote, for instance, that it was summer when she dropped in on Cudjo the second time, and that she visited him repeatedly until that October. In fact, if she did go directly from Penn Station to interview him, as she told Hughes she was going to, this means their conversations started in December of 1927 and continued until the end of January 1928. They may have resumed when Hurston returned to Mobile several months later, but she left again long before that October.

Boas, for one, would not have been surprised by these apparent factual discrepancies. He warned a colleague to "check on Miss Hurston for accuracy" while partnering with her on a 1929 project. "I have no reason to doubt her," he added, "but temperamently [sic], she is so much more artistic rather than scientific that she has to be held down." Hurston's manuscript also seems to repeat the plagiarism of her 1927 article in at least five instances. However, it's important to remember that any factual errors, and any instances of plagiarism, come from an unfinished manuscript—one that Hurston herself never carried through to publication. And more important, these aspects of the book pale in comparison to its achievements as a work of anthropology. The major events are confirmed by other sources, and Hurston managed to correctly get down certain words Cudjo taught her in Yoruba. In her attempt to capture "essential truth," her success is undeniable.

With those caveats in mind, what follows is the story as Hurston told it.

When she approached Cudjo's house that first morning, after some months away, the gate surrounding his house was unlocked, and the door was wide open. She walked toward the porch and called out his Yoruba name. Cudjo appeared in the doorway. He was eating his breakfast with his hands, out of a round enameled pan—the way he would have done back home. When he saw her, he froze. Then she saw tears well up in his eyes.

"Oh Lor', I know it you call my name," he said. There was no one else who addressed him by his former name. "You always callee me Kossula, jus' lak in de Affica soil!"

Cudjo's two-room house by this time was likely in disrepair. Another visitor several years later noticed bits of old saws, the broken handle of an ax, a bicycle sprocket, ragged quilts stuffed halfway into boxes, faded calendars hanging on the walls, empty fruit jars, buckets with the bottoms hollowed out, pillow cases filled with clothes, and a mattress in the corner, suspended on some crates. In the front room, chipped and broken dishes were piled up on a table.

Hurston noticed another man in the house behind him. She remarked that he had company.

Cudjo explained that he'd been sick and bedridden for five months. His guest was a full-time caretaker. But he was feeling better now. (Hurston didn't record it, but Cudjo's great-grandson, Johnnie Lewis, who had been born to his grandson Emmett in 1920, was also living with him in these years. Emmett, one of Aleck's children, died in 1921.) While he lit his pipe, Cudjo asked Hurston some questions about New York. "I lakee have comp'ny come see me," he told her. He admitted that he'd been deeply lonely since Celia's death. Anyway, he asked, what did she want with him?

Hurston said she wanted to know about his life: about where in Africa he came from, the customs of his people, the story of his journey to America, and his experiences since the Civil War. After a little more back-and-forth, he apparently realized his visitor could serve a valuable purpose. "Thankee Jesus!" he said. "Somebody come ast about Cudjo!" He wanted to tell his story, he said, in the hopes that his name might travel back to his homeland and someone there would remember him. He asked Hurston to spread his name everywhere she went. Then he began talking about his old life. On that first day, according to Hurston, he described his grandfather and some of the customs of their town, including the way they built their homes, the way husbands and wives paired up, the division of household labor. After a little while, he sank into silence, immersed in his thoughts. He seemed to forget she was there. When he remembered, he dismissed her tersely, saying he was tired. He suggested she come back the next day, after he was finished working in the garden.

Hurston did return the next day, bearing a basket of Georgia peaches. Cudjo gladly took them and bit into a peach. His great-granddaughters, Mary and Martha, wandered up. They were the daughters of Cudjo's granddaughter Angeline (who was also one of Aleck's children). His love for the girls was obvious, Hurston noticed. He picked out four of the best peaches and handed two to each little girl, then playfully scolded them to go play. "See dat cane?" he said to Hurston, pointing to a clump of sugarcane in his garden. He said he grew it because the girls like to chew on the stalks. He showed Hurston around the garden and gave her some clingstone peaches from his own tree, but he wasn't in the mood to talk about himself. So she kept at it, coming back the next day with insect powder to drive the mosquitoes away from his hut. Over the weeks that followed, Hurston said, Cudjo became increasingly comfortable with her, and he revealed his whole story: the raid on his town, his trek to the Dahomean coast, his years of enslavement, the founding of African Town, his train accident, and the deaths of his family members.

Part of the reason for Hurston's success was her patience. One Saturday, Cudjo seemed a little grouchy, so she didn't press him for information; she simply helped him clean the church and then drove him into town so he could buy some turnip seeds. Another day, at his request, she drove him to Mobile Bay, where his friends caught them a pile of blue crabs. She continued plying him with gifts, including an enormous watermelon, a Virginia ham (which made him "delighted beyond his vocabulary"), and a late-season melon they bought from a vendor on the roadside.

Another factor in getting him to open up was Charlotte Osgood Mason's largesse. By February 1928, and possibly earlier, Mason was sending Cudjo a monthly allowance to pay for his fruit and tobacco. Hurston notes that one day she opened their conversation by talking about the white woman in New York who had taken an interest in him. Cudjo liked hearing about Mason. He said Hurston should let her know that he wanted to please her.

It's clear Hurston and Cudjo developed a loving friendship over the course of their visits. When it was time for Hurston to leave—two months after she arrived, she said—they felt close enough that Cudjo wished he could follow her to New York. He gave her two peaches from his tree and watched her depart toward the Cochrane Bridge, which had just opened nearby, connecting Plateau and Magazine Point with the nearby Blakeley Island.

As much affection as Hurston felt for Cudjo personally, however, letters from the period suggest she was less committed than her patron was to producing a manuscript from the interviews she'd done with him. Hurston became consumed with other projects as soon as she left Mobile. She spent the balance of the year in Florida and Louisiana, where she collected more folklore, some of which would end up in her 1935 book *Mules and Men*. But Mason remained preoccupied with Cudjo's story.

During the spring semester in 1928, Alain Locke was teaching at Fisk

University in Nashville. He learned there that one of his colleagues, an anthropologist named Paul Radin, had read Hurston's article about Cudjo and planned to interview him. Radin was a Jewish immigrant from Poland who had studied with Franz Boas, earning his PhD in 1911. He was in the early stages of a groundbreaking project: the first systematic collection of interviews with formerly enslaved people. When Locke heard about it, he was affronted. He thought Radin was "imposing on a Negro situation," trying to "parasitically profiteer" from African Americans. But he kept his opinion to himself. He wanted to deter Radin from going to Plateau, but he decided to take a sly approach, befriending his new colleague instead of arguing with him. "I'll scatter as much sand in the air as possible," he wrote in a letter to Mason. In the meantime, he added, "Zora must contrive to seal Cudjo's lips, and not let her material get loose." He told Mason she was apparently "right about the Jews"—even though he hated to generalize about an ethnic group, seeing how much his own people had suffered from racist stereotyping.

When Mason received Locke's letter, she was equally outraged. "Langston!" she wrote in a February 13 letter to Hughes. "I am in a state of fury at this highway robbery!" She asked the young poet to "help Godmother to try Voodoo on him to protect Cudjoe Lewis and Africa." And to Locke, she wrote: "you must pray with all your might that no white man can ever come near him again." Mason thought that if the decision was up to Cudjo, there was a good chance he'd share his story with Radin. She felt justified in intervening, if only because "American life systematically closes the door of African intuition," as she told Locke. She planned to have Hurston go back and speak with Cudjo directly, telling him the "lady in the North" who sent him money would be upset if he spoke with any white researchers. On February 24, Locke followed up with Hurston. "You have already heard I know from Godmother about the possible crossing of your lines by influences which she and I both agree should be kept entirely away not only from the project at hand but from this entire movement for the rediscovery of our folk material," he wrote. "The main thing . . . is to have C.L. entirely silenced."

But in mid-March, the crisis, as they saw it, was narrowly averted. Locke sent a cryptic telegram to Mason: HAWK SLIDES TO MOBILE TOMORROW CHICKENS SAFE LOVE ALAIN. In a letter he wrote the same day, he explained that Radin was traveling through Mobile, but was going with a group and wouldn't be able to stay long. It seems Locke had also talked Radin's research assistant into acting as a spy and deterring any future attempts to interview Cudjo.

Hurston returned to Alabama in May or June and spent at least six more weeks in Magazine Point, collecting folklore and likely continuing her conversations with Cudjo. In one letter to Locke, she enclosed a piece of wood that she said came from the *Clotilda*. In another, she told him she was "using the vacuum method, grabbing everything I see." She kept traveling and researching for the next year and a half, spending time in New Orleans, Florida, and the Bahamas. In the moments when she did find time to write, she was swamped. "I have more than 95,000 words of story material, a collection of children's games, conjure material, and religious material with a great number of photographs," she wrote to Boas in April 1929.

Still, she allowed herself enough time to write a draft of her book on Cudjo. She rendered his speech phonetically, in "dialect," rather than conventional English. This was a common technique in anthropology, which she would have learned at Barnard, but she also knew Mason wanted it this way. She titled the manuscript *Barracoon*, after the cages where Cudjo and the other shipmates had been held in Ouidah. She also wrote a dedication to her patron: "To Charlotte Mason, My Godmother, and the one Mother of all the primitives, who with the Gods in Space is concerned about the hearts of the untaught." She sent a draft to Locke for his edits, and he loved it from the start. "All of Kossula's stories are of superior stamp of imagination," he wrote in a June 1929 memo. "It is providence that Z. was sent to fasten this fast-slipping last link."

However, Hurston said that when she began submitting it to book editors, they were less impressed. She shared a draft with her friend Harry Block, an editor at Alfred A. Knopf who worked with the crime novelist Dashiell Hammett. They met to discuss some of her work in February 1931. Block didn't think *Barracoon* was ready. According to Hurston, he doubted that a book rendered in dialect would sell—and in the Great Depression, Knopf was in no position to take big risks. "He says only anthropologists have any interest in dialect," Mason wrote to Locke, summarizing what Hurston had told her.

In a June 7 letter, Mason told Locke the publisher Harper & Brothers had also rejected *Barracoon*. Once again, the word from Hurston was that editors wouldn't publish a book in dialect. Mason was furious. The stakes for her were high. None of the other Harlem-borne projects she'd sponsored were panning out. Hughes's 1930 novel, *Not Without Laughter*, had not accomplished what she hoped, and she and Locke couldn't agree on the plans for a Harlem Museum of African Art. Time was of the essence for Mason, as she was losing her hearing and eyesight. She believed "the future of the Negro in America" depended on *Barracoon* being published. As she explained in her letter, she wanted Locke to talk some sense into these publishers, persuading them it would "sell tremendously in the end." By the end of her dispatch, Mason had worked herself into a fit. "Break the stone heads of these publishers," she concluded, "and throw them into the debris heap!"

Locke wasn't about to lecture the senior editors at Knopf or Harper. Instead he decided to try Viking Press. He was acquainted with an editor there, apparently Harold Guinzburg, and he would have known the publisher was actively seeking out Black authors. He sent Guinzburg a copy of *Barracoon*. In a letter he attached, he explained that other publishers had rejected it because of the dialect, but he hoped Viking would have better judgment. He added that he'd be traveling through New York several days later, and if Guinzburg didn't mind, he would stop by the Viking office. He was hoping for a quick yes or no. "There's nothing to love in a swift attack like this," he told Mason, but he felt optimistic.

On the day when Locke arrived in New York, he used a pay phone at Penn Station to call Viking. The receptionist said Guinzburg was just then coming through the door. "Could I come see him right away?" Locke asked. Guinzburg himself got on the phone. There was surely no need to drop by, he said. He was seriously interested in the manuscript, dialect and all; but Hurston's agent had already swooped in and taken his copy. She'd explained that Hurston wanted to make "considerable revisions" before she let Viking review it. Locke was "befogged," as he put it later. He couldn't go against the young author's wishes, so he simply urged Guinzburg to give *Barracoon* his "personal and immediate attention" when a new draft was ready. After he hung up, he called Hurston again and again at her New York apartment. She didn't answer. As it happened, she was not in the city at all; she was on a road trip through New England, with an old friend, the novelist Fannie Hurst.

Mason was still bent on seeing the book published—but as it turned out, she was the only one. It slowly became clear Hurston was not going to make the "considerable revisions" her agent had promised. Hurston sent Mason an update in the fall: "The Viking press again asks for the Life of Kossula, but in language rather than dialect." She knew how Mason felt about that, "so I do not answer them except with your tongue."

How to explain this turn of events? It's possible, in theory, that Guinzburg changed his mind for some reason and told her the dialect was a deal-breaker. But another possibility is that Hurston simply wanted to prioritize her other projects and wasn't inclined to put in the time it would take to revise *Barracoon*. Perhaps she'd lost faith in it after the earlier rejections. Or perhaps she had other reservations that she never expressed in writing. Whatever the case, she never wrote another draft, despite continued pressure from Mason. "You do not seem to realize that I made a contract with you," her patron wrote in a draft of a letter to Hurston in April 1932. "All of 1930 you were supposed to be getting your books ready." Mason felt she had "nothing to show" for the money she'd given Hurston. In October of that year, she sent her last payment to the young author, and the manuscript languished in her safe-deposit box.

All through this time, Cudjo was still receiving money from the Park Avenue address. The letters he sent Mason show the depth of his gratitude. "Since I ben in this country no one has thought enough of me to look out for my wellbeing as you has," reads a letter he sent her in 1930, likely penned by someone who took his dictation. "I don't know how to thank you but the Lord says whatsoever you do for one of his little one you [do] to him and he says he will reward you." He hoped that if they didn't meet face-to-face, they would encounter each other in heaven, "where there no more parting."

For Mason, of course, their arrangement wasn't only about friendship. She expected some control over Cudjo in return. She continued fretting that his story would get out. Cudjo apparently had a copy of Hurston's manuscript, which made Mason especially uptight. In the same 1930 letter, he promised he wouldn't show it to any more white visitors. The "young lady told me you said not to," he wrote, "therefore I don't let anyone see it anymore." However, Mason couldn't keep Cudjo a secret forever. About the same time the *Barracoon* manuscript was shelved, he became the subject of some national press coverage. Just as Mason had feared, he was introduced to the world in the terms of white bigots, with none of the depth or subtlety Hurston had brought to the subject.

It seems the catalyst was his ninetieth birthday party. The *Mobile Press-Forum*, a Black weekly newspaper, organized the celebration in the fall of 1931, and Big Zion A.M.E. Zion Church, in downtown Mobile, agreed to host it. The secretary of the chamber of commerce worked to drum up interest among white Mobilians. Tickets were sold for 15 cents and 25 cents, about $2.50 and $4.25 now. When the event started, at eight P.M. on a Wednesday in October, the church's big sanctuary was full, with the crowd overflowing to the balcony. The white section was a who's who of Mobile society. A senator, the mayor, and the city commissioners were there, along with business leaders, educators, doctors, lawyers, and ministers. Several gave speeches in Cudjo's honor. Benjamin Baker, Isaiah Whitley's successor as the principal of MCTS, was also invited to make a tribute. A dentist presided over the ceremonies, and vocal quartets from all over the city performed. The centerpiece was a presentation by Cudjo himself. He recounted his life story and sang a song in Yoruba, then explained its meaning in English. Two bakeries donated cakes, decorated elaborately. "Birthday greetings to Uncle Cudjoe" was written on one.

The event was tinged with more than a little paternalism. The money it brought in—$65.72, which would be a little more than $1,100 now—was not given to him directly, but was instead placed in a "Cudjoe Lewis Fund" and doled out in a weekly allowance, with some cash held in reserve for his future medical bills.

Within weeks after the event, the old man had another visitor. "Cudjo!" he heard one day while he was tending his garden. "Here's a man who wants to talk to you." He turned to see an acquaintance accompanied by a white man he didn't recognize. It was Walter Hart Blumenthal, a writer for the New York *Evening Post*. Blumenthal asked him the usual questions: about life in his hometown, the Dahomeans' raid, the experience of the Middle Passage, and his conversion to Christianity. When the article came out later that year, it identified Cudjo as "The Most Historic Negro in the United States." It was the epitome of Jim Crow journalism. "Anyone who desires may meet him," Blumenthal wrote, as if Cudjo were a tourist attraction. The story included a photo of the old man drawing water from a well, grinning broadly. The article was also reprinted in *The Literary Digest,* another New York publication. Soon Cudjo received a lucrative offer to come to New York and appear in a vaudeville show. He turned it down.

The renewed interest in the *Clotilda* story was not limited to Cudjo. In December 1931 and January 1932, journalists upstate made another discovery: there were at least two other survivors, each living on separate plantations near Selma. They had both been separated from the other shipmates in 1860. Though the news articles contain some willful embellishments and distortions, they seem to be accurate in most respects, and given their length, they're relatively thorough. As the only surviving interviews with women who survived the Middle Passage, the information they contain is invaluable. Since 2019, the scholars Hannah Durkin and Sylviane Diouf have uncovered more about the women's lives.

The first survivor to appear in the news was Matilda McCrear, who went by Tildy. She was about seventy-two. A week before Christmas in 1931, she traveled the fifteen miles from her rural cabin to the county courthouse in Selma. She was there to ask for compensation for her kidnapping and enslavement as a little girl. Octavia Wynn, a *Selma Times-Journal* reporter with a keen interest in southern history, managed to interview her. McCrear's nearly white hair was done up in bright-colored string, and she spoke in a low, husky voice. She explained that when the Dahomeans had raided her village, she was only about two. Her mother, who later took the name Gracie, gathered as many of the children as she could. Besides McCrear and her ten-year-old sister, who would become Sallie Walker in America, two other sisters joined them on the trip to America. Their two brothers were left in West Africa. McCrear said one of her cousins and another boy from their town became sick on the *Clotilda* and were thrown overboard.

Wynn reported that Gracie paired up with another captive named Guy during the voyage (though in reality, the two may have been paired up in America, by the men who bought and sold them). Once they reached Alabama, Gracie, her new companion, and her two younger children were sold to a planter named Memorable Walker Creagh, who lived near Tuscaloosa. They lost touch with the two older girls. McCrear learned English quickly. When her mother and stepfather needed goods from the store, they brought her along as their translator. Their typical shopping list—"two yards of calico, a plug of tobacco, some snuff, and meat and meal"—hints at the extent of their poverty.

When McCrear grew up, she had a long-term relationship with a German immigrant named Jacob Schuler. They couldn't get legally married, and it was dangerous for them to live together. Had they been prosecuted, they would have each faced two to seven years in prison. Nevertheless, McCrear bore fourteen children with Schuler, of whom ten survived. It seems McCrear was evasive when the reporter asked about her children's father. Wynn reported only that she "never took a husband" and that "she laughs lightly if the question of marriage is introduced." Though she didn't take Schuler's name, she did modify her inherited name, Creagh, perhaps to distance herself from her former owner.

She and Schuler apparently made their living as sharecroppers. Wynn reported that as of 1931, McCrear was still hoeing cotton. That day at the courtroom, the judge denied her request for money, which she took in stride, according to Wynn. She lived another nine years. In the years after the interview, like many tenant farmers during the Great Depression, she and her family moved out of the countryside and into the city, almost certainly to find work. At the time of her death, in January 1940, she was living in her youngest daughter's house, in Selma, and was getting by doing housework.

The other shipmate was a woman named Redoshi. Her father, the *Montgomery Advertiser* reported, had been something like an attorney in their West African town. The *Advertiser* said she'd been twenty-five and married at the time of her capture, though another person who interviewed her later in life reported that she'd been only twelve. According to the *Advertiser*, Redoshi remembered waking her husband in the middle of the night to tell him about a strange dream: she pictured them both sailing across a huge body of water on a winged canoe. At the moment when she finished narrating, the *Advertiser* claimed, the Dahomeans burst into her hut, killed her husband, and took her away. Once they reached the coast, Redoshi and the other captives were taken in small boats to the slave ship. She remembered the captain's name—she pronounced it "Wa-Yam"—and the way he peered through his eyeglass throughout the trip, watching for other ships that might give them trouble.

After the voyage, a man named Washington Smith bought Redoshi and another captive named Billy, whom she married. Smith was a Kentuckian who had moved to Alabama shortly before the Civil War. He founded the Bank of Selma, and he owned a plantation near Selma. After emancipation, at first the couple stayed at Smith's plantation upstate—where, she told the reporter, they knew people would treat them decently. Ultimately they bought their own land in Bogue Chitto, an unincorporated Black community twenty miles west of Selma. They raised one child, a daughter whose name was listed as Lethe, Lethia, and Letia, among other spellings. In her old age, Redoshi became known around Selma as Sally Smith, or Aunt Sally. Billy died in the 1910s or '20s, and Redoshi died in 1937.

Hurston's letters reveal that she knew about Redoshi but tried to keep her existence a secret. "Oh! almost forgot," she wrote to Hughes in July 1928. "Found another one of the original Africans, older than Cudjoe about 200 miles up state on the Tombighee [*sic*] river. She is most delightful, but no one will ever know about her but us. She is a better talker than Cudjoe." The *Advertiser* reported that Redoshi and Cudjo knew each other well and had seen each other roughly a month before the article was published. At some point, perhaps on that same visit around the end of 1931, McCrear had also traveled to Mobile County and had met with Cudjo and Redoshi together. The meeting was "one of the great events" in her life, her interviewer wrote, because Cudjo represented "a link to her childhood."

As Cudjo aged, Plateau and Magazine Point were continuing to evolve around him. The region had always had an industrial element, at least since Tim Meaher set up his operations there. One reason the shipmates had chosen the area for their settlement was to be close to the sawmills and shingle mills where they worked. In the years since, sawmills had continued to draw new residents, and a hardwood and veneer plant was built at Hog Bayou in 1915. But 1928 was a turning point. It was when the Meaher family and other white power elites gave the area over to the paper industry.

That July, International Paper (IP), a massive corporation that had been formed in the merger of seventeen northeastern paper mills, announced that it was interested in building a plant in Mobile County. The company had been selling so much paper that the forests of New England could no longer supply it with enough pulp; and the Gulf Coast states, with their vast, untapped forests and their networks of rivers, had been beckoning. Already a broader geographical shift was under way. Since roughly the 1870s, when the Atlanta newspaperman Henry Grady had issued the call for a "New South," the entire region had been desperate to recruit northern industry. Southern states would "take a noble revenge" on the North, Grady promised, by competing with the region's textile mills and iron factories. As state and local governments, from Texas to Virginia, tried to rebuild their economies and get out of debt, they came to see the appeal in Grady's vision. They did everything they could to attract manufacturing. Some communities went as far as promising to pay companies' legal expenses, should they ever be sued for pollution.

In Mobile's case, by the time IP announced its interest, it had already found a site it wanted, with help from the chamber of commerce. The site bordered Plateau's residential area on the north, and was adjacent to the new Cochrane Bridge, which would be critical for the company's transit needs. The property belonged to Augustine Meaher, who had already agreed to sell it. But before IP's executives committed, they wanted to see Mobilians come up with $100,000 (more than $1.5 million now)—not as a loan, but as a donation, which would cover the property purchase and other costs. IP's representative assured the community that other southern cities had offered even larger amounts to recruit paper plants (which was true). In exchange, IP promised to spend $1 million on the annual payroll, most of which would stay in the area, plus $5 million on construction. Politicians and business leaders launched an aggressive campaign to raise the money by the end of that week. "Citizens of this city will be glad to put up this small sum," the *Mobile Daily Register* declared. "They ought to be glad to do it."

The fact that the chamber of commerce chose Plateau as the factory site represented a new stage in a long history of abuse and exploitation. It was the same history that involved the neighborhood's being denied sewers and plumbing, being excluded from the city limits, and briefly becoming the county's lynching capital. The role of the paper mill is obvious. The amount of pollution it emitted would be staggering. Granted, it's unlikely that anyone in local leadership was thinking about environmental consequences at the time; on the contrary, the *Register* predicted that the mill's presence would "encourage the building up and conservation of natural resources" outside the city limits. But it must have been obvious that the paper mill would give off a putrid smell. Had it been built anywhere near downtown, it might have given the city a bad reputation and stymied future development—not to mention that white residents would surely have protested. The residents of Plateau and Magazine Point, of course, had no say in the matter. The only way the neighborhood could have exercised power was by incorporating as a town of its own—but since Black residents couldn't register to vote, this was a nonstarter.

By Thursday night in the week of the fundraising campaign, two days before the deadline, the fund was only up to about $40,000. The *Register* resorted to shaming the residents, declaring in a front-page banner, "Mobilians Fail to Realize Big Opportunity." Authorities were predicting the mill would launch a new era for Mobile, potentially doubling the population within a few years. Ultimately the city did reach its goal, with some magnates putting up as much as $1,500, and scores of others donating just $5 or $10. A man named Harry Simon contributed $2.50. Production started at the mill fifteen months later.

At the time when the mill started up, the tradition of superior public education that Isaiah Whitley had inaugurated in Plateau still persisted. Whitley had died in 1923, but his successor, Benjamin Baker, who took over in 1926, was more than his equal. It's safe to say that in Plateau's history, no one apart from the shipmates is more revered than Baker. "He was the innovator," said

Valena McCants, a retired educator in her mid-nineties who studied and then taught under Baker. "He was class." Under his leadership, MCTS made the transition from being a training school in Booker T. Washington's sense into being an academic powerhouse. The hog farm on its campus became a distant memory, and sociology classes were added to the curriculum. So esteemed was the school in those days that McCants, as a teenager, opted to commute there all the way from Mobile proper. This meant catching a streetcar at 5:30 every morning, then transferring to a bus, and finally trudging her way down a long, muddy hill. Often she didn't get home until it was nearly dark, but it was worth it for the education. Baker recruited teachers from Black colleges throughout the United States, including Fisk University in Tennessee, Wilberforce University in Ohio, and Hampton in Virginia, and his alma mater, the Tuskegee Institute. Every high school teacher there had a college degree, a situation practically unheard of at rural Black schools in the South.

To the extent that MCTS was still oriented around "training" while Baker was in charge, the school prepared students more for leadership than for wage work. Under his guidance, the student body became mostly self-governing. When kids got into fights or otherwise misbehaved, discipline was generally meted out by the student council, not by teachers. But of course the students' authority was underwritten by Baker, who was simultaneously adored and feared. He was rumored to carry a pistol. "They didn't want Dr. Baker to do anything but say good morning and good afternoon to them," said his daughter, Jane Nettles. Each year Baker selected the most promising seniors for his "Big Ten" group. He took some of them on a tour of Black colleges and universities, introducing them to recruiters. "Everybody would want the students from Mobile County Training School," McCants recalled. The trip sometimes culminated in a visit to Atlanta or Washington, D.C. "Travel was not like it is now," Nettles said. "For them to get that experience"—coming, as they did, from modest households in the rural Deep South—"was exceptional."

It's hard to say how long Cudjo stayed in touch with Mason and Hurston. His last surviving letter to Mason is from May 12, 1932. He had stopped receiving mail from her, and she hadn't responded to his last several notes, so he wanted to make sure she was in good health. It turned out there had been delivery problems. On May 26, Hurston wrote to Mason, saying she'd asked an acquaintance to check on Cudjo. She also asked the post office in Plateau to keep an eye out for any letters addressed to him from New York.

"You are quite right in not trusting his daughter-in-law and grand daughter," she wrote. Hurston suspected they were hard up because of the Depression and were intercepting his money.

White visitors in these years reported that Cudjo seemed joyful when he greeted them, but that he broke down in the course of conversation—probably because they always asked about the great tragedies of his life. James Saxon Childers, a literature professor and writer for the *Birmingham News* who visited in 1934, reported that Cudjo no longer wanted to go back to Africa. He knew there was no family waiting for him there, he told Childers, and he didn't know how to find his hometown. Childers also observed that Cudjo was becoming frail. He was about ninety-four. His joints seemed stiff, and he moved about slowly. He had an elderly Black caretaker, and his daughter-in-law brought him food, but his clothes were in tatters: not only were his shirts thick with patches, but the tops and bottoms of his shoes flapped as he walked.

In late 1934 and early 1935, Cudjo was visited often by his old friend Emma Langdon Roche. (Roche had kept herself busy promoting the arts and the preservation of local history, and in 1935, she was appointed as the state director of the Federal Art Project, which had been launched under the New Deal.) She typically found his shutters closed. "Opening a door, I'd call 'Kazoola,' and out of the gloom a low moan and a 'Thank God' would answer me," she wrote in a 1935 article. But late one afternoon, Roche found Cudjo sitting in an old rocking chair, with his back arched, watching the sunset through his window. He told her he was preparing for death. Back home, he explained, when a person was sick, the custom had been to carry them out before sunset, then take them back to bed when it was dark.

He sang Roche a Yoruba song about death, for which he, Pollee, and Charlie had come up with new words. "Jesus Christ, Son of God," he sang. "Please, Jesus, save my soul. / I want to go to heaven / When I die / Jesus Christ, Son of God." He asked Roche to take a pencil and paper and write down the place and date of his conversion to Christianity: the Stone Street Baptist Church in Mobile in 1869.

On July 29, 1935, a sweltering Monday morning, Union Baptist was filling up with mourners. They came from all over southern Alabama. Knowing seating would be scarce, many carried crates and short benches into the church. Little girls dressed in bright colors came in with bouquets of wildflowers they had picked outdoors. They dropped them around the coffin. Their mothers, dressed in black velvet in spite of the heat, dabbed the sweat from their faces with handkerchiefs. The ten preachers who'd been invited were clustered in a little room near the rostrum.

Cudjo had suffered a cardiac incident the previous Thursday. He died around five P.M. on Friday, July 26. The cause of death was arteriosclerosis—a narrowing and hardening of his arteries. Given the Alabama heat, the body was bound to decay quickly, so his family had scheduled the funeral right away, allowing just enough time for the word to get around. No doubt his name had rung out from many pulpits that weekend.

A pew near the front had been reserved for white attendees. Only five were present, including the lone journalist covering it. His name was Merlin Hanson, and he was an idealistic young man who had recently been fired from the *Mobile Register*—for writing about people of mixed racial heritage, according to his account. The only surviving description of Cudjo's funeral is Hanson's dispatch for a publication called *Globe*. The journalist noted with scorn that Mobile's dignitaries weren't showing Cudjo the same respect in death that they had at his 1931 birthday benefit. Bakeries had been glad to donate cakes when they saw a chance for free publicity, but on Cudjo's coffin there was only one floral design. (The mourners, however, had more than made up for this with flowers they brought from the woods and their gardens.)

The service started at eleven, with the choir leading the mourners in singing "Nobody Knows the Trouble I've Seen." A dozen soloists had been invited. The congregation became boisterous, a change from the usually sedate atmosphere at Union Baptist. The thin floor of pine vibrated with all the stomping. For two hours the service alternated between songs and prayers. Then the preaching started. One minister announced that "Uncle Cudjo" had "done no wrong," that he'd never been a "backslider." Congregants called out in affirmation: "Amen, brother, amen."

After they took up an offering for the funeral expenses, Cudjo's body was carried toward the little cemetery where his wife and children were buried. The coffin was covered with clumps of dry clay. By then, the living presence of the last local *Clotilda* survivor was already giving way to legend.

PART III

PRESERVATION AND DEMOLITION: 1950–2008

11

KING COTTON, KING PULP

Every Sunday in the mid-1950s, Joe Womack's family hustled to arrive at Yorktown Missionary Baptist Church by nine A.M. Womack's grandfather was the Sunday-school superintendent, and he expected them to be on time. Along with a couple dozen other boys, Womack would shuffle into a classroom, where they'd sit on the floor and listen to Mr. Henry Williams tell stories from the Bible. Williams, who was a welder by trade, didn't need any teaching aids or props; the way he way paced back and forth, gesticulating, with his eyes shining, was enough to hold the kids' attention. Over the three years Womack was in his class, they cycled through the classic Old Testament tales, including Adam and Eve eating the forbidden fruit, Noah and his family waiting out the flood, and David killing Goliath.

But when Womack looks back on those classes now, what he remembers best are the special lessons Williams delivered about once each month, when he'd talk about a band of heroic Africans who had once lived in their neighborhood. In anecdotes that chimed with the Bible, he narrated how they'd been taken away from their families and carried across the ocean on a ship. Once they gained their freedom, he said, they had come to Plateau and established their own community. There they had taught the American-born freedpeople how to live independently.

The way Womack and others from his generation remember, most adults didn't care to hear these stories, and some doubted whether they were true at all. "They said, 'Don't listen to Henry Williams; he's crazy,'" said Darron Patterson, who was in the same classes with Womack. "So I kind of wrote

Henry Williams off. Wish I had listened to him more." The adults' attitude was understandable. Williams was brilliant in his way but was not always a reliable source. He claimed credit for such inventions as toilet paper and the jungle gym, and he told variations of a story about getting his fingers blown off in World War II—even though all ten of his fingers were still intact. Besides, the surviving documentary evidence of the *Clotilda* story was scattered far and wide. No historian had ever pulled it together and subjected it to scrutiny. The one book that detailed it all, Roche's *Historic Sketches of the South*, had long since gone out of print, and no copies circulated around Plateau.

At the same time, the neighborhood had been transformed since Cudjo's death. A second mega-factory, Scott Paper, had opened there in 1940, leasing another 134 acres from the Meaher family (with an option to purchase after sixty years). Also by 1941, the regional company Gulf Lumber had established a major sawmill beside Lewis Quarters, between the houses and the main road that led into Mobile. And a meat processing plant, Haas-Davis Packing Company, operated near the lumber mill. The local population had boomed as African Americans from all over Alabama and the Gulf Coast moved there for factory jobs. The streets were now packed tight with houses, and a bustling service industry had sprung up, with supermarkets, clothing stores, laundromats, nightclubs, hotels, a movie theater, a hardware store, a pharmacy, and a service station. The sight of this modern community made it hard to imagine that a fabled African settlement had once been there.

Some of the shipmates' descendants did learn the history at home. Lorna Gail Woods, for instance, who was born two years before Womack, grew up hearing about her great-great-grandfather Charlie Lewis. Her grandmother told her how he'd bought the land for Lewis Quarters, where their family still lived, and built his own home there. Cudjo Lewis's descendants still lived in the area as well. His great-grandson Johnnie lived in Magazine Point, where he was raising nine children and working for a railroad. Johnnie's daughter Cassandra Lewis Wallace, who was born in 1964, remembers sitting on the floor with her siblings and listening to her father's stories about Cudjo, including one where "Cudjo gave him the baddest whipping of his life." He also taught the kids songs Cudjo had passed along and imitated the old man's speech. Cudjo's granddaughter, Angeline, still lived in his old house, and Garry Lumbers, Cassandra's cousin, lived there with her.

But even among descendants' families, attitudes varied about this collective heritage. Patterson, a descendant of Pollee Allen, didn't find out about his family history until he was an adult. He believes his mother felt ashamed of it. "She was dark-skinned, had African features," he said. "I would tease her sometimes and say, 'Ma dear, you're an African.' And she says, 'I'm *not* an African!' And she was adamant about it." He wishes she had been forthcoming. "Nobody in our house sat me down and said, 'I want to tell you about who you are. You're a Yoruban prince.' I would have loved that." Some members of the generation that grew up in these years now believe their elders may have kept quiet because they felt intimidated by their landlords, the Meahers, who still owned more residential properties in the neighborhood than anyone else. As for Johnnie Lewis, Cassandra says, he was not embarrassed or intimidated, but he forbid the children to go around announcing their connection to Cudjo. He preferred to keep a low profile.

In the wider world, academic historians had doubts about the *Clotilda* story. The historian Warren S. Howard dismissed it in his 1963 book *American Slavers and the Federal Law, 1837–1862*. Howard noted that scholars before him had accepted it as true, "but no good evidence of it has ever been found." The three accounts Howard could find all contradicted one another on various details, and none of them cited reliable sources. He pointed to the editorial in the *Mobile Mercury* from the summer of 1860 that argued the whole story was a hoax. Henry Williams, however, took it upon himself to keep the stories alive. He would tell the children how the Africans' traces were everywhere, for those who knew where to look. Hog Bayou, where neighborhood kids went to fish and swim, acquired its name because the Africans had hunted hogs there after the Civil War. The shipmates' church, Union Baptist, was still thriving, and the cemetery where some of them were buried was nearby. The bell next to MCTS, which was used to announce all manner of community events, from funerals to football games, was said to have come from the *Clotilda*. And Meaher State Park, which was on an island in Mobile Bay, consisted of 330 acres that Tim Meaher's descendants had donated to the state in 1952. It was named after Augustine Meaher, Timothy Meaher's son.

In August 1959, on what Williams mistakenly thought was the hundredth anniversary of the *Clotilda*'s landing, Williams and some others established a monument to the shipmates outside of Union Baptist. It was a bronze bust of Cudjo, mounted on a small pyramid of bricks, and was meant to honor the entire group. "Any one of them could have been the symbol of all the African natives," Williams wrote in a program for the dedication ceremony, but "Uncle Cudjoe (Kazoola) Lewis lived the longest and it is our feeling that he is the symbol of all the African natives." It was done under the auspices of the Progressive League, a group Williams had created in 1957 for the purpose of preserving local history. Cudjo's grandson, Motley Lewis, had posed for the sculptor Eugene Rhodes, as Rhodes fashioned a wooden model. The bulletin lists numerous sponsors, including Scott Paper and some local grocery stores. The Meahers contributed the bricks.

Womack doesn't know how deep his own roots in the Plateau area go. One of his cousins has taken a DNA test and learned that 20 percent of her blood is from Benin; but Womack has never felt the need to be tested himself. ("If someone says, 'Everyone who can prove they're a descendant gets a $10,000 check,' I'll get tested.") All he knows is that his great-grandfather, William Brown, was born in Plateau in roughly 1880, and that William's son, Isaiah Brown, was born there in 1907.

While Womack was growing up, his grandfather worked for a lumber company, driving a supply truck and working in the back of the shop. He would ride out with customers to their property and assess what size house they ought to build. He could calculate in his head how much wood and mortar they needed—"and most of the time," as Womack remembers, "they wouldn't have to come back for more." Isaiah Brown built his own house on Edwards Street, around the corner from Yorktown Baptist, along with a neighboring house where Womack and his five siblings were raised.

His father, Joe Womack Sr., was a Plateau transplant. He was emblematic of the thousands of newcomers who arrived in those years. The youngest of ten children, Joe Sr. grew up in a tiny town south of Montgomery. He quit school after sixth grade to work in the fields. When he was sixteen, word reached his community that International Paper in Mobile was hiring at high wages. "They said, 'As long as you live in the community, we'll hire you,'" as Womack understands the story. So Joe Sr. and his friends climbed into a station wagon and drove to the coast. They all stayed in the house of someone's relative or acquaintance, sleeping on top of one another, and used the address on their job applications. As soon as they received their first paychecks, they rented their own places.

On Joe Womack Sr.'s walking route to the paper mill, from Magazine Point, he typically cut through Isaiah Brown's yard. Before long he noticed Annie, Brown's oldest daughter. She had an infant son named Jesse, born in 1948. They started to flirt, and "things evolved," as Womack puts it. The couple were married in 1949. Womack was born on October 5, 1950. Unlike so many of the kids he grew up with, who were brought into the world by the neighborhood's midwife, Womack was delivered at Mobile General Hospital, the only facility in town that admitted patients of color.

However high the paper-mill wages may have seemed, Plateau was still a poor community. As of the early 1970s, the median family income there was only $3,000, the equivalent of $20,000 now—which was 44 percent less than the median income for the city ($5,400). During Womack's childhood, the neighborhood was still outside the city limits, so it still lacked basic municipal services. Only a few roads were paved. The Womacks had electricity, but their water came from a pump in their yard, and instead of a bathroom they had an outhouse. In the rare instances when they needed a phone, they had to use a neighbor's. For Womack and his friends, though, the place seemed idyllic. They stayed out all day on weekends, swimming in the creeks, fishing and crabbing and collecting oysters. There was a porousness between households that rarely exists in suburbia. Children were welcome at their friends' dinner tables, and it wasn't uncommon for a woman to breastfeed her neighbors' kids if the mother was away. "Nobody cared about private property," said Valerie Hayes, who was born in Plateau in 1967. "Nobody would say, 'This is my land; this is yours.' It didn't matter whose was whose."

Womack's favorite pastime was fishing. His grandfather had no sons of his own, only daughters, so he loved taking the boys out in his twelve-foot boat. They would row to his favorite spot on the Mobile River and fish for bream, catfish, and speckled trout; and on Sundays, they would often come home with a tub full of crabs, which Womack's grandmother would use to make gumbo.

The neighborhood kids were mad for baseball. While Womack was growing up, there were four Black players in the major leagues who hailed from Mobile County, including the legendary Henry "Hank" Aaron. By the time he was twelve, two more had graduated from MCTS: Cleon Jones and Tommie Agee, both of whom would play on the Miracle Mets team that won the 1969 World Series. Womack learned the game in a makeshift neighborhood league. The kids played without mitts, and they could only afford 10-cent rubber balls that were always splitting in half. But some mornings a man named James Robertson, known around the neighborhood as Fats, would pull up in his station wagon, with its frame tilting toward the driver's side, and deliver a trunk full of equipment for the kids to borrow. After a day of endless innings, they would leave it in the dugout, and Robertson would pick it up in time to run practice with the team he coached.

It's hard to overstate the enormity of the two paper mills that hedged Plateau. Not only did they dwarf every other factory in Mobile County, but they were also among the largest paper mills in the country. Each one was a sprawling compound with numerous buildings. The IP facility employed 2,700 people as of 1948, with a payroll of $7.9 million. And in 1959, the Scott mill had 1,500 workers. As of 1962 it was the largest of Scott Paper's sixteen mills in the United States.

A Georgia scientist had predicted in 1933 that "King Cotton," the South's chief export, would be replaced by "King Pulp," and this turned out to be correct in more ways than one. To IP and Scott, the men of Plateau and Magazine Point made an ideal labor force. The companies were "very particular" about those they brought on, said John Bacot, a Plateau native and descendant of Pollee Allen, who worked as a recruiter for Scott. "They didn't necessarily care too much about people from the city—they couldn't be cowed. They wanted to hire people who were manageable." And they worried that if they brought in college graduates, they'd have "trouble with the union, or trouble with them recommending new ideas and muddying the water, so to speak." They hired workers of both races, but Black men were kept in low-level positions as a matter of policy, upheld jointly by the unions and the management. Workers in the Black unions and white unions had separate "lines of progression," and Black workers could not be promoted into the jobs that paid best and were less physically demanding. "The Blacks were on the bottom," recalled Bill Sullivan, a white worker who started at IP in 1957. "They stayed there. They didn't move up."

When Bacot took a job at the Scott mill in 1966, as a consumer representative, he was the first Black worker ever hired there in a management role. It was a difficult balancing act. He felt the need to "represent as best I could," so he wore sharp suits and carried an attaché case. He insisted on being addressed as "John," not "Johnny," by his white peers. But he didn't want to seem snobbish toward the other Black workers. "They understood the position I was in. But at the same time, they hated that I was in this position and they weren't. The mill could be cruel out there."

But despite the discrimination, Plateau families were grateful for the mill jobs. For the plants to be unionized was a rare condition in the South, and besides pushing up the wages, this also provided job security—which was critical for Womack's father, who was always getting into fights on the job. "He'd tell me, 'Old such-and-such said somethin'. I had to knock the crap out of him,'" Womack recalled. "He didn't smoke, he didn't drink, but he would fight." Joe Sr. would sometimes be suspended for two or three days, but the union always helped him get back to work. Womack remembers his mother saying, "The only reason your daddy's still working is because of the union."

Even for families who did not get their income from the mills, there were benefits to living nearby. IP would throw a community picnic every year for the Fourth of July, and it always put up an elaborate Christmas display, with a colossal Santa Claus on the roof of one building—a marvel to local children. Bacot ran a program for several years where Scott Paper supplied gifts for all the workers' children. "It was good for the community," Bacot said. "It was a blessing as well as a curse."

The full dimensions of the curse would not become clear until Womack was an adult, when the science of environmental health had developed far enough. But there were a few indications in the 1950s and '60s.

The first was the odor, which resembled the smell of rotten eggs. Paper mills are notorious for smelling bad; but Plateau, sitting between two of the largest mills in the South, had it worse than most mill towns. The residents became mostly inured to it, but when the odor was strongest—especially when a hard wind pushed the vapors through the neighborhood streets—it became difficult to breathe, and no one wanted to be outside. "It would stick to your clothes and hair," Bacot recalled. When friends got a whiff of him after a shift, they'd exclaim, "You came from Plateau!" It was so bad that in 1976, two new residents in Fairhope, a more affluent town eighteen miles away, across Mobile Bay, wrote to the county's air inspector to say they found it unbearable. "Four days in a row last week the stench was so disgusting we found it necessary immediately on arising in the morning to close the windows and use the air conditioning," they wrote. The inspector wrote back that the odor had been reduced more than 90 percent from its 1972 levels.

The typical way of coping, both in Plateau and throughout the South, was to dismiss the problem with a wry remark. In 1941, for instance, after the city of Tuscaloosa gave a paper mill $15,000 in tax incentives, a local official quipped that the people were getting their investment back "scent by scent"; and in 1970, when the state's on and off governor George Wallace visited a paper mill outside Montgomery, he declared, "That's the smell of prosperity!" Over the years Mobilians came up with their own variations: "That's the breath of life," "That's bacon and eggs," or simply, "It smells like money."

The second warning sign was the flaky white ash, technically called salt cake, that would blow from the mills and rain down on Plateau. Whenever it was spotted, someone would ring the bell at the school to alert the whole neighborhood. Children were expected to run home and help their mothers pull clothes off the lines. The ash floated down on their cars, creating a film. Residents found that if they didn't wash their vehicles constantly, the metal would rust over within two or three years. Ultimately International Paper installed a car wash that locals could use for free anytime day or night. But the residents couldn't stop the ash from blanketing their roofs, and they found themselves endlessly replacing shingles that had been eaten through.

Still, if they had misgivings about how the ash affected their bodies, they tended to tamp those down. When ash fell on their vegetable gardens, they were more likely to wash away the white flecks than to throw out the produce. Eventually residents did complain (Womack suspects it was Henry Williams who led the charge), and the mills changed their practices. They started releasing the ash at night, and they tried to "play the wind," so it would blow away from Plateau, Bacot recalls.

A third cause for concern was the effect paper-mill pollution was having on the waterways. During the early decades of the mills' existence, it was standard practice to dump 95 percent of the water used in production back where it came from. The company executives called this "borrowing," but because the water was untreated, it was toxic to marine life. The waste absorbed oxygen from the rivers, making it impossible for fish to breathe. It would take many more years for scientists to realize the paper mills' bleach was also filling the water with dioxin—one of the most toxic compounds ever tested, one that persists in the environment for long periods and accumulates in food chains and living tissues. But from the beginning, local residents knew something was wrong. As early as 1930, the district game warden in Mobile was called out to investigate the killing of hundreds of game fish in Chickasabogue Creek and Hog Bayou, near the IP mill. He found that IP had dumped a "poisonous substance" into the water, and following his report, the company was indicted.

This charge came at a time in the 1930s when criminal cases and lawsuits against paper mills were being filed all over the South. Fishermen accused the companies of endangering their livelihood; neighbors said they were hurting land values. The courts, however, tended to take the mills' side. A judge in Louisiana who shot down a suit against an IP plant wrote that paper-mill sludge seemed to be "beneficial" to plant life, "rather than deleterious." And in Mobile County's case, IP ducked prosecution by pointing out that it had sold the plant before the waste was dumped. The company entered a plea of abatement. That the new owner was simply an IP subsidiary somehow made no difference.

In 1949, Alabama passed a law that legislators claimed would regulate water pollution. But in practice, thanks to the industry's lobbying efforts, it only guaranteed the mills' right to dump whatever they wanted. Plateau's waterways, like many others around the state, were officially designated "industrial streams" by the new law, meaning they were off limits for further regulations. Since no public agency was keeping track of the pollution, it's impossible to say exactly how much was being discharged, but there is at least one clue. In 1962, Scott Paper announced it was installing a waste-treatment system at the Mobile plant, which it said would process 35 million gallons of wastewater a day—implying that the mill had been dumping 35 million untreated gallons each day up to that point. IP, which processed almost 60 percent more pulp than Scott, was likely dumping a great deal more.

The results were predictable. In 1965, tests were done on the water in Chickasaw Creek, which borders Plateau on the east, and Threemile Creek, which runs below it on the south. Healthy bluegill were held in the water in baskets, and nearly all of them died within three hours. And during half the years between 1954 and 1967, the state had to shut down the entire region's oyster industry, out of concern that the oysters were carrying diseases from the pollution. These shutdowns led to a federal investigation. The government found that industrial plants were the biggest source, and that IP topped the list, with a total waste discharge of 34 million gallons each day. Scott was also a top contributor, though its emissions were only a fraction of IP's. The government called for the polluters to install more treatment equipment.

But as far as residents can recall, no signs were ever posted, nor were any flyers distributed, to warn residents that the fish in Threemile Creek were not safe to eat. Not that it would have come as a surprise. The water sometimes had a slight odor or a foam on top—"like you could tell something was in it," Jesse Womack said. But for poor residents, eating the fish seemed like a matter of necessity. Valerie Hayes remembered fishing in the creek with her siblings every week when she was a child. Her mother, who was single, was raising their family of eight on a bus driver's salary. Often, when they got back home and started filleting the fish, they turned out to be black inside. Hayes and her siblings threw those ones out—unless they hadn't caught enough that week, in which case, "You'd fry it real, real hard."

*   *   *

When Womack was a child, his grandfather was part of a small council of neighborhood elders. The group had formed in 1933 at the urging of Benjamin Baker, the MCTS principal, during a meeting at Yorktown Baptist. It called itself the Citizens' Committee. Its roots, however, went deeper than that; it was effectively the successor to the governing body established by the shipmates, which had Gumpa as its chief. Among the other members were Edley Hubbard, who owned one of the local supermarkets; John Randolph, who owned the other; and Nelson Adams. It seems Adams was the group's unofficial leader. As a young man, he had worked as a stevedore, hauling logs to one of the paper mills. He became a community organizer, and neighborhood tradition holds that he secured early funding for what became the Mobile County Training School and helped recruit Isaiah Whitley to teach there. He was sometimes regarded as the unofficial mayor. (His son, Clifton, was equally influential in the neighborhood's development. Clifton built much of the local housing—at one point he owned roughly 30 rental properties—and ran a grocery store, a dry cleaner, a barbershop, and a movie theater.) The group of elders would often meet at Isaiah Brown's house. Womack's grandmother would set out a tray of biscuits, and Womack would sit at the table, sipping a lemonade, watching the men deliberate.

The most pressing need in those days was proper infrastructure. Letters from Plateau residents to Mobile's city commissioners, dating from the mid-1950s, make this clear. A 1954 letter from the Citizens' Committee pointed out that hundreds of children attended the schools in Plateau, and "they have to drink this pump water, which is really unfit to drink." The neighborhood also remained vulnerable to fires. "We are suffering out here for lack of hydrant water for domestic and fire fighting purposes," reads a letter from 1955. "We need water badly, the only way that we can obtain water is to be taken into the City of Mobile." Besides all this, the sanitary conditions remained poor, and there is evidence that disease outbreaks persisted. Some residents were also getting tired of driving on dirt roads and using outhouses. "I tell kids nowadays, they don't know what it's like when the weather is twenty-five, thirty degrees outside," said Ron Davis, another Plateau native of Womack's generation, "and you have to go outside to use the restroom."

The geography of Mobile was being transformed during the postwar era, and there the members of the Citizens' Committee saw an opportunity. Mobile's population had boomed during World War II, as workers had poured in for jobs at Brookley Air Force Base, south of downtown, and at the docks. By the fifties, the city's physical resources were overburdened. The schools needed more money to accommodate all the new students; the hospitals were packed; the recreational facilities were lacking; and the streets were jammed with traffic. In 1955 and '56, the city annexed fifty acres, mostly on the western side, enlarging the landmass from roughly twenty-five square miles to ninety-two. Much of the land was already suburbanized; and interstate highways, a shopping mall, and more housing were soon built. Local banks were keen to loan money for white home buyers in this new area, but at the same time, they started refusing loans to residents who wanted to restore old houses. The white population fled en masse to the suburbs, and the city center was effectively relocated. The downtown area began to deteriorate.

Magazine Point was annexed by Mobile in 1945, and the 1955–56 annexation brought part of the Scott Paper compound into the city limits; but in both rounds, Plateau was left out. In 1959, Plateau's residents hired Vernon Crawford, Mobile's predominant Black attorney, to help them engineer an annexation. Womack remembers hearing Brown explain the decision to his mother: "The time for the outhouse is gone." In early 1960, Crawford presented the city commissioners with a petition, signed by some three hundred Plateau residents, saying they wanted to join the city limits and were willing to be taxed. It apparently didn't take much to persuade the commissioners. They were already looking to expand the industrial footprint along the northern part of the Mobile River, and they realized the undeveloped marshland around Plateau could accommodate any number of factories. The leaders of Prichard, a smaller city that bordered Plateau, tried to block this annexation in court, saying Plateau should be part of their city instead. But this challenge was rejected by the Alabama Supreme Court, and in February 1960, Plateau became part of Mobile.

Even after the annexation, it took several more years of lobbying by neighborhood leaders for sewers and plumbing to be installed. Ordinarily, under state law, municipal taxes couldn't kick in until these services were installed; but somehow, in Plateau's case, the taxes were imposed first. By the mid-1960s, residents were upset that the city wasn't holding up its end. Finally, in June 1967, the water and sewer board voted to move ahead with the improvements. It raised most of the money for water and sewer lines by assessing the homeowners, and the U.S. Department of Housing and Urban Development contributed a sizable grant. The end result was a vast improvement in quality of life for Plateau families.

However, at least one person was unhappy about the change: Augustine Meaher Jr., Tim Meaher's grandson, who went by Gus. He was sixty at the time of the vote, and he owned scores of properties in Plateau and Magazine Point, at least some of which had belonged to his father, who had died in 1938. Augustine Jr.'s wife, Margaret Lyons Meaher, also came from a prominent family; she'd been the queen of Mobile's Mardi Gras court in 1935, and her stepbrother, a physician, had chaired the National Library of Medicine. Together Augustine and Margaret Meaher had raised three sons, Augustine III, Joe, and Robert, who were all in their twenties.

City records show that Augustine Meaher Jr. signed the petition agreeing to the annexation terms. But in interviews with the *Southern Courier*, a civil rights newspaper, which were published in 1967 and 1968, he was startlingly candid about his feelings. He was upset about having his property assessed for the improvements, and he thought it was all unnecessary, as "people have lived perfectly healthy and happy for years without running water and sewers." Meaher said in June 1967 that he had recently worked out an agreement to lease seventeen acres of residential land to Scott Paper, and this meant he'd be kicking off the families who lived on that tract.

Meaher said he was also moving forty-two rental houses to another town farther north, where he wouldn't have to install plumbing. He predicted the tenants would be just as happy there. "You know, that's the way it is with n—ers, they'll be happy in a community—everybody together," he said. "They try to go back to African tribal life. He don't need no garbage service—a darkie will feed it to his pigs. He don't need a bathtub—he'd probably store food in it. Wouldn't know how to use it."

Meaher said that as a younger man, he'd spent some time in Plateau. "They always had a great time out there," he said, "laughing and singing from Saturday night to Monday morning." He had visited on weekends and had "some of the best times ever." At least one of these *Southern Courier* interviews occurred in Meaher's twenty-sixth-floor office in a new building downtown. Meaher posed for a photo beside one of his wall decorations—an old advertisement for one of his grandfather's ships, the *Southern Republic*.

On a fall day in 1960, Womack was on the grassy playground of Whitley Elementary during recess. It was still in that early part of the school year, when boys were testing one another's limits, sorting out the social hierarchy. "If you walked away, that was weak," Womack recalled. "If you tried to fight and you lost, that was weak. But if you hung in there for a while and looked presentable, that was okay. And of course if you beat him, you're a tough guy." His friend Terry Boyd, who he knew from the neighborhood, was a bit of a bully. That day at recess, Boyd picked a fight with another fourth grader named Anderson Flen, a wiry kid who lived near Magazine Point. Boyd swung first. Flen ducked, leaned into Boyd's torso, and picked him up, dropping him onto the grass. Boyd scrambled up and swung once more, and again Flen dodged him and knocked him onto the ground. It went on like this, with Boyd never landing a blow, and soon he gave up. Womack was impressed with this new classmate.

Flen, as Womack would learn, was an unusually serious kid. Flen attributes it partly to his hardscrabble surroundings. His parents had migrated to Mobile County from a rural area near Montgomery, and he was the third of their seven children. No Man's Land, their neighborhood, was poorer and less developed than Plateau; there were no street signs, and some of their neighbors lived in abandoned boxcars. (It was the same area that Augustine Meaher Jr. would lease to Scott Paper in 1967.) Flen's father worked on the railroad, and his mother was a "cutter" at a chicken factory, responsible for hacking off chickens' necks as they moved by on a conveyor belt. Conditions at the factory were dismal. Water from the factory's sprinkler system, which was designed to cool down the machinery, would pool up around the women's ankles as they worked, and they often cut themselves as they tried to keep up. Flen remembers his mother coming home with bloody hands. He resolved that when he grew up, he'd leave Mobile and invite his mother to come stay with him, where she could have a more comfortable life.

The friendship between Flen and Womack developed gradually. A couple of years after the schoolyard fight, when they had both started junior high at MCTS, they landed in the same homeroom. They were both diligent students, and their teachers wanted to keep the "smart group" in the same classes. Womack began taking a slight detour home so he and Flen could walk together every day.

Benjamin Baker had left MCTS in 1947, fifteen years before Womack and Flen started classes there. He'd been recruited to run a new Black public school in Mobile. He was still sorely missed. However, the school had been shaped by Baker's design, and the campus leadership structure remained intact. Flen was a natural leader; he became president of the student body their junior and senior years, and he's still on the books as the only graduate who started as football quarterback three years in a row.

If Womack didn't encounter Baker in the hallways, he encountered

Valena McCants, Baker's protégée, every day in the classroom. She was an innovative teacher. The textbooks were lacking Black history ("You looked like a fool as a Black teacher, telling them about cotton," she recalled), so she and other teachers taught history and civics using the periodicals they received at home: *Jet, Ebony,* and *The Chicago Defender.* She required students to read *Time* every week and quizzed them on the stories. She was a tough grader. "You can't forget her, man," said Cleophas Armstead, who graduated in 1962. "The reason was, most everybody flunked."

When it came to discipline, McCants followed Baker's lead. When students talked out of turn, she'd stand on their toes, in her high heels, leaning into their faces like a drill sergeant, and ream them out in front of their classmates. "Our thing was, we had these Thom McAn shoes," Womack recalled. "The boys would really take pride in shining those shoes. You would shine your shoe and you could see your face in it. And she would come and put her heel on it, mash it in. It would ruin the shoe. It ruined the shoes, man! I mean, you could push it out, and you could shine it, but it would still be wrinkled."

McCants and other teachers did what they could to get their students into colleges. Womack was planning to attend a junior college in Baldwin County, across Mobile Bay. He wanted to study computers, which were starting to be deployed throughout the business world, and was looking forward to playing on the basketball team. But McCants intervened with a different plan. She and a football coach, Curtis Harden, connected Flen and Womack, along with three of their classmates, to the dean of St. Paul's College, a small Black school in southern Virginia. The dean had a Plateau connection and was offering scholarships.

The young men agreed to enroll there. It sounded like an adventure; they had never spent much time outside of Mobile. In the summer of 1968, they caught a plane at the Mobile airport and flew to Virginia.

12

"RELOCATION PROCEDURES"

In the years when Womack was away at school, Henry C. Williams, his old Sunday-school teacher, was doubling down on his political activism. To Williams, the neighborhood's situation seemed increasingly urgent. Like everyone else in the area, he saw the industrial blight and the intense factory pollution (for which the Meaher family, as lessors of the land, were largely responsible). But unlike most of his neighbors, Williams understood this as a scandal of epic proportions. To him, Plateau was more than a tight-knit community—it was a unique historical treasure. There was "no place in America," he wrote in 1967, "with the historical value for the Negro as Plateau and Magazine hold." He also realized the only hope of protecting it from further industrial encroachment was to make other people see it the way he did. It was in this context that he started calling the area Africatown (or AfricaTown, U.S.A.), a name he must have plucked from one or more of the journalist accounts written at the turn of the century. Williams would eventually become known as "the father of Africatown," and though it seems he may have come up with this name for himself, hardly anyone would dispute it.

Williams was the product of an unusual upbringing. "He was a little odd," said Barbara Wheat, who knew Williams in the 1980s, "because his father was a little odd." His father was Edward Williams, known around northern Mobile County as "the root doctor," or more crudely, "the witch doctor." Ed Williams had learned hoodoo as a young man, reportedly by studying with some Haitians who lived nearby. For a Black Mobilian of his generation, this was not unheard of. In the early 1930s, Zora Neale Hurston wrote in an academic article, "shreds of hoodoo beliefs and practices" still survived in Black communities everywhere, but the tradition "had its highest development along the Gulf Coast," between New Orleans and Florida.

Throughout Henry Williams's lifetime, his father treated patients from all over the country. The root doctor's reputation spread by word of mouth. "From one state to another, somebody knows me," he told an ethnographer in the early 1980s. Near the family's house in Magazine Point, he had a small facility where his patients could stay during treatment and recovery. He guarded his secrets closely. "People practiced evil," he said, "so I will not spread my wisdom to everyone." He divulged only one formula: for gonorrhea, pellagra, and tuberculosis, he would make a "blood medicine" out of pokeweed and elderberry shrubs. But people who knew him remember other examples. Robert Moore, who lived nearby, and was Ed Williams's godson, said he went to the root doctor once because he was having marital problems. "Godfather had a vision of what was going on." He said someone had put a curse on Moore, and he advised him to swim across the Mobile River to cleanse himself. Moore believes the treatment saved his marriage.

Others are skeptical. "He was a charlatan," Darron Patterson said, laughing. When Patterson was a kid, he told Ed Williams once about a girl he had a crush on. "So he made up this thing for me. It had chicken feet in it, lizards, gizzards. He said, 'Throw it on top of her house.'" Patterson did as he was told. After a few days it stank horribly. "My daddy had to get it off the roof. And the girl never did like me." Ed Williams also kept an alligator in his backyard, with a pen that extended into the nearby creek, so the gator had water access but couldn't swim away. Williams nominally gave it to Patterson as a pet. "I would walk down there to see my alligator, 'cause I couldn't bring it to the house." The doctor used the alligator's droppings in his medicines, mixing them with feces from the farm animals he kept in the backyard. Moore also remembers him keeping poisonous snakes around, which he'd squeeze by their heads to make their venom drip into jars.

Henry Williams absorbed both his father's interest in root medicine and his mystical understanding of the world. Another formative influence for Henry Williams was Cudjo Lewis, who was still a fixture in the neighborhood while he was growing up. Williams claimed he'd been with Cudjo just before he died. He said the old man whispered to him, "Will you see that Cudjoe gets back home?" It's likely he was stretching the truth; but there's no reason to doubt he and Cudjo knew each other. Williams may have attended the funeral, which happened when he was fourteen.

Besides being a professional welder, Williams was an outsider artist in the best sense. His workshop itself was a wonder; he built it with fifty-five-gallon oil drums that he bought from Standard Oil, $30 for a heap of three hundred. He welded them together in the shape of a barn. His yard was decorated with a gallery of metal, life-size silhouettes of his heroes, including Sojourner Truth, Nat Turner, John Brown, Martin Luther King Jr., and Mohandas Gandhi. His calling card was a steel buffalo, also welded together from oil drums, that he mounted onto his truck bed, as a tribute to the Buffalo Soldiers, the African Americans who fought on the Civil War's western front. Williams was proud of the fact that at least one Buffalo soldier, Emperor Green, was buried in the same Plateau cemetery where some of the shipmates were interred.

In spite of Williams's tendency to embellish, his knowledge of local history was formidable. He was reputed to know the origin of every street name and the history of every parcel of land. One of his friends later told the *Mobile Press-Register* (the newspaper formed after the merger of the *Mobile Register* with its onetime competitor, the *Mobile Press*) that in Williams's house, there were "books on top of books," and that Williams could recite the contents of each one. In the 1970s, Williams started publishing his own findings in booklets, each one dealing with a facet of the neighborhood's past. He also talked about local history to most anyone who would listen. "He wasn't just going to walk away once he got your attention," said Ron Davis, a 1981 MCTS graduate and a deacon at Yorktown Baptist. "When you were a teenager, when you saw him coming, you started to go the other way." Many adults had similar reactions. "Some called him a genius," said Charles Porter, who ran the *Inner City News*, a Black newspaper, "and others called him an idiot. Sometimes he would mix the two into one conversation."

In 1977, Williams also told the Associated Press he spoke sometimes with Augustine Meaher Sr., though he was clearly referring to Augustine Meaher Jr., Timothy Meaher's grandson. "He and I laugh and talk," Williams said. "I may accuse him of being a land thief but we're friendly." Williams said he occasionally brought up the subject of "reparations," which he thought the Meahers owed to the shipmates' descendants. "He will not talk about it," Williams added.

Williams took a liberal approach to determining Africatown's boundaries. His definition seemed to include nearly every site in Mobile where any of the shipmates had ever lived and more places where they hadn't. These boundary lines never caught on, but a simpler set of boundaries did. A sign on the edge of Plateau now defines Africatown as a cluster of five smaller neighborhoods: Plateau, Magazine Point, Happy Hill, Kelly Hills, and Lewis Quarters.

One of Williams's early clashes with the local authorities began in 1972. It dealt with the MCTS bell, the one said to have come from the *Clotilda*. The saga gives a sense of what Williams and his allies were trying to achieve and the resistance they encountered.

No one explains the bell's significance better than Womack. "Every boat had a bell on it," he said on a neighborhood tour in 2020, "and that bell actually came off the ship."

> If the bell was silent, the sea was calm. If the bell clanged, you knew a storm was coming and the sea was rough. And because [the shipmates] were basically young children, when they heard the bell clanging, they got closer together—even though they were from different tribes . . . When they let 'em off the ship, some kind of way they knew they were about to scuttle that boat. They burned it and sank it. So one of the good acts of the captain, he gave them the bell. So they dragged the bell with them wherever they went, and when they built the first church, and when they built the school, they put it here. They rang the bell in the morning to tell people the school was ready to take in, and in the evening to let the people know the kids were ready to get out. And they also rang the bell for emergencies. If somebody's house was on fire, people would come out in the middle of the night, to put out the fire with buckets and water.

The bell, in other words, was regarded as a vestige of the neighborhood's roots, but also had a central role in the ongoing life of the community.

In November 1972, a professor at Alabama State University, a predominantly Black school, wrote to the Alabama Historical Commission with a request. ASU's History and Political Science Club had been trying for "some time" to obtain the bell, in hopes of displaying it on campus. He wondered if the state could help. Taking up this request, the historical commission composed a letter to the Mobile County school superintendent. "We understand that the bell now lies in neglect at the former Mobile County Training School," it read. (In reality, MCTS was still functioning, but in the wake of desegregation, in 1970, it had been reduced to a middle school.) The letter suggested that putting the bell on the campus would be a powerful gesture. "Enshrined at a predominantly black institution, located at the State Capital which lies in the heart of the principal antebellum plantation and slavery (we speak, of course, in the past tense) area in Alabama, the bell would be a meaningful aspect of black history and Alabama's heritage." But in December, the school superintendent wrote back that the bell had been moved to Mobile's history museum, and that it would stay there. Other correspondence shows the museum had received it in February of that year, and had cleaned it and put it on a mahogany base.

One year later, several dozen alumni from the MCTS class of 1958 met for a reunion. They were surprised to learn the school district had taken the bell—for repairs, as they understood—and had not yet returned it. They agreed to have Charles Porter, who was part of their class and was working as a publications editor at Northwestern University, ask the administrators what was going on. Porter composed a note, which he sent the administrators in January 1974. "When we visit the campus—or just in passing—we would like to see something that helps us recall the beautiful history of a school with which we have had a passionate love affair," he wrote. "However, with the developments over the past few years, nearly all that we can grasp is purely nostalgia, and the missing bell appears to be an attempt to take part of that away." He asked politely but firmly that it be returned. James Benson, an assistant superintendent, wrote back nine days later. "I know that you will be delighted to know that we have enshrined the bell in the City Museum," he said, "so that the proper honor can bestowed upon it." He mentioned the request to display it in Montgomery and the school district's decision to keep it in Mobile. He closed by thanking Porter for his interest.

Porter, of course, was *not* delighted with this news. He followed up with a letter to the museum. "I understand that the Museum has purchased a bell from the Mobile County Public Schools that came to America on the slave ship Clotilde," he wrote. He asked what price had been paid and what condition the bell was in. Caldwell Delaney, the museum director, sent back a snotty reply. Since the *Clotilda*'s voyage had started in the United States, he said, the bell "did not 'come to America.'" He said Africatown already had a "very fine" bronze bust of Cudjo—implying that Plateau didn't need the bell (which, he added, was in pristine condition).

At this point Williams, who had received copies of the letters from Porter, intervened with a more confrontational approach. "Your action of moving the Historic Bell," he wrote to Delaney on February 18, "leaves us with no

other alternative than to demand that you replace the bell." He told Delaney
that Africatown's history needed to be preserved by the community itself—
"and not by you, for this is why it is presently distorted today."

Delaney was affronted. "I am amazed by the rude language of your letter,"
he wrote back. "As you well know I have gone far beyond the call of courtesy
or duty in supplying you with the fruits of my years of research." (He mentioned in another letter that he'd once lent Williams the notes from his own
interviews with Emma Langdon Roche, and they had never been returned.)
At any rate, he said, the bell wasn't his responsibility, since it was the school
board, not the museum, that had removed it from the school in the first place.
"I do not wish to hear from you again," he wrote. At the same time, he wrote
to Benson, suggesting the school district take the bell back, so the museum
could duck further conflict. Benson agreed.

What ultimately became of the bell is a mystery. A letter Benson wrote
to Williams that May makes it sound as though the district was preparing to
give it back. "We have not been able to find the missing parts," Benson wrote,
and he wondered if Williams could share any photos so they could have those
parts fabricated. He also inquired about the date of an upcoming reunion, as
if he hoped to get it ready in time. But it was apparently never returned to
the school. The school district's personnel have turned over many times since
1974, and no one currently working there knows of its whereabouts; nor does
the district keep internal records dating back so many decades. One local
historian suggested that it could be in "somebody's back yard in Spring Hill,"
a historic neighborhood where many of the prominent white residents live,
including one of Timothy Meaher's great-grandsons. Womack has thought
the same. "Somebody's got that bell," he said. "They probably bring it out
every year and have a big dinner around it."

By the time of the bell controversy, Womack and Flen had graduated from
St. Paul's College. Womack's degree was in business administration. He
knew exactly what he wanted to do for a career—he had known since his
teens. "I wanted an office," he said. "A desk. A sit-down, white-collar, tie-
type job." He thought he'd go into accounting. In the long run, he wanted to
become a supervisor. As he was leaving Virginia, he still saw this kind of job
in his future; but first, he knew, he was almost certain to be drafted into the
military. Given the ongoing war in Vietnam, and the timing of his birthday,
his number was sure to come up. His older brother, Jesse, urged him to vol-
unteer before it happened. That way he'd be able to choose his branch; and

with his college degree, he had a likely shot at becoming an officer. Womack decided to join the Marine Corps, if only to show his friends he could do it. "Everybody told me not to join. 'You're not a Marine!' 'You're not Marine material!' I kept hearing that. It pissed me off. You know how it is—you want to prove folks wrong."

As it turned out, he would never be sent to Vietnam. He split his time between Camp Lejeune, in North Carolina, and Camp Courtney, in Okinawa, Japan. When he returned to Mobile, he joined the Marine Corps Reserve and became a lieutenant. He also took a job at Shell Chemicals, north of Mobile, as an accountant. When his paychecks started coming in, he moved to an apartment in the suburbs of West Mobile, across town from Plateau.

Flen, meanwhile, was in Atlanta, where he'd found his calling as a public health worker. He was hired to do contact tracing for the Centers for Disease Control. Most of his work was responding to sexually transmitted diseases. "You had to deal with every element of society, from pimps to prostitutes to politicians and business owners." He and his college sweetheart, Lynn, were married and had a young daughter. But many nights, as late as eleven or midnight, Flen had to go out and find people so he could interview them and take blood samples. He got used to having guns and knives drawn on him. One of his favorite anecdotes evokes what the job could be like on the liveliest days. He and a colleague were at a bar, looking for someone who didn't want to be found. His colleague had spent time there before, trying to cultivate sources. A woman who knew him came up and quietly told the pair they should leave right away. As soon as they were gone, a Molotov cocktail sailed through the window, and the place went up in flames. Flen later found out the bar owner was convicted of hiring an arsonist and committing insurance fraud.

But it was through Flen's work at the Georgia statehouse that he learned the most. His investigations there gave him a deep education in psychology, politics, and power. Every year, when the legislature was in session, sex workers poured in from other states. They had regular clients among the lawmakers who came to Atlanta from small towns. "In our world of epidemiology, it's a known thing that goes on every year," he said. "They call it The Circuit." One of the hardest parts of the job was getting politicians to talk about their sexual liaisons. They were always afraid that whatever they said would leak to the public and ruin their careers. Flen learned he could get to them by going through pimps, who kept books on them. "The pimps knew everything," he said. And unlike politicians and businessmen, "they would never lie to you."

For a time in the mid to late 1970s, African American history was having a heyday in pop culture. The biggest factor was the 1976 publication of Alex Haley's novel *Roots,* the seven-hundred-page saga of Kunta Kinte, a West African man who is sold into slavery at age seventeen, and of his descendants, who live in North Carolina and Tennessee. Though *Roots* was billed as fiction, it tracked closely with Haley's research about his own ancestors. It was a stunning commercial success, with a forty-six-week run on the *New York Times* bestseller list. The TV miniseries based on the book, which aired on ABC in 1977, racked up thirty-seven Emmy nominations. Eighty million people tuned in for the finale, shattering all previous viewership records.

At the same time, tourism at historic African American sites was starting to burgeon, thanks in part to the federal government. For decades, the national monuments program had been mostly devoid of Black history sites; but in 1972, the National Park Service gave a private group, the Afro-American Bicentennial Corporation, the funding to carry out a sweeping survey of these landmarks. An early ABC report made a stinging critique of the park system's criteria for designating historic sites. "It is organized to cover American history from a white American's perspective," the group wrote in 1973. "There appears to be a marked reluctance on the part of NPS to openly deal with some of the less appealing aspects of American history, especially slavery . . . Although the past cannot be changed, it can be honestly faced, and the future can be made differently." ABC's work led to a number of Black history sites being added to the National Register of Historic Places, including the Dexter Avenue Baptist Church in Montgomery, which Martin Luther King had once pastored, and the Battle of Rhode Island site in Portsmouth, where the all-Black 1st Rhode Island Regiment fought in the American Revolution.

Africatown was not included in ABC's surveys, and in the late seventies, Henry Williams resolved to fix the oversight. No doubt one reason was that he wanted the validation it would bring. Getting that kind of a nod from the federal government would be a rebuke to Caldwell Delaney at the history museum, to the Mobile city government, and to everyone else who treated Williams with disrespect. He also recognized the economic benefits it might bring. Starting at least as early as 1974, he'd been calling for an "AfricaTown, U.S.A." attraction that would bring money into the neighborhood and jobs for the residents, while also generating the kind of press that would make the *Clotilda*'s story known to the world. Alex Haley had said that African Americans needed a "Pilgrim's Rock." And why not Africatown? It was not the first place on the continent where enslaved Africans had landed, but it was definitively the last; and the settlement they had created was a powerful symbol of Black self-determination.

However, there was also a more pressing reason. The city was continuing to expand the industrial footprint along the Mobile River. Brookley Air Force Base, which had been Mobile's largest employer for years, making up roughly a third of the local GDP, had shut down in 1969. Over time, factories and other industrial businesses settling in the area around Plateau—much of which belonged to the Meahers—were helping to replace the lost jobs and tax revenue.

As a result, Africatown's periphery was becoming more of an industrial hub. As of 1978, there were three oil-tank farms there, plus a chemical manufacturer and a cement company. The industrial traffic meant residents had to deal with a constant parade of cargo trucks carrying toxic chemicals, idling and giving off fumes, and releasing more pollution into the atmosphere. Williams worried that one day the neighborhood itself would be taken over. His fears were intensified by three proposals that came along that year. One proposal was to tear down his own workshop, where he also taught welding classes. City inspectors said that March that it was badly rusted and might collapse anytime. They ordered him to make repairs that he said would cost at least $4,000—nearly $16,000 now (though he may have been exaggerating). Given how little concern the city showed about industrial hazards nearby, which posed far greater danger to local residents, it's hard to believe this was a good-faith effort to keep the community safe. "I will say it was a pretty unsound building, but there was history there," said Barbara Wheat, who got to know Williams during this period. She believes the true purpose was to cow Williams or teach him a lesson. After a months-long battle, Williams managed to assuage the city government by making small-scale repairs.

A second proposal was to rezone seven acres of residential property in Plateau so a realty company could build an industrial warehouse there. When the city commission took it up for a vote, in July 1978, Williams and more than a hundred other residents showed up to protest. The proposal failed, 2–1. Still, the residents knew they had only gotten lucky. It was clear they had no leverage over the commissioners. (Thanks to the Voting Rights Act, signed by Lyndon Johnson in 1965, Black Alabamians were once again able to vote. But Mobile still chose its commissioners in citywide elections, and no Black candidate had ever won a seat on the commission.)

The third project was the largest in scale. The state wanted to replace the Cochrane Bridge, which had corroded, thanks largely to the emissions from the paper factories and other plants. The new bridge would be much taller than the old one, rising 140 feet above the river at its apex. This was necessary so that industrial ships would be able to pass beneath it, without the bridge constantly being raised and lowered. To support the new structure, longer approaches would be needed along Bay Bridge Road, which ran east and west through Africatown, marking the border between Plateau and Magazine Point. Part of the road would also have to be widened from two lanes to four. It was estimated that thirty-one homes, nearly all of them owned or occupied by African Americans, would need to be demolished to make room.

Williams believed roughly half of these homes had been built by the shipmates, and it's likely he was correct. One of the city's architectural historians surveyed several of them in the early 1980s and couldn't date them precisely, partly because there were no records of their construction. But Cudjo's old house, which stood at 500 Bay Bridge Road and was along this corridor, was probably typical. The house didn't resemble a nineteenth-century dwelling because the family had remodeled it in the late 1960s, adding several bedrooms and a living room, installing a porch, and putting bricks on the exterior. Martha West Davis, Cudjo's great-granddaughter, was living there in the eighties. The architectural historian, for her part, erred on the side of caution. She recommended that more research be done on the homes and that at least some of them be preserved. An archaeologist working for the state also visited in 1980 and '81. He believed the property tract most likely to have historical significance was an elevated piece of land on Scott Paper's property. He couldn't survey it properly, he wrote, because as of 1980, the company was using it as a dumping ground for industrial waste.

It was clear that this highway project, if it were carried out, would also be devastating to the daily life of the community. The street in question was home to Africatown's central business district. Fourteen small businesses, nearly all of them Black-owned, were in jeopardy, including a grocery store, a jewelry and furniture store, and the beloved restaurant Slay and Earl's. ("They made the best hamburgers," Cassandra Lewis Wallace said, adding that she and her siblings called them "greaseburgers.") The area was pedestrian-friendly, and most of the clientele came and went on foot. With those businesses gone, the many residents who didn't own cars would be left with few options.

In 1978, an engineering firm released a report on the community that was intended to help with construction plans. It contains some noteworthy statistics. Just over half the neighborhood residents over age twenty-five had never completed elementary school, which meant there was the potential for a high rate of illiteracy. As a result, the residents were likely to have a hard time participating in meetings about the possible highway, the firm noted. "Since many can't read, they will not hear of the project and may be 'surprised' by any actions, or they will garner information by word of mouth with its concomitant risk of misinformation and rumor." Income levels were also low: the median was $5,375 (the equivalent of $21,700 now), one-third less than the median for Mobile. As for home values, the neighborhood median was $8,600 as of 1970 (which now translates to around $58,000). These numbers represent more than a snapshot of the community; they also had important ramifications for highway planning. Elected officials might have concluded that building the highway through Africatown would be cheap—which is to say, an efficient use of tax dollars. Thanks to the "misinformation and rumor" that would circulate, the firm thought condemnation proceedings and "relocation procedures" might involve some hassles; but all told, the community was unlikely to put up a serious fight. The state would not face the prospect of expensive lawsuits, nor would it have to spend a fortune on property acquisitions.

In 1978, Henry Williams and his allies called an assembly at Union Baptist, to talk about how they could protect Africatown from the threats it was facing. They brought in William Harris, a young lawyer who was relatively fresh out of law school. Harris was on staff at the Legal Services Corporation of Alabama, a scrappy nonprofit firm that advocated for the rights of African Americans and poor people. He'd grown accustomed to hearing stories of not-so-legal shenanigans being perpetrated against African Americans, often by judges, elected officials, and the police. He told the crowd at Union Baptist that its best hope of resisting unwanted developments was to get Africatown legally recognized as a historic district, by either the state or the federal government. In the months afterward, Williams followed up on this suggestion. He needed help, so he wrote to John Henry Smith, a thirty-one-year-old graduate student at the University of Wisconsin, asking him to spearhead the project.

*   *   *

John Smith was Williams's perfect counterpart. He had grown up in Prichard, the city of forty thousand adjacent to Plateau. His father ran a barbershop in Mobile's Black commercial district. Smith had been a star fullback in high school, and in 1967, he'd been recruited to play football at the University of Wisconsin. His wife, Barbara Wheat, who was also from Prichard, joined him there after finishing her bachelor's degree at Tuskegee. The young couple were swept up in academic life. African American studies programs were on the rise, and it was a thrilling time to be a young Black intellectual. Smith and Wheat each enrolled in graduate programs. Smith started in anthropology but bobbed around between departments. "He loved history, first of all," Wheat said. "Wherever he went, he was going to a museum. But John was like an octopus. He had that big head, and it had all these tentacles going out, and all of them were strings of ideas." He was most drawn to West Africa and the history of Blacks in America—interests that had been bolstered by his reading of Haley's *Roots*. In 1978, Smith paused his studies to come back to Mobile and work on the campaign of Michael Figures, a thirty-year-old Black attorney who was running for state senate. In the course of that campaign, Smith learned about the *Clotilda*. "It became an obsession with him," Wheat recalled.

    Smith and Williams hit it off immediately. In Williams, Smith found a singular wealth of information. And in Smith, the welder found someone with the youth and vigor, and the political and academic connections, to help advance his Africatown project. With help from other graduate students, Smith wrote an application to have Africatown included in the National Register of Historic Places. It was submitted in June 1979. It was not successful. Reading it several decades later, it's not hard to understand why. Smith's enthusiasm could not make up for his lack of professional experience. The document lists twenty-six sites that supposedly merit federal recognition, including some of the shipmates' original houses, but it provides no evidence or documentation of its claims. The list also includes sites that obviously were not connected to the shipmates, such as the Cochrane Bridge (built in 1927) and Williams's welding shop. Still, these efforts yielded some short-term results. City records include a letter from the Alabama Historical Commission to the mayor of Mobile, in July 1979, explaining that the Progressive League was still doing research on the neighborhood. "This agency would greatly appreciate your withholding demolition permits of structures within this historic area until such time as the survey and inventory project is completed," it reads.

Smith's involvement in the project was far from finished. Michael Figures, who had won his election to the state senate, had plans for him. The mayor's seat in Prichard was opening in 1980, and Figures wanted Smith to run. "I was *not* in agreement with that, I will tell you," Wheat recalled. She wasn't ready to move back to Alabama, nor did she think it was the right move for her husband. But Smith decided to go for it. His mind was reeling with the possibilities of what he could do for his hometown. His campaign manager was Merceria Ludgood, a law student who had run Figures's 1978 campaign as well. Her description of Smith syncs up with Wheat's. "He was a technocrat, as opposed to a stump-speech politician," she said. "He liked working out the solutions. He never met a chart or a diagram or a layout he didn't like. He kind of worked and thought like an engineer."

Prichard was the second largest city in Mobile County and the ninth largest in Alabama. Increasingly, since World War II, it had been a destination for the county's rising Black middle class. By 1972, there were enough Black residents to elect a Black mayor: A. J. Cooper, a twenty-six-year-old attorney whose family owned a local funeral home and an insurance company. Before he took office, the city had a long history of budget problems. Cooper, who had worked on Bobby Kennedy's 1968 campaign and was well connected in Washington, D.C., brought in a significant amount of federal money and built several new public facilities. But the budget troubles persisted, in part because of white flight. Throughout the seventies, roughly half of the 20,000 white residents left town. After two terms, Cooper stepped down for a job in Washington, D.C.

In July of 1980, Smith won the mayoral election by a landslide, collecting more than 3,000 votes, while the runner-up took only 962. He put the Africatown project at the center of his economic development plan. Never mind that the historic core of Africatown was outside of Prichard's city limits. The city of Mobile was not embracing it, he figured, so Prichard would. Geographically, downtown Prichard was closer to Plateau than downtown Mobile was. Smith told the *Mobile Register* in 1981 that Africatown would soon become "the largest Black historic preservation district in the United States." A booklet he and Williams coauthored that year describes their vision. They planned a park that would "serve as an international heritage resource dedicated to both the past and future of African people." They wanted to build a museum complex and an education center, a replica of the *Clotilda*, and a restaurant designed with traditional West African architecture. Elsewhere, Smith also talked about making Prichard a hub for intercontinental trade. He wanted to establish a market where West African vendors could sell crafts, clothing, food, and other products directly.

In February 1982, to kick-start the project, Smith organized the first AfricaTown Folk Festival. There was a parade, where he and others rode a float, wearing traditional African garb. There was a gospel music workshop, a display of African art at city hall, and a performance by a dance troupe from Selma. The main event was a program at the city's auditorium, where Smith paid tribute to several descendants of the *Clotilda* shipmates, including Mama Eva, Mable Dennison (the granddaughter of Kanko and James Dennison), and Mary Lumbers and Martha West Davis, Cudjo's twin great-granddaughters—the ones Zora Neale Hurston had met more than half a century earlier. Williams had the honor of opening the festival with an Africatown tour.

In his new position, Smith was also able to get the attention of Howell Heflin, one of Alabama's U.S. senators, who hailed from the northwest corner of the state. A second application for National Register status was submitted in 1981, this time with a narrower focus: it was for the site of the Scott Paper factory, which, according to lore, was the former location of the shipyard where Bill Foster had built the *Clotilda*. "The present condition of the site is altered," the application conceded, "due to heavy industrial use." Unsurprisingly, this application also failed to pass muster. Undeterred, Smith had another idea: creating an AfricaTown National Historical Park and District. It was to span eight hundred or more acres in Mobile and Prichard. Heflin was receptive to the idea, and his office worked with Smith to craft a Senate bill.

13

A THREAT TO BUSINESS

On a rainy Thursday morning in April 1983, Smith went into the Dirksen Office Building in Washington, D.C. He was there to testify before a Senate subcommittee regarding Heflin's bill. The timing was somewhat unfortunate. The network of national parks had been rapidly expanded during Jimmy Carter's presidency, but that trend had come to a halt the moment Ronald Reagan took office. James Watt, the interior secretary, who oversaw the National Park Service, was the most controversial figure in Reagan's cabinet. Before his appointment, Watt had been one of the country's leading opponents of the conservation movement. Once in office, he had called for a moratorium on park expansion, in order to save money, and there were reports that he'd prepared a "hit list" of urban parks that he wanted de-authorized (though he denied this). The Reagan administration also tried to slash $50 million from the department's budget and hike the fees for park visitors, saying it wanted to make the parks less competitive with the private recreation industry.

Knowing what they were up against, Heflin and his office had kept the bill modest. They estimated development costs would total $8 million (or $21 million now), but Smith was promising to raise all of this money from private investors. The federal government was only being asked to give the park a designation, a process expected to cost around $300,000. It was reasonable to think the Park Service might agree to a compromise.

The hearing was before a division of the Committee on Energy and Natural Resources. The eight senators had other business that morning, including a bill establishing a new Harry S Truman National Historic Site in

Missouri (which the Park Service "strongly" endorsed). When it was time to take up the Africatown bill, Heflin and Smith were summoned to the desk in the center of the room. The committee members sat before them at a table that curved in a broad semicircle. Heflin addressed them first.

"Good morning," he drawled. Heflin was tall and burly, with broad shoulders and an immense square jaw. He'd entered electoral politics late in life, after a stint as the chief justice of Alabama's supreme court. Senate colleagues addressed him as "Judge." He leaned into the microphone and read from his prepared remarks: "AfricaTown, U.S.A., Alabama, is an area of exceptional significance in local, national, and international history and culture." The neighborhood was a "living reflection of the Nation's heritage," he said, and "therefore should be protected and enhanced for ourselves and our posterity." Heflin understood the Park Service had objections, but he saw no reason those should derail the whole project. "We do not care whether we will end up calling it a park or a district or a landmark, site or zone." He proposed a conference between his office, John Smith, Henry Williams, and the park officials, where they could work out the details.

Smith's turn was next. He told the eight senators about the research he and the graduate students had done, which had yielded a stack of documentation on Africatown's history, including some of Zora Neale Hurston's work. The "Africatown landscape," he argued, "must be protected as an invaluable public resource." But besides historic preservation, he offered another reason to back the project: to spur economic development. At this point his language became overtly Reaganite. "Mr. Chairman, if Congress is truly serious about municipal government assuming greater responsibility for establishing self-reliant economies, reducing the incident of poverty, welfare, and unemployment, then this small effort in the city of Prichard will be recognized and supported."

Mary Lou Grier, the Park Service deputy director, followed him at the microphone. Grier was a political appointee, selected by Watt in 1981. She had no prior experience in public service, but had worked for years on Republican campaigns in Texas. "We would strongly recommend against enactment of this bill," she said. She gave two reasons. First, the government had not identified any "site, buildings or objects of national historical significance" in the area. Granted, this was only because it hadn't tried. "Mr. Chairman," she said, "while the event of the last landing is significant, the site where it occurred has been little studied." Her second objection was that Africatown lacked "historical integrity"—or in other words, that it didn't *feel* like a historical place. It was a "modern community," "impacted by modern residential and industrial construction, including many rail lines."

This assessment sounds harsh, but internal records from the Park Service show that nonpolitical staffers who advised Grier about what to say were sympathetic to Africatown's situation. The landing of the *Clotilda*, one historian wrote to a colleague that February, was clearly an event of "great importance." "American blacks had no Ellis Island," he wrote, and places like Africatown were the closest counterpart. But in the scanty applications they had seen so far, there wasn't much evidence that Africatown still had physical sites intact that would meet the threshold for a federal designation.

Their comments reflected a more deeply rooted problem. The Park Service criteria, with their focus on architecture, were inherently weighted against historic Black communities like Africatown. The *Clotilda* shipmates, like so many other freedpeople throughout the South, had lacked the resources to fashion robust buildings that would last for many generations (even if, as of the early 1980s, at least a few of their homes still stood). And in fact, in their jobs at sawmills and shingle mills, the shipmates had not only helped the Meahers and other white families to build up their wealth; they had also produced the very building materials that had been used for white people's homes and businesses. By the 1980s, for a historic Black community to be surrounded by heavy industry, as Africatown was, was not unusual, either. The end result was that while the Park Service's rules seemed neutral, in practice they tended to reinforce the historical inequities between Black communities and white ones.

As the Afro-American Bicentennial Corporation had pointed out in the 1970s, the Park Service had not always been consistent about these criteria, either. The site of the first Pacific Coast cannery in California, a restaurant where the first commercial telephone exchange had once stood in New Haven, Connecticut, and the former site of Henry David Thoreau's cabin at Walden Pond, Massachusetts, were all National Historic Landmarks—meaning the sites of these former structures were not only recognized as historic, but were also protected from further development. And the approximate site where the first Roman Catholic mass had been conducted in the northern Rocky Mountains was on the National Register of Historic Places.

What the Park Service staffers had suggested before this hearing in 1983 was further study of Africatown. No one from the agency had ever made an official visit. Grier went on to voice this recommendation. The department would be willing to investigate further, she said, if "funds were made available." She estimated a proper survey would cost $50,000 and would take three months. Judging from the subcommittee chairman's response, it sounded like the legislators were willing to take up her suggestion.

Smith must have left the hearing that day feeling buoyant. This was the best outcome he could have reasonably hoped for. But in the long run, the study was apparently never done. As the months passed, it became clear the bill would not get traction. Available records do not convey what happened. James Watt or his lieutenants may have been responsible, given their knee-jerk resistance to adding more parks, or perhaps there was some other cause. The Park Service, as it would turn out, was not the only institution skeptical of the project.

John Smith and Henry Williams had separate priorities, and after this federal legislation failed, their endeavors forked. Smith began working with Michael Figures and Bill Clark, a state representative who had coached and taught at MCTS, to create an Africatown park through the state government. The area they nominated was not in Plateau or Magazine Point; instead it was a vacant 150-acre plot in Prichard that Scott Paper had donated to the city in 1969. For Smith's purposes, this would still work. He planned to use the park as a springboard for economic development. However, the bill promised no protections for the historic Africatown. It also had an even smaller price tag: Figures and Clark promised it would cost the state nothing at all.

But this bill, too, was met with opposition from the residents of College Woods, a predominantly white neighborhood near the proposed park. To the project's supporters, it seemed clear that their objections were racially motivated. Whatever their reasons, their protests were enough to slow the project's momentum. During the 1984 legislative session, the bill passed in the state senate but not the house.

Smith was having more success with his AfricaTown Folk Festivals, which had become a yearly staple. In January 1984, Governor George Wallace issued a proclamation honoring that year's festivities. Smith and Williams were at the state capitol for the signing ceremony. This was, of course, the same George Wallace who had called for "segregation now, segregation tomorrow, and segregation forever" in 1963, and had stood in a doorway at the University of Alabama to stop two Black students from entering. More recently, Wallace had renounced his former views on race and become a born-again Christian. But this nod to the folk festival wasn't only about racial reconciliation. It was also a sign that Wallace saw economic potential in what Smith was doing.

During the celebration in Mobile, Smith was given an honorary degree from a university in Liberia. The festival's gospel concert drew a crowd of two thousand. Likely the proudest moment for Smith was when twenty-four African envoys landed at the Mobile Municipal Airport, and he was there to greet them. They came from Benin, Congo, Madagascar, and several other countries and were wrapping up a tour of the United States. "You're at home," Smith told them at the airport, "brothers among us." During a press conference, he said their visit was a "high point in the development of Prichard."

That spring, Smith doubled down on his dream of making Prichard the hub for American trade with West Africa. He knew this would require help from the federal government; and not wanting to repeat his last experience, he'd begun making connections with the Reagan administration. He went so far as to change his party affiliation to Republican, even though his local base was heavily Democratic. His efforts began to pay off. In April 1984, the federal government paid for him to visit West Africa. He met with leaders in Nigeria, Ghana, and Benin. When he returned home, after sixteen days, he announced that he'd brokered an agreement. Ouidah, the city where Cudjo and the other shipmates had been held in barracoons, and where the *Clotilda* had docked for more than a week, was going to become Prichard's sister city.

For all his progress on these long-range endeavors, however, the day-to-day administration of Prichard wasn't going well. The city was on the verge of bankruptcy, and its unemployment rate was at 18.5 percent. Smith was up for reelection in the summer of 1984. He campaigned by saying he'd laid the foundations for improvement and just needed time to build on them. He faced five challengers. Come election day, his vote tally totaled 1,908, higher than those of his opponents, but only 38.5 percent of the total. Since no candidate won a majority, a runoff was held several weeks later. Smith's top challenger was a white real estate agent and hairdresser named Margie Moberg Wilson. On August 1, Smith eked out a victory over Wilson, with a margin of just 266 votes.

While Smith was focused on Prichard, Plateau and Magazine Point were again being threatened by major construction plans. And now that the prospects for preservation status had fallen through, the outlook seemed bleak.

In 1984, design plans were released for the Cochrane Bridge replacement, and they confirmed the community's fears: twenty-seven houses, and a big part of the central business district, were set to be destroyed. And in February 1985, the old bridge was demolished. A crew placed 216 pounds of explosives at twelve strategic spots along its span. When they went off, they jarred the surrounding area like an earthquake. "The heart of Africatown has received total damage," Williams later told a reporter. He blamed the event for the cracks that were forming in the brick walls of his Chin Street office building, half a mile from the river. "Most of the houses are leaking," he said in 1988, "and the people don't know why."

By this time a second highway project was in the works that would be equally consequential for Africatown. On the opposite side of the neighborhood, to the west, the state had announced it wanted to build a new interstate spur, a proposal that would eventually be called I-165. It would run north from downtown, through Prichard, and would connect with I-65. Altogether, it was on track to wipe out 219 homes, according to an estimate released in 1984. Most of those were in Prichard; but the plans also called for a portion of Bay Bridge Road, in Africatown, to be relocated for easier interstate access. This would mean another twenty-nine Africatown homes being demolished. Assuming these plans were carried out, only a short stretch of the old Bay Bridge Road—which, as of the mid-1980s, was still the physical spine of Africatown—would be left. And its fate did not look promising.

Also in 1985, Hauser Realty, the company that had tried to build a huge warehouse in Africatown's residential zone back in 1978, started a second push. Once again, it was asking to have seven acres rezoned. The company's attorney made an audacious argument: that the Hauser family's wishes ought to trump those of the local community because their ancestors had bought the property in 1856, before the *Clotilda* shipmates came to America. The Hausers had farmed the land until 1918. An appraiser also addressed the commission. He said he'd assessed the property, and from his perspective, the most appropriate use of the land was to put a warehouse there. Since it would connect to an existing industrial zone, on the far side of the neighborhood, he argued, it would have no impact on the community.

A group of residents, no doubt including Williams, were there to protest, and they, too, had come prepared. Reverend C. L. Daniel, the pastor of Yorktown Baptist, brought a petition with 356 signatures. "We ask you to consider the voice of the people in the community," he said. "We do not want our community to become an industrial area." Arealia Craig, who lived near the seven-acre tract in question, reminded the planning commission of how the residents had fought the same effort in 1978. "What makes you think we changed our minds?" she asked. Africatown was "already surrounded by commercial and industry." The residents didn't want any more, she said, especially since it might damage the remaining historical sites. The planning commission was unmoved by these protests. It approved the application once again, forwarding it to the city commissioners.

The mood in Africatown that spring was dismal. As far as the city authorities were concerned, the rezoning was nothing to get too upset over. It was only a single warehouse, which would occupy only seven acres that no one was using anyway. But to the community, it seemed there was more at stake. A writer for a weekly newspaper, the *Azalea City News & Review*, visited shortly after the hearing, and he learned that many people believed the rezoning was part of a master plan to seize the whole area. "Rumors fly all over Africatown of industry moving in, taking their small lots and houses," he wrote. One man who had retired from Scott Paper said it was his understanding that Scott wanted to take over half the residential area and IP the other half. Another resident predicted that soon many of the neighborhood's elderly people would be homeless. "If they came in and condemned and took property here," he said, "you couldn't put the blocks under another house for what they'd give you."

On the most literal level, these residents were almost certainly mistaken. There's no evidence suggesting there was a conscious conspiracy to use their land for factories. Officials at city hall and IP expressed surprise when the reporter asked them about the rumors. "It's completely out of the blue," an IP spokeswoman said. But on another level, the residents were close to the mark. It had always been individual projects like these—a factory here, a warehouse there, a railroad passing near their homes—that had eroded their neighborhood across a period of six decades. No master plan was needed. Economic forces, channeled through a political and legal system largely shaped by Jim Crow mores, were enough to drive the transformation on their own. From this perspective, the residents understood what was going on better than the bureaucrats who looked at each construction project in isolation.

Helen Richardson Jackson, the director of a shipmates' descendants association that had started up in 1984, was working diligently to save several houses in the corridor. She told the state highway department that three of the homes slated for demolition had been built by her ancestor, Ossa Keeby, and that all three were still occupied by members of the family. It's likely she also told the highway officials about the house built by Cudjo at 500 Bay Bridge Road. A fifth house in the corridor was apparently built by Gumpa. Along with roughly thirty other residents, she and Williams also made a trip to Montgomery in April 1985, where they pleaded with the highway department's director in person. It seems he was polite but noncommittal.

In an interview with the *Inner City News*, Jackson expressed her feelings at greater length. "You get the feeling of being boxed in with no way out," she said. When she looked out her window, she now saw a parking lot where her neighbors had lived until recently. The new highway was planned to run less than two hundred feet from her house, and on her other side, a service road would soon be installed, with hazardous cargo in mind. "We need more input to find ways of keeping human beings from being completely pushed aside," she said.

On May 14, the Mobile city commission took up the proposal to rezone residential land for a warehouse. As usual, Africatown residents showed up in force to voice their objections. Williams told the three city commissioners that if the city were so bent on making money from Africatown, there were better ways. A tourism boom was coming, he said, that would overwhelm these minor industrial plans. Mama Eva, who was ninety years old, addressed the commission and identified herself as the daughter of Pollee Allen. She spoke about the hardships her father and his companions had endured before they established Africatown. "I'm begging you," she said, "with tears in my eyes, please leave us alone."

This time the commissioners could not be won over. They voted 2–1 to approve the rezoning. The loss was bitter for Williams. "We have not had one white friend stand up for us," he said.

Two months later, in mid-July, the state put out a call for construction bids for the new Cochrane Bridge. Despite the community's pleas to the state highway commissioner, the design had not been altered. The houses built by the shipmates were going to be demolished.

As the community fought the proposed development plans, Smith and Figures were still trying to establish an Africatown park in Prichard. In the spring session of 1985, Figures reintroduced his bill into the state senate. But this time, a more powerful opponent made itself known: the paper industry.

Spokesmen for Scott Paper and International Paper said they were being hypervigilant because of Scott's recent experience in the Alabama city of Demopolis. A year earlier, the company had planned to build a plant there; but before it broke ground, a Demopolis historic district was established, leading to tighter restrictions on pollution. The company had to cancel the project. Executives at both plants in Mobile said they would have "major concerns" if Africatown received any kind of historic status. They described their situation as "once bitten, twice shy." It was more than a little bold for these companies, which had released unfathomable amounts of pollution into Africatown's air and waterways, to suggest they, and not residents like Mama Eva, were the ones in danger of being "bitten."

Figures was furious. By this point, the bill had been stripped of practically any meaningful content. It would not give environmental protection to Plateau or Magazine Point; it would merely designate an "AfricaTown, U.S.A. State Park" on a vacant lot in Prichard, and would allow for commemorative markers to be put up at thirty-seven sites in the historic neighborhood. "I do not understand these last-minute unfounded concerns being expressed," Figures wrote in his *Press-Register* column on May 8, 1985. "Even Gov. George Wallace supports the bill and has been in contact with African government officials who expected to participate in the development of the park." Figures admitted that he hoped the bill would be a step toward some kind of federal recognition. Thanks to the companies' resistance, the bill failed to pass during the regular session. The *Register* reported that the matter wasn't closed. "Scott Paper Co. may still be open for discussion," a May 22 story read—as if the companies, not the elected representatives, were the ones casting votes.

In mid-August, Figures met with the executives and with other legislators at the local chamber of commerce. It became clear to Figures that the opponents still had not bothered to learn what was in the legislation. Every objection they raised, he said in his August 21 column, had already been addressed in the bill's text. The summer edition of the *Scott Government Relations Newsletter*, a bulletin apparently written by the company's lobbyists, gives some clues about what these quibbles were. Under a section titled "Africatown, USA—A Direct Threat to Alabama's Best Business Area," the newsletter claims (incorrectly) that the bill would classify 2,500 acres of mostly industrial land as a "state and federal historic area." But the newsletter also raises blanket objections. "Historic designation," it notes, "is a threat to the existence and profitable operation of any business located in or nearby such an area." The paper companies later told a reporter they had "withdrawn opposition," but they made it clear that they still did not support it.

The bill passed in a special session that August, thanks to legislative maneuvering on Figures's part. The vote in the house was 42–15, with the votes of Mobile County's representatives split almost precisely down racial lines. On September 26, Governor Wallace signed it into law. "Africatown U.S.A. is finally on the map," the *Mobile Register* declared. Williams must have felt mixed emotions. He was not mentioned in the story, and neither were any of the construction projects that were destroying parts of the historic neighborhood. Smith, however, was thrilled. His ideas for the new park were still blossoming. He announced in the story that it would include a theater, a library, and a zoo.

The AfricaTown Folk Festivals, meanwhile, were mounting in scale. They reached their apex with the 1986 celebration. That year's festival opened on February 23, a Sunday, with a "Season of Prayers" ceremony at an auditorium. The keynote speaker was Isidore de Souza, the Roman Catholic archbishop of Benin. He was there representing the descendants of the Dahomeans who had sold the *Clotilda* shipmates into slavery. "Who would think that I would be welcome here?" he said in French, speaking through a translator. "God guides history," he went on. "I am thankful to the savior for bringing us together as brothers." After he finished speaking, Smith and Reverend Oscar Lipscomb, the archbishop of Mobile, gave him a gold ring, as a gift to Benin.

Later that week, Prichard welcomed a fifty-person delegation from Benin, including the foreign minister and other diplomats. On February 26, during a ceremony at the Prichard Municipal Complex, Smith and a Ouidah official cemented their partnership as sister cities. "Long live Prichard," they each intoned. "Long live Ouidah; long live the United States; and long live the People's Republic of Benin, West Africa." Smith wore a dashiki and a kufi. A visiting dance troupe—"the best we have in Benin," one of the diplomats said—gave a performance. Also there to witness it were two African American celebrities: Dick Gregory, the comedian and civil rights activist, and Alex Haley, the author of *Roots* and *The Autobiography of Malcolm X*, who gave an address to the crowd. The following day, Benin's minister of commerce announced that his country was ready to open a trading company in the United States. The base of operations, the official said, would be in Prichard.

By 1988, when Smith was up for reelection, however, these development plans were still just prospects. Nothing had been built. The AfricaTown, U.S.A. park was still a vacant lot, and ground had not been broken for a museum or library or zoo. Landmarks had not been erected in Plateau and Magazine Point. There were no trade outposts belonging to West African countries. Smith hadn't been able to raise the needed capital for development, and Prichard was in as poor shape as ever.

By this time, Smith's relationship with Figures had fractured. Acquaintances don't know exactly what led to the split, but everyone agrees they had personality conflicts. Over the previous decade, Figures and his associates had been successful in building something like a Black political machine in Mobile. They had gotten African Americans elected to more offices, including in the county government and the state legislature. Wheat remembers Figures calling himself the "kingpin." "Anybody Black running for office had to come through him, and he would tell that person what was going to be their agenda," she said. Her husband was too headstrong to take orders from someone else, and the two men started to resent each other. "They still worked together," she said, "but it wasn't the same."

But Merceria Ludgood, who had run Smith and Figures's first campaigns and was Figures's law partner, said the senator was driven by strategic concerns. It seemed to Figures, Ludgood, and others in the Black political establishment that Smith was not a viable candidate in '88. His support among voters had sunk. Prichard "needed mayors who wanted to get in the trenches, and roll up their sleeves and do that hard, dirty work," Ludgood said. "Because John's focus was so big-picture, so aspirational, that's not what he wanted to do." They recruited Jesse Norwood, a Prichard native who was living in Birmingham, to run for the seat. Norwood was persuaded to move back home, having been assured that Smith was going to step down and devote himself full time to developing trade relations with West Africa. But after the two of them met, the incumbent mayor said to him, "'I hate to tell you this, brother Norwood, but I think I'm going to run.'" (Wheat's memory is that Smith never wavered in his intentions to run for a third term. "I say this because I was against it," she added. "I was trying to get him to move on.") Margie Moberg Wilson, the hairdresser who had run against Smith in 1984, also entered the race.

The election was on August 23. Smith hosted a party at Prichard's city hall. As the election results came in that night, the incumbent mayor's odds looked worse and worse. It became clear that the presence of two Black candidates was splitting up what had once been Smith's base. In the end, 30 percent of the total went to Norwood, 18 percent to Smith. Wilson got 42 percent.

Smith's son Yuri, who was eleven at the time, recalled going to his grandparents' house after the party and finding all the adults in the back room. Yuri slipped in between them, and as he approached his father to give him a hug, he realized his dad was crying. "It really broke him as a man," Yuri reflected, "as a confident man, as a Black man, as a political man."

In a newspaper interview after the election, Smith said he believed the Africatown development would still pan out. He was confident in the groundwork he had laid. At the same time, though, he couldn't help lapsing into bitterness. He predicted in the same conversation that Prichard would become a "permanent ghetto." "All the programs I started were designed to stimulate economical growth in Prichard," he said, but he felt the residents had not been ready.

Smith refused to endorse Norwood in the September 13 runoff, and Wilson was victorious. Only 6,194 of Prichard's 40,000 or more residents cast ballots. In the weeks after the hairdresser's victory, numerous people in Prichard told Barbara Drummond, a *Press-Register* reporter and columnist, that they heard Wilson say she planned to "squash Africatown." When Drummond called her, Wilson replied, "Whoever said that is a bald-face liar." But if Wilson didn't like the project, there was no need for her to squash it; all she had to do was let it die out. The 1989 festival was an all-around failure. The organizers couldn't recruit any African dignitaries or African American celebrities to come speak. Turnout was nil, and several events were canceled at the last minute. Eventually, plans for the development of a trade hub at the state park fell apart.

By 1986, Africatown's central business district had collapsed. Old city directories give a picture of what was lost. Among the businesses on the strip in 1983 were Slay & Earl's Lounge, the Williams Lounge, the Williams Motel, Rigsby's Barber Shop, Randolph's Variety Store (which sold "everything from nails to meat," according to Deborah Randolph, the owner's daughter), Peoples Grocery, a post office, the Culliver Service Station, and the Bryan Service Station. Among these, the Williams Motel appears to be the only one that survived. But there were other businesses that operated off the books, out of people's homes. Many residents in that area had built additions to their shotgun houses or put up shacks in their yards, where they sold beer and cigarettes to factory workers finishing their shifts. At intervals throughout the day and evening, tired workers would stand around their friends' trucks or sit on the curbs, tying a few on before they walked home.

Letters from 1985 and 1986 show that the state gave the okay for the descendant-occupied homes along the corridor to be moved before highway construction started, as long as the owners, rather than the state, covered the costs. Helen Richardson Jackson successfully had one historic home moved to an adjacent property belonging to her family, but she was having hang-ups with two other homes and needed to ask for more time. By June 1986, state officials were becoming impatient, worried about the costs of delays. It was "imperative" that the remaining homes "be removed from the State right-of-way or demolished as soon as possible," an official from the state highway department wrote to Jackson that month. In the end, the two remaining homes were torn down. Years later, an archaeologist examined what was left of Gumpa's house, which was also in this area, and found that at least half of it had been destroyed in the highway construction. (Garry Lumbers, Cudjo's great-great-grandson, believes the house his ancestor built along this corridor was bulldozed before the highway construction started, because he'd fallen behind on the tax payments. State records are not clear on this point.)

The bridge was finished by 1991. It stood 350 feet above the river, supported by concrete slabs that were connected to neat rows of arcing steel cables. Henry Williams opted to make the best of a bad situation. That spring, before the bridge was opened to the public, he organized a "pre-dedication" ceremony. He knew that when the old bridge had opened, in 1927, the governor's wife had "christened" it with a bottle of orange juice grown in Mobile County (in lieu of champagne, since Prohibition was in effect). It was important to Williams that this ritual be repeated. "Here in Africatown, we believe in spiritually dedicating something," he told a reporter. On a humid Sunday afternoon in April, several dozen people from the community gathered at the new bridge. Reverend Bob Hope, the assistant pastor of Yorktown Baptist, was the emcee. Singers from Africatown's choirs, wearing their robes, led the group in singing "God Bless America." Homegrown orange juice was not available, so they poured out a carton from the regional brand Dairy Fresh.

Williams also had the idea of renaming the structure the Cochrane-Africatown USA Bridge, and this went over surprisingly well. Two days after the ceremony, the *Mobile Register* announced its support for the idea. "We hope the Legislature will find time to approve the appropriate resolution to accomplish this simple but historically significant act," the editors opined. Figures introduced a bill to the state legislature, and it cleared both chambers on May 7. As it turned out, it was easy to get support for gestures toward Africatown as long as there was no cost to industry.

Demolition of the neighborhood continued on. That same spring, construction began on I-165, the new interstate spur west of Africatown. It was on track to open by the mid-1990s. And that spring, another project was announced, one that would complete the destruction of Africatown's main corridor. The rest of Bay Bridge Road would be widened into a full-scale five-lane highway and upgraded for industrial traffic. State officials were clear that this was not being done with commuters in mind. It would be "a facility for the transporting of hazardous materials" to the opposite side of the river, said Malcolm Risher, one of the state's engineers. He said the point was to divert the traffic away from "small towns and heavily populated areas" elsewhere in the county. No mention was made of the inhabitants of Prichard or Africatown.

The proposed highway would be paving over part of the Old Plateau Cemetery, the same cemetery where Cudjo and some of the other shipmates are buried. State highway records do not reflect this, but longtime residents remember it clearly. Burials there were often done on the cheap. Some people were interred in homemade wooden boxes, which were prone to rotting, and many of the graves lacked headstones. Construction on this final section of the highway was carried out later in the nineties. Residents believe a number of graves were dug up in the process.

By the time the bulldozers and cranes were gone, Williams found himself in the same position he'd been in twenty years earlier. Africatown had been celebrated internationally and had received considerable press coverage and the attention of U.S. senators. But on the ground, from Williams's workshop on Chin Street, it all amounted to nothing. The prospect of a heritage-tourism development that would honor the shipmates, while also renewing the neighborhood, was still only a prospect—if anything, a more distant one than before. At the same time, many of Williams's fears had been borne out. The neighborhood's footprint was smaller, and the noise, the fumes, and the environmental hazards were worse than ever. "Henry was a really good guy, but there was a part of him that was bitter," said Merceria Ludgood, the attorney and sometime campaign manager. "And I could understand it."

As for John Smith, he had long since left the region. Smith and Wheat divorced around 1989, and within a few years he was remarried. The family lost track of him for a time. In 2006, Bill Clark, one of Smith's longtime allies in the state legislature, successfully introduced a ballot measure that would have allowed the city of Prichard to create a "Foreign Trade Investment Zone," making good on one of the former mayor's longest held dreams. The small city's best prospect was to import agricultural products from Benin, with which it still had a relationship. Voters turned the project down—but Smith did not live to see the result. Seven weeks before the election, he died of a massive heart attack. He was only fifty-nine. His principal request was that his ashes be scattered in West Africa. Leaders in Benin did him one better, establishing a shrine for him in Ouidah. As of 2019, there were plans to add on a memorial library. Wheat said Smith's efforts to create a trade partnership had always been more appreciated overseas than at home. "My sister becomes very angry every time she sees something on the news about Africatown," Wheat said. "And she says, 'They're not talking about what John did!' I said, 'But you know, the legacy is 'I might not finish . . . but somebody else can pick it up and carry it on.'"

On a chilly December morning in 1996, three men motored an open-top boat up the Mobile River, past Twelvemile Island, into one of the narrow bayous that ribbon off to the east and west. The two younger men, Michael Krivor and Michael Tuttle, were clad in jeans and sweatshirts. They worked for Panamerican Consultants, an archaeology firm. They had hauled the boat down earlier that week from their office in Memphis, bringing along their expensive equipment, which included a magnetometer (to detect ferrous metals on the river bottom) and a sidescan sonar (to capture images of whatever was beneath their boat). The third man, dressed in khakis and a button-down shirt with a safari vest, was Jack Friend. He was a sixty-seven-year-old retired entrepreneur and an amateur historian. Finding the *Clotilda* was his obsession.

Friend had grown up in Mobile, where his father had been an executive at the International Paper plant. He had a deep love for the bay. In his retirement, he'd taken up two projects. The first was a definitive book on the 1864 Battle of Mobile Bay, which he researched so compulsively that his friends thought he'd never finish. "He used to tell me, 'I believe I can just about tell you what they had for breakfast,'" said John Sledge, the author of several books on Alabama history, who knew Friend well. Friend's other project was finding the *Clotilda*'s remains. Sometimes he lay awake in bed, trying to imagine Bill Foster's thought process on the night when he scuttled the ship.

In 1993, Friend got a leg up—or at least thought he did. Robert Meaher, one of Timothy Meaher's great-grandsons, kept an office in the same downtown building where Friend was laboring on his book manuscript. The two men talked several times each week, and Robert Meaher knew about Friend's interest in the *Clotilda*. One day Robert's father, Augustine Meaher Jr., unfurled a property map and showed Friend exactly where the wreckage had sunk.

In 1994, the Maritime Museum of Mobile received a grant for underwater exploration. Friend wrote to Robert Meaher that October, telling him the *Clotilda* was sure to be a major target and might well be found during the expedition. "With this in mind," he asked, "does your family, because of its past association with the *Clotilde,* want to be involved in the project, and, if so, how?" But the Meahers were not interested. Ultimately Friend began working with Panamerican Consultants, the archaeology firm, to find the ship. (Whether or not the maritime museum had any role is unclear.)

The expedition that morning in 1996 was the culmination of all Friend's research and preparation. The trio made long passes through Big Bayou Canot and Little Bayou Canot, motoring up one side and down the other, the water beneath them black and opaque. Their printer rolled out sheets of paper showing the read from the magnetometer. Whenever they passed a spot that Friend thought was promising, he'd lean over Krivor's and Tuttle's shoulders. "Are we getting a hit, boys?" he'd ask. "Are we finding it?" Occasionally they exited the boat and walked the bayou shoreline to take readings on the land. They encountered what were obviously alligators' nesting spots. "We never saw the alligators, thank God," Krivor said, "but I'll tell you what, it was not an area where you would want to spend a lot of time." They returned the next day, and again the next, marking spots where they planned to send a diver. The hours were long. "Jack would be very keen to have us work as much as possible," Tuttle recalled with a laugh. By the time they were finished, they'd identified thirteen areas that warranted a closer look.

Krivor and Tuttle's firm did more surveying in 1997. But in June 1998, when they went back with a diver, the results were disappointing. At one site they found a sunken barge; at another, a wooden plank; and at a third, there were no foreign objects at all.

Friend put the project on hold for several years while he finished his book, but he gathered enough funds for another search in 2003. Again he contracted with Panamerican Consultants. This time Krivor and Tuttle were not involved, but Stephen James, the firm's owner, came along for the search. The deeper into the bayous they went, the more James doubted they were looking in the right place. "If you go just half a mile north of the city, you're in a backwoods swamp," he recalled. "There's nothing but alligators. It's a jungle out there." But to Friend, it seemed like the perfect place to hide evidence. They had a diver search three more targets. One turned out to be a fifty-five-gallon drum, and the others appeared to be debris.

There were still a few promising spots they hadn't assessed, but after this, Friend never went back. The expeditions were costly, and the preparations, which included a permitting process with the state, took a great deal of time.

Friend died in 2010. "It's too bad," Tuttle said, "because Jack was a damn good guy, and if anybody should have found it, it was him." At the same time, Tuttle always saw it as a long shot. "About once in every hundred targets you dive, you find the shipwreck," he said. The bay and its offshoots are incredibly vast, and only so much territory can be covered in a day.

In this case, however, the vastness of the bay was not the only hindrance. It seems Friend may have been deliberately deceived. In November 1994, Augustine Meaher III, Robert Meaher's brother, apparently wrote a revealing memo to their father. A copy is included in Friend's own papers at an archive in Mobile, but how and when he got hold of it remains a mystery. The date suggests it was written after Augustine Jr. had given Friend advice about where to look, but well before the search began. The author—identified as AMIII, presumably Augustine Meaher III—wrote in the memo that he'd just received a call from an R. V. Williams, a diver in Pensacola. Williams had recently gone diving for the ship and had no trouble finding it. Its bow was pointing upstream, and the masts were tall enough that their stubs still peeked above the water during low tide. The deck and at least one side of the hull had apparently been burned away, and the cabin was charred. After clearing away some mud, Williams had been able to swim inside the ship, through its back end.

The author makes it clear he had spoken with the diver in advance of this expedition—which suggests that the Meahers knew the true location. Williams "commented that it was too cold for him to dive beneath the hull and verify the condition of the copper bottom which you had discussed with him," the memo reads. But Williams hoped to return in the spring, when the weather was warmer. He planned to call the memo's recipient (AMJR, apparently referring to Augustine Meaher Jr.) in case he wanted to join. The diver also said he'd been contacted for information about the ship, but before disclosing anything, he wanted to speak with AMJR. "After speaking with you," Gus noted, "I informed him that you felt the vessel simply should be left to rest in peace and he seemed to agree."

From reading the letter, it's unclear what spurred Williams to start looking for the vessel in the first place, and how he got connected with the Meaher family. But another letter in the same archive, at the History Museum of Mobile, seems to shed some light on the events that followed. In 2011, Robert Meaher wrote to a museum employee, saying that in the nineties, he'd had several conversations with a "salvage man in Pensacola" who had dived down to the *Clotilda* wreckage and wanted to remove the copper around the hull. They made plans for the diver to show him the wreckage, but before this was to happen, the man died of a heart attack.

As Augustine Meaher Jr. aged, it seems his three sons wavered on the question of whether they should speak to the press. In a 1998 interview, one member of the family (reportedly Augustine III) told a local journalist that in twenty years, the family would tell its side of the story. But this interview came just a matter of weeks after the release of *Amistad,* Steven Spielberg's movie about a slave revolt near the coast of Cuba. In the wake of its release, Joe Meaher reportedly made his brothers promise they would do their part to keep the Meaher name out of the news media.

Augustine Meaher Jr. died in 2001, at age ninety-four, and their mother, Margaret, died in 2007, leaving the three sons with the family's land.

The women warriors of Dahomey—who were nominally the wives of the king—were recruited from all over the country and put through rigorous training. They participated in the raid in which Cudjo Lewis was captured and his family members killed. *(Alpern, Amazons of Black Sparta)*

The "indomitable Timothy Meaher" (as he was described by Mobile's *Weekly Advertiser* in 1857) (left) and William Foster, a ship carpenter from Nova Scotia, were the principal culprits behind the *Clotilda*'s ghastly, illegal voyage to Ouidah.

(Mobile Public Library, Local History & Genealogy Division, left; History Museum of Mobile, right)

THE SLAVE-SCHOONER AT PORT ROYAL.

The *Clotilda*'s design had a rare combination of speed and holding capacity. It may have been used for other illicit slave voyages before 1860. The ship above, the *Zeldina*, is a similar schooner that was captured on a slave voyage in 1857.

(www.slaveryimages.org/s/ slaveryimages/item/2740)

Kossola, or Cudjo Lewis, as he became known in the US, lived near Mobile until his death in 1935.

(Roche, Historic Sketches of the South)

Zuma was also among the last surviving shipmates. She was photographed by the local writer Emma Langdon Roche for Roche's 1914 book, *Historic Sketches of the South.* *(Roche, Historic Sketches of the South)*

The original Cochrane Bridge opened near Africatown in 1928, making the area a convenient hub for industrial companies that needed to ship materials across the Mobile River. *(Azalea City News Collection, The Doy Leale McCall Rare Book and Manuscript Library, University of South Alabama)*

Cudjo Lewis lived until 1935 in the home that he built himself. The house remained standing until the 1980s, when the state government had it torn down. *(Erik Overbey Collection, The Doy Leale McCall Rare Book and Manuscript Library, University of South Alabama)*

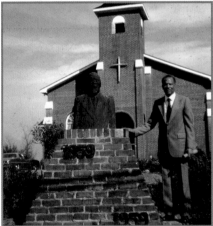

Henry Williams, a welder and folk historian, became known as the Father of Africatown. He may have coined the name for himself, but hardly anyone would dispute it. The bust of Cudjo Lewis at Union Missionary Baptist Church, seen next to him, was based on Williams's design and was installed in 1957. Williams's workshop (above) was a Magazine Point landmark. He built it by welding together oil drums that he'd bought for 10 cents each.
(William Tishler)

Scott Paper's compound, which bordered Africatown, was built on land that previously belonged to the Meaher family. Along with International Paper, it brought jobs but also emitted untold amounts of pollution over six decades.

(Scott Paper Company Collection, The Doy Leale McCall Rare Book and Manuscript Library, University of South Alabama)

After the original bust of Cudjo was stolen, the Mobile artist April Terra Livingston worked with Union Missionary Baptist Church to replace it with a new one. *(Mike Kittrell)*

Joe Womack, a retired Marine Corps major and unlikely environmental-justice advocate, in his element—at Hog Bayou, giving a tour.

(Nick Tabor)

Despite the presence of heavy industry, Africatown still has elements of breathtaking natural beauty. Three Mile Creek is pictured above. *(Mike Kittrell)*

The Old Plateau Cemetery, where many of the shipmates and their families are buried, fell into neglect for years, but has been largely restored since the early 2000s.
(Mike Kittrell)

After a sweeping survey of shipwrecks in Mobile Bay, archaeologists announced in 2019 that they had identified the remains of the *Clotilda* "beyond reasonable doubt." At left, archaeologist Alex DeCaro prepares to dive while archaeologist Kyle Lent stands by as his dive tender.

(SEARCH)

Bay Bridge Road was once the heart of Africatown—a pedestrian-friendly corridor filled with restaurants and shops. In the 1980s, numerous businesses there were destroyed, along with several homes built by *Clotilda* shipmates, to build a highway for "the transporting of hazardous chemicals." *(Mike Kittrell)*

Garry Lumbers, Cudjo Lewis's great-great-grandson, grew up in the house his ancestor built. Above, he poses beside Cudjo's gravestone.

(Garry Lumbers)

The descendants of Cudjo Lewis pose around the bust commemorating their ancestor, at a family reunion in 2021.

(K.C. Photography, Graphics, Printing LLC)

Joe Womack (left) and Anderson Flen (right) have been friends since fourth grade. Flen, a veteran public-health administrator, also helps to spearhead restoration efforts in Africatown.

(Meg Parker)

14

GOING BACK TO CHURCH

In 2000, three days before Christmas, a couple hundred International Paper workers huddled inside the fence line at their plant, behind the main gate. They had received the bad news weeks earlier: after years of downsizing, IP was shutting down the entire Mobile operation, putting the remaining 790 staffers out of work. They had been summoned on this freezing winter morning to pay their last respects. On the way in, they had driven past a sign that read THANKS FOR THE EFFORT.

To some of the workers, the timing seemed needlessly cruel. "It's a terrible thing for people to wake up on Christmas Day and not know where their next paycheck is coming from," a ten-year veteran named Angela Adams told a *Press-Register* reporter that week. "That's no way to treat people." It didn't help that when employees had tried to buy the mill, so they could run it themselves and keep their jobs, IP executives rejected the proposal out of hand. "They don't want anybody putting more of these products on the market," the union representative told the Associated Press. On the other hand, the closure didn't come as a complete surprise. IP had laid off thousands of people around the country in recent years, and Kimberly-Clark, which had purchased Scott Paper, had also closed its Mobile pulp mill in 1999, leaving only its tissue mill there.

At eleven A.M., Walter Brunson, the mill's manager, went in front of the crowd, wearing a black overcoat and scarf. "Reflect on your first day here," he suggested. "Remember who mentored and trained you, who helped you and who didn't. We all have some great memories that we can take with us as we leave here today and move on with our lives." With the audience shivering, Brunson kept his remarks short. There was a moment of silence, then a worker gave a benediction. At 11:15, the mill's American and Alabamian flags were lowered and presented to longtime staffers. Then the two hundred workers exchanged hugs and shuffled off, many knowing they'd never see one another again.

For Africatown, the legacy of the mills was mixed. The benefits they brought the community over the years should not be discounted. On a historical level, they were the biggest reason Plateau and Magazine Point had burgeoned as residential areas. If not for them, men like Joe Womack Sr. would not have moved there by the hundreds during the postwar era—and instead the neighborhood might have emptied out, as so many other historic Black towns did across the South. There is no telling how many Africatown residents bought their first homes and first cars and raised their big families with income from the factories.

On the other hand, the amount of pollution the mills had released over the years was enough to raise serious questions about the worthiness of the trade-off. A brief accounting of the emissions since the time Womack left for college helps round out this picture. In 1971, Mobile was roughly on par with Birmingham for having the dirtiest air in the state, and on at least thirteen days that year the air pollution was rated "critical" by the authorities. Some days the county health department warned everyone to stay inside to protect their lungs. There was no monitoring post in Africatown, but the nearest one, in Prichard, picked up more pollution than any other station in the county. In 1972, the state issued new regulations that were meant to cut the area's pollution in half. IP fought these rules, saying it couldn't afford the associated costs. The rules did take effect, and the IP and Scott plants were forced to make upgrades; but even so, in 1988, when the Environmental Protection Agency compiled a list of 205 plants nationwide whose air emissions seemed to pose elevated cancer risks, both IP and Scott were included.

The federal government started making a systematic accounting of emissions, called the Toxics Release Inventory, in 1988. During the first several years, IP and Scott both ranked among the country's top two hundred air polluters. In 1988, they released 964,000 pounds of chloroform and 1.8 million pounds of hydrochloric acid, both of which are known to cause cancer. TRI data released in 1992 also showed that Mobile County ranked first in the nation for the discharge of chemicals linked with birth defects. Its levels were twice those of Harris County, Texas, the second highest county on the list. Mobile also ranked first in the state for cancer-causing chemicals, and the Scott Paper plant beside Africatown was the top culprit.

The mills also continued polluting Africatown's waterways. In 1979, IP was penalized for illegally dumping waste into Chickasaw Creek sixteen times in a fourteen-month period. (The case was assigned to Brevard Hand, a far-right federal judge who had once hung a huge Confederate battle flag on his office wall. He fined the company just $47,750, less than a tenth of a percent of the plant's annual payroll.) And in 1990, the EPA tested the fish downriver from nine Alabama paper plants. They found the fish near Africatown had more dioxin than those anywhere else in Alabama. The state warned Alabamians to limit their consumption of fish caught near the plants, but this news never reached most Africatown residents. Again, no signs were ever posted along the creeks. "I don't remember hearing about none of that back then," Jesse Womack said.

By the time of the mill closures, the term for what Africatown was experiencing, environmental racism, had become widely recognized. The person responsible for popularizing this term was Robert Bullard, a sociology professor at Texas Southern University. The story, as Bullard tells it in his landmark 1990 book *Dumping in Dixie*, begins with his wife, an attorney. In 1979, she was representing the residents of a Black suburb in Houston who were trying to fight off a landfill. She asked Bullard to look at Houston's other landfills and see whether they were concentrated in Black areas. He found that they were—and that in every case, the place had been a residential area well before industrial facilities had come in. Bullard later expanded his research beyond Houston and found that the pattern held throughout the American South. In some cases, the polluters in question were dumps and landfills; in others they were incinerators, smelter operations, paper mills, or chemical plants. Bullard and others refer to the neighborhoods given over to this kind of pollution as "sacrifice zones."

Bullard's findings sync up neatly with Africatown's history. "These industries have generally followed the path of least resistance," he wrote in *Dumping in Dixie*, "which has been to locate in economically poor and politically powerless African American communities." Africatown residents accepted the mills' pollution for years without protesting, effectively gagged because they needed the jobs, which reflects a pattern that is repeated in many communities of color. As Bullard notes, Black workers tend to be overrepresented in low-wage, low-skilled occupations, where there's an abundance of people who could replace them. They often have little choice but to accept safety and environmental risks. Bullard has a term for this as well, which he has borrowed from other scholars: job blackmail. When communities overcome these barriers and achieve some measure of equitable treatment, it's known as environmental justice.

The mechanisms of environmental racism have been more or less the same all over the country, especially in the South. But Alabama's Jim Crow constitution, which still remains in effect, has played a distinct role in stripping Black residents of civic power. When the modern geography of Mobile was shaped, the state constitution denied Black residents any voice in local or state government. The constitution also prevented counties from making any decisions about land use, which meant there could be no zoning—no policy to block a massive factory from being built beside a neighborhood.

Making matters worse, the constitution cemented a tax system that deprives the state government of the funds it would need to take proper care of the environment. As of 1920, property taxes provided 63 percent of state revenue; but by 1978, that figure had been reduced to 3.6 percent, and by 1992, it was down to 2 percent, thanks mostly to the state constitution. That year, the next lowest state's property taxes were 30 percent higher than Alabama's, and the national average was 375 percent higher. The most direct beneficiaries of this tax system are families like the Meahers, who own vast tracts of Alabama land (roughly 22,000 acres). The cost is borne by other residents, who pay some of the highest sales taxes in the country—including on groceries. (It's been estimated that the poorest Alabamians pay more than 7 percent of their household income in sales taxes.) But the tax system is also one of the reasons the Alabama Department of Environmental Management (ADEM) receives only $10.85 per person each year—less funding per capita than any counterpart in any other state. The agency's budget in the 2015 fiscal year was about $55 million, compared to $141 million in Georgia, $259 million in Mississippi, $489 million in Texas, and $1.4 billion in Florida. ADEM, as a result, has a poor record of enforcing regulations. "I would characterize it as just terrible," said David Ludder, an attorney who once worked for the organization and now handles many environmental cases.

Ludder said another problem is that the constitution still prohibits local governments from imposing their own regulation, mandating that everything has to go through the state legislature in Montgomery instead. "The legislature is very favorable to the business community," he said, "and all legislation regarding environmental matters has to be passed by the state legislature." ADEM is more beholden to the legislature than it is to big business, "but it translates to the same thing." Other state agencies are crippled in similar ways. Several national surveys by nonpartisan professional groups, including the magazine *Governing*, have found Alabama's legislature to be the least effective in the nation. The surveys generally have not blamed the lawmakers themselves; instead they've located the problem in the size and quality of staffs, among other systemic issues. This deficiency has made legislators deeply dependent on lobbyists for data and information. As of 2001, there were 550 registered lobbyists in Montgomery, nearly four for every lawmaker. "The result," writes the Alabama historian Wayne Flynt, "was government of, by, and for special interests."

And what was the toll of all this pollution in Africatown? Did the elevated cancer risks translate to a cancer epidemic?

There's no way to say with scientific certainty. Given that the pollution started in the late 1920s, and that for decades, Africatown residents had limited access to medical care, early cancer cases would not have been diagnosed, let alone entered into any database. Moreover, in recent decades, a vast share of the population has moved away, and there's no way of tracking how many of those people have contracted the disease. To the extent that any cancer data exists, the state divulges only the number of cases per county; it does not release figures at the level of zip codes or census tracks.

However, many Africatown residents feel certain there is a cancer epidemic. Most everyone in the neighborhood can rattle off a list of family members who have been felled by cancer, many at young ages. Ruth Ballard and Washington Taylor, a sister and brother who grew up in Plateau, have each survived cancer twice. Their mother died of a brain tumor, and three of their siblings have also died with the disease. Another Africatown resident, Charlie Walker, said five of his family members died from it. "I had two sisters die from cancer, I had a brother, I had a dad and a mother," he said in 2018. "I got a brother with cancer now." He and his friends all feel like it could come for them at any time. "You go to the doctor, you get a clean bill of health. Three months later, you're dying of cancer." The list of cancer victims and survivors also includes many shipmate descendants, including Joycelyn Davis and Garry Lumbers, who both contracted the disease in middle age (and lived through it). And Womack's sister, Portland, died in 2004, at age forty-five, from a respiratory illness. She never smoked, and Womack has always wondered if her death was connected to the neighborhood pollution. Like so many other residents, he and his family members are now haunted by their memories of the paper-mill ash eating through their roofs and corroding their cars.

The closest attempt at a comprehensive survey was made by Reverend Christopher Williams, who became the pastor of Yorktown Baptist Church in 2006. His first week on the job was punctuated by a funeral, and by the end of his first year, he'd delivered about twenty eulogies. "I knew right away there was something strange about that—because it wasn't only elderly people who were passing away," he said. "Their ages were all over the place. Sixteen all the way up." The other two Plateau churches were experiencing it as well; some weeks there would be two or three funerals in the neighborhood. "Everybody I went to see had cancer," Williams recalled. One day he typed up a short survey and ran off hundreds of copies for distribution around Africatown. It asked about life-threatening illnesses that respondents and their loved ones had experienced. Williams knew this method was imperfect, but his resources were limited, and this was a start. When the forms came back, they seemed to validate his suspicions. Almost every sheet mentioned some form of cancer: most often breast cancer, but also cancer of the lungs, stomach, liver, prostate, and pancreas.

Unfortunately, reports of cancer clusters are exceedingly common, especially in the communities Bullard calls sacrifice zones, but the claims are almost never proven. A study released in 2014 showed that among 576 cancer clusters reported over a twenty-year period, only 72 could be confirmed, and only 3 could be linked to exposures to certain chemicals. There was only one case where the cause could be identified with certainty. Even with the most famous alleged cancer cluster, the one in Hinkley, California, which was depicted in the 2000 film *Erin Brockovich*, doubts still linger among epidemiologists about whether there was a true link between the pollution and the disease.

One possible explanation is that residents in places like Africatown are not exposed to toxic chemicals at a high enough rate to give them cancer. Eating fish from polluted creeks two or three times a week, for instance, is not on par with inhaling toxic chemicals constantly as a factory worker, and may not be enough to cause the disease. Besides, to the extent that those chemicals do contribute to cancer cases, they don't operate in isolation. Hereditary conditions, environmental factors, and lifestyle choices can all work in tandem. A person might smoke heavily, *and* live near a polluted site, *and* have a history of breast cancer in her family. In a situation like this, it's usually impossible to tease out how much pollutants alone were responsible.

Another theory, which is affirmed by the authors of the 2014 study, is that scientists don't have the tools to identify cancer clusters where they do exist.

The challenges of nailing down Africatown's cancer rate point to the deficiencies here. People's exposure levels to dangerous chemicals are almost never tracked closely; residents often move away from polluted areas; and cancer can take years to develop. By the time the disease shows up in a person's body, the cancer-causing agent may no longer be in the bloodstream. Carcinogens themselves can also disperse in the atmosphere, making it difficult and expensive (if not impossible) to trace them after the fact. "There are fundamental shortcomings to our current methods of investigating community cancer clusters," the authors concluded. They called for new research approaches that would reveal more about how and why cancer clusters form.

Reverend Williams, the Yorktown pastor, worked for several years to find a law firm that would sue IP for its history of pollution. In 2017, a suit was filed by Donald Stewart, a former U.S. senator who successfully sued the Monsanto Company for PCB dumping in Anniston, Alabama. There were 248 plaintiffs listed in the International Paper complaint. Stewart's firm had soil and water testing done by a local lab, and it found high levels of contaminants; but a second test, conducted by a lab Stewart had worked with before and trusted, found only background levels of contaminants—meaning they weren't higher than normal. But given that it had been roughly thirty years since the factory was operating at full capacity, this doesn't mean residents weren't harmed by IP's pollution in the past. It would take more extensive (and costly) testing to determine whether and at what level contaminants had made their way from the topsoil into local rivers and creeks. But instead, the case was settled in 2020, with plaintiffs receiving payouts on the basis that their property values had been degraded—not on the basis of a cancer link.

After losing the battle over the highway and the bridge, Henry Williams continued fighting for neighborhood improvements. One of his struggles was to arrange for ongoing maintenance of the remainder of the cemetery. It seems the new bridge was displacing stormwater, causing it to regularly flood the cemetery grounds; and this was causing the rapid growth of grass and wetland trees and shrubs. The city parks department calculated that maintenance would cost about $18,000 a year—a sum the leadership apparently thought was too high. In August 1997, E. Ashton Hill, an assistant city attorney, wrote to a colleague, saying Williams had recently called to ask for an update. "He sometimes lists a litany of 'historical' individuals who are buried on the grounds," Hill remarked. Williams had suggested the grass be cut every three months or so, but Hill thought this would not be cost-effective, seeing that the grass would grow high during the interim and would be hard to cut. "I tried to make it clear to Mr. Williams that the City was not inclined to undertake this project if it involved a continuing obligation," he wrote. "That did not suit Mr. Williams' needs." He wondered if the city could scrounge up some discretionary funds and help Williams find volunteers.

The result of failing to maintain the cemetery was that twelve years later, when the archaeologist Neil Norman came to do research in Africatown, the grounds were in worse shape than ever. Not only were many gravestones wrapped with grass and weeds, but in some cases, the roots of nearby trees had pushed around graves and headstones, sometimes as far as a foot. Many of the earliest burials were marked only by "slight depressions" in the ground, where coffins had collapsed. At some sites, coffins and vaults had been pushed to the surface, and the remains inside had been exposed to the elements; and at others, the headstones had sunk far beneath the ground. Some graves had also been vandalized—coffin lids opened, human remains removed. (Norman's group gave the cemetery the cleanup it needed, mowing the grass, clearing brush, thinning trees. The team also made a thorough examination and discovered roughly two hundred unmarked graves that had been overgrown.)

Also in 1997, efforts were renewed to make Africatown a tourism destination. Robert Battles, a community organizer in Mobile, planned several meetings in the neighborhood, where he invited Williams and other activists, along with local ministers and shipmate descendants. Jack Friend, who also attended, thought the Alabama Historical Commission could help find money for an Africatown park. In the end, these efforts produced a makeshift Africatown welcome center, near the cemetery, consisting of two trailers. (These would be battered in Hurricane Katrina and rendered unusable.) All the while, the AfricaTown Folk Festivals continued, but a *Press-Register* reporter said the 1997 festival resembled "an afternoon tea more than a major cultural affair."

Williams received some validation when historian Sylviane Diouf's book, *Dreams of Africa in Alabama*, came out in 2007. It was the first scholarly treatment of the *Clotilda* and Africatown ever published. Diouf's thorough research dispelled any notion that the story was only a myth. "Far from being a hoax," she wrote, "the last slave voyage to the United States—and the lives of the people on board—is probably the best-documented story of the American slave trade." Her book also revealed a great deal about the shipmates that had not been previously known. Diouf cited Williams as a source on the oral traditions of Africatown. The following year, the historian Natalie Robertson published her book *The Slave Ship* Clotilda *and the Making of AfricaTown, USA*, which was based on her 1996 dissertation. Also in 2008, Union Baptist was incorporated into Mobile's African-American Heritage Trail. Diouf, whose book on the shipmates had won an award from the American Historical Association, was there to unveil the plaque.

Henry Williams died in September 2008. He was eighty-eight and had been fighting cancer. By then he was living in Chastang, in far northern Mobile County. Surviving him were a brother, his daughter, and his son, who went by the name C. Charles Porter remembers C. being upset about the funeral turnout. "The upper-echelon community leaders—they were not there," Porter said. "I know he felt that Henry deserved better than just the people who showed up." Porter wanted C. to appreciate that many of the mourners had been his father's stalwart supporters. But he also reminded him that Williams's personality had been divisive. "He would put thorns in your pocket."

The year of Williams's death was also the year that would mark Joe Womack's reengagement with Africatown. Since Womack had moved away several decades earlier, his involvement with the neighborhood had been uneven. In 1977, he had married a woman he met through his former teacher, Valena McCants. They raised a son together and bought a house in the suburbs of West Mobile. Between his salary from Shell and his income from the Marine Corps Reserve, Womack was making the kind of money in those years that his parents had only been able to daydream about.

At the time, he felt a pull to go back to his old church, Yorktown Baptist, and to get more involved with the community. In fact he had what he considers a vision, circa 1980, while he was in bed one night. He saw something like an orb—a radiating mass—coming down the hallway toward him. Looking back, it reminds him of the biblical episode where Moses encountered God in a burning bush. He heard an audible voice say, "Go back to church."

At the time, he resisted. He took this as an order to become a preacher, which didn't suit him. "I told him, 'Look, I'll go back to church, but not now, man. I've got this new wife and new kid. I'll get back to you.'" The glowing mass disappeared. The episode was repeated roughly five years later, and the message was the same: "Go back to church." Again his immediate reaction was to dismiss it. But he heard the voice say, "If I have to come back a third time and get you, you ain't going to like it." This time the voice was so clear, the experience so vivid, that he got out of bed and checked the hallway to make sure there wasn't another person in his home.

The experience did happen a third time. Not long afterward, his wife told him she wanted a divorce. They separated, and she took their son with her. Meanwhile, he began having troubles at work. The Shell plant where he worked was bought out by DuPont in 1986. Womack didn't get along well with his new bosses, and he wound up quitting. He also experienced some heart troubles. "Everything that I put in the way was taken out of the way over time," he said. "My family, my wife, my job, even my good health."

He ultimately received full custody of his son. The two of them began attending Yorktown Baptist, and Womack joined the choir. His son sometimes fell asleep beside him in the pew. "I believe you can read into something more than it is," Womack said in an interview. "It didn't say, 'Go back to church and preach,' or 'Go back to church and take over.' It said simply, 'Go back to church.'" In this period, he also got involved with Henry Williams and the other activists, joining them for meetings and protests. He saw a different side of his old Sunday-school teacher, and it made a searing impression. Womack's political sensibilities were defined more by these encounters than by any other experience in his life. "Henry Williams said, 'As long as this land is here, and it's available, there will always be a struggle,'" he recalled. "You just can't back down, and you can't be weak. You always have to have a sort of loud voice. You just never back up. And you always have to know that it is never over. It is never over."

Womack scaled back his neighborhood involvement again in the 1990s, when he started working as a truck driver. For the most part, he enjoyed life on the road; the long hours didn't faze him. But he was often away on the weekends. He still visited his mother in Plateau regularly, but his routine of attending church and civic meetings was no longer workable.

His career came to an end in 2007. At an annual checkup, required by his employer, the doctor detected some blockage in his arteries. He was sent to the hospital for stents, but he ended up getting a quadruple bypass. "Have y'all had many drivers have heart bypasses?" he asked his bosses afterward.

"Not many, but we have had some."

"What was their experience when they came back to work?"

"Well, none of 'em ever came back to work."

The management suggested he apply for disability insurance benefits.

When those payments ran out, he applied through the Social Security Administration—"and I got it, just like that." He also had retirement income from the Marine Corps Reserve (from which he'd been discharged with the rank of major) and from DuPont. "So that was it, man. I was done working." He was only fifty-nine.

Retirement allowed Womack to spend more time in Africatown. By this time, the neighborhood was fairly debilitated. No Man's Land, the area where Anderson Flen had grown up, which the Meahers had leased to Scott Paper, was now the Kimberly-Clark distribution center. Gulf Lumber, the factory beside Lewis Quarters, was a behemoth, hedging the little neighborhood in. Seven or so houses remained there, but the only way to get in or out was through the lumber company's property. Africatown's population had dwindled, and there were dozens of abandoned houses and vacant lots. Hardly anyone walked around these days, if only because there were no stores, restaurants, laundromats, or beauty parlors left to walk to. At the same time, the factory presence was continuing to grow. Among the newcomers were a metal fabricator, a truckload carrier, several chemical companies (at least one of which was on Meaher property), and an asphalt plant.

In early 2008, Womack's mother received a letter about Boyd Bros. Transportation, a Birmingham company, wanting to build a trucking depot in Africatown. If the depot were approved, it would be a breach of what she and her neighbors had long regarded as the tacit compromise: that heavy industry would stay on the north side of Paper Mill Road, so the highway and the railroad tracks could provide at least a thin buffer. The company was asking to have a tract of residential land, south of the buffer, rezoned. The proposed site was only six hundred yards from her house. She called her younger son, thinking his experience as a trucker might be valuable. "I need you to go out there and find out what's going on," she told him. "Don't let them take my property."

As Womack considered the next steps, he immediately thought of military exercises. "In my mind, my mother's house was the headquarters," he explained. "So in order to keep it safe, I got to keep the neighbors safe, I got to keep people a mile away safe, I got to keep everybody safe. I got to establish a demilitarized zone around the headquarters so their long-range weapons can't get in." The community, according to this strategy, could "not give up an inch."

That February, William Carroll, the city councilman representing Africa-town, called a meeting at a church in Magazine Point. Some residents came with complaints about police response times, others about abandoned houses and overgrown weeds (which were so high on some lots that children had to stand in the street while they waited for school buses, so the drivers could see them). Carroll, who was a contractor by trade, told everyone the city was doing what it could, but he explained that some lots were so overgrown, they had legally reverted to their "state of nature," meaning they were exempt from regulations. "All we can do is continue to request that they do something to their property," he said.

The residents also presented Carroll with a petition bearing two hundred signatures, saying they didn't want the trucking depot in their neighborhood. Womack thought Carroll seemed annoyed when the subject came up. "This could mean jobs! Jobs for y'all!" he remembers the councilman saying. Womack turned to his brother. "The only jobs they could give them, if they didn't have a commercial driver's license, would be washing trucks or cleaning up the buildings." This meeting harked back to the ones he'd attended twenty years earlier, but the difference was an absence of grassroots leadership. Everyone he had once looked up to—not only Henry Williams, but also Nelson Ad-ams, Edley Hubbard, John Randolph, and Womack's grandfather, among others—was gone. The only crusader from the older generation still left was Arealia Craig, who was still fiery at age seventy-nine. When Craig had an opportunity, she stood up and denounced the proposed depot. "We had to smell the paper mills," she said. "We're going to get the dust from the people making the pipes" (she was referring to a new pipe fabricator occupying the old IP land), "and we're not going to be able to sleep if a trucking company goes there."

Womack also spoke up. "I just retired from the trucking business," he said. "I know how a trucking company brings a lot of things the community has to put up with, and one of them is diesel, the other one is noise. And you'll get some trucking person coming in there late at night, and he'll get lost and go throughout the community and tear up the streets. This is gonna happen more than once." He predicted the depot would also attract drugs and prosti-tution, which he had seen at countless truck stops during his travels.

When he was finished, he heard people around him whispering: *Who is that? Who is that?* and *That's Jesse's brother.*

Before the meeting was over, Carroll said he would make sure the resi-dents had a chance to express their concerns to company representatives. And two weeks later, after another town hall meeting, where company representatives answered questions from the residents, they agreed to withdraw the application, saying they wouldn't set up shop where they were not wanted. For Womack, the experience was pivotal. No longer could he take comfort in thinking someone else was advocating for his old neighborhood. He now felt the weight of responsibility himself.

PART IV

FROM THE BRINK: 2012–2022

15

ONE MOBILE

At the end of 2012, four years after Henry Williams's death, one of the welder's great ambitions was borne out: Africatown was added to the National Register of Historic Places. The federal government acknowledged at long last that the place was "worthy of preservation" and had "significance" in American history and culture. It was the 135th site in Mobile County to make the register. In the three and a half decades since Williams and Smith had begun working on the first application, 102 others had been added before Africatown.

Africatown's inclusion was part of a broader project to recognize Mobile's Black history. The city's first Black mayor, Sam Jones, was elected in 2005, and he appointed a Black president to the Mobile Historic Development Commission. Commission staffers, whose backgrounds were mostly in architectural history, were unsure at first whether Africatown would qualify for the NRHP, given that so few of the neighborhood's early buildings survived. But they learned it could be nominated based on its archaeological treasures, including the cemetery and the sites where the shipmates' houses had once stood. In 2007, two archaeologists visited from the NRHP office in Washington, D.C., and commission staff took them around the neighborhood. "We got in a van, and we started driving," said Devereaux Bemis, who was director of the commission at the time. "They were going, 'Oh, this! This! This!' We're going, 'Really?' We were looking at 1940s houses, and they were talking about archaeology and the stories the landscape tells." Later the city received a federal grant to do research for the nomination.

In the spring of 2012, Bemis called a meeting to inform Africatown residents about the process. Some people, Womack included, were disappointed to learn that only Plateau and Magazine Point would be nominated, and that Happy Hill, Hog Bayou, and Lewis Quarters would be left out. Those areas still had vacant land, and Womack suspected industrial developers had their eyes on it. It sounded to him like a deal had been brokered by the local power elites. The parts of Africatown that belonged to the Meahers, for instance—which amounted to 15.2 percent of Plateau and 11.8 percent of Magazine Point, as of 2020—were being skirted in the nomination. Bemis, however, said in an interview that it was strictly a question of which sites met the requirements, something the city had worked out with the state and federal governments. "To be on the National Register, there's got to be something there," he said. "You can't say, 'These are the woods that my ancestors hunted in,' when it's just woods, and there's nothing there"—no artifacts to be unearthed. "That was the problem we had." Lewis Quarters does have archaeological resources, but it was considered a distinct community by city workers. They noted that there is a sign at the entrance of Lewis Quarters, identifying it by its own name (with no mention of Africatown) and stating its founding date (1870).

Perhaps because of their conservative approach, the application sailed through with no trouble. The city sent it to the Alabama Historical Commission in September 2012, and it was forwarded to Washington, D.C. with the state's recommendation. Africatown was officially added to the NRHP that December. Bemis reasoned that the boundaries could always be expanded in the future. Womack was happy as well; he took comfort in thinking that at least the historic heart of the neighborhood would now be protected. But he didn't realize that when a site becomes part of the program, the federal government doesn't impose new restrictions on what can be done with it. From a legal standpoint, all options remain open, according to the government's literature—"up to and including destruction."

A radically different set of plans, meanwhile, was being drawn up for the area surrounding Africatown. The oil market was experiencing a boom of historic scale. As of 2012, crude was selling for around $97 a barrel, up from an average of $31 in the 1990s. Countries around the world were recovering from the 2008 financial crisis, and they all wanted more petroleum. Energy companies, in turn, were scrambling to increase their output.

One of the world's largest oil reserves is in Alberta, the Canadian province known as the Texas of the North. Starting five hundred miles north of the Montana border, there are sedimentary deposits that span a landmass larger than the state of New York. They consist of tar sands, a sludgy mixture of sand, clay, water, and bitumen, in some parts going as deep as half a mile underground. When the bitumen is separated out, with the aid of heat and chemicals, it can be refined into crude and used for gasoline and other petroleum products. All told, Alberta has more than 170 billion barrels of oil waiting to be harvested. The only catch, for the industry, is how much the harvesting process costs with tar sands, in some cases upward of $50 a barrel. It doesn't make good business sense unless the price of oil is extremely high.

In 2011 and 2012, it made sense, so oil companies were shipping all the tar sands they could to refineries along the Gulf Coast. A top priority was the building of the Keystone pipeline. Proposed in 2005, it was designed to run from Alberta to Saskatchewan, then south through Montana and the Great Plains, ultimately reaching Houston. Once it was finished, industry leaders announced, it would have the capacity to deliver nearly 35 million gallons of oil to Texas each day.

But the pipeline promised to be disastrous for the environment. By 2011, many scientists were convinced that for climate change to be significantly slowed down, fossil fuels had to be phased out altogether. Introducing tar sands on a large scale, the Columbia climatologist Jim Hansen warned, would be "essentially game over." In the summer of 2011, environmentalists declared war on the Keystone proposal. There were mass demonstrations against the pipeline in Washington, D.C. that August, lasting four weeks and leading to some 1,250 arrests. Resistance also took hold at the local level, in communities that found themselves along the Keystone's 1,200-mile path. For these residents, it was often less about the big-picture threat of climate change and more about fears of having their towns flooded with oil. Their concerns were well founded. Between 2010 and 2012, pipelines in the Upper Midwest, the area where the greatest volumes of tar sands had been moved during the longest time period, spilled 3.6 times more crude per mile than the national average. And in 2010, a tar sands pipeline broke open in southern Michigan, pouring some 843,000 gallons of bitumen into the Kalamazoo River.

Following the demonstrations in 2011, the Republican governor of Nebraska asked Obama's administration to shift the Keystone pipeline so it would avoid a critical source of the state's drinking water. That November, the Obama administration agreed to rethink the route, which meant delaying the project indefinitely.

As the oil industry waited for a decision, its leaders came up with an alternative plan: shipping the tar sands on railcars instead. By March of 2013, Canada's railways were handling 150,000 barrels of oil a day, up from 70,000 in 2012, and were on track to reach 300,000 by the year's end. "Oil will get to market," Canada's U.S. ambassador told *The Washington Post.* "This is clear." This was where Mobile came in. The Canadian National Railway's transcontinental line, which runs through Detroit and St. Louis and Memphis, terminates near the Mobile River, only two miles from Africatown.

From the industry's perspective, Mobile was an ideal place to stockpile oil. Freight railways connect the city to Birmingham, Pensacola, and New Orleans. A massive Chevron oil refinery, one of the largest in the country, is only forty miles away, on the Mississippi coast. Because Mobile sits on the water, barges can easily move oil in and out, whether to import it from Mexico, carry it to Texas or Louisiana for refining, or export it to international markets. And industrial regulations in Mobile are about as loose as they get anywhere. As of 2013, oil storage tanks were already abundant in Mobile County. Driving across the Cochrane-Africatown bridge, it was easy to spot them—gray cylinders, some of them several hundred feet wide and sixty or seventy feet tall, arrayed in rows near the waterfront.

In late 2012, two companies announced plans to build tank farms in the city, where they would store tar sands on their way to refineries. The tar sands would have to pass near Africatown several times, first on railcars and then on trucks, to reach their final destination. They said the added capacity would let them ship 75,000 barrels of oil into Mobile every day.

There were also plans to start harvesting tar sands within Alabama. The Hartselle Sandstone formation, which spans a large share of northern Alabama and Mississippi, is the third largest tar sands deposit in the United States. Since roughly 2010, a shell company called MS Industries had been buying up rural property that sat on top of the formation. It had workers stationed in a mobile home outside a vacant gas station, in the town of Wolf Springs, three hundred miles north of Mobile, where they were drilling hundreds of holes, looking for the best spots to begin strip-mining. The governors of Mississippi and Alabama, both eager to develop the mining industries in their states, were openly supportive of strip-mining projects. It seemed there was a good chance that once the harvesting began in earnest, the oil would go through Mobile en route to a refinery.

Joe Womack first heard about these oil developments from a seventy-two-year-old local activist named David Underhill. Underhill was the conservation chair for the Alabama branch of the Sierra Club, one of America's largest environmentalist groups. He was white, but he had a keen interest in civil rights and Black history. He had first come to Mobile in the sixties, after graduating from Harvard, to run the local bureau of *The Southern Courier*, a combative civil rights newspaper. He had settled in Mobile permanently and devoted most of his life to environmental activism.

Underhill was also concerned about another oil development. A Houston-based company called Plains All American was planning to build a pipeline from a tank farm it already operated, near Prichard, to the Chevron refinery on the Mississippi coast. The pipe would be forty-five miles long and two feet in diameter, wide enough for 6 million gallons of oil to pass through every day. It was set to be installed close to Big Creek Lake, the sole source of Mobile's drinking water, eight miles outside the city limits. It would run beneath a creek that branched off from the lake—raising concerns that if it ever ruptured, the water supply could immediately be poisoned.

Plains's safety record did not inspire confidence. Between 2004 and 2007, according to the federal government, the company was responsible for ten spills in four states, with a total discharge of 273,000 gallons of oil. In 2012, a Plains pipe spilled 122,000 gallons into an Alberta river; and in February 2013, the company was responsible for at least 12,000 gallons of crude spilling into a creek in Mississippi. Granted, most or all of these spills involved aging pipelines that Plains had bought from other companies; but they were still vivid illustrations of the worst-case scenario for Mobile County. Plains itself, in documents filed with the federal government, predicted that it would have more "releases of hydrocarbon products into the environment" in the future, and said its existing assets along Gulf Coast were "particularly vulnerable to hurricane or tropical storm risk."

Plains said it planned to use its new pipeline only for light crude, not for tar sands oil. It insisted it had no connection to the corporations building the new oil tanks. But Underhill, who died in 2019, felt certain the projects were connected. He believed Plains intended to channel tar sands oil from the new tanks to Mississippi. The theory seemed plausible on its face. Plains already did a big business in tar sands transporting. Under the company's arrangements with Alabama's government, there were no restrictions on what could go through the new pipeline, nor was Plains required to notify anyone if it switched out the products. There was no evidence that the Chevron refinery had the capacity to handle tar sands, but in recent years, Chevron had sought to expand other refineries and add this capacity, and there seemed to be no reason the Pascagoula site couldn't be upgraded as well.

No connection was ever proven. One person who insists Underhill was mistaken is Casi Callaway, who was the director at the time of the organization Mobile Baykeeper. In that capacity, she was an advocate for environmentally responsible policies, but unlike Underhill, she often took an insider tack, cultivating relationships with political and business leaders. (She later took a job with the city government.) Callaway said in an interview that some of the companies involved showed her enough about their plans that it became clear the projects were unrelated; they involved different technology and different personnel. She understands why Underhill was suspicious. "We certainly researched it," she said. "Like, 'How many of these things can we have at one time? What's going on?' But the 'going on' was $100 a barrel."

Setting these questions aside, what mattered most was that Underhill's theory linked the concerns of Africatown to those of other Mobilians. On its own, the small Black community had no chance of stopping the tank farms. This was not like the trucking company's proposal in 2008; this time Africatown was up against the global oil industry. The corporations involved had endless money to spend on litigation and political influence, and they were settled on Mobile—no other Alabamian city would do. For once, however, Africatown was not on its own. The rest of the city had a material interest in helping.

Early one evening in July 2013, Womack drove out across Interstate 10, swooping through the south side of Mobile and taking one of the twin bridges across the river. He passed the petrochemical plants near the coast and the half-dozen seafood shacks perched along the water. He was headed to a meeting of the Sierra Club, where Underhill was going to present his findings to a wider audience. He'd suggested Womack speak on Africatown's behalf. Several elected officials would also be there.

The meeting was at a state facility near the Meaher State Park. The sun was shining through floor-to-ceiling windows when Womack entered the lodge. The place was packed; all told, some two or three hundred people were in attendance, the demographics skewing gray-haired and white. Soon a trim, bespectacled man approached the microphone up front. He introduced himself as Tom Hutchings, an environmental consultant who was working with the Sierra Club. When he had learned about the oil developments from Underhill, he said, he'd been "absolutely dumbfounded—and mad." "This had been going on for a year and a half," he said, "and how come the public did not know?" He made it clear where his main concerns lay: "Our drinking water supply," he said, "is something that's very, very personal to all us. I mean, air quality, water quality—we're all for that. But when it comes down to our drinking water"—he held up a water glass—"it becomes very, very personal."

For Africatown, of course, it had always been personal. Now everyone else in the room was getting a sample of how Womack felt.

Sam Jones, Mobile's mayor, also spoke up. He reiterated the importance of protecting the water supply. The state had bypassed the local government in approving the pipeline, he said, but there was still time for state representatives to demand it be routed away from the watershed.

Underhill was in his element that night. He came to the mic with a sheaf of papers in hand. The sky behind him was a deep shade of blue, getting deeper. He was concerned, he said, that amid all the talk about the pipeline, the group was forgetting about the tank farms, which were set to be installed only a couple feet above sea level. "Imagine a hurricane storm surge twenty-five to thirty feet high—that's what happened with Katrina—coming up the bay and up the river, to these tank farms." Also looming in Mobilians' memories was BP's Deepwater Horizon spill, in 2010, which occurred only about 140 miles from where they were sitting that night. It had resulted in 200 million gallons of oil being leaked—a fraction of the amount already stored on Mobile's waterfront.

But Womack was haunted by a different disaster. In 1988, while he'd been working for DuPont, a Shell plant in Louisiana had exploded, killing seven workers and blasting debris for a five-mile radius. Nearly fifty people who lived nearby were injured. There had been stories about the plant burning for eight hours and thousands of people being forced to evacuate their homes in the middle of the night.

When Womack took his turn at the microphone, it was getting late. His aim was simply to remind everyone that his old neighborhood existed and was already bearing the brunt of their city's pollution. "We grew up in Africatown with two paper mills, International and Scott Paper." He described the pollution that he'd seen every day growing up and the apparent cancer epidemic that was now ravaging the community. "We're still burying most of our people between the age of forty and fifty," he said, not mentioning that his sister had been among the casualties. "We don't want this hazardous stuff around Mobile. We want it stopped."

All evening, a young man had been standing near the front with a serious expression. He wore his dark hair in a long braid, and his faded green tanktop was almost threadbare at the shoulders. Near the end of the night, he introduced himself to the crowd.

"My name is Ramsey Sprague," he said, adjusting the microphone. "I came here from Texas. I've been part of the tar sands blockade—the Keystone XL blockade in Texas." The crowd erupted in applause when he said this. He explained that his own ethnic group, Native Americans, were suffering "slow industrial genocide" because of tar sands oil. He felt a connection to the poor Black communities at risk in Mobile County. "I'm here to help," he said. "We want to stand up for Prichard; we want to stand up for Africatown; we want to stand up for Eight Mile; we want to stand up for these long-term communities that are suffering." They were experiencing environmental racism, he said, and it was critical to recognize it that way. He warned the group not to depend too much on elected officials, because even if they meant well, there would be limitations on what they could do. But that was no reason to give up hope. "The fact that there are so many people here is a powerful statement to these companies," he said. "For what it's worth, we're going to shut them down."

For Womack and many others, the meeting was invigorating. They understood they were up against extraordinarily powerful interests. But seeing all the people who had turned out, from all across coastal Alabama, and seeing the range of skills and knowledge represented by everyone who had taken to the microphone—and knowing they had some support from elected leaders—they felt it was possible that Sprague's prediction would be borne out.

Later that week, it became clearer exactly how the public had been bypassed in the permitting process. County commissioners admitted that they'd known about the pipeline since March. They had approved Plains's application, not realizing the pipe would run so close to the lake.

The commissioners blamed the Alabama Public Service Commission (PSC). And not without reason. Most every state government has a public service commission, or something like it, that is tasked with regulating electricity, gas, and water utilities. But in most states, the members are appointed by the governor. In Alabama's case, they're elected by the public—which means they depend on campaign donations to stay in office. This opens up a way for corporations to try to curry their favor.

In the case of Plains's application in Mobile, the PSC had only one responsibility, said David Rountree, its spokesman: to decide whether the pipeline would "further industrial development." The agency was interpreting this criterion in a narrow way; it didn't assess how the project might affect Mobile's industrial economy overall, weighing the benefits against potential costs. This seems to explain its reasoning in keeping the public out. If residents don't want a pipeline running through their water supply, that has nothing to do with whether or not the pipeline "furthers industrial development" in the most limited sense. In response to the uproar in 2013, the PSC said that if Mobilians felt like their democratic process was being thwarted, their local officials were the ones at fault.

The only agency that had not greenlit the pipeline was the water utility, MAWSS (Mobile Area Water and Sewer System). In 2012, when Plains had asked for permission to start construction through the watershed, the MAWSS board had denied the request. In July 2013, it was waiting on a third-party study on whether the pipeline would be safe. The day after the big Sierra Club meeting, MAWSS officials and county commissioners met with Plains representatives and expressed concerns about the pipeline's route. The company would not change its plans.

Mobilians wasted no time getting organized. A core group started meeting regularly; its ranks included Womack, Underhill, Carol Adams-Davis (one of the leaders of the local Sierra Club chapter), and Thayer Dodd, a horticulturalist. Their aim, in the short term, was to keep the broader public engaged. At the end of July, they recruited about twenty people to picket a MAWSS meeting while Plains representatives walked in. The following day they protested outside a city council meeting. WAKE UP, MOBILE, one protester's sign read; ONE SPILL WOULD KILL OUR WATER, read another. But in a city where politics are so often racially segregated, the diversity of their group spoke louder than the placards. "See, that was something that Mobile had never seen before," Womack recalls. "When we went down to those city council meetings, white and Black, those folks were surprised. You could see it in their eyes."

White members of the coalition, for their part, remember it as a time of genuine education. Before that point, the only association they had with Africatown was the Cochrane-Africatown Bridge. Most of them had not realized it was a living, functioning neighborhood. When Thayer Dodd started going there regularly, she sometimes heard acquaintances disparage the place. "Most people were like, 'What's Africatown?' and 'Why is Africatown any different from Prichard? Prichard's full of crime.'" They questioned whether it was safe for Dodd to attend meetings there. But for her and others who were intimately involved with the pipeline fight, the neighborhood's interests were becoming a bigger priority. "I think once we figured out what Africatown was, and how it fit in the big picture, and who the people were, and how they'd been treated, we all wanted to fight for Africatown."

They were also becoming aware of how big an invisible footprint heavy industry already had in their city. As they did more research and as the proceedings went on, they found out there were already at least nine oil pipelines running beneath the Mobile River, funneling the product into tanks on Blakeley Island. There were also two Plains pipelines near the Big Creek Lake area, which had been in place since before the lake was created (as a public works project, in 1952). And there were more than a hundred tanks on or near the waterfront, with a combined capacity of more than one billion gallons—five times the amount spilled in the BP incident.

A safety report commissioned by the water utility came out in August 2013. Out of the 111 pages of dense engineers' language, a catalog of horror scenarios emerged. A pipeline rupture, the report said, could be caused by external or internal corrosion, third-party damage, construction-related issues, manufacturing-related issues, incorrect operation, or weather events, among other phenomena. Erosion in the creek could cause "scour damage" and "possible catastrophic failure." A nearby car accident or the toppling of a power line or a derailment on the train tracks running overhead could break the pipe open. In any of those situations, oil could surge into the creek until the flow was shut off; and after that, as much as 2,100 barrels more could come gurgling out. The authors were clear: "The only option that would remove all of the risks," they said, "would be to completely relocate the pipeline route out of the watershed."

Plains was having an easier time going directly to individual homeowners, getting clearance to use their front and back yards, which avoided the hassle of dealing with the local governments and commissions. For those homeowners who wouldn't be bought out, the company went through condemnation proceedings. Out of roughly 115 properties the pipeline would traverse in Mobile County, by August the company had rights to build on 95 of them, and construction was already 70 percent finished.

As for the oil tanks, the scope of what was being proposed kept growing. In early August, a local company called American Tank and Vessel announced plans to build a tank farm at the old International Paper site, starting within a few hundred feet of Africatown's residential zone. Each tank would be sixty-four feet tall, the size of a small building, and altogether they'd have a capacity of 100 million gallons. The company's CEO refused to say at first whether they would hold light crude oil or tar sands. The plans also included ten new railroad tracks, an administrative building, a pipeline station, and other infrastructure. It was unclear who was really behind this project, but Underhill and the others suspected it was Plains. American Tank and Vessel was only in the business of building tanks for other companies—it didn't operate tank farms itself. The CEO of American Tank and Vessel would reveal only that he was working with unnamed business partners in Houston—the city where Plains, along with the rest of the petroleum industry, was headquartered.

The more time Joe Womack spent at meetings and protests, the more he was hearing the term *environmental justice*. *What the hell is environmental justice?* he remembers thinking. One day he looked it up on the internet—he had just gotten his first computer—and he was stunned at what he found. "It said, you know, 'You can't keep beating down the same communities.' I said, 'This is us! They were writing this thing for us!'"

By the end of the summer, this battle had become almost an obsession for some of the pipeline opponents. They were getting a deep education—both in civic engagement and in the workings of the oil industry. Members of the group would do extensive research, poring over company reports and public records, and share their findings, whether in presentations or emails. Despite the recent setbacks, the mood was no less hopeful than it had been that spring. At the same time, their work was starting to produce small victories. For instance, Mayor Sam Jones's administration came out against the tank farm at the International Paper site; and before the application came up for a planning commission vote, the company backed out on its own.

Jones, who had aligned himself with the protesters throughout the summer, was up for reelection on August 27. The Black Democrat was seeking a third term. His challenger was Sandy Stimpson, a sixty-one-year-old white Republican. Stimpson was an heir of Gulf Lumber, one of Mobile's most successful family businesses. Stimpson had never held public office, but his other civic roles reflected his place in Mobile society: he had served on the boards of a local bank, a finance company, and the elite private school he once attended, and had chaired the local chamber of commerce in 2009. (He was also a leader in the development of Prichard Preparatory School, a private preschool and elementary school where students' tuition is supplemented by donations.)

Mobile has a coterie of wealthy white families, including the Meahers, who can trace their local lineage back to the nineteenth century. Residents refer to them as "Old Mobile" (as in, "She's Old Mobile"). City streets bear their last names, and their influence in the local economy and government runs deep. They're said to form the membership of the oldest, most prestigious Mardi Gras societies (though the membership lists are kept secret). Within this rarefied world, there are those who regard the Stimpsons as nouveau riche. The family's history in Mobile extends back to 1868, when Sandy Stimpson's great-grandfather, James Herbert Stimpson, moved to the area from Massachusetts, taking advantage of the fractured southern economy to buy a plantation for the equivalent of $44 an acre. During the 2013 mayoral race, Joe Meaher surprised friends by saying he planned to vote for Sam Jones. "Well, I'm not gonna vote for a carpetbagger," he told them. But to most voters, Stimpson was Old Mobile incarnate.

Stimpson raised about $1.5 million that summer, smashing Mobile's previous records. He outspent Jones's campaign by a ratio of more than three to one. Come election day, he won by a comfortable margin, taking 53 percent of the vote to Jones's 47. Racial tensions had been evident throughout the race, and both candidates had run on slogans that were clearly meant to downplay it. Jones's mantra was "Too busy to be divided" (an echo of Atlanta's civil rights era slogan, "Too busy to hate"), and Stimpson's was "One Mobile." But exit polls showed that neither candidate had met with much success across the color line. White voters "went emphatically" for Stimpson, the *Press-Register* noted, but his support among Black voters was in single digits. Given that Black voters in Mobile marginally outnumbered whites, it was clear that Jones had lost largely because of low turnout among his base.

Up to that point, Stimpson had been vague about where he stood on the oil developments. He said in a summer debate that he wanted to "reserve judgment." His résumé gave clues, however, about where he might come down. He had close ties with the veteran politician Jeff Sessions, a longtime foe of environmentalists. In Sessions's first campaign for U.S. Senate, Stimpson had chaired his operation in Mobile, and in later races he'd been the senator's state finance chair. Stimpson had also chaired the board of a right-wing think tank, the Alabama Policy Institute, which routinely opposes environmental regulations. More to the point, Gulf Lumber, his family's business, was the one situated practically on top of Lewis Quarters, the oldest part of Africatown. It was hard to imagine him seeing industrial encroachment on Africatown as a pressing issue. As one of his political allies told a reporter that summer, "He just approaches things with a CEO's mindset."

* * *

In September, activist Ramsey Sprague came back to Mobile. He and his friends from Texas had agreed to give a workshop on the tactics they'd used to block the Keystone pipeline. "We don't shy away from controversy," he remembers telling the Mobilians. "They said, 'Bring it.'" So on a Saturday and Sunday, about three dozen residents, including a number from Africatown, gathered at the MCTS auxiliary building to learn how to get arrested.

Sprague is a Louisiana native, but he grew up with his grandparents near Fort Worth. While he was in high school, his love for punk and industrial music led him into left politics, and he embraced protesting at the same time that he was taking an interest in performance art. His focus on environmentalism developed gradually. One factor was his Native American heritage. His ancestors are the Chitimachas who inhabited the Mississippi River Delta for thousands of years before Europeans arrived. Another factor was his experiences in Texas. When he was younger, the air around Fort Worth would become so thick with smog every summer, thanks mostly to emissions from cement plants, that sometimes the authorities warned everyone to stay inside.

Sprague became more serious about activism throughout his twenties. By the time demonstrations started up against the Keystone pipeline, he was ready for a leadership role in Texas. He was arrested at a pipeline conference in early 2013, after he chained himself to the audio equipment, interrupting an executive's speech. Shortly before he came to Mobile, Sprague spent time training Indigenous groups in South Dakota. He and David Underhill were acquainted, and it was Underhill who'd first invited him to Mobile in the summer.

In the training session that September, Sprague and his friends demonstrated different kinds of blockades: linking arms, going limp, sitting down. "He said, 'Do not hit back,'" even if they were beaten or spit on, recalled Ruth Ballard, an Africatown native in her eighties. They discussed the philosophy of civil disobedience and did team-building exercises. By the end, some of them were feeling charged up. Womack, Underhill, Ballard, and several others, mostly from Africatown, met with Sprague after the event and agreed to formalize their little group. They settled on the name MEJAC, for Mobile Environmental Justice Action Coalition. It would be the first organization uniting Black and white Mobilians under the banner of environmental justice. Sprague volunteered to set up a website, a blog, and social media accounts. "With good leadership, you can move a mountain," Ballard said several years later. "Ramsey was willing, so we became gung ho."

16

HOUSTON-EAST, CHARLESTON-WEST

On a Saturday morning in late September 2013, Womack found himself stomping through the rain downtown. In all the years he'd spent working in the petrochemical industry, this was never how he'd pictured his retirement. He was marching with a couple dozen others, from Cathedral Square up to the old GM&O railroad building, where Arc Terminals planned to build an unloading depot for oil shipments. It was MEJAC's first official event, part of a national day of tar sands protests organized by the environmentalist group 350.org. At first fifty to seventy-five people had turned out; but as the downpour had become heavier, the crowd had thinned.

TV crews were there to film them. "Pipelines leak!" the protesters chanted. "Trains crash! Keep your tar sands off our tracks!" Womack had agreed in advance to be the spokesman. When it was time for his interview, he called on industry executives to cancel their construction plans. "I know you've committed millions of dollars," he said on camera, but it was their fault they had invested that money without first consulting the people of Africatown. "This is not right. We don't want it here. We definitely don't want it going through our drinking water. We don't want it going over, under, around, or through the Africatown and Prichard communities."

As the situation stood, however, it looked like Plains's pipeline was going to do exactly that. Just a few days before the protest, the company had filed paperwork that showed another dimension of its plans. Plains already had one set of oil tanks in Magazine Point and another near Prichard. There was a pipeline connecting them that skirted the border of Africatown, and it had been in place since 1973. Part of the land that it ran through was leased to Plains by the Meaher family. Now Plains was asking permission to replace it with a new pipeline that would go directly through the MCTS schoolyard and would come within a hundred yards of Ruth Ballard's home. Jarrod White, Plains's attorney, explained in an interview that much of the existing pipeline was under Paper Mill Road—and if the company had not opted for a new route, the project would have required shutting down the road for months. By shifting it a hundred feet or more to the west, he said, Plains was also avoiding further road disruptions in the future.

For Womack, the thought of the pipeline going so close to the school was chilling. Throughout the course of the protests, he had brought up the school as often as he could. "We always said, 'We don't want these dangerous tanks right across the street from our schoolchildren.'" If anything would rouse Mobilians from their apathy, he figured, it was the thought of kids being put in harm's way. Now it seemed Plains wasn't even afraid of how this would look. For its part, the company said it was making the community safer, because the new pipeline would be less prone to breaking or spilling than the old one.

MEJAC and its partners mounted an effort to get Plains's application denied. But once again they had to deal with the Public Service Commission, that notorious state agency. Their first step was to launch a letter-writing campaign, asking the PSC to come to Mobile and listen to public comments. In a rare decision, after receiving dozens of letters, the commission gave in, and one afternoon in October, its three members held a meeting in the port city. For almost three hours, concerned citizens railed against the project, describing the hazards it could pose and the historic resources it could endanger. Instead of engaging with these arguments, however, the commissioners insisted the decision wasn't up to them. "The Public Service Commission here has a very small role," said Twinkle Cavanaugh, the PSC's president. "We don't make laws. Whatever the legislature says is the law, we follow it."

Although it was painful for the residents to hear, there was truth in Cavanaugh's statement. Thanks to state laws, there are limits on the PSC's power to approve or deny applications like this one. On the other hand, the PSC was showing no interest in using the power it did possess. The organization Mobile Baykeeper made the case that this pipeline would not "further industrial development" in Mobile overall, because if a rupture or spill ever occurred, it would be disastrous for other industrial operations. The commissioners said they had no formula for factoring this in. "They did nothing that would showcase economic impact," Callaway recalled. "Everything that had potential to go wrong was a drain on the economy, and they refused to take it into account."

A few days later, some forty or fifty residents went to Montgomery for a more formal hearing, most of them riding together in a bus. Per usual, the group was racially mixed. They were ushered into a room where the three commissioners and a judge sat behind a long bench in the front. Brenda Bolton, a former school administrator who had been involved with the environmentalist group since Sprague's workshop, had submitted legal paperwork in advance, asking for the chance to address the commission. Ruth Ballard and two other Africatown residents, Mae Jones and Charles Hope, had done the same.

"All right," the judge, John Garner, intoned. "Thank y'all for being here this morning." He mentioned that Jarrod White, Plains's attorney, had filed an objection to Bolton speaking. He asked White to stand up and explain his reasons.

"Yes, sir," White said. "A party only has a right to intervene if they're directly affected by the proceedings." Bolton didn't own property within the pipeline route, he said, so she didn't qualify.

Bolton was dazed. She had been clear in her petition that she wouldn't be speaking only for herself; she represented many Mobilians, including some who lived in the pipeline area. She stood up and reminded the judge about this. She had brought a statement, she added; but if she couldn't read it out loud, perhaps someone from Africatown could.

No dice, Garner said. "The problem that we have is that we have procedures in place so that we can expeditiously consider this application." Every speaker had to get legal clearance in advance.

White also objected to Ballard, Jones, and Hope speaking. Again, he said, their property was not directly in the pipeline route, so they had no legal standing to weigh in. The residents' attorney, who worked for a nonprofit, argued that they lived close enough to qualify. Ballard would be able to see the pipeline's path from her yard.

"But it does not touch her property?" Garner clarified.

"No, sir."

Garner said it was a situation where "we have to do what is legally required rather than probably what we would prefer to do." The Africatown residents had not demonstrated a "personal interest," he said. And again, the only question at issue was whether the pipeline would "further industrial development." But if the residents wanted to sit up front and listen, they were more than welcome.

The bulldozers came four months later. They rolled through the north end of Plateau in February 2014, roaring and sighing and spewing exhaust. MEJAC members were expecting them. They had scheduled a press conference near the school, hoping to at least publicly shame the pipeline company. Womack started it off. "Good afternoon," he said. Ballard, Jones, Underhill, Adams-Davis, and Womack's brother Jesse stood behind him. The day was cool and cloudy, and the wind whipped at their faces. "The people in Africatown, we've paid our dues," he said. "We've paid our part." He spoke about his family's military service, and about the ash that used to fall on the neighborhood when he was a kid. Then he attacked the ads that had been running in recent days, claiming the oil developments would bring jobs to the city. In truth, the vast majority of those were projected to be temporary, and most of the permanent jobs would not be suited to most Africatown residents, because they would require technical expertise. Ballard and Jones spoke as well.

Before the bulldozers moved onto the baseball field, the group staked out a space there to picket. Eventually the massive vehicles started moving toward them. At first Womack wasn't alarmed. As far as he knew, they were supposed to be digging behind the school. But soon the bulldozer was getting closer than he'd expected. *Wait a minute now,* he remembers thinking. *Aren't they going to stop? Aren't they going to take a left turn here?* When it became clear that they weren't turning, the group rushed out of the way, and the machine plowed into the backstop. "If we hadn't moved," he remembers, "that sucker would have ran us down." The situation was worse than he'd thought. The pipeline would run beneath a spot where kids routinely went to play.

One person not present that afternoon was Ramsey Sprague. Since the workshop in September, Sprague had spent nearly all of his time in Mobile working with MEJAC. This was not what he'd pictured when he first came. At the time, he'd been thinking of moving to the Dakotas and continuing to fight pipeline developments there. "But I couldn't take my eyes off of Mobile," he remembers. He happened to be up in the Dakotas for two weeks that winter, and it was during his absence that the pipeline was built through the schoolyard.

When Sprague heard the news, it clinched his decision to move to Mobile and devote himself to Africatown and MEJAC for the long term. "I knew there wasn't going to be a cavalry," he said. It seemed the only outside support Africatown was going to get would be whatever he could bring. "I could not know what was impending here and leave." If he did, he thought, it was all the more likely that the tank farms would be built. Womack and the others were grateful he decided to stay. "I have nothing but the utmost respect for him," Ballard said. At the same time, his presence provoked hostility and suspicion on the industry side. There was speculation among business leaders that he'd been sent there by the Sierra Club's national organization, or by some wealthy environmentalist, akin to George Soros, as part of a plot to bring down Mobile's entire port operation. "I don't think Sprague was here for the right reasons," White said in an interview. But in reality, Sprague did not have powerful backing; he was barely scraping by. His allies in Mobile had found a place for him to stay where he didn't have to pay rent or utilities. He got around on a bike, because he didn't own a car, and he went without health insurance.

Later in February, Womack received a call from Martha Peek, the superintendent of the county school system. She wanted to address Africatown directly, and she wondered if Womack could set something up. On the day of the meeting, residents and alumni packed a room at MCTS. Peek stood before them, with Womack to her left. "I want to give you a little background information," she said. From outdoors, they could hear the clanking of the pipeline being installed. "When you move into a superintendency, sometimes you inherit things, and then you leave a legacy too. But the work that has taken place here was actually work that was approved in 1951."

September 18, 1951, to be exact—nearly two decades before Mobile County's schools were desegregated. That was the day when the superintendent signed an agreement allowing Plains's predecessor to run a pipeline through the MCTS property. In exchange the company paid the county school system $310. After thirty years, the agreement said, it would have the right to renew for the same fixed price. The company had taken that option in 1981; and then Plains, after acquiring the pipeline, renewed it again in 2011, the year before Peek became superintendent.

"In those days, environmental issues and concerns were not at the forefront," Peek went on. "I don't think that my predecessors had any intent of not being cognizant of the neighborhood." Of course, she was talking about a decision made during the Jim Crow era, one that clearly reflected the mores and political structures of that time. No one interrupted to point out this irony, but it was surely not lost on many people in the audience. Next Peek brought up the matter of money. Plains had announced it would give the district $50,000, apparently to offset the bad publicity. Peek said $20,000 would go to academics and school programs, and the rest would cover a restoration of the baseball field, which had long been neglected.

Peek offered to take questions. Given that the new pipeline took a different route than the old one, someone asked, why didn't the school district ask for local input before giving its approval? "Hindsight is twenty-twenty," Peek replied. "When we looked at this I'm not sure we realized how important that area was." She promised the district would do better in the future. Another person asked whether school administrators had tried to alter or void Plains's legal agreement before it was renewed in 2011. According to a dispatch David Underhill later wrote, Peek said they had not. She also said they had not consulted the Alabama Historical Commission or done archaeological surveys or spoken with Plains officials about emergency plans. "All I can do is apologize" for not approaching the community earlier, Peek said, "but now we need to establish that dialogue and move forward."

Plains seemed to be winning on every front. Around the same time, in early 2014, a judge ruled that the company couldn't be stopped from building its pipeline through the watershed. The judge's legal reasoning seemed debatable, and at a MAWSS meeting that February, residents urged the utility's leadership to appeal. "Don't be bullied," Womack said, "and we'll continue to support you in any kind of way." Instead the utility settled out of court, saying an appeal would be pointless and expensive. After all, Plains had at least two former Alabama Supreme Court justices on its legal team. Plains paid MAWSS $40,000 for rights to 4,000 acres of watershed property, plus an undisclosed amount in damages; and it promised, with the backing of a court mandate, that the pipeline wouldn't carry tar sands and wouldn't be heated. The pipeline was finished in March.

The band of environmentalists were disappointed but not defeated. The threat of tank farms being built up around Africatown still lingered. And if they could stop those, they thought, they'd be limiting the industry's overall footprint in Mobile, and maybe avoiding future pipelines. Thayer Dodd, the horticulturalist, and Brenda Bolton, a former public school administrator, were spearheading the group's research. "We would read about other locations that were fighting pipelines," Bolton said, "and we would see, 'Oh, their city council did this,' or 'They changed their zoning law.'" They discovered that the Mobile city council had legal authority to ban new oil tanks. So as early as the fall of 2013, they'd been lobbying certain council members to take up their cause.

Soon the city council was talking about rewriting the regulations for new tanks, and in the meantime imposing a moratorium on tank projects. Stimpson, the new mayor, clearly didn't favor the idea. While he didn't want to see the city sacrifice its "quality of life" for industrial developments, he said, "For the same token, we cannot deny any business the right to be here." Business leaders opposed the idea, too. Jimmy Lyons, the president of the State Docks, said a moratorium was unnecessary because the petroleum trade was an "inherently safe industry"; and the chamber of commerce president fretted that it would send "a message that we are closed for business," as if the city were a retail store for oil corporations. But the council pushed ahead and passed the measure in December 2013. It ruled that no new tanks could be installed for six months unless the council gave special permission. To keep the business community happy, everyone agreed not to call it a "moratorium," but the effect was the same.

In early 2014, the city appointed a committee of ten residents to draft a new set of tank regulations. Levon Manzie, the councilman whose district included Africatown, chose Bolton. Not a single person from Africatown, the community that stood to be most affected, was on the committee. But Bolton did her best to represent the neighborhood's interests.

The group's proposal, which was released that April, was quite robust. It called for every new tank near the waterfront to be at least 1,500 feet from any residential community, private business, house, or historic district—a distance large enough to block the tank farm from being built on the old International Paper site. It also discouraged developments that would only move petroleum through Mobile, on its way to other markets. It said tank companies should have to disclose exactly what kind of oil they were storing and should submit yearly lists of potential hazards. And it called for capacity limits, odor-control technology, and verified emergency plans. (Several members also added personal statements to the final draft, saying they preferred the regulations be stricter still, especially where Africatown was concerned. Bolton's comments were so thorough they added up to nine single-spaced pages.)

However, the proposal had to go through the planning commission before it reached the council. And during that interim, Stimpson stepped in. On July 17, he replaced the majority of the planning commission's members, saying he wanted to bring more "balance" between industrial and environmental interests. There was a common trait among most of the people he ejected: they had failed to support the construction of a controversial coal terminal that spring. (Stimpson denied that this had anything to do with his decision.)

Womack and the others braced themselves for the worst. But before the planning commission could make any moves, Africatown caught a huge break: the price of oil started to drop. At first it went down gradually, from $106 in June to $104 in July and $97 in August. Then the price plummeted. By November, it was down to $76, and in January 2015, it hit $47. This was all a matter of supply and demand. It turned out that the United States and Canada had ramped up their crude production so quickly that both countries had gotten ahead of the market. As they watched these numbers, oil companies started to reassess their construction plans. As of June 2015, with the price hovering around $60, oil infrastructure projects worth a total of $200 billion had been canceled around the world. Rail shipments were also declining. Plans for the new tank farms around Africatown were also revoked. It wasn't exactly the victory Womack and the others had pictured, but it was a victory all the same.

All along, the activists had been saying that pipeline and tank companies couldn't be trusted—that their leaders might try to cover up public health risks. In the summer of 2015, they felt vindicated. Early that year, Arc Terminals began submitting paperwork to store asphalt and sulfuric acid, rather than petroleum, in tanks along the riverfront. The application came up before Mobile's planning commission in June. At two consecutive meetings, residents passionately argued against it, saying the acid would be roughly as dangerous as the petroleum. The planning commission gave its approval all the same. But on August 11, when the matter came up for a city council vote, one councilwoman asked whether the company was already storing sulfuric acid in its tanks. "Correct," the company's vice president replied. Most everyone in the room was stunned. The executive added that Arc hadn't known it needed permission until it already had the tanks. He also said that as far as the company knew, the public had been aware all along. The council voted to let the company store asphalt but demanded that it remove the acid.

The activists had begun framing the debate over regulations as a question about Mobile's identity. What would the place look like in twenty or thirty years? Should it focus on attracting tourism, by promoting its waterfront, its historic architecture, and its seafood? If it were to choose this route, it made sense for Africatown to be the centerpiece; nothing else in the area came close in terms of historical significance. Or was it a bigger priority to be seen as "business-friendly" and to attract more heavy industry? In other words, as Sprague puts it, did Mobile want to be Charleston-West or Houston-East? Mayor Stimpson and the chamber of commerce rejected this framing, insisting that Mobile could have it both ways. Stimpson's hope was to make Mobile the most "business and family friendly city in America."

The chamber hired two consultants, paying them $30,000 to quantify the role of oil storage tanks in the local economy. The consultants found that the storage tank industry employed more than 1,800 people in the area (some by contract) and had a GDP of $688 million. All told, between oil, gas, chemical manufacturing, and coal, the energy industry had a $4 billion to $5 billion impact on Mobile's economy each year. The chamber's president touted the study as evidence that storage tanks were critical to Mobile's business network. Many local companies relied on "the availability of affordable and abundant energy options," he said.

Concerned citizens fired back with their own report. In March, they distributed a sixty-six-page document titled "No More Petro-Chemical Storage Tanks on Our West Bank." It opened with a letter from Peter Burns, a downtown attorney, arguing that the chamber was giving a skewed picture of the city's interests. "Of course the petroleum industry is valuable," he wrote, "but that is not the issue. The question is what economic impact this particular project will have on our community." It would also be a mistake, he said, to consider only the benefits—namely the bumps in tax revenue and job numbers—and ignore the downsides. In the testimonies that followed, contributors spelled out these costs. Bernard Eichold, a health officer of the Mobile County Health Department, warned that oil tanks could pose "significant" health hazards when the chemicals inside them made contact with sunlight. Wladimir Wertelecki, a pediatrician, noted that petrochemical pollutants had been known to cause miscarriages, birth defects, and childhood leukemia, and that Mobile's pollution levels were already "severe." And several small-business owners outlined how installing more storage tanks could hurt their operations. Did Mobile want "a growing vibrant downtown full of people, restaurants and shops?" asked John Serda, a coffee-shop owner—or "a downtown full of industry? You cannot have both." As it was, Serda said, he had to power-wash his café every month to remove the dust from a nearby coal terminal.

The last letter in the packet was from Joe Womack. A few weeks earlier, he wrote, a friend in Africatown had told him he was looking forward to his sixty-second birthday. The friend was planning an early retirement. Then on the same day when Womack was writing this letter, he'd received a call from his friend's sister. The man had died suddenly from a lung disease. Womack blamed it on factory pollution. "The Africatown Community is tired of being the dumping ground for heavy industries," he wrote. Besides the health consequences, he said that additional storage tanks would drag property values down farther, and would inhibit plans to bring heritage tourism. "NO MORE TANKS ON OUR BANKS, is the rallying cry of ALL Africatown residents, natives, descendants and friends."

Over these past three years, Womack had been giving car tours of his old neighborhood. "When people got here, I wanted them to see Africatown the way I saw it," he said. "Then I found out that what I knew, and the way that I see it, was unique." In his telling, every part of the geography had several layers. One level consisted of his own childhood memories. He'd point out where he and his friends had once fished and swam, where they had played baseball. A second level dealt with the *Clotilda* story and the early days of Africatown's history. This part was informed by the folktales he'd heard from Henry Williams and his grandfather, as well as the books by Sylviane Diouf and others. A third level was Womack's idea of how it might look in the future: where a museum could be built, where the boat tours could depart, where new housing could be set up and old houses could be renovated. And increasingly, there was a fourth layer that dealt with environmental justice and the ongoing fight against the tank farms.

In the fall of 2015, he gave a tour to a distinguished guest: Robert Bullard, the father of environmental justice.

The Alabama NAACP was hosting its annual conference in Mobile that October. MEJAC members saw it as a chance to highlight the connections between civil rights and the environment. Working with the NAACP, they declared it the "No More Tanks on Our West Bank" week of action, and planned a rally in Africatown, a picket at Government Plaza, and a march downtown. They also recruited Bullard to come speak. He gave a fiery presentation explaining how Africatown's experiences fit into a broader pattern. "Having the facts is never enough!" the professor shouted, waving his arms in broad gestures. His energy could be felt throughout the room. "Having the proof, having the documentation, is never enough to get justice for

African Americans and other people of color and poor people. You've gotta have mobilization behind that information!"

That weekend, Womack took Bullard around the neighborhood. The professor took photos of historical sites, including Cudjo Lewis's grave, and posted them on Twitter and Facebook. Womack told him about the pollution and the threat of more tank farms being built. Bullard's visit bolstered the sense that this struggle in Africatown represented a cause much larger than Mobile. Because of its unique history, the neighborhood was perhaps the most dramatic illustration to be found anywhere of environmental racism. A victory there had the potential to inspire activists in similar straits throughout the country.

Around that time, negotiations on the tank regulations had come to a standstill. City officials turned to Casi Callaway, the director of Mobile Baykeeper, to get the process moving again. Baykeeper is southern Alabama's most influential environmental organization, thanks largely to Callaway's leadership. Unlike the Sierra Club, Baykeeper works hand in hand with business leaders, to foster what Callaway calls "responsible growth." Explaining her strategy, she said that when environmentalists and industry clash over a policy issue in Alabama, industry almost always wins. The laws are structured in their favor, and it's all too easy for corporations to buy political influence. Sometimes Baykeeper does file lawsuits to stop projects it deems environmentally unsound. But in many cases, Callaway said, the only way for environmentalists to get even a partial victory is to negotiate. Underhill used to criticize Baykeeper, Callaway recalled, even as he dutifully wrote checks to support its work. He called Callaway a "blue-suit" (rather than "grassroots") environmentalist. "He meant it disparagingly," she said, "but I loved it."

In this case, Callaway collaborated with Jarrod White, who was working with an industry coalition called Keep Mobile Growing, to broker a compromise on the regulations. By November, they had a proposal both sides could live with. But when it was released to the public that fall, MEJAC members and other agitators were upset. To them it seemed most of the valuable recommendations had been stripped away. As Sprague wrote on MEJAC's website, the possibility remained that if developers wanted to build a tank farm and found out there were homes nearby, all they'd have to do was buy those houses and bulldoze them. (However, Callaway and White both argue that in practice, this would be next to impossible—because there are too many houses nearby, and the homeowners might not agree to sell, and even if they did, demolition permits would be required.) Other recommendations had been disregarded as well; for instance, there was no requirement for tank companies to have financial bonding that would cover cleanup and other costs, in the event that something went wrong. In fact, the new ordinance said nothing about companies' responsibilities in the event of a disaster. The tank companies and their allies were also unhappy with the new ordinance. They attacked it, saying it still put too many restrictions on them.

By the end of March 2016, the ordinance was in the hands of the city council. At this stage, the representatives of heavy industry had mostly come around. Council members were also increasingly supportive. They said it represented a compromise; neither side was getting exactly what it wanted, but each side was getting something. But the residents who had been protesting for three years didn't feel that way. At the council meeting on March 29, concerned citizens pleaded for a delay so the ordinance could be revised or rewritten. On the environmental side, the only person who spoke in support of the ordinance was Casi Callaway of Mobile Baykeeper. She argued that if the council simply passed a decent ordinance, it could always revise it in the future. Baykeeper's support was a significant factor. As Callaway said, reflecting on the meeting, no one on the council wanted to be seen as "solely pro-industry." Having buy-in from the area's biggest environmental organization made it seem more politically acceptable.

When it was time for council members to speak, Levon Manzie, the councilman representing Africatown and downtown Mobile, led off. He explained why he'd be voting in favor. "This is by no stretch a perfect solution," he said. In the gleam of the overhead lights, it looked like he was sweating, and his microphone picked up on the clicking of his pen. "We have to come together to try to cobble together an ordinance that will provide further protection for our communities while also being respectful to future business growth, positive business growth, in the city of Mobile. So it's with great reluctance that I'm going to support this compromise."

A few minutes later, the ordinance passed, 6–1.

For the environmental justice crowd, it was felt as a bitter loss. There was still a technical possibility, however unlikely, that someone could develop a tank farm at the International Paper site. Womack felt sure the matter would come up again sooner or later. Brenda Bolton had similar worries; she felt, during the aftermath, like she was "waiting for the other shoe to drop." "Even today," she wrote in an email in 2021, "as I wash coal dust off my house or take in the horizon crossing the bay headed west, I am constantly aware of the ever-present environmental threat, and wondering how many times we can roll the dice, how many floods and hurricanes we can withstand, how many times we can avoid the big explosion."

However, another way of seeing it is that the group had been more successful than the members gave themselves credit for. In the short term, the installation of new oil tanks near Africatown had been halted, and they had played a major role. The city had also imposed a requirement for 1,500-foot setbacks from residential buildings—and Bolton, in all her research, had not found examples of stricter setback requirements anywhere in the country. In all the years Henry Williams and his allies had fought unwanted developments, they'd never won such a victory. If it felt like a letdown, that was partly because the horizons of possibility had shifted so much in just three years. At the same time, immense strides had also been made in community organizing. MEJAC was now a force to be reckoned with, and Sprague was in Mobile to stay. The political atmosphere was no longer so welcoming for would-be industrial developers near Africatown. Partnerships had been developed with the Sierra Club and the NAACP. There was a semblance of neighborhood leadership. Those achievements were intangible, but they would soon pay off.

17

RECONSTRUCTION

On a frosty morning in January 2018, archaeologists from the University of West Florida traveled by boat to a swampy part of the Mobile Delta, a mile downstream from where Jack Friend and his companions had stopped their search fifteen years earlier. Their guide was Ben Raines, a longtime reporter for the *Press-Register* (and the son of Howell Raines, the former executive editor of *The New York Times*). Ben Raines moonlighted as a tour guide in the delta, taking sightseers and fishermen on boat trips, and he knew the territory well. Earlier that month, when the tide was exceptionally low, Raines had set out looking for the *Clotilda*. He'd come upon a wreck that he believed might be the one.

Raines took the men to a muddy bank, thick with driftwood. The sunken vessel was near the shore, rising partially above the murky water. There wasn't much the archaeologists could do that morning. They didn't have a permit to dive in and examine the ship closely or measure its full dimensions. But from what they saw on the surface, it seemed likely the vessel had been built between 1850 and 1880. They agreed it ought to be investigated further. "We didn't see anything that screamed, no, it couldn't be" the *Clotilda*, John Bratten said in an interview.

Two days later, after they'd returned to Florida, Bratten was surprised to see a story Raines had written for the *Press-Register*'s website. "Wreck Found by Reporter May Be Last American Slave Ship, Archaeologists Say," read the January 23 headline. Raines was careful in the story not to make definitive claims. "You can definitely say maybe," he quoted one of Bratten's colleagues saying, "and maybe even a little bit stronger, because the location is right, the construction seems to be right, from the proper time period, it appears to be burnt." Even so, the whole world immediately took notice. Within two days of the announcement, the news had been covered by *The New York Times, The Washington Post,* NPR, and CNN, among many other outlets.

Joe Womack and Anderson Flen were also caught off guard by the news. For months, the two men had been in discussions with the National Park Service and the Smithsonian Institution about getting a team to search for the *Clotilda.* Identifying the ship, they thought, would be an incredible boost in their efforts to bring tourism to Africatown. They had felt they were getting close; already researchers had begun poring over the files from Jack Friend's expeditions, and a grant application was in the works. When they heard Raines's announcement, both Womack and Flen had mixed reactions. They were relieved and excited, but this was not the way they'd intended for it to happen. They were concerned that they might be left out of further discussions, and that Africatown's interests would become an afterthought.

Flen still lived in Atlanta, but since 2015, when he'd retired from the Georgia Department of Public Health, he had been a frequent presence in Africatown. He and Womack remained close friends. While Womack had been crusading against the oil developments, Flen had been trying through other means to improve the neighborhood's conditions. For instance, under the auspices of the MCTS Alumni Association, of which he was the president, he had started an annual kite day, where local kids learned how to make their own kites and how to fly them. And his leadership committee had found a new bell for the school grounds, resembling the one that had been taken in the 1970s. The committee had the new bell cleaned and painted and installed on a cement pedestal. Flen set a goal of making sure something encouraging happened in the community every three to six months, "because people need hope." It was a way of bringing residents together and fostering connections, while also cultivating support for the more ambitious projects that he and Womack (and other allies) had in mind.

The discussions about launching a search for the *Clotilda* had grown out of a longer-term collaboration with the National Park Service. Along with the Park Service's Mississippi field office, Africatown supporters were trying to develop a blueway, a path through the community waterways that would be accessible for nature walks, swimming, fishing, canoeing, and kayaking. Part of the plan was to put up markers at important historic sites, such as the spot on Threemile Creek where the shipmates had once done baptisms.

They also hoped to put a boat and kayak launch at the AfricaTown, U.S.A. State Park in Prichard—the one John Smith had labored to establish in the eighties.

Following the news of Raines's discovery, Flen spoke with his federal contacts about how to ensure the community would be kept in the loop. Dave Conlin, the chief of the National Park Service's Submerged Resources Center, told him the state would have final legal authority over the shipwreck site. So Flen sent a letter to the Alabama Historical Commission (AHC), asking that if there were any more announcements to be made, they be made onsite in Africatown, so the residents would be the first to know. The AHC's leadership agreed. "Archaeology has a huge and really terrible history," Conlin said, where "we extract the history of a place and appropriate it for our own good." But in this case, the archaeologists were determined not to let this happen.

By then, the AHC was already putting together a team of experts to investigate the wreck Raines had found. Besides personnel from the Park Service and the Smithsonian, this team included James Delgado, one of the world's leading experts in maritime archaeology. Delgado had been the chief scientist on the RMS *Titanic* mapping expedition, among many other exploits, and much of his work had focused on nineteenth-century ships. Both Delgado and Stacye Hathorn, the state archaeologist at the AHC, say they already knew this ship was not the *Clotilda*. From the images they'd seen online, they'd been able to tell it was too large. But "by the time we found out about it, it was already international news," Hathorn recalls, "and the community had already been told this was the *Clotilda*." The state had a responsibility to investigate thoroughly. So in March 2018, nine archaeologists, all working pro bono, went to the site of Raines's discovery, bringing along scuba gear. Raines also joined the expedition. It turned out the timbers were too large to have been used by nineteenth-century shipmakers, and the fasteners appeared to be steel, rather than iron, the kind Foster would have used. After two days on the river, the team had confirmed that it was not the right ship.

As Flen had requested, the state broke this news at the community center in Africatown. Officials urged the residents not to despair; they promised the research wasn't over. "The last thing anybody wanted to do was just show up and say, 'Nope, that's not it,'" Delgado recalls. It was clear how much the project meant to the neighborhood.

That spring, there was another encouraging development. *Barracoon*, the manuscript based on Zora Neale Hurston's conversations with Cudjo

Lewis—which had been shelved for almost ninety years, most recently among Alain Locke's papers at Howard University—was published. For the first time ever, Cudjo's own narration of his story was made available to the masses. Due to his skill as a storyteller, the richness of his voice (which Hurston captured far better than other interviewers), and the excruciating nature of his experiences, it's hard to read *Barracoon* without feeling moved. The book became a massive bestseller. Thanks in part to its success, national press coverage of Africatown continued for months; and Womack offered tours in his pickup truck to most every journalist and camera crew that came into town, seizing every chance to highlight the ongoing pollution and industrial blight.

On present-day maps of the Mobile Delta, the water on each side of Twelve-mile Island is shown as a channel for ships to pass through. But by examining maps and charts at the Library of Congress, the researchers realized that back in 1860, the waterway on the eastern side had been a bayou, not a channel. It seemed that it had functioned for decades as a "ship graveyard." Nearly every major port and waterfront has one, Delgado said in an interview. In the nineteenth and early twentieth centuries, when a ship was no longer useful, it was easier to abandon it in this bayou than to break it apart. The bayou was close enough to Mobile to be convenient, but far enough away that it wasn't closely monitored or patrolled; and the traffic there was minimal, because ships passing through had always used the other side. The old charts showed that more than a dozen wrecks were down there in the river's depths.

There was evidence to suggest the *Clotilda* might be among them. Throughout the early months of 2018, several people told the AHC that in years past, they had personally explored the *Clotilda* wreck and had tried to recover materials from it. These informants confirmed that it lay on the eastern side of Twelvemile Island. Moreover, this area was the only viable spot that had not been covered in previous searches. To Delgado and the other archaeologists, it seemed increasingly likely that the ship was down there, "hiding in plain sight." Not long after they'd finished assessing the wreck Raines had found, Delgado's team submitted a proposal for a comprehensive survey. The state agreed to cover the cost.

In the meantime, Raines resumed searching as well. Not long after the letdown about his first discovery, he got in touch with the head of marine sciences at the University of Southern Mississippi, who was an old friend. Raines asked if the university could send a research crew to do a full survey of the eastern channel. The team came a week later. It ended up investigating a dozen targets within a two-mile section of the river. Most of these wrecks were too large to be the *Clotilda* or had the wrong construction materials; but one seemed especially promising. Raines eventually swam out to the vessel and felt around. He found a thick piece of lumber, held down by some large, rusty nails. With a little prying, it came loose. On the bank nearby, there was a concrete survey marker, painted red. Its vertical letters said MEAHER, a reminder that the family still owned this part of the shoreline, which it had acquired in the 1850s. It used the area as a fish camp. Raines later called the AHC again. This time, he said, he was quite sure he'd laid his hands on the *Clotilda*.

Delgado and the others took note, but they still moved ahead with the comprehensive survey they'd been planning. That summer, they scanned the channel and produced a high-resolution map that showed many objects immersed in the mud. They identified fourteen targets for investigation. "We started at the top, Target 1, and went all the way through to Target 14," Delgado said. Ultimately, they zeroed in on Target 5, the same one Raines had singled out. When Delgado dove down and examined this wreck himself, he was astonished at the vessel's craftsmanship, which seemed worthy of a yacht. The attention to detail was remarkable, down to the way the builder had lined up the grain on different pieces of wood. He was also surprised to see that three sides of the hold, where the captives would have been kept (if this was indeed the *Clotilda*), were still intact. "When you go to it, you're actually entering the hold itself," he said. There's no other known slave wreck where this is the case. "I don't think a single one of us who's been in there has not been chilled by that thought, and horrified—because it is a small, confined space. And we could stand right up and get out of the hold and swim to the surface." Foster and his crew had evidently installed walls within the interior to fashion a temporary holding cell. The team made repeated trips to the site, collecting wood and iron hardware for testing, along with samples from the mud nearby. When the lab results came back, they strongly suggested the ship in question had been burned. They also showed signs of dynamiting, possibly from the Meaher family's attempts to extract the copper from the hull.

At this point they confronted a new challenge. "If every Gulf schooner looks more or less alike, other than size," Delgado said, "how can you tell whether what you have in the river, in other terms, is a 1945 or a 1946 Chevy?" Their only option was to create a database of more than a thousand Gulf schooners built between 1813 and 1893 and compare their precise features. To do this, Delgado and his wife met up with Hathorn, Alabama's state archaeologist, at the National Archives in Atlanta, where the three of them went through massive bound volumes that clearly had not been opened in decades. So thick was the dust that soon their cotton gloves were blackened, as if they'd been gardening. Hathorn said she went in feeling doubtful—but what they found in the archives changed her perspective. "I knew the wood was right," she said. "The size was right; the location was in the ballpark. But I wasn't sure what the universe of ships like *Clotilda* was. I mean, was *Clotilda* a rare vessel? Or was *Clotilda* one of a dozen that were just the same vessel?"

It turned out only eight schooners from the right time period had the qualifications they were looking for. These ships had larger cargo capacity than all the other Gulf-built schooners of the 1800s. They had also been insured in New York, which suggested they'd been designed for something more than coastal trade, and built to exacting standards, approved by the insurance company's inspectors. Meanwhile, their research also revealed that the *Clotilda*'s dimensions were unique among the thousand-plus vessels in their database. In other words, the wreck they had singled out in the Mobile Delta could only be one ship. "That was the tipping point for me," Hathorn said.

The objective, at this stage, was to prove the wreck was *not* the *Clotilda*. But by the fall of 2018, the researchers felt they had exhausted every avenue and hadn't been able to do this. They wrote up their findings in a thick report and sent it around for peer review. They were careful to avoid any leaks to the press; every recipient was asked to keep it confidential. The feedback they received was universally encouraging. Their peers agreed with the team's conclusions. Delgado's suspicion that the *Clotilda* had been hiding in plain sight had apparently been correct. Images of the wreck had been captured by Google Earth during low tide. And in *Historic Sketches of the South*, Emma Langdon Roche's 1914 book, there's a black-and-white photo of a partially submerged ship. Roche claimed it was the *Clotilda*. Delgado now believes she was right. (He and Hathorn, following the conventions of archaeology, are careful to say the ship was "identified," rather than "discovered.")

In the spring of 2019, Flen received calls from his contacts at the Smithsonian, the AHC, and the National Park Service, all asking how soon he could be down in Mobile. He had a hunch about what was coming. A community meeting was scheduled for the morning of May 2. There Delgado, along with representatives from the state, informed Africatown residents that the ship had been identified. They were overjoyed. Later that day, *National Geographic* broke the news internationally. "Last American Slave Ship Is Discovered in Alabama," its headline read. Delgado was quoted saying the ship had been identified "beyond reasonable doubt."

A week later, the AHC had a press conference at the community center in Africatown. A huge crowd assembled in the gymnasium, where a stage had been set up. Flen gave the opening remarks. Stimpson, the AHC chair, and an envoy of Alabama's governor also addressed the crowd. The full 172-page report on the *Clotilda* research was made available. Afterward there were ceremonies and a party under a big tent outdoors.

Throughout the rest of 2019, there was a vast flourishing of projects surrounding Africatown. A clearer vision for heritage tourism developments started coming into focus. It was inspired by the National Memorial for Peace and Justice in Montgomery. Womack, Flen, and their allies imagine that visitors will come prepared for a somber experience. They picture exhibits that will explain the *Clotilda*'s voyage in the broader context of the transatlantic slave trade and of antebellum Mobile. No doubt it will depict the horrors of Dahomey's slave raids in West Africa, as well as the horrors of the Middle Passage. But if their vision is borne out, it will also depict the establishment of African Town and the shipmates' lives in America. It will tell a story of survival and triumph as well as suffering and oppression.

In connection with the tourism plans, discussions began in earnest about what ought to be done with the ship. From the start, there was talk of dredging up the vessel and putting it on display. "My ultimate dream would be to have it raised," state senator Vivian Davis Figures told *National Geographic* days after the announcement. But some archaeologists had doubts about this prospect. One of the challenges, said Christopher Dostal, a marine archaeologist at Texas A&M University, was that the wood was liable to fall apart if it were dried out. A complicated, expensive process would be necessary to keep it intact. Delgado estimated that a full-scale recovery would cost tens of millions of dollars. "And where would that money better be spent?" he said in an interview. "Very quickly it can all become about the ship, as opposed to the community." One alternative, suggested by *National Geographic,* was a memorial at the site of the wreck, like the one in Pearl Harbor commemorating the USS *Arizona.* Others thought a replica should be built when Africatown finally got its own museum.

The exact site of the wreck was not announced, lest anyone vandalize it or take away pieces to keep or sell. The state also banned boat traffic in the surrounding area and put marine police there on patrol. Meanwhile, the AHC filed a claim with the federal government, asking for ownership of the vessel, and in the spring of 2020 this request was granted. Afterward the state set aside $1 million for further preservation efforts, including the retrieval of artifacts.

In 2018, local and state officials budgeted $3.6 million to build a welcome center near the Old Plateau Cemetery. The money came out of a $4.4 billion fund created by BP after the 2010 Deepwater Horizon oil spill. The plot of land near Plateau's cemetery was tiny, so plans were drawn up for a small building that would function as a "landing point" for tourists. The design contract went to a firm that had worked on the Historic Bethel Baptist Church in Birmingham. But after the ship was identified, it was clear that Africatown couldn't wait for the welcome center to be finished—it needed a place to start receiving visitors as soon as possible. In 2020, Merceria Ludgood, an attorney with a long history in local Black politics, was a county commissioner, a post she'd held since 2007. She announced plans for the Africatown Heritage House, which would hold more than a dozen artifacts from the *Clotilda*, and would have a "meditative garden" with plant species native to the area. The construction was fast-tracked, set for completion in the spring of 2022. There was discussion about land and boat tours as well.

In 2020, Senator Doug Jones secured a grant of $500,000 for excavation, education, and community engagement involving the *Clotilda*. He entrusted this money to the Smithsonian Institution, and Smithsonian leaders promised to work with the community to identify specific priorities. Other organizations across the country also lined up to help. The National Association of Black Scuba Divers launched a swimming and scuba program for kids living in Africatown. David Padgett, a geography professor at Tennessee State University, volunteered to create a digital "story map" of Africatown, in connection with the blueway project. Vanderbilt University also came in to help with the blueway, joining Mississippi State University, which had been involved in the design work since 2018. Oberlin College, in Ohio, had also been helping the community for several years. During spring break trips, Oberlin students had done oral history interviews with residents, with plans to make these interviews available online. Half a dozen other schools, including Penn State University and the University of Virginia, offered their resources as well.

The shipmates' descendants also banded together in a way they hadn't done since the 1980s. Joycelyn Davis, a sixth-generation descendant of Charlie Lewis, and Darron Patterson, a fourth-generation descendant of Pollee Allen, led the effort, along with descendants of Ossa Keeby and James and Lottie Dennison. For the first Spirit of Our Ancestors festival, in 2019, more than two hundred descendants of the shipmates gathered in Africatown, and Natalie Robertson gave a keynote presentation. *National Geographic* covered the event. Turnout was even larger at the 2020 festival, when Deborah Plant, the editor of *Barracoon*, gave the main address. Garry Lumbers, Cudjo Lewis's great-great-grandson, was among those in attendance. Also there was Michael Foster, a descendant of one of Captain William Foster's uncles. Michael Foster lived in Montana and had recently learned about the *Clotilda* story through a relative's genealogical research. His travel expenses were paid by CBS, which filmed the reunion for a *60 Minutes* segment that aired later in 2020. In a tearful encounter (most of which did not make the cut for TV), Foster apologized on his family's behalf to several of the shipmate descendants.

Flen, who was always thinking about long-term strategy, decided Africatown needed one organization that could tie together all the ongoing projects. Throughout 2020 and 2021, amid the COVID-19 pandemic, he worked to establish the Africatown Heritage Preservation Foundation. The foundation accumulated grant money to hire a full-time executive director and to launch an international fundraising campaign.

There's no detailed blueprint for how Africatown advocates want the neighborhood to look in the long term. But almost all of them agree it should involve old houses being restored, and new ones built to match the existing architecture—places that young families will want to move into; small, locally owned businesses; more protection from heavy industry, if not a significant scaling down of the industrial presence; and abundant access to the waterways. Flen hopes to see open areas repopulated with orchards. They hope tourism will be a springboard for some of this redevelopment. However, in the way Flen pictures it, the Mobile County Training School will be at the center. He imagines unoccupied parts of the main school building could be used as work spaces for entrepreneurs. One day, he hopes, the foundation will be able to offer artist residencies. He has secured a house, near the school, where artists will be able to stay, and he hopes to convert the main floor into a coffeehouse. "I want to see that community teach the world how to reinvent itself," he said, "by actually reinventing *it*self."

* * *

Three people who stayed noticeably quiet after the *Clotilda* was identified are Gus, Joe, and Robert Meaher, Timothy Meaher's great-grandsons. The pact they reportedly made circa 1998, after the release of *Amistad*, was generally kept, up until two of the three brothers, Joe and Robert, died (in 2020 and 2021, respectively). For some people in Africatown, as well as for the shipmates' descendants, the three brothers have always been cloaked in mystery. There are virtually no photographs of them on the internet, and when they've had property interests at stake in public proceedings, their attorneys have generally gone in their stead. They have apparently not sat on many boards or appeared on stages at political events or galas. Their standard response to the press has been complete stonewalling; rarely have they even acknowledged inquiries. However, from a broad array of public records and other documents, and from interviews with people who know them, it's possible to assemble a portrait of their lives and personalities.

Gus Meaher, the oldest son of Augustine Jr., was born in 1939. He attended University Military School, the academy where almost all of Mobile's elite families send their children. There he edited a school publication, the *Battalion Review*. He graduated in 1957, then earned a bachelor's degree and a law degree from Tulane University in New Orleans. He served as a transportation officer in the Army before starting his civilian career as an attorney. In legal directories he's listed as a specialist in corporate law, probate, wills, trusts, and real estate. Acquaintances describe him as quiet and taciturn. His wife, however, is reported to be the opposite. "Mary Lou Meaher is *not* a Stepford wife," said a Mobilian who knows the couple. Another friend of the couple said Mary Lou is a liberal Democrat. This person said Gus Meaher does not seem especially interested in politics, but may not share his wife's liberal views. The couple lives at the Springhill Avenue house that once belonged to Augusta Evans Wilson, the nineteenth-century novelist, and Lorenzo Wilson, her husband. They have six children, five of whom have also graduated from Tulane.

Robert Meaher, the youngest brother, was born in 1946. He left Mobile when he was young to attend the Darlington School, an elite boarding school in Georgia. He returned home for college, graduating from the University of South Alabama in 1969. In 2001, months after their father's death, Robert Meaher sold his share in the family estate to his brothers. A family friend said they had a falling-out. "I always felt he was uncomfortable," another person said, describing Robert's personality. "He may not have fit with what everybody expected."

The middle brother, Joe Meaher, who went by the name Cap'n Joe, died in 2020, apparently in his late seventies. He had the most vivid personality by far—and was also "the most unreconstructed," as one acquaintance puts it. A common refrain among those who knew him is that he was born in the wrong century. He lived on a family property called Promise Land Plantation. Cap'n Joe spent his career managing the family's land, timber, and mineral resources (and may have had other clients as well). His manner was at once roughhewn and aristocratic. Every day at lunch, he and some of his workers used to pile in at Bienville Bistro, a downtown restaurant that served sophisticated French cuisine, wearing their khaki forestry uniforms. An acquaintance describes him as "courtly," if not refined—adding, "I don't know if 'refined' would ever appear in a sentence with Joe."

In certain circles, stories about Cap'n Joe are easy to come by. Suzanne Cleveland, a lifelong Mobilian, went on a date with him in the late 1970s. She remembers him saying, "Miss Suey, I'm gonna have to fatten you up." They went out to dinner and then to his home. At the first opportunity, he threw her onto the bed. In a fluster, she fended him off. (Cap'n Joe never married, and in spite of this anecdote, rumors long flourished that he was gay.) He had Black men working for him, Cleveland said, "And he always said the 'niggroes' had to go to the back door if they came for anything." Another anecdote comes from Robert Allen, an attorney, who once partnered with Cap'n Joe to explore a forestry tract that one of his clients had an interest in. The two of them spent a day traipsing around a swamp along the Mobile River. At one point Joe asked whether Allen was hungry. Not far ahead, one of his hired men was waiting in a clearing with their lunch. "And lunch consisted of fried chicken and bourbon," Allen recalls. "No vegetables." A third person recalls meeting Joe and Gus Meaher for lunch, in the 2010s, after they had donated money to an organization where this person served on the board. The source was scandalized by Joe Meaher, who spoke about his "plantation" and used the n-word repeatedly. "Truly, I would not have been surprised to go up there and find somebody shackled to a tree, and him whipping them, from the way he talked about it," this person said. "There's just no common decency there. I hate to say it, but there's just no common decency to the man."

In his 2015 book *The Mobile River,* the historian John Sledge writes about being treated to a river tour in what Cap'n Joe called his "haul-ass boat." He gave a running commentary as they sped along. "Pointing toward a non-descript section on the city side," Sledge writes, "Joe began dog-cussing a family that had done the Meahers wrong during Reconstruction." His will, which he devised in 2006, called for his property to be left with J. Heath Eckert, his close friend and business partner, or to Eckert's descendants. But in the unlikely event that he outlived the Eckert family, he wanted his estate donated to Beauvoir, the Jefferson Davis home and presidential library in Biloxi, Mississippi (which the will refers to as "the Jefferson Davis Shrine"). It also specified that under no circumstances should Robert Meaher or his family receive a cent. After Joe Meaher's death in March 2020, his obituary identified him as Timothy Meaher's great-grandson.

The Meaher family's property holdings are immense. In 2012, the last time a full appraisal was done, the assets they shared were worth $35.5 million, with real estate accounting for $28 million and timber making up another $6.8 million's worth. In 2011, a fairly typical year, they brought in $985,600 in rental income and another $144,768 from timber sales, according to court filings. One local attorney, Herndon Inge, recalls that when he was growing up, in the 1950s and '60s, the Meahers were seen as slumlords. The perception was that most of their money came from renting out cheap, poorly kept housing to Black Mobilians. "They weren't rich," Inge said. "Nobody really knew about the *Clotilda,* so the Meahers just rocked along, probably lower-middle-class." He believes most of their wealth came from marshland they owned in the Mobile Delta, where oil was discovered in the 1970s. A 1981 lawsuit confirms that they made "substantial" royalties by leasing out some property to the Getty Oil Company, beginning in 1978. Another acquaintance, however, said they were "always considered to be wealthy people," but may have become much wealthier after the oil was discovered. There's little doubt that they reaped immense profits by leasing land to industrial clients. It's clear that in at least one of these land deals, when they agreed in 1937 to let Scott Paper build a factory on their land, the family drove an extremely hard bargain.

Property records show that the Meahers have continued buying land in Africatown as recently as 2017. Sometimes when an elderly resident dies, ownership of the property is divvied up among several heirs who don't live in the neighborhood. When they fall far behind on taxes, the state eventually takes ownership and sells the lot. In cases like these, the Meahers have acquired properties for as little as $250. Joe Meaher's name is typically the one listed on the deeds. What exactly the Meahers want with this land is unclear. For someone like Womack, their buying pattern looks like evidence of a long-term plan to seize the neighborhood and turn it over to heavy industry.

But others have suggested, quite plausibly, that they have no particular plan and have bought the properties only because they've been available. "They probably think, *If I can acquire a big tract of land, it will be easier to sell*," said one acquaintance of the family. The Meahers also own a substantial amount of the industrially zoned land around Africatown, and their lessees there include two oil tank farms, two trucking facilities, the tissue mill, a metals supplier, and at least one chemical manufacturer.

Before Joe Meaher's death, there was also turmoil between him and his older brother. For years, the brothers' holdings company, Chippewa Lakes, had no staff of its own, and Joe handled the day-to-day management of their assets. He knew the land well enough, an appraiser wrote in 2013, that the company would be "significantly disadvantaged" when the time eventually came for him to step down. In 2015, the brothers agreed that his management fee would be $240,000 a year. But at some point, his forestry company, J. L. Meaher & Associates, began operating at a loss, and family members say he started using money from Chippewa Lakes's accounts to pay his debts and expenses. They also say he siphoned off company profits and then falsified records to make it look as if the money had gone where it was supposed to.

In 2016 or thereabouts, Gus Meaher became concerned about the accounts. Chippewa Lakes was low on cash and had to borrow money to meet its obligations. One of Gus's daughters, Meg Meaher, an accountant living in Charlotte, reviewed the tax records and concluded her uncle had taken roughly $1.5 million. She and her sister, Helen, sued Joe Meaher in 2017, with their father's support. (Together the girls had a 4 percent stake in the company.) Joe said that years earlier, he and Gus had agreed they would have a "true-up" one day, where they'd settle the books amicably. Had he known that they'd have to answer to Gus's children for how they managed the company, he said, he never would have agreed to form Chippewa Lakes in the first place.

The lawsuit carried on after Joe Meaher's death. Eckert, his heir, stood in as the executor of his estate. As of 2022, the litigation was still ongoing.

Though the Meahers have been quiet since 2018, they have not been completely silent. Gus Meaher told the website SFGate in 2018 that his great-grandfather was not responsible for the *Clotilda*'s voyage; he blamed Foster instead. And Robert Meaher gave brief comments to *National Geographic* for a 2020 story about Africatown and the *Clotilda*. "Slavery is wrong," he told the magazine, but "if your brother killed somebody, it would not be your fault." Still, he added: "I'll apologize. Something like that, that was wrong." At the same time, he was defensive, noting that his family had once donated church property and land for a park in Africatown. He questioned whether the ship that archaeologists had singled out in 2019 was truly the *Clotilda,* and he mentioned that his ancestor had never been convicted of a crime. When the magazine asked whether he'd consider meeting with the shipmates' descendants, he replied, "I'm not open to it."

In years past, Robert Meaher has made similar comments in private. "It is my position to keep a low profile at all times in the community here," he wrote to a staffer at the History Museum of Mobile in 2011. "Mobile needs good jobs here and not racial tension or labels." He said that in the past, his father had received demands for restitution, accompanied by threats, and said he knew the Foster family had also been threatened. He doubted much of the accepted history about the *Clotilda* saga, he said, and questioned whether William Foster's diary, one of the principle sources of information on the voyage, was authentic. He mentioned that he'd done some historical research himself. He once called the Department of Justice in Washington, D.C., inquiring about any records they had on his great-grandfather.

In all that had been written about Cudjo Lewis, Robert Meaher said, he'd never seen anyone note that Cudjo was glad he'd been brought to Mobile, because it had given him the opportunity to become a Christian. (This is a distortion of comments Cudjo made in various newspaper stories, where he said he cherished his Christian faith but also expressed a desperate longing to be back home.) Robert Meaher closed the letter almost cryptically. Looking at photos of Cudjo, he wrote he realized the two of them had something in common: they'd both lost their right index fingers. "The Lewis family lived on Conception Street Road where Gulf Lumber is today and Henry Williams, a black historian, told me Cudjoe is buried there."

For several years, Robert Meaher was reportedly in discussions with the history museum about the prospect of donating some artifacts from the *Clotilda,* including a pistol and an ornate drinking cup; but in the end, this donation never occurred. A more intriguing question, however, is what kinds of documents the family might possess and what they could reveal about the *Clotilda* story. "They never throw anything away," said one person acquainted with the family.

In 2021, however, there was a development that led some Mobilians to wonder if a new era might be dawning for the Meahers. The family owned a building in Africatown that had once housed Scott Paper's credit union. For some time, Womack, Flen, and others had been vocal about wanting to see the building converted to a food pantry or something else the community could use. In 2021, Stimpson got in touch with the family, after discussing the matter with Merceria Ludgood and other local leaders. The Meahers agreed to sell it for $50,000. This was billed as a steep discount; though the property had been vacant for decades, its appraised value was $300,000. The city used federal funds to cover the purchase price, and Ludgood promised the county would handle the necessary repairs, including a new roof and HVAC system. Yorktown Baptist and other organizations agreed to run a food bank there. However, seven months later, Ludgood made another announcement: after assessing the building, design contractors had found that the necessary repairs would cost at least $700,000. It would be more cost-effective to demolish the credit union and build a new facility.

A press release by the city, issued when the sale was announced, included a statement from the Meaher family. When Stimpson had contacted them about selling or donating the property, they said, "we could not think of a better way to give back to the community." They added, "We all look forward to watching this endeavor become a reality with a lasting positive impact on the community for years to come." The press release did not name any individual family member. However, it seems doubtful Joe Meaher would have agreed to this gesture if he were still living. With Gus Meaher's children apparently poised to inherit half of the property in the coming years, they may well have played a role in the decision. Eight months later, Helen Meaher and employees of Chippewa Lakes, the Meahers' company, made a quiet appearance in the neighborhood, helping to distribute food at a bi-weekly pantry event. But whether or not these gestures augur bigger changes remains to be seen.

It's commonly assumed in Mobile that the reason for the Meahers' reticence has been a fear that if they speak up or start a dialogue with the Africatown and descendant communities, they'll be pressured to "pay reparations"—to part with more of their holdings, whether in the form of cash payments or property transfers. If this is true, it speaks to a phenomenon larger than their family. For all the help Africatown has received from outside of Alabama since 2018, the record of the city and state governments has been mixed. The trouble is that some of the reforms Womack and others have requested would cost significant amounts of money, and in some cases would pose a threat to deeply entrenched business interests. This is a paradox the neighborhood has faced at least since the eighties. No one objects to the community celebrating its heritage, but when discussions begin about redevelopment—which, inevitably, comes with substantial costs—local support tends to wither.

Mayor Sandy Stimpson, who was reelected in 2017 and 2021, has made supportive gestures. He has visited Africatown for occasional events, such as the unveiling of the new bell on the school grounds, the press conference about the *Clotilda* finding, and the announcement about the new food pantry. His staff organized a cleanup day in the community in 2020, and the city government has agreed to chip in $250,000 for the Heritage House (with the county covering roughly $1 million more). In 2021, the city used $72,000 in federal grant funding to bring in some 230 out-of-state volunteers, who re-roofed ten homes and made siding repairs to seven others. Perhaps the city's most significant achievement has been obtaining a $300,000 grant, under the Environmental Protection Agency's Brownfields Program, to study contamination levels at certain sites in Africatown and clean them up, so they can be put to new uses. As of 2021, a few of the sites slated for assessment were the old International Paper property, some vacant lots near one of the neighborhood entrances, and a three-story house where there was talk of establishing a bed-and-breakfast.

At the same time, a feeling persists among many residents and supporters that Africatown's redevelopment is not a high priority for Stimpson's administration. It's hard to deny that the city could be doing much more. The city government has barely been involved in the planning of the blueway, despite overtures made by the blueway committee. And a project to add Lewis Quarters to the National Register of Historic Places, as part of the larger Africatown site established in 2012, was nixed shortly after Stimpson took office. The contract with Shaun Wilson, the researcher working on the application, was terminated.

More important, apart from applying for the EPA grant, the Stimpson administration has done little to support environmental justice for Africatown. This has been a live issue since 2016, when the city started working on new development regulations. Mobile's code has not been revised since 1968, a time when Black residents were systematically excluded from holding office in the city. The decision to revise it was spurred by the 2016 fight over tank farm regulations. Throughout the process, Ramsey Sprague has led the charge for better protections around Africatown. Given the scope of the overhaul, he and other MEJAC members opted to be ambitious: they've asked that the tank farms surrounding Africatown be phased out over time.

The city could achieve this by rezoning the land where the tank farms sit, so that when the existing tanks became too old to use, they could not be replaced with new ones. Besides this, however, MEJAC has also made a number of more modest requests. In comments Sprague has submitted to the city, he's asked for ten-foot-high walls around all new industrial operations bordering Africatown's residential streets, and for buffers of trees and bushes around factories, among other amenities.

During the drafting process, the city has incorporated some of these requests but refused to grant others. For instance, city leaders reportedly told MEJAC it was too hard to source ten-foot-tall barriers that would shield residents from floating dust. (Stimpson's administration also said in an email interview that the walls could have the effect of "carving up the urban fabric" and could lead to "social exclusion rather than environmental protection.") The request to phase out the tank farms has been a nonstarter. In the near-final draft that came out in 2021, only four pages of the new code dealt with Africatown specifically, compared to a thirty-one page section on Spring Hill, the area where Old Mobile families are concentrated.

When the planning commission took up the document in February 2021, pandemic restrictions were still in effect, so the main hearing was live-streamed online. Stimpson, in his introduction, said the new code represented "balance" between different interests, including those of historic neighborhoods and the industrial sector. Later, when the floor was opened for public comment, several people criticized the portion of the code dealing with Africatown. One eloquent speaker was Lella Lowe, a West Mobile resident who has long been involved in MEJAC. She raised the question of what tourism in Africatown would look like if the conditions there didn't improve. She asked the planning commission to picture a tour group passing an Africatown home, where only a chain-link fence stands between the yard and an industrial site, and "where trucks travel in and out, all day long, over a dusty dirt road, creating dust and debris that falls on top of the homes in this historic area." Clearly, she said, this would be a showcase of environmental *in*justice. "Now reimagine," she said, "that there are ten-foot-tall concrete barriers between those same two zoned areas, and that there are odor-abatement requirements." In this version of the future, tour guides would be able to talk about how Mobile had recognized its past mistakes and tried to do right by Africatown. Under those conditions, Lowe suggested, visitors might be impressed enough to recommend the tour to their friends.

In the weeks after this hearing, the city amended the code slightly, adding stronger landscaping requirements for the buffer zones in Africatown. But other requests, including a mandate for taller and stronger barriers, still went unaddressed. From Sprague's perspective, the code offered virtually no support for the blueway project. In the fall, the code was rejected by the city council, in part because of the concerns Africatown supporters had raised, and was sent back to the planning commission for revisions.

To some extent, the city's actions here simply reflect its general priorities. Early on, under Stimpson's leadership, the city slashed its allocations to the Historic Mobile Preservation Society, the Mobile Arts Council, the Mobile Opera, the Mobile Symphony Orchestra, and a museum of Black history, cutting them roughly in half. Stimpson also spun the city history museum off as an independent organization, so it would no longer be the local government's responsibility, which led to much of the staff being laid off. "He's not a fan of the arts," said one former colleague, echoing an observation that is often made by the mayor's critics. "He's not a fan of history. He's not a fan of preservation."

When it comes to housing, Stimpson has spoken about residential blight in alarmist terms. "It's like having stage four cancer, and we're trying to save the patient right now," he told a local TV reporter in March 2021. "And we're throwing everything we can at it." By and large, however, this has meant tearing houses down instead of fixing them up. As of mid-2019, two years into the city's blight removal program, 887 structures had been demolished or were scheduled to be, and preservation advocates believe several hundred more have been torn down since then. Jarrod White, who is involved in preservation projects (even if he has sometimes found himself at odds with environmental justice advocates), believes at least 700 of those homes were more than a century old. In the 2020 and 2021 fiscal years, Stimpson's administration has budgeted an extra $570,000 for demolitions, in addition to federal funds that can be used for the same purpose. Another person involved in preservation suggested that if blight is like a cancer, the city's response has been like giving the patient cyanide.

The city's actions also stem from its reluctance to impose burdens on heavy industry. Its refusal to require sight and sound barriers around Africatown is a little puzzling; but as for MEJAC's most radical request, that the city phase out the tank farms around Africatown, the reluctance is understandable. It could mean major costs, not only for the tank farms, but for the other businesses that depend on them for petroleum, as well as for the city (in the form of tax revenue). There's little doubt that it would also be challenged in court. However, this speaks to why environmental racism is so hard to uproot. It has been a factor in shaping Mobile's very geography. Given Africatown's historical import, relocating the petroleum tanks may seem well worth the cost, especially from an outsider's perspective. But many locals don't see it that way.

Perhaps there's also some resistance, or at least a lack of enthusiasm, for the Africatown project in particular. If the vision of Womack, Flen, and the others is ever borne out, the story of Africatown will likely end up overshadowing the rest of Mobile's history. Many Mobilians, white ones especially, take great pride in the city's past, including its years under French and Spanish rule, its maritime history, and its elaborate Mardi Gras traditions. Some residents are reluctant to accept what now seems, to many outsiders, an obvious fact: that none of this history compares, in national or international significance, to the *Clotilda* landing and the founding of African Town. (At least one local historian has complained that in his decades working in the city, he's always had to field inquiries about the *Clotilda*. In 2020, he expressed the counterintuitive hope that the identification of the ship would finally put the matter to rest.) This may be less about the shamefulness of the *Clotilda* story, and more because Africatown simply doesn't excite these Mobilians in the way that Mardi Gras does. For the most part, they didn't hear about Africatown growing up. It's a counterpoint to the other stories Mobile tells about itself, and might even be seen as an indictment of the city.

At the same time, a threat also looms at the state level. Since the 1990s, the Alabama Department of Transportation has talked about building a new Interstate-10 bridge across the Mobile River. Traffic congestion on the existing bridge is a serious problem; the structure was designed to handle thirty-six thousand vehicles a day, but as of 2019, the daily average was around seventy-five thousand. In 2020, the state was moving ahead with plans to install a new six-lane bridge, which it intended to pay off by charging tolls of $3 to $6. It was clear that if this happened, tens of thousands of drivers would take the Cochrane-Africatown Bridge instead, which had no toll—and this meant traffic through the center of Africatown would surge. This would in turn create more noise and more fumes, and would make it more dangerous than it already is for residents to cross the street. In the spring of 2019, the state held a meeting at Union Baptist, and roughly fifty residents and allies turned out, mostly to express their opposition.

The plan was ultimately canceled, but only because a massive number of residents from elsewhere in Mobile and Baldwin counties protested the tolls.

As of 2021, a new plan was being floated: to build a separate bridge just for cargo trucks, funded by a $10 to $15 toll. The state predicted it would divert hazardous cargo away from Africatown, but Womack, for one, remained skeptical. He remembered from his trucking days that many drivers have to pay their own tolls. He compared the bridge plans to a film franchise, "where the writers keep bringing the bad guy back from the dead to keep the movie going."

For Africatown residents and supporters, the years since the *Clotilda* announcement have been hopeful but tense. To understand the mood, it helps to go back to the celebration that happened in May 2019, the week after the news broke about the ship. Hundreds of people were gathered under a massive tent, in the heart of Plateau, with many, including Joe Womack, clad in traditional West African garb. The sun was shining, and the day was warm. During the ceremonies, portions of William Foster's memoir were read, a dance troupe performed, and prayers and rousing speeches were delivered. Reporters and camera crews were everywhere. It felt as if the eyes of the whole world were on the place—almost like the future that Womack and others pictured was already at hand.

But of course, when the party was over, the crowds departed, leaving the streets mostly empty. The run-down houses were no less run-down, the community was no less poor, and the pollution remained. This may have been how Henry Williams and John Smith felt in the eighties, when the crowds of the AfricaTown Folk Festivals died down. In a way, the whole question, at this stage in Africatown's history, was whether this time would be different. Would the broader outcome from the eighties be repeated as well? Would another new highway disrupt the community? Would all the press attention amount to nothing? Certainly the stakes this time were higher. The residential population was aging and contracting. Without redevelopment, it was conceivable that before long, there would be no Africatown left.

Merceria Ludgood, the county commissioner, who witnessed all the events in the eighties, remained hopeful. In an interview in the spring of 2021, she pointed out two advantages that Africatown had gained in recent years. One was money. The millions that had been secured for the heritage house and the welcome center had no parallel in the neighborhood's history. The other advantage, she said, was that thanks to the *Clotilda*'s wreckage being identified, Africatown was on an international stage like never before. "It's kind of like what happened on the Edmund Pettus Bridge," she said, referring to one of the pivotal events of the civil rights movement. On March 7, 1965, hundreds of protesters, led by John R. Lewis and Reverend Hosea Williams, marched across the steel bridge in Selma, where they were attacked by police carrying clubs and tear gas. Images of the attack were televised across the country, putting pressure on President Lyndon Johnson to do more for the protesters' cause. "I mean that was the impetus that got the Voting Rights Act of 1965 passed," Ludgood went on. "When the world was watching. 'What are y'all gonna do now?' Well, we saw."

Ludgood takes an optimistic view of the tourism question. She predicted that after the opening of the heritage house, an influx of visitors to Mobile would create similar pressure locally. "They're going to look at more than the cemetery," she said. "They're going to look around that community and say, 'Oh my god, how have you allowed this international treasure to deteriorate in this way?'"

When Womack and Flen are asked about the future, their perspectives diverge. Although Womack is hopeful about certain projects, it's doubtful that he'll ever feel like the crusade he's part of has succeeded. He has a reflexive pessimism and sense of combativeness. "They keep coming, and they keep coming, and they keep coming," he sometimes says, repeating the mantra he learned from Henry Williams. "You can never rest, because they'll keep coming."

Flen has a different touchstone—a favorite anecdote from his years at MCTS. He was a sophomore, and the football team had just lost a game in Montgomery, where he'd been the quarterback. "I was looking kind of down and despondent," he recalls, "and the referees had cheated, the whole nine yards." Curtis Harden, his coach, noticed his demeanor and walked up to him. "He said, 'Anderson Flen, I want you to know something.' He said, 'You've got two choices in life. You can have a pity party, or you can beat 'em with success. The easiest one is to have a pity party. The hardest one is beating them with success—but that's what you get the most joy from.' And I have never forgotten that."

ACKNOWLEDGMENTS

When I think about all the support I received in the research and writing of this book, I'm overwhelmed with gratitude. It's hard to know where to begin.

Laurie Abraham, my editor at *New York* magazine in 2018, has a rare gift for brainstorming ideas. She had the inspiration to ask for a piece on what had become of Cudjo Lewis's descendants. The genealogist Angela Walton-Raji played a critical role by connecting me to Garry Lumbers. The rest of that experience I describe in the prologue.

In early 2019, Audrea Lim commissioned me to write a chapter about Africatown for *The World We Need*, an anthology dealing with grassroots environmental groups throughout the United States, which she was editing for the New Press. It was in the course of writing that chapter that I realized Africatown's 160-year history demanded an entire book of its own.

I would not have embarked on this project if not for the encouragement I received in those early stages from Africatown residents and their allies in Mobile. When I told them what I had in mind, the response I got, almost universally, was "Come on down! We need all the help we can get." Once I moved to Mobile, Reverend Christopher Williams was one of the first people to welcome me and help me make connections. Before the pandemic, he introduced me one Sunday from the pulpit at Yorktown Missionary Baptist Church. Mae Jones, Ruth Ballard, Washington Taylor, Anderson Flen, Joycelyn Davis, Darron Patterson, and many others trusted me with their personal stories and helped deepen my understanding of Africatown's history. I hope my respect for them comes through in these pages. Besides Joycelyn and

Darron, numerous other descendants of the shipmates, particularly Garry Lumbers and Cassandra Lewis Wallace, have also entrusted me with elements of their family history, for which I feel honored beyond words.

Several community groups—MEJAC, CHESS, the MCTS Alumni Association, and the Africatown Community Development Commission—allowed me to sit in on meetings before COVID-19 forced us all into lockdown. Later, when the restrictions were relaxed, Reverend Derek Tucker also introduced me to his congregation at Union Missionary Baptist Church and allowed me to examine some of the church's oldest records. As for Ramsey Sprague, his research on pollution, zoning issues, and neighborhood history has been extremely formidable—to say nothing of his other work as an activist. He could have a remarkable career in any number of fields, and it's a testament to his moral devotion that he's committed so much of his life to this project.

No one was more giving of his time and knowledge than Joe Womack. Besides inviting me into his home and introducing me to his family, Joe also let me shadow him when he gave speeches and made presentations—in Mobile and beyond. I'll never forget the untold hours we spent together in the course of my research.

I am also indebted to many archivists and librarians: Elizabeth Theris-Boone, Valerie Ellis, and Denisha Mosley-Logan at the Local History & Genealogy Library in Mobile; Michael Campbell and Vicki Tate at the University of South Alabama; Sonja Woods at the Howard University Moorland-Spingarn Research Center; Marye Newman at the History Museum of Mobile; Edward Harkins, Pamela Major, and Tamara Callier at the Mobile Municipal Archives; Bob Peck and Robert Allen at the Historic Mobile Preservation Society; Tracy Neely of the Mobile Creole Cultural and Historical Preservation Society; Courtney Pinkard and Kayla Scott at the Alabama Department of Archives and History; and Cynthia Walton at the National Park Service. I'm also grateful for the digital resources of the New York Public Library, which is an extraordinary institution—like a university library for the rest of us.

David Alsobrook is one of the finest historians Mobile has produced. We never met in person, on account of the pandemic, but I kept him on speed dial for most of my time living in the city. He was the first to review the manuscript for accuracy, and he made helpful notes and corrections no one else would have been positioned to make. His death in late 2021 came as a shock. I wish he'd lived long enough to see the book in its final form, which bears many traces of his influence. Two other scholars provided me with similar help. John Sledge fielded my questions for the better part of two years and opened up to me the records of the Mobile Historic Development Commission, which contain treasures that had never been unearthed. And James Delgado not only walked me through many aspects of maritime archaeology, but was also the ideal fellow traveler in my efforts to get at the true events of the *Clotilda* plot. Their comments on the completed manuscript both saved me from some factual blunders and helped bring new depths to the narration.

Akinwumi Ogundiran and Robin Law, both giants in the field of West African history, also took time out of their schedules to review portions and offer valuable comments, as did my friend Garry Mitchell, who covered Mobile for thirty-one years as an Associated Press correspondent. In addition, Kern Jackson, Scotty Kirkland, Gregory Waselkov, and Wayne Flynt (who may well know more about Alabama history than anyone else alive) generously lent me their support and knowledge.

It hardly seems necessary to say that this book wouldn't have been possible without the prior work of Emma Langdon Roche, Zora Neale Hurston, Natalie Robertson, Sylviane Diouf, and Deborah Plant. They all have my respect and gratitude. The work of many local journalists over 160 years also undergirds this book. John Sharp, who has covered the city government and Africatown for the *Press-Register* since 2012, especially deserves recognition.

I'd also like to thank several other friends I made in the course of my reporting. Suzanne Cleveland resents being called the Gertrude Stein of Mobile, but based on my experience, the description suits her in the best possible way. Before I met Andrew Tumminia and April Terra Livingston, during a cleanup day in Africatown, the three of us were on a collision course. Our long conversations on their porch, in their backyard, and during strolls through Magnolia Cemetery are now some of my happiest memories in the city. When I first called Wanda Cochran, it was to ask a single question about zoning law; but I got more than I bargained for, with her deep knowledge of local politics and history, and with the rapport we immediately established. Though Margaret Brown no longer lives in Mobile, she and her crew visited often to shoot *Descendant*, which shaped up to be a masterpiece of documentary film. Margaret became a close collaborator and a trusted friend. Thanks also to Florence and Mike Stratas, Tom Mason, Joe and Donna Camp, John Coleman, and John and Celia Mann Baehr.

My agent, Jane Dystel, did much more than sell the book proposal. Since she took me on as a client in 2013, I've benefited often from her vast knowledge of the publishing world and her wisdom. Thanks to Stephen Power, who acquired the book, and to Anna deVries, who has been a consistent source of much-needed advice, and whose keen editing has improved my drafts immeasurably.

A grant from the Economic Hardship Reporting Project was most helpful in funding the intensive research this book required.

The editors to whom I owe the most are Tony Gonzalez, Jennifer Brown, David Haskell, Genevieve Smith, and Maxwell George. Over the years, Daniel Silliman has often been the ideal reader I've had in my head. He's inspired me to be at once more critical and more generous. Thanks also to my dear friends Mike Chalberg, Maggie Downham, Andreea Drogeanu, Jonathan and Naomi Dunn, George Fillingham, Andy and Courtney Gillies, Zach and Heidi Hendrickson, Luke and Mary Heyman and their kids, Jack Hittinger, Benjamin Joubert, Adam Valen Levinson, Dan Miloch, Joel Myers, Jon Oatess, Rob Ogden, Stephen and Sarah Petrie, Matt Schonert, Patsy Sims, Neda Toloui-Semnani, Nathaniel Swanson, and my church family at the Cathedral of the Holy Virgin Protection in New York.

Throughout our lives, my sister Erin Tabor and I have grown intellectually, spiritually, and in every other way on parallel tracks. She's given me the kind of moral support that only a sibling could provide. My parents, John and Karen Tabor, have been my most enthusiastic readers since this book was in its conceptual stage. I'm grateful as well to my grandparents, Gerald and Sandra Smith, and Delores Tabor. No one has inspired me more than my grandfather, Fred Tabor. I was in the middle of my move to New York, in 2013, when I heard he was going into hospice, and I happened to have Philip Levine's book *The Simple Truth* open on my lap. The title poem said more than I possibly could have.

A NOTE ON SOURCES

Before the 1990s, the story of the *Clotilda*'s voyage was only ever recorded by unreliable narrators. This is a pattern that goes all the way back to that week in the summer of 1860 when the ship was brought up through Mobile Bay and set on fire. The first news report that traveled across the wire was wrong about the number of captives and—in some of the newspapers where it was printed—about the name of the ship as well.

As I mentioned in the prologue, there are limits to how much the true events of the *Clotilda* saga, particularly the deeds of Timothy Meaher and William Foster, can be separated from mythology. I admit the question did occur to me, from time to time, whether the story is mythology all the way down. But in those moments, I reminded myself that there *is* a bedrock of documentation. There are many newspaper reports on Meaher and his business operations that were published in his lifetime, both before and after the *Clotilda*'s voyage. There are census records showing where he and Foster lived, property records showing what they owned, and maritime records showing when the *Clotilda* was built and where it traveled on its many voyages. And there's a half-burned ship lying in the muck, beside Twelvemile Island, that has now been shown to match—precisely—the descriptions in that old paperwork. Similar statements can be made about the shipmates. Many reporters visited them while they were alive, and they always told the same story about their arrival in Mobile and their experiences after the war. This book has aimed to lay out all of that evidence, in a comprehensive way. But it has also aimed to trace the development of the story to show how it has served different interests at different times. Toby Green has written that all "sources" on the past represent political projects, and I hope this book has demonstrated how that principle can work in action.

Let me begin, however, with the sources on West African society in the 1850s. Reconstructing the internal life of places like Yorubaland (which was a vast area, containing multitudes) and Dahomey is a challenge, because these were predominantly oral cultures, where communication was generally not done in writing. Most of the descriptions we have from the nineteenth century were written by European visitors. These were men (almost never women) who didn't speak the local languages, spent relatively little time in the societies they wrote about, and were restricted, while they were there, to what the authorities allowed them to see. Even so, their writings are invaluable, because they're the only ones we have. Following the lead of contemporary scholars, I drew heavily on those eyewitness accounts; but also from those scholars, I took cues about where to give credence to the Europeans' reports and where to distrust them. I am also indebted to the historians Robin Law, whose knowledge of the Kingdom of Dahomey is unsurpassed, and Akinwumi Ogundiran, the author of an outstanding 2020 volume on the Yoruba people, for reviewing my sections on West Africa and giving valuable suggestions.

Of course, my chapters on West Africa center on the biography of Kossola. Though Kossola spoke with many visitors during his years in the United States, the only detailed account of his life is the one composed by Zora Neale Hurston, published as the book *Barracoon*. As I indicated in chapter 10, it's possible that Hurston was not always perfectly reliable herself. Besides the red flags described in that chapter, there is another concern to keep in mind. Hurston presented her dialogue with Cudjo as if she'd transcribed it verbatim—but this is unlikely. In one scene, for instance, she quotes a monologue he supposedly gave while she was driving, when she couldn't possibly have been taking notes. Even when she was undistracted, her transcription would have been imperfect at best. Portable tape recorders didn't yet exist in the late 1920s, and Hurston was not skilled at shorthand. In fact, she was once dismissed from a secretarial job, in part because her notetaking was scarcely legible. In some cases, she also quoted Cudjo reciting information that he likely wouldn't have known, such as specific dates and place names. It seems she inserted these details herself and put them in his voice.

At the same time, Hurston successfully took down some of the Yoruba words Cudjo taught her—and as Diouf has noted, Yoruba is a tonal language, difficult to record. When Cassandra Lewis Wallace, one of Cudjo's great-great-grandchildren, was growing up, her father used to imitate Cudjo's speech for her and her siblings. When Wallace read *Barracoon,* she told me, she was astonished at how closely the dialect matched her father's imitations. As for the substantive information in *Barracoon,* most of it can be confirmed through other sources. I've chosen to use direct quotations from the book, knowing they don't match the standards of precision that are expected from journalists in the twenty-first century, when digital recorders are de rigueur.

The earliest sources that describe the voyage in detail are the firsthand accounts of William Foster (as recorded in a short memoir) and Timothy Meaher (as told to a journalist). Both were composed thirty years after the fact, when the southern atmosphere was thick with antebellum nostalgia and the *Clotilda* mythology had already had time to ferment. Those accounts should be read with great skepticism. Nevertheless, with regard to the journey itself, and its aftermath, they are likely still the most reliable sources sources available. My narration of the trip, and the cover-up that followed, is drawn from those, and also from federal records that detail the investigation and halfhearted prosecution. (The original copies of those federal records are in the National Archives, but since my access to those copies was restricted, because of the COVID-19 pandemic, I relied on copies on file at the History Museum of Mobile.)

During the 1890s and early 1900s, the story was told again in numerous magazines and newspapers. Each article relates the story of Foster traveling to West Africa, bringing the captives back, and torching the *Clotilda;* and almost every one includes its own bits of information that are not found in the others. In general, I've tended to disregard these details. It's worth giving an example to demonstrate why. Roche writes that when Foster first anchored the ship near the Mississippi coast, he and Meaher waited until dark to bring it up through the bay. Later, as the *Clotilda* passed downtown Mobile, Roche writes, the clock in the old Spanish tower struck eleven. The watchman called out, "Eleven o'clock and all's well," and his voice carried across the water—or so Roche says. But she has the timing wrong. In Mobile at that time of year, it wouldn't have turned dark until nine P.M. or later, and for a tugboat to pull the *Clotilda* that many miles would have taken several hours or more. More to the point, given that she wrote her book more than fifty years after the events in question, long after the deaths of Meaher and Foster, she had no reliable way of confirming details like this one. This is the trouble with all those tidbits that appear in the later accounts: they're not to be trusted. (On the other hand, I have used several details that Roche clearly learned from Foster's widow directly, when there's no particular reason to doubt them. These are all highlighted in the endnotes.)

Of course, this book also benefited from the scholarship of Sylviane Diouf and Natalie Robertson. In virtually all cases, I have consulted primary sources instead of depending on their summaries; but where it's been appropriate, I have cited their interpretations of the events, and being able to compare my findings against theirs was also a major help.

Skipping ahead to the twentieth century, there's an unfortunate paucity of records dealing with Plateau and Magazine Point. Another lesson here is that preserving historical records tends to cost money. In general, poor communities are often forced to use cheap materials to build houses, schools, and churches; and especially in a hurricane-prone area like Mobile, many of those buildings cannot stand the test of time. In Africatown's case, the history of industrial development hasn't helped, either. When the buildings get torn down, whatever records they may have housed are frequently lost. At the same time, the white historians of Mobile's past, such as Caldwell Delaney, clearly didn't care enough about Africatown to help preserve the neighborhood's history, or to store many of those records for safekeeping in the museums and libraries downtown. When they did, it was done more in the spirit of extraction than collaboration. To the extent that I managed to fill this void, I'm indebted to current and former Africatown residents who took the time to share their memories, and to contemporary Mobile historians (in particular David Alsobrook and John Sledge), who pointed me in new directions for my research. Over time, I did find many records on this period as well, as the bibliography indicates.

When it came to narrating the debacle over the petroleum developments, much of the information came from troves of documents compiled at the time by Brenda Bolton, Thayer Dodd, and Casi Callaway, which they preserved and were kind enough to share. I also did my own research in public records and industry documents, and I filled in the rest with interviews and news coverage. In the last chapter, my narration of the *Clotilda* being identified again came from published reports and from interviews with the archaeologists James Delgado, Dave Conlin, Stacye Hathorn, and Kamau Sadiki. Other events described there were sourced in a similar way.

No one from the Meaher family would speak on the record.

AUTHOR'S INTERVIEWS

John Adams, Nelson Adams, Tori L. Adams, Carol Adams-Davis, Robert Allen, David Alsobrook, Cleophas Armstead, John Bacot, Ruth Ballard, Robert Battles, Devereaux Bemis, Sydney Betbeze, Teresa Bettis, Brenda Bolton, Mike Box, Walter Bracy, John Bratten, Edwin Bridges, Phil Brown, Hank Caddell, Casi Callaway, Suzanne Cleveland, Wanda Cochran, Dave Conlin, A.J. Cooper, Joycelyn Davis, Ron Davis, James Delgado, Sylviane Diouf, Thayer Dodd, Mike Dow, Troy Ephriam, Janet Fiskio, Anderson Flen, Wayne Flynt, Michael Foster, Robert Gamble, Bill Green, Palmer Hamilton, William Harris, Stacye Hathorn, Valerie Hayes, Genevieve Hubbard, Herndon Inge, Sarah Jackson, Stephen James, Emory Johnson, Cleon Jones, Mae Jones, Kimberly Kane, Ted Keeby, Michael Krivor, Carolyn Adams Lewis, Walter Lockwood, Cindy Lowry, David Ludder, Garry Lumbers, Valena McCants, Ellen Mertins, Robert Moore, Sheila Mosley, Gloria Nault, Jane Nettles, Jesse Norwood, Akinwumi Ogundiran, David Padgett, Darron Patterson, Sharon Patterson, Addie Pettaway, Isaiah Pinkney, Charles Porter, Deborah Randolph, Fred Richardson, Willie Roberson, Kamau Sadiki, John Sledge, Afra Smith, Daryl Smith, Yuri Smith, Liz Smith-Incer, Ramsey Sprague, Al Stokes, Bill Sullivan, Daniel Tait, Washington Taylor, Lucy Thomas, Michael Thomason, William Tishler, Charles Torrey, Derek Tucker, Michael Tuttle, Charlie Walker, Cassandra Lewis Wallace, Barbara Wheat, Jarrod White, Christopher Williams, Shaun Wilson, Jesse Womack, Joe Womack, James Woods, Lorna Gail Woods, Donnie Woodward

(And others who requested anonymity)

ABBREVIATIONS

- ADAH: Alabama Department of Archives and History
- ADEM: Alabama Department of Environmental Management
- ALP: Alain Locke Papers, Howard University
- AP: Associated Press
- EOA: Encyclopedia of Alabama
- HMM: History Museum of Mobile
- HMPS: Historic Mobile Preservation Society
- *MA: Montgomery Advertiser*
- MCPC: Mobile County Probate Court
- *MDI: Mobile Daily Item*
- *MDR: Mobile Daily Register*
- MHDC: Mobile Historic Development Commission
- MMA: Mobile Municipal Archives
- *MP: Mobile Press*
- MPL: Mobile Public Library
- *MPR: Mobile Press-Register*
- *MR: Mobile Register*
- *NG: National Geographic*
- NPS: National Park Service
- *NYT: New York Times*
- PSC: Alabama Public Service Commission
- *TD: Times-Democrat* (New Orleans)

- USA: McCall Archives, University of South Alabama
- *WP: Washington Post*

A note on citations: Mobile's principal newspaper has changed its name numerous times since its first issue was published (under the name *The Mobile Commercial Register*) in 1821. Often these changes have accompanied mergers and changes in ownership. It became the *Mobile Daily Register* in 1849, and the name was shortened to the *Mobile Register* in 1905. Another paper, the *Mobile Press,* was launched by a separate publisher in 1929, and it acquired the *Register* in 1932 and became the older paper's afternoon counterpart. In 1997, the afternoon edition was eliminated, and the morning paper became the *Press-Register.* For a breakdown of the paper's evolution, see "Mobile Press-Register 200th Anniversary: A Timeline of Mobile's Newspaper," *MPR,* June 10, 2013.

BOOKS CITED IN TEXT

Akintoye, S. Adebanji. *A History of the Yoruba People*. Dakar: Amalion Publishing, 2014. First published 2010.

The Alabama Negro, 1863–1946. Mobile, AL: The Gulf Informer Publishing Co., 1946.

Alpern, Stanley B. *Amazons of Black Sparta: The Women Warriors of Dahomey*. New York: New York University Press, 1998.

American Anti-Slavery Society. *The Anti-Slavery History of the John-Brown Year*. New York: American Anti-Slavery Society, 1861.

Baker, Jean H. *James Buchanan*. New York: Henry Holt, 2004.

Baptist, Edward E. *The Half Has Never Been Told: Slavery and the Making of American Capitalism*. New York: Basic Books, 2016. First published 2014.

Baquaqua, Mahommah G. *The Biography of Mahommah Gardo Baquaqua: His Passage from Slavery to Freedom in Africa and America*. Edited by Robin Law and Paul E. Lovejoy. Princeton, NJ: Markus Wiener Publishers, 2001.

Bay, Edna G. *Wives of the Leopard: Gender, Politics, and Culture in the Kingdom of Dahomey*. Charlottesville: University Press of Virginia, 1998.

Beckert, Sven. *Empire of Cotton: A Global History*. New York: Vintage Books, 2014.

Bergeron, Arthur W., Jr. *Confederate Mobile*. Baton Rouge: Louisiana State University Press, 2000. First published 1991 by University Press of Mississippi.

Boyd, Valerie. *Wrapped in Rainbows: The Life of Zora Neale Hurston*. New York: Scribner, 2003.

Boyd, William. *The Slain Wood: Papermaking and Its Environmental Consequences in the American South*. Baltimore: Johns Hopkins University Press, 2015.

Bullard, Robert D. *Dumping in Dixie: Race, Class, and Environmental Quality*, 3rd ed. New York: Routledge, 2018.

Burnett, Lonnie A. *The Pen Makes a Good Sword: John Forsyth of the* Mobile Register. Tuscaloosa: University of Alabama Press, 2006.

Burroughs, Richard. "Suppression of the Atlantic Slave Trade." In *The Suppression of the Atlantic Slave Trade: British Policies, Practices and Representations of Naval Coercion*, ed. Richard Burroughs and Richard Huzzey, 1–13. Manchester: Manchester University Press, 2015.

Burton, Richard F. *A Mission to Gelele, King of Dahome*, 2nd ed. (two volumes). London: Tinsley Brothers, 1864.

Calonius, Erik. *The Wanderer: The Last American Slave Ship and the Conspiracy That Set Its Sails*. New York: St. Martin's Griffin, 2006.

Campbell, Robert. *A Pilgrimage to My Motherland: An Account of a Journey Among the Egbas and Yorubas of Central Africa, in 1859–60*. New York: Thomas Hamilton, 1861.

Chester, Greville John. *Transatlantic Sketches in the West Indies, South America, Canada, and the United States*. London: Smith, Elder & Co., 1869.

Clapperton, Hugh. *Journal of a Second Expedition into the Interior of Africa*. London: John Murray, 1829.

Cobb, James C. *The Selling of the South: The Southern Crusade for Industrial Development, 1936–90*, 2nd ed. Urbana and Chicago: University of Illinois Press, 1993.

Columbus, Christopher. *The Journal of Christopher Columbus*. Translated by Clements R. Markham. London: Hakluyt Society, 1893.

Cumming, Kate. *Gleanings from Southland*. Birmingham: Roberts & Son, 1895.

Curtin, Mary Ellen. *Black Prisoners and Their World: Alabama, 1865–1900*. Charlottesville: University Press of Virginia, 2000.

Davis, Jefferson. *Jefferson Davis, Constitutionalist: His Letters, Papers and Speeches*, Volume 3. Edited by Dunbar Rowland. Jackson: Mississippi Department of Archives and History, 1923.

De Leon, T. C. *Belles, Beaux, and Brains of the '60s*. New York: G. W. Dillingham Company, 1909.

Dennison, Mable. *A Memoir of Lottie Dennison*. Boynton Beach, FL: Futura Printing, 1985.

———. *Biographical Memoirs of James Dennison*. Boynton Beach, FL: Futura Printing, 1985.

Deutsch, Stephanie. *You Need a Schoolhouse: Booker T. Washington, Julius Rosenwald, and the Building of Schools for the Segregated South*. Evanston, IL: Northwestern University Press, 2011.

Diouf, Sylviane A. *Dreams of Africa in Alabama: The Slave Ship* Clotilda *and the Story of the Last Africans Brought to America*. New York: Oxford University Press, 2007.

Doss, Harriet Amos. *Cotton City: Urban Development in Antebellum Mobile*. Tuscaloosa: University of Alabama Press, 2001. First published 1985.

Du Bois, W.E.B. *Black Reconstruction in America, 1860–1880*. New York: The Free Press, 1998. First published 1935 by Harcourt, Brace.

Duncan, John. *Travels in Western Africa, in 1845 and 1846*, Volume 1. London: Richard Bentley, 1847.

Ellis, A.B. *The Yoruba-Speaking Peoples of the Coast of West Africa*. London: Chapman and Hall, Ltd., 1894.

Equiano, Olaudah. *The Life of Olaudah Equiano*. London: Equiano, 1789. Project Gutenberg, March 17, 2005. https://www.gutenberg.org/files/15399/15399-h/15399-h.htm.

Falconbridge, Alexander. *An Account of the Slave Trade on the Coast of Africa*. London: J. Phillips, 1788.

Fauset, Arthur Huff. "American Negro Folk Literature." In *The New Negro: Voices of the Harlem Renaissance*, ed. Alain Locke, 238–44. New York: Atheneum, 1992. First published 1925.

Feldman, Glenn. *Politics, Society, and the Klan in Alabama, 1915–1949*. Tuscaloosa: University of Alabama Press, 1999.

Fitzgerald, Michael W. *Urban Emancipation: Popular Politics in Reconstruction Mobile, 1860–1890*. Baton Rouge: Louisiana State Press, 2002.

Fleming, Walter L. *Civil War and Reconstruction in Alabama*. New York: Columbia University Press, 1905.

Flynt, Wayne. *Alabama in the Twentieth Century*. Tuscaloosa: University of Alabama Press, 2004.

———. "A Tragic Century: The Aftermath of the 1901 Constitution." In *A Century of Controversy: Constitutional Reform in Alabama*, ed. Bailey Thomson, 34–49. Tuscaloosa: University of Alabama Press, 2002.

Foner, Eric. *Reconstruction: America's Unfinished Revolution, 1863–1877*. New York: Harper & Row, 1988.

Forbes, Frederick E. *Dahomey and the Dahomans*, Volume 1. London: Longman, Brown, Green, and Longmans, 1851.

Foster, James Fleetwood. *Ante-Bellum Floating Palaces*. Edited by Bert Neville. Selma, AL: 1967.

Fuller, Hiram. *Belle Brittan on a Tour at Newport, and Here and There*. New York: Derby & Jackson, 1858.

Garrett, William. *Reminiscences of Public Men in Alabama*. Atlanta: Plantation Publishing Company's Press, 1872.

Garrison, William Lloyd. *Thoughts on African Colonization: An Impartial Exhibition of the Doctrines, Principles and Purposes of the American Colonization Society*. Boston: Garrison and Knapp, 1832.

General Assembly of Alabama. *Acts of the Session of 1865–66.* Montgomery, AL: Reid & Screws, 1866.

Going, Allen. *Bourbon Democracy in Alabama, 1874–1890.* Tuscaloosa: University of Alabama Press, 1951.

Green, Toby. *A Fistful of Shells: West Africa from the Rise of the Slave Trade to the Age of Revolution.* London: Penguin Books UK, 2019.

Hackney, Sheldon. *From Populism to Progressivism in Alabama.* Princeton, NJ: Princeton University Press, 1969.

Hamilton, Peter J. *Mobile of the Five Flags: The Story of the River Basin and Coast About Mobile from the Earliest Times to the Present.* Mobile, AL: Gill Printing Company, 1913.

Harlan, Louis R. *Booker T. Washington: The Making of a Black Leader, 1856–1901.* New York: Oxford University Press, 1972.

Harris, Joel Chandler. *Life of Henry W. Grady.* New York: Cassell Publishing Company, 1890.

Hartman, Saidiya. *Lose Your Mother: A Journey Along the Atlantic Slave Route.* New York: Farrar, Straus and Giroux, 2007.

Hemenway, Robert E. *Zora Neale Hurston: A Literary Biography.* Urbana: University of Illinois Press, 1980. First published 1977.

Hoffschwelle, Mary S. *The Rosenwald Schools of the American South.* Gainesville: University Press of Florida, 2014.

Horton, R. G. *The Life and Public Services of James Buchanan, President of the United States.* New York: Derby & Jackson, 1857.

Howard, Warren S. *American Slavers and the Federal Law, 1837–1862.* Berkeley: University of California Press, 1963.

Hughes, Langston. *The Big Sea.* New York: Hill and Wang, 1993. First published 1940 by Alfred A. Knopf.

Hurston, Zora Neale. *Barracoon: The Story of the Last "Black Cargo."* New York: HarperCollins, 2018.
All citations of Zora Neale Hurston refer to *Barracoon* unless otherwise noted.

———. *Dust Tracks on a Road.* New York: HarperPerennial, 1996. First published 1942 by J. B. Lippincott.

———. *Mules and Men.* New York: HarperPerennial, 1990. First published 1935 by J. B. Lippincott.

Hutchinson, George. "Publishers and Publishing Houses." In *The Encyclopedia of the Harlem Renaissance,* Volume 2, eds. Cary D. Wintz and Paul Finkelman, 1000–1004. New York: Routledge, 2004.

Ingraham, J. H. *The Sunny South: Or, The Southerner at Home.* Philadelphia: G. G. Evans, 1860.

Jackson, Harvey III. *Rivers of History: Life on the Coosa, Tallapoosa, Cahaba, and Alabama.* Tuscaloosa: University of Alabama Press, 1995.

―――. "Mobile Since 1945." In *Mobile: The New History of Alabama's First City,* ed. Michael V. R. Thomason, 277–314. Tuscaloosa: University of Alabama Press, 2001.

Johnson, Samuel. *A History of the Yorubas: From the Earliest Times to the Beginning of the British Protectorate.* London: Lowe and Brydone (Printers) Limited, 1921.

Kaplan, Carla, ed. *Zora Neale Hurston: A Life in Letters.* New York: Anchor Books, 2003.

―――. *Miss Anne in Harlem: The White Women of the Black Renaissance.* New York: HarperCollins, 2013.

Kennett, Lee. *Marching Through Georgia: The Story of Soldiers and Civilians During Sherman's Campaign.* New York: HarperCollins, 1995.

Law, Robin. *Ouidah: The Social History of a West African Slaving 'Port,' 1727–1892.* Athens: Ohio University Press, 2004.

―――. *The Slave Coast of West Africa, 1550–1750: The Impact of the Atlantic Slave Trade on an African Society.* Oxford: Oxford University Press, 1991.

Lee, Antoinette J. "Discovering Old Culture in the New World: The Role of Ethnicity." In *The American Mosaic: Preserving a Nation's Heritage,* eds. Robert E. Stipe and Antoinette J. Lee, 180–205. Detroit: Wayne State University Press, 1987.

Lerner, Stephen D. *Diamond: A Struggle for Environmental Justice in Louisiana's Chemical Corridor.* Cambridge: MIT Press, 2005.

Lewis, Cugo (Cudjo). "T'appin (Terrapin)." In *The New Negro: Voices of the Harlem Renaissance,* ed. Alain Locke, 245–47. New York: Atheneum, 1992.

Locke, Alain. ed. *The New Negro: Voices of the Harlem Renaissance.* New York: Atheneum, 1992. First published 1925, Albert and Charles Boni (as *The New Negro: An Interpretation*).

Lynn, Martin. *Commerce and Economic Change in West Africa: The Palm Oil Trade in the Nineteenth Century.* Cambridge: Cambridge University Press, 1997.

May, Robert E. *Manifest Destiny's Underworld: Filibustering in Antebellum America.* Chapel Hill: University of North Carolina Press, 2002.

McCrary, Peyton. "History in the Courts: The Significance of *The City of Mobile v. Bolden.*" In *Minority Vote Dilution,* ed. Chandler Davidson, 47–63. Washington, DC: Howard University Press, 1984.

McKiven, Henry M., Jr. "Secession, War, and Reconstruction." In *Mobile: The New History of Alabama's First City,* ed. Michael V. R. Thomason, 95–125. Tuscaloosa: University of Alabama Press, 2001.

McMillan, Malcolm Cook. *Constitutional Development in Alabama, 1798–1901: A Study in Politics, the Negro, and Sectionalism.* Chapel Hill: University of North Carolina Press, 1955.

Minchin, Timothy J. *The Color of Work: The Struggle for Civil Rights in the Southern Paper Industry, 1945–1980*. Chapel Hill: University of North Carolina Press, 2001.

Moore, Albert Burton. *History of Alabama and Her People*, Volume 2. Chicago and New York: The American Historical Society, 1927.

Nicholls, Keith. "Politics and Civil Rights in Post–World War II Mobile." In *Mobile: The New History of Alabama's First City*, ed. Michael V. R. Thomason, 247–76. Tuscaloosa: University of Alabama Press, 2001.

O'Connor, John. *Wanderings of a Vagabond: An Autobiography*. New York: O'Connor, 1873.

Oldmixon, John W. *Transatlantic Wanderings: Or, A Last Look at the United States*. London: Rutledge & Co., 1855.

O'Meagher, Joseph Casimir. *Some Historical Notices of the O'Meaghers of Ikerrin*. New York: O'Meagher, 1890.

Owen, Thomas McAdory. *History of Alabama and Dictionary of Alabama Biography*, Volume 4. Chicago: S. J. Clarke Publishing Company, 1921.

Perman, Michael. *The Struggle for Mastery: Disfranchisement in the South, 1888–1908*. Chapel Hill: University of North Carolina Press, 2001.

Polk City Directories. *January 2008 Polk City Directory: Mobile County, AL*. Livonia, MI: Polk City Directories, 2008.

Rediker, Marcus. *The Slave Ship: A Human History*. New York: Penguin Books, 2008.

Reid, Whitelaw. *After the War: A Southern Tour*. New York: Moore, Wilstach & Baldwin, 1866.

R. L. Polk & Co. *1983 Mobile (Mobile County, AL) City Directory*. Richmond, VA: R. L. Polk & Co. Publishers, 1983.

Robertson, Natalie S. *The Slave Ship* Clotilda *and the Making of AfricaTown, USA*. Westport, CT: Praeger Publishers, 2008.

Roche, Emma Langdon. *Historic Sketches of the South*. New York: The Knickerbocker Press, 1914.

Rogers, William Warren, Robert David Ward, Leah Rawls Atkins, and Wayne Flynt. *Alabama: The History of a Deep South State*. Tuscaloosa: University of Alabama Press, 1994.

Russell, William Howard. *My Diary North and South*. Boston: T.O.H.P. Burnham, 1863.

Schurz, Carl. *Report on the Condition of the South*. New York: Arno Press and *The New York Times*, 1969. Project Gutenberg, August 18, 2003. https://www.gutenberg.org/cache/epub/8872/pg8872.html.

Shackelford, R. B. *People & Paper: A History of Scott-Mobile, 1939–1989*. Daphne, AL: The New Providence Trading Company, 1989.

Skertchly, J. A. *Dahomey As It Is: Being a Narrative of Eight Months' Residence in That Country.* London: Chapman and Hall, 1874.

Sledge, John S. *The Mobile River.* Columbia: University of South Carolina Press, 2015.

———. *These Rugged Days: Alabama in the Civil War.* Tuscaloosa: University of Alabama Press, 2017.

Smith, John H., and Henry C. Williams. *Africatown, U.S.A.* Madison, WI: American Ethnic Science Society, 1981.

Soumonni, Elisée. "The Compatibility of the Slave and Palm Oil Trades in Dahomey, 1818–1858." In *From Slave Trade to 'Legitimate' Commerce: The Commercial Transition in Nineteenth-Century West Africa,* ed. Robin Law, 78–92. Cambridge: Cambridge University Press, 1995.

Stanfield, James Field. *The Guinea Voyage: A Poem in Three Books.* Edinburgh: J. Robertson, 1807. Project Gutenberg, September 28, 2014. https://www.gutenberg.org/files/46990/46990-h/46990-h.htm.

State of Alabama. *Official Proceedings of the Constitutional Convention of the State of Alabama, May 21st, 1901 to September 3, 1901.* Wetumpka, AL: Wetumpka Printing Co., 1940.

———. *Third Biennial Report of the Inspectors of Mines.* Birmingham: Dispatch Printing Company, 1900.

———. *Third Biennial Report of the Board of Inspectors of Convicts.* Montgomery: A. Roemer, 1900.

Stimpson, William H., and Richard W. Price. *A Stimpson Family in America.* Salt Lake City: Price & Associates, 2004.

Stokes, Melvyn. *D.W. Griffith's* The Birth of a Nation: *A History of the Most Controversial Motion Picture of All Time.* Oxford: Oxford University Press, 2007.

Taylor, Yuval. *Zora and Langston: A Story of Friendship and Betrayal.* New York: W. W. Norton, 2019.

Thomson, H. Bailey. Introduction to *Ninety Degrees in the Shade,* by Clarence Cason, v–xxvi. Tuscaloosa: University of Alabama Press, 2001.

Trefousse, Hans L. *Andrew Johnson: A Biography.* New York: W. W. Norton, 1997.

United States. Naval War Records Office, 1894–1922. *Official Records of the Union and Confederate Navies in the War of the Rebellion,* Series 1 (27 vols.) Washington: U.S. Government Printing Office.

U.S. House of Representatives, Legal and Monetary Affairs Subcommittee of the Committee on Government Operations. *Overview Hearing on Operations of the Department of Housing and Urban Development.* 92nd Congress, 1st session. Washington: Government Printing Office, 1971.

U.S. Senate, Subcommittee on Public Lands and Reserved Water of the Committee on Energy and Natural Resources. *Proposed Additions to the National Park*

System and Miscellaneous Public Land Legislation. 98th Congress, 1st session. Washington: Government Printing Office, 1983.

Walther, Eric H. *The Shattering of the Union: America in the 1850s.* Oxford: SR Books, 2004.

Washington, Booker T. *Booker T. Washington's Own Story of His Life and Work.* Naperville, IL: J. L. Nichols & Co., 1915. First published 1901.

———. *The Story of the Negro: The Rise of the Race from Slavery.* Philadelphia: University of Pennsylvania Press, 2005. First published 1909 by Doubleday, Page & Company.

Wiggins, Sarah Woolfolk. *The Scalawag in Alabama Politics, 1865–1881.* Tuscaloosa: University of Alabama Press, 1977.

Williams, Henry C., and Charles W. Porter. *A History of Mobile County Training School.* Mobile, AL: Williams, 1977.

Woodward, C. Vann. *Origins of the New South, 1877–1913.* Baton Rouge: Louisiana State University Press, 1971.

NOTES

PROLOGUE

2. The church the shipmates had built: Joe and Jesse Womack interviews.

2. In 2019: Joel K. Bourne Jr., "Last American Slave Ship Is Discovered in Alabama," *NG*, May 22, 2019.

4. some 400,000 visitors: *NYT*, May 21, 2019.

7. "Pilgrim's Rock": *Sunday Times* (London), April 10, 1977.

CHAPTER 1: THE LION OF LIONS

11. Kossola's grandfather: Hurston, *Barracoon*, 23.

11. Mahommah Baquaqua: Baquaqua, *Biography*, 120.

11. trading with European: Akintoye, *History*, 178.

11. But parents often let the rumors flourish: Diouf, *Dreams*, 54.

12. His favorite pastime: Hurston, 43.

12. It would have been in the center of town: Johnson, *History*, 91; Akintoye, 151.

12. Palm trees probably surrounded the square: Ogundiran correspondence; Johnson, 91, 110; Akintoye, 151, 182. Clapperton's *Journal* describes specific markets on 12, 59, and 74.

12. an elderly man, who wielded some influence: Hurston, 41.

13. The historian Sylviane Diouf: Diouf, 40–41.

13. Kossola said in 1906: S. H. M. Byers, "The Last Slave Ship," *Harper's Monthly* 113 (October 1906): 742–46.

13. this has led another historian: Robertson, *Slave Ship* Clotilda, 80.

13. a network of autonomous kingdoms: Akintoye, 186–87.

13. Kossola was the second of six children: Hurston, 38.

13. It was likely a modest place: Johnson, 98–99.

13. Kossola remembered later: Hurston, 38.

13. A Yoruba mantra: Johnson, 95.

13. Besides the tropical fruit: Hurston, 20; Roche, *Historic Sketches,* 75; Johnson, 110.

14. The town's main industry: Roche, 75; Campbell, *Pilgrimage,* 51–52.

14. The palm nuts: Campbell, 51–51; Lynn, *Commerce and Economic Change,* 47; Skertchly, *Dahomey,* 33–34.

14. It was sent to port cities: Skertchly, 34.

14. Yoruba towns: Akintoye, 199.

14. The greatest prestige: Ibid., 166.

14. On a ceremonial level: Ibid., 140.

14. Every king was chosen by a council: Ibid., 142; Ellis, *Yoruba-Speaking Peoples,* 164.

14. The economy, too: Akintoye, 206–7.

14. Criminal defendants: Hurston, 30–31.

14. After the chiefs took their turns: Ibid., 32.

14. Kossola's grandfather loomed large: Ibid., 20.

14. His status conferred some small measure: Ibid., 23.

15. The custom was: Ibid., 21.

15. The old man fell ill: Ibid., 33–34.

15. Kossola's training as a warrior: Ibid., 40.

15. Defense, in Kossola's town: Ellis, 35; Johnson, 26; Akintoye, 48.

15. Instead the people devote themselves: Ellis, 44.

15. Shango, the god of thunder: Ibid., 46, 49.

15. Ogun, the patron of hunters: Ibid., 67.

15. Their shrines were everywhere: Ibid., 110.

15. In his town: Ibid., 109–110.

15. On days set aside: Ibid., 111.

16. Or else the only trace: Ibid., 110.

16. After the day: Ibid.; Hurston, 29; John Parkinson, "The Legend of Oro," *Man* 6 (1906): 103–105.

16. Kossola was led into a house: Hurston, 41–42.

16. They led him to the place: Ibid.; Ellis, 110; R. Braithwaite Batty, "Notes on the Yoruba Country," *Journal of the Anthropological Institute of Great Britain and Ireland* 19 (1980): 159–64.

16. Before the banquet was over: Hurston, 42.

17. The king, Glèlè: Law, *Slave Coast,* 270–72.

17. A British visitor: Burton, *Mission,* vol. II, 231.

17. Throughout the 1700s: Forbes, *Dahomey*, 12. Burton, who visited in 1864, however, thought the kingdom's size had been "grossly exaggerated." He put its size at only four thousand square miles (vol. 2, 230–32).

17. Prior to their arrival: Green, *Fistful of Shells*, 265, 271–295.

17. Warmaking, in turn: Law, *Slave Coast*, 269.

17. The military was the pride of the land: Alpern, *Amazons*, 95.

17. Most fearsome were the women: Alpern, 38–39.

17. The kingdom's calendar year: Law, "Human Sacrifice in Pre-Colonial West Africa," *African Affairs* 84, no. 334 (January 1985): 53–87.

18. Palm oil wasn't necessarily as lucrative: Soumonni, "Compatibility," 89.

18. And if the economy: Bay, *Wives*, 231–32.

18. Glèlè had seen what happened: Alpern, 72.

18. But in 1852: Soumonni, 83.

18. There is also some evidence: Law, "The Politics of Commercial Transition: Factional Conflict in Dahomey in the Context of the Ending of the Atlantic Slave Trade," *Journal of African History* 38, no. 2 (1997): 213–233.

18. Ghezo faced a backlash: Law, "Politics," 227.

18. "ferocious lion of the forest": Robertson, 84.

18. the aphorism *Glelile ma hnn ze*: Law, "Politics," 213.

19. He was tall, athletic, and broad-shouldered: Skertchly, 142.

19. He dressed with an understated elegance: Burton, vol. I, 238.

19. "truly kingly dignity": Skertchly, 142.

19. His only fancy accoutrement: Ibid.

19. "I have seen him turn from the execution scene": Ibid., 235.

19. "no mere lust of blood": Burton, vol. I, 176.

19. the king had little choice: Burton, vol. II, 275–76.

19. If he tried to cease the military campaigns: Burton, vol. I, 176.

19. Glèlè planned to sacrifice more than two thousand people: "West Coast of Africa: The Slave-Trade—A Stupendous Human Sacrifice," *NYT*, August 27, 1860.

19. the numbers were wildly exaggerated: Burton, vol. II, 18–19.

19. Predawn raids were Dahomey's hallmark: Alpern, 141–42.

19. The campaigns themselves: Forbes, 15.

20. The troops moved in great secrecy: Burton, vol. II, 128–130; Skertchly, 416–18.

20. three strangers came into the market: Hurston, 43–45.

CHAPTER 2: "THEY'LL HANG NOBODY"

21. The steamer's torchlights: Meaher made trips like this every week, as attested by the weekly advertisements in Mobile newspapers and by several sources related to the burning of the *Clotilda*. This description is based

principally on William Howard Russell's description of a separate trip on one of Meaher's ships (*My Diary*, 184–89).

21. around 300 miles: Byers, "Last Slave Ship"; weekly advertisements published in Mobile newspapers; U.S. Army Corps of Engineers, "Alabama River Navigation Charts," https://www.sam.usace.army.mil/Missions/Civil -Works/Navigation/Black-Warrior-and-Tombigbee-River/BWT-Alabama -Rivers-Navigation/ALR-Charts/.

21. Given his immense workforce: "Home Enterprise," *The American Cotton Planter* (June 1853), 191.

21. The ship swaying beneath his feet: *Clarke County Democrat*, May 14, 1857.

21. "the indomitable Timothy Meaher": *Weekly Advertiser* (Mobile), May 27, 1857.

21. At the time when Meaher came down: *Clarke County Democrat*, June 12, 1890. Two other sources (Joseph Casimir O'Meagher's *Some Historical Notices of the O'Meaghers of Ikerrin* and Timothy Meaher's obituary) claim he moved there in 1836 (O'Meagher, 177), but in the *Clarke County Democrat* story, Meaher himself said he had his first ship assignment in 1835.

21. still belonged to Native Americans: The expulsion of Native Americans, mainly Creek and Cherokee tribes, happened mostly in the 1830s. See Christopher Haveman, "Creek Indian Removal," EOA, January 28, 2009, http://encyclopediaofalabama.org/article/h-2013, and Sarah E. Hill, "Cherokee Indian Removal," EOA, January 16, 2008, http://encyclopediaofalabama.org/article/h-1433.

21. James Meaher (who went by Jim): *Mobile Item*, February 14, 1885; O'Meagher, *Some Historical Notices*, 176.

22. as glamorous a profession back then: Sledge, *Mobile River*, 105–06.

22. At first he was only a deckhand: "Capt. Tim Meaher's Sketch of His River History," *Clarke County Democrat*, June 12, 1890.

22. By this late date: "Mobile—Its Past, Present, and Future," *De Bow's Review* 1, no. 1 (January 1859), 81.

22. It was all on a rugged piece of property: Roche, 103.

22. Jim had moved back down in 1850: O'Meagher, 176–77.

22. overseeing their finances: *MDR*, February 10, 1885.

22. Their younger brother, Burns: New Orleans *Daily Picayune*, November 30, 1890; O'Meagher, 178.

22. Three of Tim Meaher's younger brothers: O'Meagher, 177–78.

22. "gray eye full of cunning": Russell, 184–85.

22. "severely injured by a knife": *Cahaba Gazette*, July 7, 1854 (reprint from the *Selma Sentinel*).

22. he was accused of ramming one of his ships: Ibid., July 17, 1857.

22. the banks on both sides: Russell, 184–85.

22. at least a few the passengers on board: Richard Hines Jr., "The Last Slaver," New Orleans *Daily Picayune*, November 30, 1890.

22. this scenery could have an exotic appeal: Oldmixon, *Transatlantic Wanderings*, 161.

22. But the novelty tended to wear off: Russell describes this feeling on a different ship (89).

22. Sleeping on the ship must have been almost impossible: Russell, 186–87.

23. Meaher sometimes regaled them with stories: Ibid., 185. It seems that Meaher fabricated this story of the massacre. It's true that untold numbers of Muscogee people were killed throughout southern Alabama in the early 1800s, as American settlers were claiming the territory; but none of the anecdotes on record match the description Meaher gives here.

23. Passengers also told stories among themselves: Ibid., 187–88.

23. The wreck of one of his first ships: *Louisville Daily Journal*, December 6, 1847; Jackson, *Rivers of History*, 88.

23. In the spring of 1850: Foster, *Ante-Bellum Floating Palaces*, 53.

23. The river was high that week: Jackson, 90.

23. Soon the entire boat was up in flames: Foster, 51; Jackson, 94.

23. For his reported efforts to save the passengers: Foster, 51; Jackson, 95.

23. a rumor was sometimes passed around: *Tuskegee Republican*, March 14, 1850.

23. The gold had never been recovered: Jackson, *Rivers of History*, 95.

24. Standing on the deck: Russell, 185.

24. According to an interview he gave in 1890: Hines.

24. Worldwide consumption of the fabric: Baptist, *Half*, xx, 350.

24. If the average worker could produce a pound: Jerrell H. Shofner and William Warren Rogers, "Sea Island Cotton in Ante-Bellum Florida," *The Florida Historical Quarterly* 40, no. 4 (April 1962): 373–80.

24. enslaved people had learned to work faster and faster: Baptist, 138–39.

24. the men and women at the barracks in downtown Mobile: Hamilton, *Mobile of the Five Flags*, 284; Diouf, 15.

24. Lately some of Mobile's hotels: Ingraham, *Sunny South*, 504; Oldmixon, 155; Doss, *Cotton City*, 94.

25. "From the West coast of Africa": *MDR*, November 9, 1858.

25. In the spring of 1859: Walther, *Shattering*, 165–66.

25. "Now is it consistent": Quoted in American Anti-Slavery Society, *Anti-Slavery History*, 16–17.

25. "They buy cotton, sell cotton, think cotton": Fuller, *Belle Brittan*, 112.

25. Throughout the 1850s: Doss, 18–20.

25. The editorial was a hit: American Anti-Slavery Society, 17.

26. He and his brothers: Diouf, 11; Russell, 186.

26. A few years earlier he had dubbed one: *Clarke County Democrat*, May 14, 1857; *Cahaba Gazette*, July 17, 1857; Roger Brooke Taney and Supreme Court of the United States, *U.S. Reports: Dred Scott v. Sandford*, 60 U.S. 19 How. 393, 1856, https://www.loc.gov/item/usrep060393a/.

26. Meaher had also lent resources: May, *Manifest Destiny's Underworld*, 40–58, 262.

26. Meaher was among their ranks: Ibid., 50.

26. The *Susan* had successfully sneaked out of Mobile Bay: *NYT*, December 10, 1858, and December 22, 1858.

26. The plan was to sail to the Honduran coast: *NYT*, January 3, 1859, and January 11, 1859 (reprint from the *Mobile Mercury*).

26. In the spring, a Texas paper: American Anti-Slavery Society, 23; Diouf, 21.

27. On a four-month voyage: Calonius, *Wanderer*, 121–24. The definitive book on these illegal slave voyages in the nineteenth century is John Harris's *The Last Slave Ships: New York and the End of the Middle Passage* (New Haven, CT: Yale University Press, 2021).

27. President James Buchanan: Baker, *James Buchanan*, 82–85; James Buchanan, "Mr. Buchanan's Inaugural," in Horton, *Life*, 438–46.

27. Buchanan had joined with the proslavery faction: Baker, 102–03.

27. His vision, however: Ibid., 111.

27. The *New York Times* opined in the spring: *NYT*, April 22, 1859.

27. some of Meaher's passengers that night: The scene was first described by Meaher in Hines's story "The Last Slaver." The dialogue here is a dramatic re-creation that appears in Byers's 1906 article.

28. But it wasn't just the South that depended on slavery: Baptist; Beckert, *Empire of Cotton*.

28. The captain and crew of the *Wanderer*: Calonius, 218.

28. Jefferson Davis, a U.S. senator from Mississippi: "Speech of Jefferson Davis Before the Mississippi Legislature, November 16, 1858," from *Jefferson Davis, Constitutionalist*, 356.

28. To prove he was right: Hines reported that the conversation on the *Taney* happened in 1858, rather than 1859. On finer details like this, however, Hines's story is no more reliable than the others. It said the *Clotilda* landed in 1861, but there is no question that it actually landed in 1860. Given the timing of the other events that probably informed Meaher's decision, such as the landing of the *Wanderer* and the publication of the *Register* story about captives being sold in Dahomey, it seems most likely that this conversation occurred in 1859. Also, legend has long had it that the conversation ended with a bet— according to Byers, Meaher put down $1,000—but in Meaher's own account from 1890 ("The Last Slaver"), he says nothing about this. Henry Romeyn,

who wrote about the episode in 1894, was ambiguous on the matter of betting ("Little Africa: The Last Slaver Landed in the United States," *TD*, April 1, 1894). Roche, in her 1914 book *Historic Sketches*, said the tradition held that a bet had occurred. However, Roche also said that according to lore, the conversation happened along a wharf (71)—when Meaher himself said it had occurred during a voyage on one of his ships.

28. Late on the night of March 3: Roche is the only source on this late-night journey (84). It seems plausible that she could have learned about it from Foster's widow, whom she interviewed—but it should be noted that Foster didn't mention it in his own brief account of the voyage.

29. Foster was about thirty-five: The 1900 census says he was born in August of 1825, and the 1860 census is consistent with this. However, the 1870 census suggests he was born circa 1829, and the 1880 census suggests 1822. (U.S. Federal Census, 1860, Mobile, Northern Division, 172; 1870, Mobile, Beat 5, roll M593_30, 380A; 1880, Mobile, Whistler, roll 24, 100B; 1900, Mobile, Whistler, 5.)

29. Foster had lived in this town for sixteen years: According to the 1900 census, he migrated in 1844.

29. The population shot up from 300: Doss, 1; U.S. Federal Census 1940, "Population, Volume I: Number of Inhabitants," Alabama section, Table I, 69.

29. ships were usually lined up by the dozen: Ingraham, 507.

29. There was a world-class hotel: Doss, 42–43.

29. Rarely had a city depended so heavily on a single crop: Doss, 81.

29. He was a skilled ship carpenter: William Wallworth, "The Foster Family of Fisher's Grant, Pictou County, Nova Scotia," October 20, 2020, http://www.deadfamilies.com/Z3-Others/PDF-Files/Book-The-Foster-Family-Of-Fishers-Grant-Nova-Scotia-W-007-01.pdf. 17, 60–61.

30. The city consciously competed with New Orleans: Doss, 46.

30. The downtown area was stacked with brothels: O'Connor, *Wanderings*, 460–62.

30. there were streets lined with villas and palatial mansions: Doss, 67; De Leon, *Belles*, 182–86.

30. Mobile's temperature was often balmy: Oldmixon, 166.

30. In the summertime, everyone who could afford it: Hamilton, 228; Doss, 43, 78.

30. Amid the distractions: Registration of *Clotilda*, April 19, 1855. National Archives and Records Administration, Southeast Region (Atlanta). RG 36 U. S. Customs Service, Collector of Customs. Copy in possession of HMM.

30. The two-masted schooner had ribs of oak: James Delgado, "Archaeo-logical Investigations of 1Ba704, a Nineteenth Century Shipwreck Site in the Mobile River, Baldwin and Mobile Counties, Alabama," SEARCH Inc., May 2019, 34. Available at https://ahc.alabama.gov/press/FINAL _1Ba704%20Report_SEARCH_redacted.pdf.

30. The design was novel: Registration of *Clotilda*; Delgado, "Archaeological Investigations," 22, 24.

31. The first time he rigged it: Quoted in Delgado, "Archaeological Investi-gations," 18.

31. Foster had hired a captain: "National Archives at Atlanta, The *Clotilda*: A Finding Aid," U.S. National Archives and Records Administration, https://www.archives.gov/files/atlanta/finding-aids/clotilda.pdf.

31. For years, however, local legend held: Roche, 71–72.

31. It was fairly common for an American ship: Delgado interview; *New York Herald*, August 29, 1858; John Harris, "Voyage of the Echo: The Trials of an Illegal Trans-Atlantic Slave Ship," Lowcountry Digital History Ini-tiative, https://ldhi.library.cofc.edu/exhibits/show/voyage-of-the-echo-the -trials.

31. The *Clotilda*'s final voyage in the Gulf of Mexico: "Action to Recover Damages for Loss of Slave," *Foster v. Holly*, Supreme Court of Alabama, June term, 1861.

32. As the captain later told Foster: Ibid.

32. It turned out the Black man: Ibid.

32. Foster must have been hard-pressed to afford it: Diouf, 23.

32. most did not have holds large enough: Delgado, "Archaeological Investi-gations," 8.

32. With room enough for about 190: Diouf, 24.

32. They re-rigged it with broad sails: Foster, "Last Slaver from U.S. to Africa A.D. 1860" (handwritten manuscript), MPL.

33. notorious for their filth: Sledge, *Mobile River*, 90.

33. Foster had recruited two northerners: A handwritten note on file at the History Museum of Mobile, which has been assumed to have been written by Foster, identifies the first mate as George Duncan and the second mate as J. B. Northrop, who were both experienced mariners from Rhode Island. It also says there were nine other crew members. However, it seems likely that the official records are more reliable here. The story Foster told later on was likely meant to provide cover for his local partners.

33. Sailors generally knew: Stanfield, *Guinea Voyage*, Letter II.

33. According to one version: Hines.

CHAPTER 3: CARAVAN

34. Kossola woke to the sound of shrieking: Hurston, 45–46.

34. Kossola knew he had to make a run for it: Ibid.

34. But on the other side: Ibid.; Roche, 81.

35. In that moment, all Kossola could think about: Hurston, 46.

35. While Kossola was being held: Ibid., 47.

35. The whole attack was over within a half-hour: Byers, "Last Slave Ship."

35. When the Dahomeans were finished: Skertchly, 448.

35. They set out for Dahomey as the sun was coming up: Hurston, 47.

36. The stress of the voyage was getting to Bill Foster: Foster, "Last Slaver"; Roche, 84–85. Meaher, in Hines's story "The Last Slaver," claims the crew did stop in St. Thomas, but Meaher was not on the voyage, and Foster himself makes no mention of it in his memoir.

36. Ultimately the stars had tipped him off: Roche, 84–85.

36. As he tossed and turned: Ibid. Again, Roche is the only source for this anecdote about the gold. Foster's memoir doesn't mention it.

37. Christopher Columbus found that his compass acted strangely: Columbus, *Journal*, 23–24, 36.

37. a U.S. Navy ship, the USS *Pickering*, disappeared near Bermuda: Delgado, "Missing and Presumed Lost," *Naval History Magazine* 30, no. 4 (August 2016): 56–63.

37. the legends can be explained by the extreme weather: NOAA, "What Is the Bermuda Triangle?" National Ocean Service, https://oceanservice.noaa.gov/facts/bermudatri.html; Howard L. Rosenberg, "Exorcising the Devil's Triangle," *Sealift* 6 (June 1974): 11–15.

37. Foster's memoir describes another episode: Foster. Note that the captain's statements about the time of day when various events occurred ought to be treated with skepticism. Even if he did carry a pocket watch on the voyage, it seems unlikely he would have remembered the time stamps when he recorded his memories three decades later. Nevertheless, I have reproduced them here as he gave them.

37. By mid-century, Britain's West Africa Squadron: Burroughs, "Suppression of the Atlantic Slave Trade," 4–5.

37. Its sailors were intensely devoted to their work: Ibid., 8.

38. he may have added the detail to heighten the drama: Diouf, 28–29.

38. Once they were on land, the crew mutinied: Foster.

38. By one later account: Roche, 85.

38. Financially, they lived voyage to voyage: Rediker, *Slave Ship*, 225–30.

38. In the bleak conditions that dominated these trips: Ibid., 204–205.

38. As for sailors' pay: Ibid., 125.

38. Foster instantly agreed to give them a raise: Roche, 85.

38. Meanwhile, Foster introduced himself: Ibid.

38. The American consul quickly ascertained: Foster.

39. The *Clotilda* sailed out after eight days: Ibid.

39. On May 15: Ibid.

39. Since daybreak they'd been marching: Hurston, 31–32. See Skertchly, 23–24, and Duncan, *Travels*, 119, on how hammock transportation worked.

39. Kossola looked at the hammocks: Hurston, *Barracoon*, 47–48, and *Dust Tracks*, 143.

39. Later in life he would blame it on a former resident: Hurston, *Barracoon*, 44–45.

39. They typically marched several thousand strong: Duncan, 92; Skertchly, 166; Alpern, 69.

39. Many shaved their heads entirely: Alpern, 58.

39. Across their backs they carried giant machetes: Ibid., 66.

40. To anyone seeing the army for the first time: Law, "The 'Amazons' of Dahomey," *Paideuma: Mitteilungen zur Kulturkunde* 39 (1993): 245–260.

40. Such was the "size of the female skeleton": Burton, vol. I, 169–70.

40. "'We are men,' say they": Forbes, 23.

40. they were nominally the "king's wives": Alpern, 44–45.

40. On the march from Kossola's town: Hurston, 47.

40. Before sunset, they reached a town: Ibid., 48.

40. That night, likely after ten or eleven hours: Burton, vol. II, 128–29.

40. Kossola and the other captives: Hurston, 48.

40. After the sun came up: Ibid.

41. Before long, the severed heads began to stink: Ibid., 48–49. The description of how the memory affected Kossola echoes Roche, 82.

41. The next stop was one of Glèlè's palaces: Diouf, 49.

41. Or it may have been Cana: Hurston, 52; Diouf, 48; correspondence with Robin Law. Hurston wrote in *Dust Tracks on a Road* that the city they visited was Abomey, rather than Cana (165–67), but she couldn't have known for sure. Natalie Robertson believes the city they visited was Cana (99–101).

41. They beat the drums so much: Hurston, 52.

41. The procession was undoubtedly similar: Burton, vol. I, 315–16.

42. The compound at Abomey: Lynne Ann Ellsworth Larsen, "The Royal Palace of Dahomey: Symbol of a Transforming Nation," unpublished PhD dissertation, University of Iowa, 2014, 10.

42. There were six palaces: Ibid., 12.

42. The buildings were made of red clay: Ibid., 16–17.

42. Burton described a long shed: Burton, vol. I, 349–50.

42. The men and women wept and pleaded: James Saxon Childers, "From Jungle to Slavery—and Freedom," *Birmingham News Age-Herald*, December 2, 1934.

42. "After singing for a while": Burton, vol. I, 362.

42. In the spring, there was a festival: Law, "My Head Belongs to the King," *Journal of African History* 30, no. 3 (1989): 399–415.

42. Even joyful ceremonies in Dahomey: Burton, vol. II, 10.

43. "comparatively kingly and dignified": Ibid., vol. I, 62.

43. For one Dahomean royal funeral: Law, "Human Sacrifice in Pre-Colonial West Africa," *African Affairs* 84, no. 334 (January 1985): 67–68.

43. Dahomean kings had collected the skulls: Law, "Head," 401–406, 413.

43. Tradition held that Ghezo's predecessor was deposed: Law, "Human Sacrifice," 53–87.

43. Four years into Glèlè's reign: Bay, *Wives*, 268.

44. European influence had also played a role: Law, *Slave Coast*, 271.

44. "shouts and trills": Burton, vol. II, 222.

44. It seems Dahomean soldiers: Ibid.

44. Following the sale: Diouf, 50.

44. There was one more ritual: Ibid.

45. After Abomey, there were several more stops: Ibid.

45. The term *barracoon*: Louis P. Nelson, "Architectures of West African Enslavement," *Buildings & Landscapes: Journal of the Vernacular Architecture Forum* 21, no. 1 (spring 2014): 88–125.

45. Through his bars: Hurston, 53–54.

45. Another captive held at that port: Baquaqua, 150–51.

CHAPTER 4: BARRACOONS

46. Between the 1670s: Law, *Ouidah*, 2.

46. For Glèlè's, the city was a critical source: Ibid., 29–30.

46. The Hueda, the Indigenous people: Ibid., 50, 53.

46. Decades later, as the international demand: Ibid., 227.

46. The Dahomean government: Ibid., 128.

47. No Dahomean king ever set foot: Ibid., 28–29.

47. Ouidah had a long-standing culture: Ibid., 75–76.

47. On the afternoon when Foster arrived: Foster.

47. Most likely these men were professionals: Skertchly, 6–7.

47. Once on land: Foster.

47. Foster may have seen enormous alligators: Skertchly, 8–9.

47. The crooked streets there: Burton, vol. I, 82; Law, *Ouidah*, 71–72.

47. There were big open stretches: Skertchly, 11–12.

48. The buildings, composed of mud: Burton, vol. I, 66–67; Law, *Ouidah*, 78–79.

48. On the ground, deep holes: Burton, vol. I, 59–60; Skertchly, 11–12; Law, *Ouidah*, 79–80.

48. "splendid accommodations": Foster.

48. Burton found him amiable: Burton, vol. I, 109–10.

48. Foster and Adoke shared a drink: Foster.

48. Foster had no clear idea: Ibid.

48. stocked with all manner of exotic products: Duncan, 121.

49. Above all, there was a bounty of fish: Ibid., 121–22.

49. workers would catch meals: Burton, vol. I, 77.

49. There was a constant rattle of cowries: Ibid., 80–81.

49. Ouidah was home to a vast cross section: Law, *Ouidah*, 88.

49. Dangbe was understood to be incarnated: Ibid., 23.

49. Dangbe had a thousand devotees: Burton, vol. II, 139.

49. The worshipers who were present: Foster.

49. Foster was glad: Ibid.

49. The days there were breezy: Skertchly, 15.

49. Sailors heard tell about "Guinea worm": Rediker, 257.

50. In Ouidah, the biggest threats: Law, *Ouidah*, 80.

50. And on the eighth day: Foster.

50. Kossola's conditions in Ouidah: Hurston, 53.

50. Some locals now believe: Law, *Ouidah*, 137.

50. However, it seems to sync up: Diouf, 51.

50. "driven like cattle": Duncan, 104.

50. But another observer: Law, *Ouidah*, 139–40.

50. In the middle of the nineteenth century: Ibid., 140.

51. There were other barracoons: Hurston, 53.

51. Language barriers between regions: Diouf, 53; Akintoye, 186.

51. One young woman confined there: Diouf, 34–35.

51. Or her name may instead be linked: Robertson, 122–23.

51. Another woman in the barracoons: Diouf, 35; Robertson, 108–11.

52. She later told her grandchildren: Dennison, *A Memoir of Lottie Dennison*, 19.

52. Jaba—or Jabbar, Jaybee: Diouf, 38.

52. There is evidence that Ossa Keeby: Ibid., 36–37.

52. Kuppollee, who would shorten his name: Ibid., 44–45.

52. After three weeks: Hurston, 53; Foster.

52. local traders had been known: Law, *Ouidah*, 140–41.

52. The buyers were given broad leeway: Ibid.

53. "He lookee and lookee": Roche, 86–87; Hurston, 53.

53. By the time he was finished: Foster; Hurston, 34.

53. It was rare for natives to be sold: Law, *Ouidah*, 148.

53. Adoke, flattering Foster: Roche, 86.

54. For professional dealers: Duncan, 143; Law, *Ouidah*, 141–42.

54. Baquaqua recalled: Baquaqua, 149–50.

54. As the sun came up: Foster.

54. Duncan, who witnessed a similar caravan: Duncan, 201.

54. Baquaqua described it the same way: Baquaqua, 151.

54. Since the 1990s: Law, *Ouidah*, 152–53.

54. Given the importance of hairstyles: Diouf, 57.

55. In one, he was "stolen": Roche, 113–14.

55. In the second version: Hurston, 54.

55. On the other side: Ibid.

55. On board the *Clotilda*: Foster; Roche, 88–89; Romeyn, "Little Africa."

56. Kossola and the others: Hurston, 54–55.

56. The captives stepped on board: Ibid., 55.

CHAPTER 5: ARRIVAL

57. West Africans were susceptible: Falconbridge, *Account*, 24.

57. In terms of ship construction: Rediker, 241.

58. The captives spent their first thirteen days: *MA*, January 31, 1932.

58. The ceiling was higher: Delgado interview.

58. Baquaqua recalled: Baquaqua, 153.

58. Just as bad was the endless rocking: Falconbridge, 25.

58. "It is not in the power": Ibid., 27.

58. The odor that wafted out: Ibid., 38.

59. "I so skeered on de sea!": Hurston, 55.

59. the "Ruler of the seas was angry": Equiano, *Olaudah Equiano*, 59.

59. Besides the seasickness: Hurston, 55.

59. to "the extreme of existence": Stanfield, Letter III.

59. On Baquaqua's ship: Baquaqua, 154.

59. On a voyage in the 1770s: Stanfield, Letter III.

59. While the captives were suffering: Foster.

59. When this last patrol ship: Hurston, 55.

60. They spent much of their remaining time: Hurston, 55; Roche, 90.

60. It's likely they also sang: Rediker, 287.

60. When captives refused to eat: Falconbridge, 23.

60. Judging from the Africans' later accounts: Roche, 123.

60. In a separate conversation: Hurston, 56.

60. A ship doctor on his morning rounds: Falconbridge, 28.

60. Kossola reportedly said: Hurston, 56; Childers, "From Jungle to Slavery." Romeyn, in his 1894 account, also wrote that two people died on the voyage.

60. Another survivor recalled: Flock, "Last Survivor."

60. The mortality rate on slave ships: Slave Voyages Consortium, Trans-Atlantic Slave Trade-Database, https://www.slavevoyages.org/voyage/database#tables.

61. After six or seven weeks: Hurston, 35; Roche, 90–91; Foster.

61. While the captives were hidden: Foster.

61. It was a Sunday or Monday: The immediate news reports said the ship arrived in Mobile on July 9, 1860, which was a Monday (see the New Orleans *Daily Delta* and the *Louisville Daily Journal,* July 10, 1860). But within days, other papers started reporting it had landed on July 10 (e.g., *Fayetteville Semi-Weekly Observer,* July 12, 1860). Foster, in the account he wrote decades later, said the ship arrived on July 9. Hines's 1890 story, based on an interview with Meaher, says it was a Sunday in 1861, but there is no question that the year was actually 1860. Romeyn and Byers said it was a Sunday but didn't specify the date. Roche reported that it was a Sunday in 1859.

61. Kossola would be convinced: Hurston, 56; Foster; Diouf, 69.

61. The delta would be the *Clotilda*'s destination: Foster; Byers.

62. There are at least eight accounts: Hines/"The Last Slaver" (1890); Foster/"Last Slaver" (1890); Mary McNeil Scott, "Affika Town," *Fetter's Southern Magazine* 3, no. 13 (August 1893): 58–65; Romeyn/"Little Africa" (1894); Byers/"The Last Slave Ship" (1906); Roche/*Historic Sketches* (1914); G. Lake Imes, "The Last Recruits of Slavery," *Southern Workman* 46, no. 6 (June 1917); and Hurston/*Barracoon* (c. 1928).

62. Foster wrote that when he arrived: Foster.

62. Foster reasoned with them: Ibid.

62. Once on land: Ibid.

62. Foster wrote that he found a tugboat: Ibid.

62. Foster took the tugboat back: Ibid.

62.63. Meaher said he learned from a messenger: Hines; Scott, 60. I have chosen not to spell out this racial slur, particularly in instances where the speaker is an avowedly bigoted white person (in this case, it's Meaher himself). As a narrator, once again, I've tried to avoid participating in the tropes of Jim Crow source material, even from a distance.

63. Meaher said *he* was responsible: Hines. Meaher was also interviewed by an Alabama reporter earlier in 1890, and the resulting story was published in the *Clarke County Democrat* on June 12, under the headline "Capt. Tim Meaher's sketch of his river history," but it makes no mention of the *Clotilda*.

63. Below deck, on the slave ship: Roche, 95–96.

63. Foster said the mates and crew: Roche writes that here the crew mutinied once more. This time Foster was not interested in bargaining, she said. He pulled two guns, both six-shooters, and brandished them at the sailors,

telling them to "hit the grit and never be seen in Southern waters again" (97). Foster's account does not mention this episode.

63. Meaher said the crew rode along: Foster; Hines; *MDR*, March 19, 1870 and April 23, 1870.

63. According to Meaher: Hines.

64. Meanwhile, Foster took his ship: Foster; Delgado interview. Again, the detail about the amount of firewood comes from Roche (97), who presumably learned it from Foster's wife, rather than from Foster's own account.

64. Meaher said that when the *Taney:* Hines.

64. Meaher claimed he had bought it: Ibid.; Roche, 97.

64. On Tuesday, July 10: See the *Oxford Intelligencer, Daily Constitutionalist* (Augusta, Georgia), *Alexandria Gazette, Richmond Dispatch, Daily Exchange* (Baltimore), *Evening Star* (D.C.), *Syracuse Daily Courier and Union, Fall River Daily News* (Massachusetts), *Burlington Times, Muscatine Evening Journal* (Iowa), and *Huddersfield Chronicle and West Yorkshire Advertiser* (UK).

65. The local authorities were likely reluctant: Ling-Pei Lu, "Sound at Heart and Right in Hand: Mobile's Road to Secession," unpublished PhD dissertation, Auburn University, 2006, 84, 180–83.

65. Its editorials had argued: Ibid., 180–83.

65. Sanford had sold the paper: Ibid., 84; *New Orleans Times,* May 3, 1867; *MPR*, June 10, 2013.

65. The U.S. marshal, Cade Godbold: Garrett, *Reminiscences,* 531; United States Confederate Officers Card Index, 1861–1865.

65. Both he and Sanford: U.S. Federal Census (Slave Schedule), 1860, Mobile, Fifth Ward, 5; Doss, 87–88; U.S. Federal Census, 1840, Mobile, roll 10, 97.

65. On that Thursday: Thaddeus Sanford to Howell Cobb, July 13, 1860, NARA (copy in possession of HMM).

65. The day after Sanford sent his telegraph: Quoted in American Anti-Slavery Society, 17.

66. Sanford dispatched Godbold: Sanford to Cobb, July 17, 1860, NARA (copy in possession of HMM).

66. For Kossola, Keeby, Zuma, and the others: Hurston, 56.

66. The shipmates' crude tents: Imes.

66. On top of the mosquitoes: Diouf, 76.

66. James Dennison, Meaher's enslaved riverboat pilot: Roche, 98–99.

66. It was later reported: Ibid., 98.

67. In 1890, Meaher claimed: Hines.

67. There the Africans were introduced to plantation life: Imes.

67. Thaddeus Sanford, the customs official: Sanford to Cobb, July 18, 1860, NARA (copy in possession of HMM).

67. Godbold sought out the acting district attorney: Ibid.

67. At least twice before: William G. Jones, "Opinion," *United States v. Gould*, U.S. District Court for the Southern District of Alabama, 1860, https://cite .case.law/f-cas/25/1375/; American Anti-Slavery Society, 29.

68. The district attorney had forwarded the case: Sanford to Cobb, July 18, 1860.

68. As of the eighteenth: Ibid.

68. Sanford's prediction: Roche, 99–100.

68. Burns had a volatile temper: Ibid., 99.

68. "We cain help but cry": Hurston, 56.

69. Foster took at least ten: Roche claims he took ten (97), but in *Barracoon*, Hurston reports that Kossola remembered him taking eight couples (56).

69. On July 23, the *Mobile Mercury:* Quoted in American Anti-Slavery Society, 127.

69. On or before July 25: A. J. Requier, "Information" (undated), and William Jones, "Judge's Order," July 27, 1860, *United States v. John M. Dabney*, record group 21, Records of the District Courts of the United States, Final Record Book for the Southern District of Alabama, box 46, Mobile, Mixed Cases, 1820–1860, NARA (copies in possession of HMM).

69. Foster's charge: Summons, August 7, 1860, *United States v. William Foster*, record group 21, Records of the District Courts of the United States, Final Record Book for the Southern District of Alabama, box 46, Mobile, Mixed Cases, 1820–1860, NARA (copies in possession of HMM).

69. Years later, he claimed he had been arrested: Hines.

69. Noah, the enslaved man: Scott, 61.

69. Sanford wrote to the treasurer: Sanford to Cobb, August 10, 1860, NARA (copy in possession of HMM).

70. Meanwhile, Sanford continued: Ibid.

70. In early September: *Prichard Herald*, February 1901.

71. His party's official platform: "The Platform," *NYT*, May 18, 1860.

71. An order was issued: Summons, August 7, 1860, *United States v. William Foster*; summons, July 27, 1860, and dismissal, January 10, 1861, *United States v. Burns Meaher*; summons, July 27, 1860, *United States v. John M. Dabney*; minutes, January 10, 1861, Records of the District Courts of the United States, Southern District of Alabama, NARA (copies in possession of HMM).

71. A newspaper reporter wrote in 1890: Hines.

71. As for Foster: Minutes, January 10, 1861, Records of the District Courts of the United States, Southern District of Alabama.

CHAPTER 6: WARTIME

72. As of the early 1860s: Roche, 102–10.

72. In this rugged setting: "Home Enterprise," *The American Cotton Planter*, June 1853, 190–91 (reprint from the *Mobile Evening News*).

72. As of the late 1850s: "Mobile—Its Past, Present, and Future," *De Bow's Review* 1, no. 1 (January 1859): 81–82.

72. Census and tax records show: U.S. Federal Census (Slave Schedule), 1860, Clarke County, 36–37.

73. Noah later recalled: Scott, 62.

73. Diouf has suggested: Diouf, 85.

73. From Noah's perspective: Scott, 61.

73. "Some makee de fun at us": Hurston, 59–60.

73. Kossola and the others: Ibid.

73. Whenever one of Jim's brothers: Emma V. Berger, "Cugo Lewis, 'Free-born ex-Slave,'" *The Continent*, January 26, 1922, 93. All around, Jim Meaher's reputation was much different from his younger brother's. His obituary, published in 1885, described him as "quiet, modest, and unobtrusive," and added that he wasn't particularly social—"but to those who were admitted to his friendship he was a friend indeed." It also reported that he'd never in all his life taken a drink of liquor. See *MDR*, February 10, 1885.

73. The shipmates had never seen a mule: Roche, 101; Hurston, 59 (possibly plagiarized).

74. The Alabama soil, by comparison: Roche, 101.

74. as peaceful as lambs: Scott, 62.

74. The first time: Roche, 101; Hurston, 59.

74. The second instance involved a young woman: Scott, 63.

74. White Mobilians had mixed feelings: Bergeron, *Confederate Mobile*, 6.

74. Much like Tim Meaher: Ibid., 6–7.

75. That first summer: Cumming, *Gleanings*, 82.

75. For the shipmates: Hurston, 61.

75. As of July 1861: Bergeron, 10.

75. Those who stayed home: Ibid., 47.

75. Later, when the mayor tried to recruit white laborers: Ibid., 109.

75. "They are in such numbers": Quoted in Bergeron, 159.

75. The jobs included: Sledge, *Rugged Days*, 72–73.

76. The workers were housed near a swamp: Bergeron, 111–12.

76. Kossola told an interviewer: Berger, "Cugo Lewis," 93.

76. Kossola spent the war years: Russell, 184–85.

76. In Russell's description: Ibid., 186.

76. When Kossola reminisced: Hurston, 60–61.

76. From Russell's account: Russell, 188–89.

77. Trade in Mobile was throttled: Bergeron, 99.

77. In September 1863: Ibid., 101–102.

78. Kossola and the other shipmates: Hurston, 62.

78. Balls and parties went on as usual: Bergeron, 92.

78. Russell's travelogue: Russell, 191.

78. Scenes like the one Russell witnessed: Sledge, *Rugged Days*, 68.

78. Between 1861, when the blockade was imposed: Ibid.

79. In the first instance, a steamer called the *Gipsy*: William P. McCann to Gideon Welles, January 2, 1864, in *Official Records of the Union and Confederate Navies*, vol. 2, 752; Noah Haynes Swayne and Supreme Court of the United States, *U.S. Reports: The Gray Jacket*, 72 U.S. 5 Wall. 342, 1866, https://www.loc.gov/item/usrep072342/.

79. The commander caught up with it: McCann to Welles, January 2, 1864; H. K. Thatcher to H. H. Bell, January 3, 1864, in *Official Records of the Union and Confederate Navies*, vol. 21, 753.

79. One Navy official: Thatcher to Bell, January 3, 1864.

79. Two months later: Swayne, *The Gray Jacket*.

80. Kossola's name in America: Hurston, 20.

80. For some ethnic groups: Diouf, 92.

80. Oluale, his father's name: Ibid., 134.

80. The man named Oluale: Ibid., 91; 132–34.

80. Zuma may have shortened her name: Ibid., 91–92.

80. The shipmates also adapted: Hurston, 62.

80. Noah mentioned that whenever there was thunder: Scott, 64.

80. When there was a new moon: Ibid., 63–64.

81. According to Diouf: Diouf, 114.

81. Generally, when an African child was born: Scott, 64.

81. Diouf has concluded: Diouf, 116. In general, infertility in Yoruba societies is often addressed with herbal and spiritual treatments as well as biomedical ones. See Sonja J. Nieuwenhuis, et al., "The Impact of Infertility on Infertile Men and Women in Ibadan, Oyo State, Nigeria: A Quantitative Study," *African Journal of Reproductive Health* 13, no. 3 (September 2009): 85–98.

81. It was Noah's understanding: Scott, 64.

81. Whenever someone from their ranks died: Ibid., 63.

81. This description is entirely plausible: Diouf, 116–17.

82. Mobile played into the general's strategy: Sledge, *Rugged Days*, 124.

82. David Farragut, a Union Navy commander: Ibid., 131.

82. Working in coordination: Bergeron, 143–45.

82. By August 8: Sledge, *Rugged Days*, 141.

82. The shelling of Fort Morgan: Ibid., 142.

82. James Dennison, the Meahers' riverboat pilot: Dennison, *James Dennison*, 28, and *Lottie Dennison*, 29–30.

83. According to an account later written by their granddaughter: Dennison, *James Dennison*, 28, and *Lottie Dennison*, 29–30.

83. Elsewhere in the Confederate states: Kennett, *Marching*, 309.

83. Three days later, in the early evening on a Wednesday: Bergeron, 191.

84. Kate Cumming, the young nurse: Cumming, 259.

84. Cudjo was on one of the Meahers' ships: Hurston, 65.

CHAPTER 7: TO HAVE LAND

87. On July 4, 1865: Statement of General Thomas Kilby Smith, New Orleans, September 14, 1865, in Schurz, *Report on the Condition of South.*

87. To Ann Quigley: Russell E. Belous, "The Diary of Ann Quigley," *Gulf Coast Historical Review* 4, no. 2 (spring 1989): 88–99. Quigley made this observation after watching a separate downtown parade of freedpeople in May 1865.

87. "Almost the entire negro population": Quoted in Robertha Steele, "Some Aspects of Reconstruction in Mobile," unpublished master's thesis, Auburn University, 1937, 17.

87. By 1870: Fitzgerald, *Urban Emancipation*, 24. Fitzgerald notes that the white population dropped from 28,500 in 1866 to 18,100 in 1870—which is a drop of 10,400 people, or 36 percent.

87. But already, in this ecstatic moment: Fleming, *Civil War*, 273.

88. The Union general overseeing Mobile: *Mobile Daily News*, April 22, 1865.

88. And out in the countryside: W. A. Poillon to Carl Schurz, July 29, 1865, in Schurz, *Report.*

88. "Angry whites were also threatening:" "Statement of General Thomas Kilby Smith," in Schurz, *Report.*

88. Cudjo mentioned that someone invited them: Hurston, 63.

88. Cudjo recalled later that they were at a loss: Ibid., 65.

88. At some point the African men had a meeting: Roche, 114–15; Hurston, 66.

88. They felt a sense of urgency: Imes.

88. This fear was, in fact, well founded: Wager Swayne to George D. Robinson, September 18, 1865, Records of the Field Offices for the State of Alabama, Bureau of Refugees, Freedmen, and Abandoned Lands, 1865–1872, NARA.

89. "My warfare is against the American Colonization Society": Garrison, *Thoughts*, 2–3.

89. But throughout the years of its existence: Bernice E. Finney, "The American Colonization Society," *Negro History Bulletin* 12, no. 5 (February 1949): 116–18.

89. Up until the Civil War: Through 1860, the total was 10,595. American Colonization Society, "Table of Emigrants Settled in Liberia by the American Colonization Society," *African Repository* 48, no. 3 (March 1872): 79–80.

89. In 1867, several families: Diouf, 140–41; American Colonization Society, 79; *Charleston Daily News*, May 21, 1867.

89. There were already several industrial firms: Robertson, 139.

89. The group apparently settled on a savings target: Imes; Addie E. Pettaway, "The Folklife and Material Culture of a Historic Landscape: Africatown, U.S.A.," unpublished master's thesis, University of Wisconsin-Madison, 1983, 66.

89. They subsisted on bread and molasses: Pettaway, 57, 60–61, 72; Hurston, 67.

90. While they bided their time: Hurston, 66.

90. When they reached their $1,000 target: Imes. This anecdote does not appear in any other accounts, but Imes spoke with the surviving shipmates circa 1917 and evidently heard it from them directly. It tracks with what Roche and Hurston wrote: that the shipmates initially saved their money, planning to buy tickets for their passage back, but soon found out it would cost more than they could ever afford (Roche, 115; Hurston, 66).

90. "makee de Affica where dey fetch us": Hurston, 68.

91. The Meahers had taken a severe financial blow: Diouf, 179.

91. Business had also been bad since the war: Chester, *Transatlantic Sketches*, 221; Reid, *After the War*, 212.

91. Meaher sat down on a tree: Roche, 115–16; Hurston, 67. Hurston almost certainly plagiarized this scene from Roche, but I have quoted the dialogue from her account instead of Roche's because she had a better ear for capturing the shipmates' speech.

91. Cudjo's reaction is not recorded: Hurston, 68.

92. When the war ended: Foner, *Reconstruction*, 35–36.

92. In January 1865, Sherman called together twenty Black leaders: Ibid., 70.

92. The group's spokesman: Garrison Frazier, "Colloquy with Colored Ministers," *Journal of Negro History* 16, no. 1 (January 1931): 88–94.

92. "In the summer, the commissioner:" Four days later, Sherman issued an order: Foner, 70–71.

93. Four days later: Ibid., 158–159.

93. Lincoln himself slowly came around: Ibid., 74

93. "a morbid distress and feeling": Ibid., 179.

93. "This is a country for white men": Trefousse, *Andrew Johnson*, 236.

94. Under his Presidential Reconstruction plan: Foner, 183.

94. Johnson also annulled the order: Ibid., 159.

94. The question of Black citizenship: Ibid., 184.

94. At first his plan was popular: Ibid., 216.

94. Only the Radicals were dismayed: Ibid., 221–22.

94. One representative law in Alabama: General Assembly of Alabama, *Acts*, 128–31.

94. Another said that anyone deemed a "vagrant": Ibid., 119–21.

94. And in Mobile, a local tax of $5: Foner, 198–210; McKiven, "Secession, War, and Reconstruction," 115–16; Fleming, 382.

94. The *Clotilda* shipmates were likely exempt from this tax: Foner, 206.

94. In a speech that September: *NYT*, September 10, 1865 (reprinted from the *Lancaster Daily Evening Express*).

95. As of January, all but 223,600 acres: Rick Beard, "Forty Acres and a Mule," *NYT*, January 16, 2015.

95. There was a clash here: Du Bois, *Black Reconstruction*, 209–14.

95. "In a selfish point of view": Ibid., 213.

96. In early 1866: Foner, 237–51.

96. The Radicals were also gaining popularity: Ibid., 267–80.

96. Alabama's constitutional convention met: Joshua Shiver, "Reconstruction Constitutions," April 7, 2020, EOA, http://www.encyclopediaofalabama.org /article/h-4192.

96. "of labor, and not of race": Quoted in Foner, 310.

96. The moderate Republicans, for their part: Ibid., 466–67.

96. The elections that fall: Ibid., 314–15.

97. At least a few graduated: Pettaway, 63; Thomas D. Weise, "The Voyage of the *Clotilde*: A Short History of the Facts and Fiction Surrounding the Last Slave Ship to America and Its Passengers," unpublished paper, Xavier University, Institute of Black Catholic Studies, April 26, 1991, 7.

97. By this time Cudjo: Diouf, 137–38.

97. Approaching her directly violated every rule: Ibid., 138.

97. So one day he told her: Hurston, 71–72.

97. As a husband in Yoruba culture: Ibid.; Reva B. Siegel, "'The Rule of Love': Wife Beating as Prerogative and Privacy," *Yale Law Journal* 105, no. 8 (June 1996): 2117–207. As Siegel points out, however, a women-led campaign against domestic abuse was gaining momentum throughout the 1850s and 1860s, and an Alabama court formally repudiated husbands' legal right to abuse their wives in 1871 (2134–35).

97. Their first child was born: Aleck Iyadjemi Lewis's birthdate is inscribed on his tombstone.

97. They gave him an American name: Diouf, 136–37.

98. When they brought the last ship: Womack told this story during a neighborhood tour in January 2020.

99. took citizenship oaths: Diouf, 165.

99. where they renounced allegiance: "History of the Oath of Allegiance," U.S. Citizenship and Immigration Services, April 23, 2020, https://www .uscis.gov/citizenship/learn-about-citizenship/the-naturalization-interview -and-test/history-of-the-oath-of-allegiance.

99. The majority started attending: "History of the Union Baptist Church," as told by Eva Allen Jones, Union Baptist Church archives.

99. "we doan know God got a son": Hurston, 19.

99. "White man, yo' no t'ink God in my country same like here?": Kirk Munroe, "The Industrial South," *Harper's Weekly* 31, no. 1595 (July 16, 1887), 503. I have used this verbatim quotation, even though it's an instance of a white journalist quoting a Black person in the Jim Crow South, because it's too ambiguous to paraphrase. She could mean that God is everywhere, and thus she wouldn't have to abandon Christianity if she returned to Yorubaland; or she could be saying (as I think she is) that Yoruba people and Christians worship the same God, albeit with different imagery and language.

99. When Mobile's white churches had opened their galleries: Hamilton, 243.

99. The themes of Black Christianity: For a thorough treatment of enslaved people's faith and the ways they adapted to Christianity, see Albert J. Raboteau's *Slave Religion: The "Invisible Institution" in the Antebellum South* (Oxford: Oxford University Press, 1978 and 2004).

100. In 1869, the shipmates were baptized: Roche, "Last Survivor of Slave Ship Deeply Grateful to God, Man," *MP*, August 18, 1935.

100. But they were still uncomfortable: Hurston, 68–69.

100. They began hosting: "History of the Union Baptist Church."

100. There was an auction in 1869: "Africa Town Deeds," MHDC.

100. Then in the fall of 1872: "Africa Town Deeds" and chain of title for 500 Bay Bridge Road, MHDC. There is a discrepancy here with *Barracoon*. According to Hurston, Kossola told her that when he acquired his land, he didn't build a house at first because he was unmarried (68). But the gravestones of Cudjo and Abile's sons show that the oldest was born in 1867 and the second in 1870, and Kossola didn't purchase the land until 1872.

100. With help from the others: Roche, "Last Survivor."

100. He cut the logs himself: Motley Lewis, Cudjo's grandson, quoted in Pettaway, 110.

100. The group also bought four acres: "Africa Town Deeds" and chain of title for 500 Bay Bridge Road, MHDC.

100. Old Landmark Baptist Church: Pollee Allen's daughter, Eva Allen Jones, reported that it was called the Old Baptist Church ("History of the Union Baptist Church"), but Hurston recorded Kossola calling it the Old Landmark Baptist Church (68 and 89).

100. The first minister who agreed: There is some uncertainty about the spelling of the pastor's name. The 1870 census identifies him as Henry McCrea; but on the church's cornerstone, it is engraved as "Henry McGray."

100. Pollee Allen served as a minister: Jones, MPL Oral History Project interview.

101. Neighborhood tradition holds: Williams and Porter, *History*, 5. According to Hurston, Kossola mentioned "building" a school, but there is no other mention anywhere of a separate school structure, and it seems logical that the group would have used the church.

101. In this period, the shipmates: Roche, 117–18; Hurston, 68.

101. Ultimately they had six children: Hurston, 73.

101. "We say dat 'cause we want to go back": Ibid., 68.

101. By the summer recess: Kenneth B. White, "The Alabama Freedmen's Bureau and Black Education: The Myth of Opportunity," *Alabama Review* 24, no. 2 (April 1981): 107–24.

101. Parents were teaching themselves: Foner, 96–97, 100.

102. Democracy was flourishing: Fitzgerald, 87.

102. They met wherever: Foner, 284.

102. In 1872, the state senate: "African-American Legislators in Reconstruction Alabama," ADAH, https://archives.alabama.gov/afro/AfricanAmerican%20 Legislators%20in%20Reconstruction%20Alabama1867.pdf.

102. A land-redistribution bill: Foner, 451.

102. By the 1890s: Kenneth E. Phillips, "Sharecropping and Tenant Farming in Alabama," EOA, July 28, 2008, http://encyclopediaofalabama.org/article /h-1613.

103. Another grim development: Keith S. Hebert, "Ku Klux Klan in Alabama during the Reconstruction Era," September 14, 2010, EOA, http: //encyclopediaofalabama.org/article/h-2934.

103. Then in 1873: Foner, 512–16.

103. Over time, financiers: Du Bois, 594–96.

103. On a Tuesday in November: *MA,* February 19, 1874.

104. "Let us plant the banner": *Mobile Daily Tribune*, November 3, 1874.

104. Tim Meaher had recently stopped: Roche, 119.

104. the party's talking points: Fleming, 776–78.

104. two Republican leaders had been assassinated: Foner, 552.

104. Sometime after Meaher's visit: Roche, 119.

105. In that morning's edition: *Mobile Daily Tribune*, November 3, 1874.

105. "quit the river": *Clarke County Democrat*, June 12, 1890.

105. The tax base: AP, February 7, 2017; Trevor D. Logan, "Whitelashing: Black Politicians, Taxes, and Violence," *National Bureau of Economic Research*, June 2019, https://www.nber.org/system/files/working_papers/w26014 /w26014.pdf, 5–6.

105. When Cudjo and the other shipmates: Roche, 119.

105. They took it in stride: Ibid., 120.

105. If anything, the setbacks: Ibid.

106. Earlier that same day: Blake Wilhelm, "Election Riots of 1874," EOA, November 6, 2009, http://encyclopediaofalabama.org/article/h-2484.

106. Some seventeen miles northwest: Ibid.

106. And blood was also spilled in Mobile: Fitzgerald, 212–13; Wiggins, *Scalawag*, 97.

107. "White supremacy sustained": Quoted in Burnett, *Pen*, 179.

107. It was the greatest turnover: Ibid.; Foner, 523.

107. In the Senate: Burnett, 179.

107. The Republicans' loss: Foner, 523–24.

107. The last gasp of Reconstruction: Ibid., 555–56.

107. "out of the region of the Civil War": Quoted in Foner, 557.

107. And in Alabama: Joshua Shiver, "Alabama Constitution of 1875," EOA, April 16, 2020, http://encyclopediaofalabama.org/article/h-4195.; Rogers et al., *Alabama*, 266–68.

107. But they kept their voting receipts: Roche, 120.

CHAPTER 8: WHITE SUPREMACY, BY FORCE AND FRAUD

108. Near the end of 1890: Hines; *TD*, November 8, 1889; *MR*, February 10, 1885.

108. Over the summer: George Howe, "The Last Slave-Ship," *Scribner's Magazine*, July 1890, 113–128.

108. Ely Creek: Ely Creek to the editor of the *Glasgow Weekly Herald*, HMM; Diouf, 247–48.

108. That September: Foster. A note preceding the memoir itself marks the date as September 29, 1890.

109. a willing collaborator: Hines started his newspaper career in Meridian, Mississippi, but he spent most of it in Mobile. He started at the *Register* as a sub-printer and rose through the ranks, working as a proofreader, reporter, and section editor. He became the managing editor of the *Mobile Daily Item* in 1911. See *St. Louis Lumberman*, July 15, 1911.

109. The story was published: Among the three newspapers where it appeared, only the *Pittsburgh Dispatch* includes Hines's byline. The others are unsigned. The *Memphis Appeal-Avalanche* also reprinted the story in January 1891.

109. Throughout the South: Woodward, *Origins*, 156.

109. More than ten thousand veterans: Ibid., 156–57.

109. He died at his home: U.S., Find a Grave Index, 1600s–Current, https://www.findagrave.com/memorial/39402084/timothy-meaher/photo.

109. "Last of the Slave Traders": *NYT*, March 4, 1892.

110. Kirk Munroe, a correspondent: Munroe, 503.

110. Circa 1893, Scott had a cousin: Scott, 59.

110. Noah's carriage pulled up that afternoon: Ibid., 60–65.

111. Scott claimed her cousin: It's unclear where exactly Scott's cousin could have read this, if she did read it in a newspaper at all. Romeyn's story is the most likely candidate. Romeyn visited African Town shortly before Scott and her cousin, and his piece, which was published in a New Orleans newspaper (the *Times-Democrat*), did mention the wager. However, it seems the first time it appeared in print was in April 1894.

111. Stories about this fabled bet: Romeyn, writing in 1894, said Meaher had offered to wager any amount. Byers, in 1906, mentioned the amount of $1,000. A local reporter, Rhoda Pickett, wrote decades later that it was a "drunken bet," part of "a conversation held over a few bottles of whiskey" (*MR*, March 11, 1993).

111. On a muggy Sunday afternoon: Romeyn says he visited the neighborhood in June but doesn't specify the year. However, he mentions the World's Fair that occurred in May 1893, and the story was published in April 1894, so he must have come in June 1893.

111. in his mid-thirties: U.S. Federal Census, 1910, Mobile, Ward 3, 1; Magnolia Cemetery, record of internment, Augustine Meaher, July 30, 1938, accessed via Family Search (https://www.familysearch.org/ark:/61903 /1:1:QKMQ-2PTN).

111. coming to be known as Plateau: This name was being used in local newspapers at least as early as 1900, perhaps earlier.

111. At the 1893 World's Fair: According to promotional materials, "Dahomey Village" featured sixty-nine Dahomeans, including twenty-one women warriors, living among "native homes." The presentation was overtly racist; one poster showed a barely clothed Dahomean holding a machete in one hand and a white man's head in the other. American-born Blacks also found the exhibit galling. Frederick Douglass and the journalist Ida B. Wells were upset in general that no African Americans had been granted a role in the planning of the fair. They wrote a pamphlet, attacking the organizers, and distributed it on the fairgrounds. In Douglass's introduction, the "Dahomey Village" exhibit came in for special criticism. It seemed to him the sole purpose was to "shame the Negro" and "exhibit the Negro as a repulsive savage." (Barbara J. Ballard, "A People Without a Nation," *Chicago History* 28, no. 1 [summer 1999]: 27–43.)

112. Yorktown Missionary Baptist Church: The church was established on March 21, 1888, according to John H. Smith, in "The Voyage of the Clotilda and Africatown Settlement: An Historic Resource Inventory," June 21, 1979, MHDC, 80. The date has been reported elsewhere as 1884 (for instance, see Pettaway, 51), but Rev. Christopher Williams, the rector as of 2022, confirms the year as 1888.

112. Romeyn assessed, quite rightly: Romeyn, "Little Africa."
113. "I don't know any other place": The interviewer, Addie Pettaway, was a Mobile County native. Her research in Africatown was connected to John Smith's work there in the 1980s (see chapters 12 and 13).
113. On Saturday nights: Pettaway, 45.
113. Once it was bright outside: Jones, MPL Oral History Project interview.
113. When Jones was a preteen: Pettaway, 51.
113. "Anybody didn't have": Jones, MPL Oral History Project interview.
113. Ossa Keeby ran a vegetable wagon: Ibid.
113. Jones watched with fascination: Ibid.
114. When the adults were together: *MA,* December 3, 1985.
114. She picked up only a few words: Weise, 7–8.
114. Later in life: Jones, MPL Oral History Project interview.
114. "little Black Africans": Ibid.
114. In 1891: Diouf, 188.
114. In 1892: U.S. Federal Census, 1900, Mobile, Whistler, 7; 1900, Mobile, Precinct 9, roll T624_26, 15A.
114. The young family lived in a compound: Hurston, 88.
114. A new round of tragedies: Ibid., 74.
114. "Shall we meet there": Horace Lorenzo Hastings, "Shall We Meet?," Hmnary.org, https://hymnary.org/media/fetch/122987.
114. "we are going away": Diouf, 184.
114. He urged his wife not to cry: Hurston, 74–75.
115. As for the couple's five sons: Ibid., 73.
115. "NEGRO KILLED LAST NIGHT AT PLATEAU": *MDI,* July 10, 1899.
115. Thomas shared the last name: Diouf, 191–92.
115. Robinson was only twenty-six: Magnolia Cemetery, record of intern-ment, Edward M. Robinson, October 25, 1908, accessed via Family Search (https://www.familysearch.org/ark:/61903/1:1:QKMQ-LMD2); Owen, *History of Alabama,* 1452.
115. In 1907 he would become: Tom McGehee, "The End of the Massons," *Magnolia Messenger,* spring 2016; Mobile Bar Association, "Past Presidents of the MBA," https://mobilebarassociation.com/page/PastPresidentsofMBA.
116. The killing was not technically self-defense: Edward M. Robinson to Joseph F. Johnston, July 25, 1900, Applications for Pardons, ADAH.
116. convicted the defendant of manslaughter: *In the matter of the special venire in the case v. Cudjoe Lewis,* City Court Criminal Minute Book 18, 1899–1902, 112–13, USA; *State of Alabama v. Cudjoe Lewis,* City Court Criminal Minute Book 18, 1899–1902, 118, USA; Convict Bureau, Executive Department of Alabama, "Statement of Sentence," Cudjoe Lewis, July 31, 1900, ADAH. Oddly, the official state records refer to it as a murder conviction, but the

city court records from the trial itself show the jurors found him guilty of manslaughter in the first degree.

116. The judge gave him five years: *State of Alabama v. Cudjoe Lewis*, City Court Criminal Minute Book 18, 1899–1902, 129, USA.

116. he would be excused from this charge: Diouf, 192.

116. When the state built its first penitentiary: "History of the ADOC," Alabama Department of Corrections, http://www.doc.state.al.us/history.

116. Between 1874 and 1877 alone: Going, *Bourbon Democracy*, 176.

116. Revenue from convict leasing: Ibid., 86.

116. After Cudjo's conviction: Intake form, State Convict Records, Alabama Department of Corrections and Institutions, container SG007461, ADAH.

117. By this time a single corporation: State of Alabama, *Third Biennial Report of the Board of Inspectors of Convicts*, 8.

117. TCI supplied fuel: State of Alabama, *Third Biennial Report of the Inspectors of Mines*, 24–26.

117. Ventilation was poor: Ibid., 30–35.

117. The mines operated around the clock: Curtin, *Black Prisoners*, 99.

117. Cudjo was expected: Ibid.

117. According to an 1891 estimate: Ibid., 98.

117. Inmates also faced: Curtin, 105. For an accessible but thorough overview of the convict-leasing system, see Douglas A. Blackmon's *Slavery by Another Name: The Re-Enslavement of Black Americans from the Civil War to World War II* (New York: Doubleday, 2008).

118. By the late summer: Robinson to Johnston, July 25, 1900.

118. They all agreed to sign a statement: Augustine Meaher, et al., to Joseph F. Johnston, July 1900, Applications for Pardons, ADAH.

118. To his packet, Robinson added letters: Jabez J. Parker and Samuel B. Browne to Joseph F. Johnston, July 25, 1900, Applications for Pardons, ADAH.

118. And in a third statement: Statement Charles E. McLean, July 1900, Applications for Pardons, ADAH.

118. Johnston knew the convict-leasing system well: Michael Perman, "Joseph F. Johnston (1896–1900)," EOA, May 13, 2008, http://encyclopediaofalabama .org/article/h-1534 .

118. He was also fairly generous with pardons: State of Alabama, *Third Biennial Report of the Board of Inspectors of Convicts*, 44.

118. In Cudjo Jr.'s case: Diouf has made this observation as well (199).

118. Cudjo Jr. would have received a ticket home: Diouf, 199.

119. But that all changed in 1891: Woodward, 235–90; Tom Watson, "The Negro Question in the South," *The Arena* 6, no. 5 (October 1892): 540–550. See also Frank, *The People, No*.

119. Kolb was perhaps: Hackney, *From Populism to Progressivism*, 4–5.

119. He had tried running for governor: Ibid., 13–17.

119. When the votes were tallied up: William Warren Rogers, "Governor's Election of 1892," EOA, July 22, 2009, http://encyclopediaofalabama.org /article/h-2351.

119. By one estimate: Hackney, 23.

119. This pattern was repeated: Danielle N. Warren, "Reuben F. Kolb," EOA, January 22, 2010, http://encyclopediaofalabama.org/article/h-2523.

119. In December 1894: Flynt, *Alabama*, 6.

120. In 1890, it ratified a new constitution: Perman, *Struggle*, 316–20.

120. In 1901, Alabama followed suit: McMillan, *Constitutional Development*, 261–62.

120. On May 21, 1901: Ibid., 263.

120. He came from an old Alabama family: Moore, *History of Alabama*, 457.

120. Shortly after eleven A.M.: State of Alabama, *Official Proceedings*, vol. I, 7–10.

120. the delegates could be divided: Flynt, *Alabama*, 7–8.

121. Much of the spring and summer: McMillan, 281.

121. less than $100 a year: Flynt, 9.

121. The committee also called for a literacy test: McMillan, 281.

121. Throughout the summer debates: State of Alabama, *Official Proceedings*, vol. III, 2826.

121. the "ignorant and vicious voter": Ibid., 3391.

121. They wanted a poll tax: Ibid., 3381.

121. a vote of 95–19: McMillan, 306.

122. Under the new rules: Flynt, 9–10.

122. The delegates also reduced: Ibid., 10–11.

122. a "clean white man's document": Quoted in McMillan, 346.

122. Knox himself canvassed the state: Moore, 458.

122. "The demand for a new constitution": John B. Knox, "Speech of Hon. John B. Knox, of Calhoun County, President of the Late Constitutional Convention of Alabama, in Closing the Campaign in Favor of Ratification, at Centreville, in Bibb County, Alabama, November 9th, 1901." ADAH. Available at https://digital.archives.alabama.gov/digital/collection/voices/id /8516.

122. Black leaders fought the new constitution: McMillan, 343.

123. They also vowed: Ibid.

123. Outside the twelve counties: Ibid., 350.

123. Reports from elsewhere: Flynt, *Alabama*, 12.

123. The result was that a massive share: Flynt, "A Tragic Century," 34.

123. "against the poorer class of whites": Harlan, *Booker T. Washington*, viii.

123. Washington kept his involvement: Harlan, "The Secret Life of Booker T. Washington," *Journal of Southern History* 37, no. 3 (August 1971): 393–416.

123. In a 6–3 opinion: Oliver Wendell Holmes and Supreme Court of the United States, *U.S. Reports: Giles v. Harris, 189 U.S. 475,* 1902, https://www .loc.gov/item/usrep189475/.

124. One day in the spring of 1902: Hurston, 77–78.

124. Cudjo was several blocks west: Ibid., 79.

124. Cudjo lay there on the street: Ibid.

CHAPTER 9: PROGRESSIVISM FOR WHITE MEN ONLY

125. "for white men only": Woodward, 371–73.

125. A national railroad network: David E. Alsobrook, "Alabama's Port City: Mobile During the Progressive Era, 1896–1917," unpublished PhD dissertation, Auburn University, 1983, 2.

125. As of 1900, its population: Ibid., 24.

125. Erwin Craighead, the editor: Ibid., 13.

126. Craighead boasted in 1902: *MR,* April 19, 1902.

126. the city assigned twenty men: Alsobrook, 13.

126. It also purchased one waterworks system: Ibid., 13–14.

126. Its public parks were improved: Ibid., 7.

126. By 1915: Ibid., 271.

126. Most important for the city's growth: Ibid., 7–9.

126. It started with an ordinance : David E. Alsobrook, "The Mobile Streetcar Boycott of 1902: African American Protest or Capitulation?," *Alabama Review* 56, no. 2 (April 2003): 83–103.

126. In 1915, Dr. Charles Mohr: Quoted in Alsobrook, "Alabama's Port City," 276.

127. When an annexation bill passed: This annexation brought 708 new residents into the city, among whom only 52 were Black. But Alsobrook, the authority on this era of Mobile's past, who was highly attuned to racial matters in the city's history, told me he saw no evidence that race was a significant factor in this particular annexation.

127. Thomas W. Dixon's novel: Stokes, *D.W. Griffith,* 47.

127. the most profitable film of its time: Ibid., 3.

127. "the stamping ground": Quoted in Alsobrook, "Alabama's Port City," 156.

127. More broadly, Erwin Craighead: Ibid., 152–53.

127. Craighead was frank: *MR,* September 1, 1907.

128. However, in 1910, there was a push: Alsobrook, 236–46.

128. Cities across the nation: Samuel P. Hays, "The Politics of Reform in Municipal Government in the Progressive Era," *Pacific Northwest Quarterly* 55, no. 4 (October 1964): 157–169; James Weinstein, "Organized Business and

the City Commission and Manager Movements," *Journal of Southern History* 28, no. 2 (May 1962): 166–182.

128. Craighead championed the proposal: Alsobrook, 243.

128. After a lobbying campaign: This is not to say that at-large elections were new to Mobile in 1911. Between 1885 and 1907, the Democratic Party (in which only white men and a minimal number of Black residents were allowed to participate) held its elections on a ward-by-ward basis, but the general elections were held on an at-large basis. The city went back to the ward system for its general elections in 1908, but a large turnout in a mostly Black ward helped sway the result. This experience drove support for a return to the at-large system (McCrary, "History in the Courts," 51–56).

128. The store also served as the brothers' base: Alsobrook, 157–58.

129. In March 1902, a Hickory Club: *MPR*, March 27, 2002.

129. And in May of that year: *MPR*, May 11, 2002.

129. In the judgment of David Alsobrook: Alsobrook, 157–158.

129. But as the brothers' ties with law enforcement: Hurston is the source for this entire paragraph (165–66). The *Daily Item* and the *Register* archives from late July and early August of 1928 have no mention of someone being killed in a fight.

129. One day roughly three weeks after: Diouf heard a different account of Cudjo Jr.'s death from Henry Williams in 2002. In this version, Cudjo was involved in a barroom fight, and he rolled under a pool table with his opponent. Powe was standing nearby and shot him, evidently meaning to hit the other person. See Diouf, 300, n. 24.

129. As the family looked: Hurston, 75–76.

130. Cudjo said later that he doubted: Ibid., 165–66.

130. a "Creole of color": Alsobrook interview.

130. The 1900 census: U.S. Federal Census, 1900, Whistler, Alabama, 9.

130. Perhaps, as Sylviane Diouf has suggested: Diouf, 213.

130. Cudjo hoped to see Powe arrested: Hurston, 77.

130. The sixty-year-old attorney: Carline Jones, "Richard Henry Clarke," EOA, October 12, 2015, http://encyclopediaofalabama.org/article/h -3708.

131. Cudjo had more than one cause: Diouf, 211–12.

131. On this day in court: Hurston, 79–80.

131. The attorney representing the railroad: Ibid., 80.

131. When Clarke's turn came: Ibid., 79–80.

131. In his instructions to the jury: Jury instructions, *Cudjo Lewis v. The Louisville and Nashville Railroad Company*, Mobile County Circuit Court, December 31, 1902.

131. Court recessed: Hurston, 80.

131. the verdict was overturned: Certificate of reversal, *Cudjo Lewis v. The Louisville and Nashville Railroad Company,* Supreme Court of Alabama, November 26, 1904.

132. One evening two years after the trial: Hurston gave a slightly different account of this episode in *Dust Tracks.* According that version, the moment Cudjo accepted David's death was when "his wife persuaded him that the headless body on the window blind was their son." Hurston implied that the head was not returned to Cudjo and Celia, at least not immediately. She also wrote that Cudjo cried hard for several minutes, but she didn't mention him retreating to a pine grove (167–68).

132. "Git off my porch!": Hurston, *Barracoon,* 83–86. (I have inferred the date here. Cudjo says on 88 that it happened the same year his son Jimmy died, which was 1905.)

133. Cudjo and Celia's third son: Hurston, 87.

133. One day not long after: Ibid., 87–88.

133. Cudjo and Celia's sorrows: Ibid., 88.

133. Jimmy, who was thirty-five: Jimmy was born on December 15, 1870 (Diouf, 137).

133. He was lying around the house: Hurston, 88.

134. Diouf believes the symptoms: Diouf, 288, n. 40.

134. It seemed to Cudjo: Hurston, 87–88.

134. a form of racial terrorism: In the 1890s, one-third of documented lynching victims were white; but between 1900 and 1909, whites made up only 11 percent of the reported victims (Woodward, 351).

134. One Black man was lynched: *Lagniappe,* July 3, 2018.

134. The first victim: Alsobrook, 159–61.

134. A month later: Ibid., 162–65; *Birmingham News,* October 6, 1906.

135. Thompson and Robinson had hearings: Alsobook, 166–68; *Birmingham News,* October 6, 1906.

135. Accounts differ on who was killed first: The *Birmingham News* said Robinson was killed first. Other sources reported Thompson being killed first (Alsobrook, "Alabama's Port City, 167).

135. An Associated Press reporter was called over: Alsobrook, "Alabama's Port City," 166–68; *Birmingham News,* October 6, 1906.

135. Later in the afternoon: Alsobrook, "Alabama's Port City," 167–68; Alsobrook interview; *Birmingham News,* October 6, 1906.

135. Another lynching occurred: The victim's first name was reported by some out-of-town papers as Moses, and his last name was sometimes reported as Dossett. However, at least two Mobile papers, the *Daily Item* and the *Daily Register,* consistently identified him as Mose Dorsett. All told, the reporters' carelessness about identifying him correctly was typical.

136. Within a few hours: *MDR*, September 23, 1907.

136. Meanwhile, as word about the incident: *MDI*, September 22, 1907, and September 23, 1907; *TD* and *Richmond Times Dispatch*, September 23, 1907; Alsobrook, "Alabama's Port City," 173–74.

136. Around 12:40 A.M.: *MDR* and *TD*, September 23, 1907.

136. "So quiet were the proceedings": *TD*, September 23, 1907.

136. For a lynching to be committed inside Mobile: This was exactly what happened on January 21, 1909. Two sheriff's deputies came to serve a warrant on Richard Robertson, a carpenter of mixed race, and Robertson drew a gun. All three men were wounded in the showdown, and one deputy later died. On January 23, after midnight, a mob—probably led by other sheriff's deputies—marched Robertson out of the jail and hanged him inside the city limits, across the street from Mobile's oldest church. The city's elites were aghast. Craighead denounced the killing in his newspaper, and local attorneys pressed for the sheriff to be impeached on charges of neglecting his duties. "How could Mobile attract northern capital and innovative entrepreneurs and investors and recapture her antebellum position as a vital seaport," Alsobrook writes, summing up their position, "if lawlessness reigned in her streets?" As a rule, he writes, the city boosters "stood firmly united on any issue which promoted Mobile's image and business opportunities." See Alsobrook, "Mobile's Solitary Sentinel: U.S. Attorney William H. Ambrecht and the Richard Robertson Lynching Case of 1909," *Gulf South Historical Review* 20, no. 1 (fall 2004): 7–27.

136. Over the days that followed: Alsobrook interview. The resident in question was Ed Williams, Henry Williams's father.

137. "This was just a topic": Ibid.

137. The same day the search was ordered: Alsobrook, "Alabama's Port City," 174; *Chattanooga Star*, September 27, 1907.

137. On a chilly November night: Hurston, 71.

137. The next day, Celia wanted: Ibid.

137. The following week, according to Cudjo: Ibid.

137. His last remaining child: Ibid., 72.

137. Whitley had grown up: *MA*, April 27, 1916.

138. "Dr. Washington is our spokesman": *New York Age*, July 22, 1915.

138. Whitley believed in education: *MA*, April 22, 1916.

138. In his early months in Plateau: *Freeman*, August 21, 1915.

138. a hundred students: *MA*, April 27, 1916.

138. he organized a committee: Ibid.

138. By February 1911: *Crisis*, February 11, 1911.

138. The following year: *MA*, April 27, 1916.

138. As of 1915: *Freeman*, August 21, 1915.

138. Later Whitley also arranged classes: *MA*, January 23 and April 27, 1916.

139. He had friends in Mobile: Alsobrook, 192–98, 216–18; Washington, *Booker T. Washington's Own Story*, 435–37.

139. "When I asked this old man": Washington, *Story of the Negro*, 104.

139. He said this explicitly: *NYT*, December 12, 1909.

139. "more than anxious": Whitley to Washington, February 12, 1912; see also Whitley's letters to Washington on June 12, 1912, and December 19, 1914. Booker T. Washington Papers, Manuscript Division, Library of Congress (copies in possession of David Alsobrook).

139. Whitley also told Washington's confidante: Whitley to Emmett Jay Scott, May 22, 1912, BTW Papers, copy in possession of Alsobrook.

139. "My dear sir": Washington to Whitley, June 20, 1912, BTW Papers, copy in possession of Alsobrook.

139. In another, he addressed his response: Washington to S. S. Murphy, December 22, 1914, BTW Papers, copy in possession of Alsobrook.

139. When another fire tore through in 1915: There is no ruling out the possibility that one or both of these fires was set deliberately. Burning Black schools and churches was a common form of racial terror in the 1910s. It could not, however, have been done under the auspices of the Ku Klux Klan. The Klan's rebirth in the Jim Crow era began on Thanksgiving night in 1915, nine months after the second fire in Plateau. See Feldman, *Politics, Society, and the Klan in Alabama*, 12.

139. Soon everyone in town: *Chicago Defender*, April 17, 1915. Incidentally, the author of this story was H. Roger Williams, the second Black physician to practice medicine in Mobile.

140. In the summer of 1915: *Freeman*, August 21, 1915.

140. Rosenwald's money would fund nearly five thousand schools: Deutsch, *You Need a Schoolhouse*, 156.

140. filling a void: Hoffschwelle, *Rosenwald Schools*, 17–18.

140. The Plateau community: Fisk University Rosenwald Fund Card File Database, http://rosenwald.fisk.edu/.

140. In January 1918: *Birmingham Reporter*, February 2, 1918.

141. He cleaned the building: Pettaway, 49.

141. it was also Cudjo's singular honor: Ibid., 43.

141. The parishioners often put on picnics: Ibid., 50.

141. Mama Eva remembered: Weise, 6.

141. Twice a month: Dennison, *A Memoir of Lottie Dennison*, 35–36.

141. His other consolation in old age: Pettaway, 43–45.

141. Tending to his garments: Roche, 123–24.

142. Mama Eva sometimes saw her father: Jones, MPL Oral History Project interview.

142. Cudjo also revealed to an interviewer: Berger, "Cugo Lewis."

142. she had studied at the Art Students League: Melanie Thornton, "Emma Langdon Roche's Artistic Legacy," *Alabama Heritage* 126 (fall 2017): 6–15.

142. only nine were left: Roche, 120. Roche says eight were alive, but she leaves out Charlie Lewis, who was apparently alive as well—see Diouf, 219 and 288.

142. Their time in America, in Roche's words: Roche, 111.

142. Following the shipmates' request: Ibid., 120–21.

142. Some of her descriptions are touching: Ibid., 124–25.

143. the death of his first wife, Annie: *MA*, September 24, 1904.

143. POOR STENOGRAPHER BECOMES BRIDE OF MILLIONAIRE: *San Francisco Examiner*, October 4, 1905.

143. According to the gossip columns: *Philadelphia Inquirer*, October 5, 1905; *Brooklyn Times Union*, October 3, 1905; *Standard Gauge* (Brewton, Alabama), October 12, 1905; *Spokesman-Review* (Spokane), October 15, 1905.

143. furious about these "sensational statements": *MA*, October 26, 1905.

143. In 1909, a white rent collector: *MA*, September 10, 1909.

143. Kanko died in 1917: Diouf, 221–22; *Andalusia Star*, March 9, 1923.

143. Then Keeby died early that year: *Andalusia Star*, March 9, 1923.

CHAPTER 10: RENAISSANCE

144. Harlem had by then "brought together": Locke, *New Negro*, 6–7.

144. He'd been visited in August 1925: Lewis, "T'appin (Terrapin)," 245–47.

145. As the interviewer explained: Fauset, "American Negro Folk Literature," 241. The interviewer in question was Arthur Huff Fauset. He was the younger half-brother of Jessie Redmon Fauset, the literary editor of *The Crisis* from 1919 to 1926. Arthur Fauset would have a remarkable anthropology career of his own. His 1944 book *Black Gods of the Metropolis: Negro Religious Cults of the Urban North* was a pathbreaking work in the field of African American religion.

145. the aunt "of all black people": Alice Walker, "In Search of Zora Neale Hurston," *Ms.*, March 1975, 74–89.

145. Hurston was a thirty-four-year-old undergrad: Boyd, *Wrapped in Rainbows*, 116–17.

145. The two of them had an easy rapport: Ibid., 114–15.

145. "Almost nobody else could stop the average Harlemite": Hughes, *Big Sea*, 239.

145. "as full of things a writer could use": Hurston to Fannie Hurst, March 16, 1926, in Kaplan, *Zora Neale Hurston*, 85.

145. He wrote a letter to the historian: Boyd, *Wrapped in Rainbows*, 142.

145. "I was extremely proud": Hurston, *Dust Tracks*, 143.

145. She needed a car: Boyd, *Wrapped in Rainbows*, 143; Taylor, *Zora and Langston*, 99.

146. Knowing about the dangers: Monroe Work, "Lynchings: By State and Race, 1882–1968," Tuskegee University Archives Repository, http://archive.tuskegee .edu/archive/wayback/web/20170224184930/http%253A/archive.tuskegee.edu /archive/handle/123456789/507; Boyd, *Wrapped in Rainbows*, 144–45.

146. "I went about asking": Hurston, *Dust Tracks*, 144.

146. She was getting the "feather-bed resistance": Hurston, *Mules and Men*, 2–3.

146. In the summer of 1927: Boyd, *Wrapped in Rainbows*, 150; Hemenway, *Zora Neale Hurston*, 97.

146. Boas had specifically told her: Hurston, *Barracoon*, 6.

146. It also took time to understand his accent: Roche, 125–26; Hemenway, 98; Boyd, *Wrapped in Rainbows*, 154.

146. So to supplement her findings: Hurston identified the place she visited as the "Mobile Historical Society," but no organization by that exact name existed. Where Hurston found her information has become a matter of curiosity to board members of the Historic Mobile Preservation Society (which was not founded until 1934).

146. large blocks word for word: William Stewart to the Historic Mobile Preservation Society, January 5, 1972, HMPS; Stewart to Carter Smith, January 18, 1972, HMPS; Hemenway, 97–98.

146. Out of sixty-seven paragraphs she wrote: Hemenway, 97–98.

147. "She made a special trip to Mobile": Hurston, "Cudjo's Own Story of the Last African Slaver," *Journal of Negro History* 12, no. 4 (October 1927): 648–663.

147. was herself connected to literary and artistic circles: Thornton, "Emma Langdon Roche's Artistic Legacy."

147. she could have called attention to the plagiarism: However, it's also conceivable that Hurston met Roche while she was in town. Roche was by then running a local artists' guild, and someone could have introduced them. There is some possibility, however slim, that Roche gave Hurston permission to borrow material from *Historic Sketches of the South*.

147. Her biographers have struggled: Hemenway, 98–99; Boyd, *Wrapped in Rainbows*, 153–54.

147. She was open with Boas: Hurston, *Dust Tracks*, 144.

147. She was a seventy-three-year-old heiress: Kaplan, *Miss Anne*, 200, 230. I was first made aware of Mason's role in this story, and of the letters Mason exchanged with Hurston and Locke, through Rebecca Panovka's excellent 2018 piece in the *Los Angeles Review of Books*, "A Different Backstory for Zora Neale Hurston's 'Barracoon.'"

147. Mason had been infatuated: Kaplan, *Miss Anne*, 49.

148. Starting in her early thirties: Ibid., 206.

148. she had found a kindred spirit: Ibid., 203–205.

148. He died in 1903: Ibid., 206–207.

148. At first she dabbled in anthropology herself: Ibid., 207–11.

148. Mason was suffering from severe arthritis: Ibid., 197.

148. Mason's involvement with the Harlem Renaissance: Ibid., 214–21.

148. To the ones she favored most: Ibid., 222.

148. the only formal condition: Boyd, *Wrapped in Rainbows*, 158.

148. Either Locke or Hughes was responsible: Kaplan, *Miss Anne*, 223; Boyd, *Wrapped in Rainbows*, 156.

148. On September 20, 1927: Boyd, *Wrapped in Rainbows*, 156.

148. With its high ceilings: Kaplan, *Miss Anne*, 197, 214–15.

149. Hurston had an immediate rapport: Boyd, *Wrapped in Rainbows*, 157–58.

149. "I think that we got on famously": Hurston to Langston Hughes, September 21, 1927, in Kaplan, *Zora Neale Hurston*, 106–107.

149. "just as pagan as I": Hurston, *Dust Tracks*, 144.

149. Mason offered the young writer a stipend: Contract signed by Mason and Hurston, December 8, 1927, box 164–99, folder 5, ALP.

149. "to see the same thing done": Mason to Alain Locke, October 9, 1927, box 68, folder 18, ALP.

149. Whatever Hurston collected or wrote: Contract between Mason and Hurston; Boyd, *Wrapped in Rainbows*, 159–60; Kaplan, *Miss Anne*, 228–29.

149. Six days after the contract was signed: Boyd, *Wrapped in Rainbows*, 160.

149. her first stop would be Mobile: Hurston to Hughes, December 9, 1927, in Kaplan, *Zora Neale Hurston*, 110–11.

150. The idea, she said, was to "set down": Hurston, 3.

150. She wrote, for instance, that it was summer: Ibid., 17, 93–94.

150. In fact, if she did go directly: Another possibility, perhaps more likely, is that Hurston changed her plans after writing to Hughes and did not go to Mobile in December 1927. All around, her letters give the best evidence of her itinerary, though they do not clarify her whereabouts for most of that December or January. She sent Hughes a postcard from Florida on January 31, 1928, saying she was living in "the quarters of the Everglades Cypress Lumber Co." She continued sending letters from Florida through May. Her correspondence shows that she was in Magazine Point in June and July of 1928. Then, as early as August 6, her letters started coming from Louisiana.

150. "check on Miss Hurston for accuracy": Boyd, *Wrapped in Rainbows*, 191.

150. Hurston's manuscript also seems to repeat: See Roche, 78–79, and Hurston, 21–22; Roche, 87–90, and Hurston, 55–56; Roche, 101, and Hurston, 59; Roche, 114–16, and Hurston, 66–67; and Roche, 121–23, and Hurston, 92–93.

150. Hurston managed to correctly get down certain words: Diouf, 246.

151. Another visitor several years later: *Birmingham News*, December 2, 1934.

151. Hurston didn't record it: Cassandra Lewis Wallace interview; Certificate of Death, Emmett Lewis, State of Alabama-Bureau of Vital Statistics, April 21, 1921, copy in possession of Cassandra Lewis Wallace. Note that the spelling of Emmett Lewis's name is not consistent across public records. The 1900 census has it as "Emmet," and on his gravestone it is spelled as "Emmit."

151. Hurston said she wanted to know about his life: Hurston, 17–24.

151. Hurston did return: Ibid., 25–26.

152. One Saturday, Cudjo seemed a little grouchy: Ibid., 51.

152. Another day, at his request: Ibid., 83.

152. She continued plying him: Ibid., 37.

152. and a late-season melon: Ibid., 83.

152. By February 1928: Mason to Locke, February 12, 1928, box 68, folder 12, ALP.

152. Hurston notes that one day: Hurston, 51.

152. When it was time for Hurston to leave: Ibid., 93–94.

153. He was in the early stages: For more on Radin's remarkable work, see Jack Glazier's *Anthropology and Radical Humanism: Native and African American Narratives and the Myth of Race* (East Lansing: Michigan State University Press, 2020).

153. He thought Radin was "imposing": Locke to Mason, February 6, 1928, box 68, folder 20, ALP.

153. "Langston!": Mason to Hughes, February 13, 1928, box 68, folder 20, ALP.

153. "you must pray with all your might": Mason to Locke, February 12, 1928, box 68, folder 20, ALP.

153. "You have already heard": Locke to Hurston, February 24, 1928, box 38, folder 28, ALP.

153. HAWK SLIDES TO MOBILE: Locke to Mason, March 14, 1928, box 68, folder 22, ALP.

153. In a letter he wrote the same day: Ibid.

154. Hurston returned to Alabama: Hurston wrote a May 10, 1928 letter from Florida, a June 14 letter from Magazine Point, more letters from Magazine Point on July 10 and July 25, and a letter from Louisiana on August 6.

154. she enclosed a piece of wood: Hurston to Locke, May 10, 1928, box 38, folder 28, ALP.

154. "using the vacuum method": Hurston to Locke, October 15, 1928, box 38, folder 28, ALP.

154. She kept traveling: Boyd, *Wrapped in Rainbows*, 162–92.

154. "I have more than 95,000 words": Hurston to Franz Boas, April 21, 1929, in Kaplan, *Zora Neale Hurston*, 137–38.

154. she also knew Mason wanted it this way: Hurston to Mason, September 25, 1931, box 69, folder 8, ALP.

154. "To Charlotte Mason": Hurston, *Barracoon*, 1.

154. "All of Kossula's stories": Locke notes dated June 15, 1929, box 139, folder 8, ALP.

154. She shared a draft: Mason to Locke, June 7, 1931, box 69, folder 5, ALP.

154. In a June 7 letter: Ibid.

154. None of the other Harlem-borne projects: Kaplan, *Miss Anne*, 235.

154. Time was of the essence: Ibid., 240.

155. "the future of the Negro in America": Mason to Locke, June 7, 1931, box 69, folder 5, ALP.

155. Instead he decided to try Viking Press: Locke to Mason, June 3, 1931, box 69, folder 5, ALP.

155. apparently Harold Guinzburg: The only references to the Viking editor are in Locke's handwritten letters, and his handwriting is a bit hard to make out, but it almost certainly identifies Guinzburg. Other historical evidence also points to Guinzburg as his contact.

155. actively seeking out Black authors: Hutchinson, "Publishers and Publishing Houses."

155. He sent Guinzburg a copy: Locke to Mason, June 9, 1931, box 69, folder 5, ALP.

155. On the day when Locke arrived: Locke memo, June 12, 1931, box 69, folder 5, ALP; Locke to Mason, June 15, 1931, box 69, folder 5, ALP.

155. she was not in the city at all: Boyd, *Wrapped in Rainbows*, 221–22.

155. the "considerable revisions": Memo by Locke, June 12, 1931, box 69, folder 5, ALP.

155. "The Viking press again asks": Hurston to Mason, September 25, 1931, box 69, folder 8, ALP.

156. "You do not seem to realize": Mason to Hurston, April 8, 1932, box 164–100, folder 9, ALP.

156. In October of that year: Boyd, *Wrapped in Rainbows*, 240–44.

156. The letters he sent Mason: Lewis to Mason, September 4, 1930, box 164–99, folder 15, ALP.

156. Cudjo apparently had a copy: Ibid.

156. It seems the catalyst: *Press-Forum Weekly* (Mobile), September 17 and October 24, 1931.

157. Within weeks after the event: "Honoring Cudjo Lewis: America's Last Piece of African 'Black Ivory,'" *Literary Digest*, November 21, 1931.

157. Soon Cudjo received a lucrative offer: *MR*, August 18, 1935.

157. The renewed interest in the *Clotilda* story: O. S. Wynn, "Woman Survivor of Last Slave Ship, Erect and Vigorous at Advanced Age, Walks Fifteen Miles for Gov't Help," *Selma Times-Journal*, December 20, 1931; S. L. Flock, "Survivor of the Last Slaver Lives on Plantation Near Selma," *MA*, January 31, 1932.

157. Since 2019, the scholars: Hannah Durkin, "Finding Last Middle Passage Survivor Sally 'Redoshi' Smith on the Page and Screen," *Slavery & Abolition* 40, no. 4 (2019): 631–58; Hannah Durkin, "Uncovering the Hidden Lives of Last *Clotilda* Survivor Matilda McCrear and Her Family," *Slavery & Abolition* 41, no. 3 (March 2020): 431–57; Diouf, "The Last Slave Ship Survivor and Her Descendants Identified," *NG*, March 28, 2020.

158. Octavia Wynn, a *Selma Times-Journal* reporter: Wynn was the great-aunt of John Sledge, who has authored several books on Mobile's history. Sledge gives a portrait of her in the prologue of *These Rugged Days*. She was hired as the *Times-Journal*'s social editor in 1914 and later rose to the rank of city editor. She wrote stories on local history and architecture, and interviewed Confederate veterans, widows, freedpeople, and other civilians about their memories of the war. Sledge, who credits her with teaching him to love history, dedicated his master's thesis to her (*Rugged Days*, xvii–xxii).

158. Wynn reported that Gracie paired up: McCrear told Wynn her former owner's name was "Memorable White Frost Creagh," and Wynn reported it as fact; but as Durkin has shown, his real name was Memorable Walker Creagh, and his biography is well documented. He served six years in the Alabama legislature.

158. she had a long-term relationship: Durkin, "Uncovering the Hidden Lives," 441.

158. Though she didn't take Schuler's name: Ibid., 440.

158. That day at the courtroom: Wynn.

159. At the time of her death: Durkin, "Uncovering the Hidden Lives."

159. The other shipmate was a woman named Redoshi: Flock; Durkin, "Finding Last Middle Passage Survivor Sally 'Redoshi' Smith," 635.

159. Hurston's letters reveal: Hurston to Hughes, July 10, 1928, in Kaplan, *Zora Neale Hurston*, 121–23.

159. The *Advertiser* reported that Redoshi: Flock.

160. McCrear had also traveled to Mobile County: Wynn.

160. a hardwood and veneer plant was built: *MA*, August 15, 1915.

160. The company had been selling so much paper: Boyd, *Slain Wood*, 16–17, 120.

160. issued the call for a "New South": Harris, *Henry W. Grady*, 205.

160. As state and local governments: Cobb, *Selling the South*, 229–30.

160. In Mobile's case: *MDI*, July 4, 1928.

161. In exchange, IP promised: Ibid., July 3, 1928.

161. "Citizens of this city will be glad": *MDR*, July 4, 1928. It appears the Meahers sold the land to the state for $10,000, and on the same day of that transaction, the state entered into a 99-year lease with International Paper. It's unclear why the company did not buy or lease from the Meahers directly,

but perhaps it wanted to avoid being publicly associated with the family of a notorious slaver. See land records: "Augustine Meaher and Wife to State of Alabama," Aug. 7, 1928, deed book 220, 136–37, MCPC, and "Southern Kraft Corp. and International Paper Co. to International Paper Co.," Dec. 23, 1941, deed book 321, 276–80, MCPC.

161. "encourage the building up and conservation": Ibid.

161. "Mobilians Fail to Realize Big Opportunity": *MDR*, July 6, 1928.

161. Ultimately the city did reach its goal: *MDI*, July 9, 1928.

161. At the time when the mill started up: Williams and Porter, 8, 10; McCants interview; *The Alabama Negro* (unpaginated).

162. He was rumored to carry a pistol: Taylor interview.

162. Each year Baker selected the most promising seniors: Hubbard, McCants, Nettles, and Taylor interviews.

162. His last surviving letter: Lewis to Mason, May 12, 1932, box 164–99, folder 15, ALP.

162. It turned out there had been delivery problems: Hurston to Mason, May 26, 1932, box 164–99, folder 10, ALP.

163. James Saxon Childers: "From Jungle to Slavery."

163. In late 1934 and early 1935: Melanie Thornton, "Emma Langdon Roche's Artistic Legacy."

163. She typically found his shutters closed: Roche, "Last Survivor of Slave Ship Deeply Grateful to God, Man."

164. The cause of death was arteriosclerosis: Diouf, 299.

164. he was an idealistic young man: Thomson, "Introduction," xiii.

164. After they took up an offering: Merlin Hanson, "Burial of the Last Slave," *Globe* (undated), HMPS.

CHAPTER 11: KING COTTON, KING PULP

168. He claimed credit for such inventions: Porter interview.

168. he told variations of a story: *MPR*, September 17, 2008. Williams also claimed that before the *Clotilda* shipmates came to the Plateau area, there was a group of North Africans, or "Moors," who had settled there long before. Talk of the Moors still persists in the Africatown community, but Williams seems to have been the original source. I have not been able to find any evidence that these settlers existed.

168. A second mega-factory: Shackelford, *People & Paper*, 3–15.

168. Also by 1941: *Onlooker* (Foley, Alabama), October 16, 1941.

168. Her grandmother told her: Woods interview.

168. Cudjo Lewis's descendants: Lumbers and Wallace interviews.

169. "but no good evidence of it has ever been found": Howard, *American Slavers*, 301–302.

169. Meaher State Park: *Baldwin Times,* August 7, 1952.

170. In August 1959: "Dedication Program," Centennial Celebration of Plateau and Magazine Point, Alabama, August 30, 1959, in "The voyage of the Clotilda and Africatown Settlement: An Historic Resource Inventory," compiled by John Smith, June 1, 1979, MHDC.

170. All he knows is that his great-grandfather: Womack interview; U.S. Federal Census, 1910, Mobile, precinct 9, roll T624_26, 7B; WWII Draft Registration Cards for Alabama, 10/16/1940–03/31/1947, Records of the Selective Service System, record group 147, box 33, NARA. Retrieved via Ancestry.com.

171. Plateau was still a poor community: U.S. Congress, House of Representatives, "Overview Hearing on Operations of the Department of Housing and Urban Development," 55.

171. the place seemed idyllic: Sources on life in Plateau and Magazine Point in the 1950s, '60s, and '70s include John Adams, Tori Adams, Armstead, Bacot, Ballard, Davis, Flen, Green, Hayes, Hubbard, Jackson, Johnson, Cleon Jones, Mae Jones, Carolyn Adams Lewis, Lockwood, Lumbers, McCants, Moore, Mosley, Darron Patterson, Sharon Patterson, Pinkney, Randolph, Taylor, Thomas, Wallace, Jesse Womack, Joe Womack, and Woods.

171. The neighborhood kids were mad for baseball: Womack interview; Womack, "'Africatown Fats,'" Bridge the Gulf, June 4, 2014, https://bridgethegulfproject.org/blog/2014/africatown-fats.

172. The IP facility employed 2,700 people: *MA,* June 13, 1948.

172. the Scott mill had 1,500 workers: *Andalusia Star-News,* May 7, 1959.

172. it was the largest of Scott Paper's sixteen mills: *Baldwin Times,* March 15, 1962.

172. "King Pulp": quoted in Boyd, *Slain Wood,* 17.

172. They hired workers of both races: After the IP and Scott mills opened in Mobile, the national paper-mill unions established separate locals for Black and white workers in order to maintain peace with the whites. Scott Paper was generally seen as progressive in the way it handled race relations, but it agreed to impose segregation at its Mobile mill, in deference to local norms. Black workers there were routinely given the hardest and dirtiest jobs: cleaning bathrooms, hauling garbage, lifting pulpwood. "We used to use an old cliché," one Black worker there later said. "If you were an Afro-American, you either pulled something or pushed something."

After the passage of the Civil Rights Act in 1964, the process of integration was slow and difficult. International Paper had to close its cafeteria because white workers boycotted it en masse. The leadership at both mills agreed in the late 1960s to integrate their workforces, but management continued finding ways to keep Black workers out of the better jobs, until federal courts forced them to change their practices. The unions were not fully integrated at Scott Paper until 1972. See Minchin, *Color of Work*, 16–17, 74–75, 112, 129–31, 146, 163.

172. "The Blacks were on the bottom": Sullivan interview.

173. "Four days in a row last week": Harold and Dorothy Seymour to Johnny W. Sanders, October 5, 1976, ADEM.

173. the odor had been reduced more than 90 percent: Johnny W. Sanders to Harold and Dorothy Seymour, September 7, 1976, ADEM.

173. "scent by scent": Flynt, *Alabama*, 165.

173. "That's the smell of prosperity!": Boyd, *Slain Wood*, 149.

173. Mobilians came up with their own variations: Cleveland, Callaway, and Mitchell interviews.

174. it was standard practice to dump 95 percent of the water: Boyd, *Slain Wood*, 154.

174. The waste absorbed oxygen: Ibid., 155.

174. filling the water with dioxin: Ibid., 151.

174. the killing of hundreds of game fish: *MR*, June 28, 1930.

174. A judge in Louisiana: Quoted in Boyd, *Slain Wood*, 156.

175. IP ducked prosecution: *Alexander City Outlook*, March 26, 1931. Contemporaneous news coverage confirms that the buyer, Southern Kraft, was an IP subsidiary.

175. "industrial streams": Boyd, *Slain Wood*, 160–61.

175. In 1962, Scott Paper announced: *Atmore Advance*, April 12, 1962.

175. In 1965, tests were done: Testimony of Archie D. Hooper, in Federal Water Pollution Control Administration, Department of the Interior, "Conference: In the Matter of Pollution of the Navigable Waters of Mobile Bay and its Tributaries-Alabama," Mobile, January 27–28, 1970, transcript of proceedings, 332.

175. concern that the oysters were carrying diseases: Ibid., 25.

175. industrial plants were the biggest source: Ibid., 37–38.

175. But as far as residents can recall: Hayes, Jackson, Walker, and Jesse Womack interviews.

176. The group had formed in 1933: *Press-Forum Weekly* (Mobile), August 5, 1933. The story identifies the group as the "citizens' League"; the name "Citizens' Committee" evidently have come later. Baker turned down requests that he serve as president, saying the role should go to someone who could devote more time to it. Reverend S. R. Lee was chosen as president, James Green as vice president, and Nelson Adams as financial secretary. According to the news coverage, the group's first projects were turning out at least a hundred residents to vote, closing "immoral places" in the community, asking

the county for more help with street maintenance, and building a library and playground.

176. It seems Adams was the group's unofficial leader: John, Nelson, and Tori Adams interviews; Carolyn Adams Lewis and Womack interviews.

176. he owned roughly 30 rental properties: Records from the 1960 annexation of Plateau, group 6, box 7, MMA.

176. He was sometimes regarded as the unofficial mayor: Pettaway, 40.

176. A 1954 letter from the Citizens' Committee: Solomon Bradley Jr. to Joseph Langan, September 20, 1954, group 6, box 7, MMA.

176. there is evidence that disease outbreaks persisted: U.S. Congress, House of Representatives, "Overview Hearing on Operations of the Department of Housing and Urban Development," 55. According to the federal government, local health officials reported "widespread disease" among Plateau's residents as late as 1971. However, the Mobile County Health Department does not have records detailing the situation further.

177. the city's physical resources were overburdened: Jackson, "Mobile Since 1945," 281, 286.

177. the city annexed fifty acres: MR, February 6, 1955; Anderson Browne, "Population Hike of About 25,000 Seen If Adopted," MR, January or February 1956, MPL.

177. Much of the land was already suburbanized: Jackson, "Mobile Since 1945," 285–88.

177. The downtown area began to deteriorate: Ibid., 293.

177. Magazine Point was annexed by Mobile in 1945: correspondence with Edward Harkins, director of MMA.

177. the 1955–56 annexation: On September 12, 1956, Gov. James Folsom signed a bill that annexed four square miles to the city's area, including part of the Scott Paper factory (see Browne, "Population Hike of About 25,000 Seen If Adopted").

177. Plateau's residents hired Vernon Crawford: MR, January 20, 1960.

177. Crawford presented the city commissioners with a petition: Ibid.

177. they realized the undeveloped marshland: MP, January 12, 1960.

177. The leaders of Prichard: Ibid., February 24, 1960; MR, February 26, 1960.

177. Even after the annexation: MR, June 20, 1967; U.S. House of Representatives, "Overview Hearing on Operations of the Department of Housing and Urban Development," 55.

178. He was upset about having his property assessed: In spite of his griping, it seems Meaher could easily afford the property assessment. The same week that a board voted to build the water and sewer lines, Meaher sold a piece of property, in what amounted to the largest single land transaction in Mobile's history. He and some other landholders sold a total of seven thousand acres,

north of Plateau and Magazine Point, to a New Orleans–based industrial development firm, for roughly $3 million. (In the decades since, however, this particular tract has not been heavily developed.) See *MR*, June 20, 1967.

178. "You know, that's the way it is": *Southern Courier*, June 17–18, 1967, and March 17–18, 1968.

178. . Meaher posed for a photo: *Southern Courier*, June 17–18, 1967.

180. When it came to discipline: Armstead, McCants, and Womack interviews.

CHAPTER 12: "RELOCATION PROCEDURES"

181. There was "no place in America": *Southern Courier*, July 1–2, 1967.

182. "shreds of hoodoo beliefs and practices": Hurston, "Hoodoo in America," *Journal of American Folklore* 44, no. 174 (October–December 1931): 317–417.

182. He divulged only one formula: Pettaway, 84.

182. Others are skeptical: Moore and Patterson interviews.

182. "Will you see that Cudjoe gets back home?": AP, October 2, 1977.

183. His workshop itself was a wonder: Pettaway, 74; photo in the possession of William Tishler.

183. His yard was decorated with a gallery: Pettaway, 74–78.

183. at least one Buffalo soldier, Emperor Green: Neil Norman, "Report on Mapping and Preservation Efforts at Old Plateau Cemetery," September 12, 2010, MHDC, 4.

183. his knowledge of local history was formidable: Ralph Poore, *The Mobile Press-Register*, EOA, January 8, 2008, http://www.encyclopediaofalabama .org/article/h-1422.

183. there were "books on top of books": *MPR*, September 17, 2008.

183. "He and I laugh and talk": October 2, 1977.

183. Williams took a liberal approach: Smith and Williams, *Africatown*, 28.

184. Happy Hill: This neighborhood's name is often called Happy Hills, but Charles Porter, who grew up there and covered the community for years in the *Inner City News*, emphasized to me that the "Hill" was singular.

184. One of Williams's early clashes: I have pieced these events together using letters that are held in various archives around Mobile and Montgomery. In one case, they're stored in an aged envelope marked Do Not Open—along with a note saying they could "cause controversy in the wrong hands."

184. ASU's History and Political Science Club: Norman W. Walton to the Alabama Historical Commission, October 30, 1972, container SG016140, ADAH.

184. Taking up this request, the historical commission: W. Warner Floyd to Harold Ray Collins, November 30, 1972, container SG016140, ADAH.

185. But in December, the school superintendent: Harold R. Collins to W. Warner Floyd, December 11, 1972, container SG016140, ADAH.

185. Other correspondence shows: Caldwell Delaney to Harold R. Collins, March 3, 1972, HMM; Delaney to Gary A. Greenough, March 12, 1974, MPL.

185. "When we visit the campus": Charles W. Porter to W. O. Clark, January 15, 1974, HMM.

185. "I know that you will be delighted": James J. Benson to Porter, January 24, 1974, HMM.

185. "I understand that the Museum": Porter to Phoenix Museum, January 29, 1974, HMM.

185. "did not 'come to America'": Caldwell Delaney to Porter, February 7, 1974, MPL.

185. "Your action of moving": Henry C. Williams to Delaney, February 18, 1974, HMM.

186. he'd once lent Williams the notes: Delaney to Greenough, March 12, 1974, MPL.

186. "I do not wish": Delaney to Williams, February 20, 1974, in Williams and Porter, *History*, 34.

186. he wrote to Benson: Delaney to Benson, February 20, 1974, HMM.

186. Benson agreed: Delaney to Greenough, March 12, 1974, MPL.

186. "We have not been able": Benson to Williams, May 16, 1974, in Williams and Porter, 31.

186. "Somebody's got that bell": Womack made this remark while giving the tour in 2020.

186. "I wanted an office": Womack interview.

188. thirty-seven Emmy nominations: AP, August 4, 1977.

188. Eighty million people tuned in: *NYT*, February 2, 1977.

188. Afro-American Bicentennial Corporation: *WP*, February 20, 1989.

188. "It is organized to cover": Afro-American Bicentennial Corporation, "Beyond the Fireworks of '76," December 1973, 57–59. I am indebted to the scholar Amber N. Wiley for sharing her copy. A presentation by Wiley on the ABC's legacy can be viewed at https://www.youtube.com/watch?v=a-4aQ9 _ApAE.

188. Dexter Avenue Baptist Church in Montgomery: Marcia M. Greenlee, "National Register of Historic Places-Nomination Form: Dexter Avenue Baptist Church," July 1973, https://npgallery.nps.gov/NRHP/GetAsset /NHLS/74000431_text.

188. Battle of Rhode Island site: Lee, "Discovering Old Culture," 189.

188. Starting at least as early as 1974: Jay Higginbotham to Williams, March 13, 1974, HMM.

189. needed a "Pilgrim's Rock": *Sunday Times* (London), April 10, 1977.

189. Brookley Air Force Base: Jackson, "Mobile Since 1945," 289–90.

189. One proposal was to tear down his own workshop: *MR*, March 22, 1978.

189. A second proposal was to rezone: Ibid., June 2, 1978.

189. When the city commission took it up: Ibid., July 19, 1978.

190. had corroded, thanks largely to the emissions: U.S. Department of Transportation, Federal Highway Administration, and State of Alabama Highway Department, "Environmental Impact Statement," Cochrane Bridge Replacement, vol. 1, July 16, 1980, 20.

190. longer approaches would be needed: *MR*, January 7, 1984.

190. marking the border: Since mid-century, the Cochrane Bridge had served as the only legal route for moving hazardous cargo across the Mobile River. Following the 1949 Holland Tunnel fire in New York City, the authorities in Mobile had banned hazardous cargo from the Bankhead Tunnel, the only other route across. See David Volkert & Associates, "Cochrane Bridge Replacement: Technical Report, Volume I," March 30, 1978, container SG028332, folder 1, ADAH, 4.

190. It was estimated that thirty-one homes: Ibid., 98. Government records and news reports show that Africatown residents pushed for a route that would have gone south of the existing bridge, through industrial property. As of 1980, state officials were in favor of this proposal, but industrial business hired the attorney G. Sage Lyons, formerly the speaker of the Alabama House of Representatives, to fight it, saying it would force them to halt their operations during construction. The local chamber of commerce also backed their cause. In the summer of 1981, the governor announced the state intended to go with the route preferred by the companies. See U.S. Department of Transportation, Federal Highway Administration, and State of Alabama Highway Department, "Environmental Impact Statement," Cochrane Bridge Replacement, vol. 1, July 16, 1980, 217–18, and vol. 2, 1–11 (letter from Donald Smith of Citmoco Services, Inc., to the Alabama Highway Department and David Volkert & Associates, September 22, 1977); *MPR*, September 19, 1980, September 20, 1980, June 22, 1981, and July 14, 1981.

190. Williams believed roughly half: *MR*, May 1, 1985.

190. One of the city's architectural historians: Elizabeth Barrett Gould, architectural evaluations, February–April 1981, MHDC; Lumbers interview.

190. An archaeologist working for the state: James W. Parker, "Archaeological Reconnaissance of the Proposed Route for Replacement of the Cochrane Bridge, Mobile, Alabama," April 1980, 6; Alabama Department of Transportation. Parker wrote that all around, his survey produced no sites of archaeological or historical significance in the area singled out for construction.

190. Fourteen small businesses: R. L. Polk & Co. 1983 city directory, 44, 99, 403; Volkert & Associates, 98.

190. The area was pedestrian-friendly: Volkert & Associates, 99.

191. Just over half the neighborhood: Ibid., 82.

191. Income levels were also low: Ibid., 84.

191. As for home values: Ibid., 86.

191. Thanks to the "misinformation and rumor": Ibid., 82.

191. They brought in William Harris: Harris interview.

191. He told the crowd at Union Baptist: *MR*, June 30, 1978.

191. In the months afterward: Williams to Smith, January 24, 1979, in *Africatown*, 51.

192. Prichard, the city of forty thousand: U.S. Department of Commerce, *1980 Census of Population: Volume I, Characteristics of the Population*, chapter A, part 2, April 1982, 21.

192. His father ran a barbershop: Afra Smith, Daryl Smith, and Wheat interviews.

192. The document lists twenty-six sites: Smith, "The Voyage of the *Clotilda* and Africatown Settlement."

192. City records include a letter: Jeanette E. Barrett to Lambert Mims, July 16, 1979, MHDC.

193. Prichard was the second largest city: U.S. Department of Commerce, 1980 Census of Population, 21.

193. Cooper, who had worked: The History Makers, "A. J. Cooper, Jr.," June 21, 2005, https://www.thehistorymakers.org/biography/j-cooper-jr; MR, December 29, 1972; July 20, 1973; September 1, 1974.

193. Throughout the seventies: U.S. Department of Commerce, 1970 Census of Population and Housing, Mobile, Ala., Standard Metropolitan Statistical Area, 1; 1980 census, 19 and 80.

193. After two terms: AP, June 11, 1989.

193. In July of 1980, Smith won: *MR*, July 9, 1980.

193. "the largest Black historic preservation district": Ibid., July 5, 1981.

193. They planned a park: Smith and Williams, *Africatown*, 61.

193. They wanted to build a museum complex: Ibid.

194. In February 1982: *MR*, February 4, February 11, and February 25, 1982.

194. "The present condition of the site": Michael I. Burt, "National Register of Historic Places Inventory—Nomination Form: Foster Ship Yard and Land Site (1859)," National Historic Landmark Program regional files, NPS.

194. It was to span: U.S. Senate, *Proposed Additions*, 97.

CHAPTER 13: A THREAT TO BUSINESS

195. On a rainy Thursday morning: U.S. Senate, *Proposed Additions*, 88.

195. prepared a "hit list": Despite Watt's denials, it was widely believed that the hit list was real. See George C. Coggins and Doris K. Nagel, "'Nothing Beside Remains': The Legal Legacy of James G. Watt's Tenure as a Secretary of the Interior on Federal Land and Law Policy," *Boston College Environmental Affairs Law Review* 17, no. 3 (1990): 473–550.

195. The Reagan administration also tried: *NYT*, February 9, 1982.

195. They estimated development costs: U.S. Senate, 80.

195. Harry S Truman National Historic Site: Ibid., 99.

196. "Good morning," he drawled: Ibid., 74–75.

196. He'd entered electoral politics: James T. Gibson, "Howell T. Heflin," EOA, March 5, 2008, http://encyclopediaofalabama.org/article/h-1485.

196. Smith's turn was next: U.S. Senate, 87–88.

196. Grier was a political appointee: *NYT*, February 6, 1983; *San Antonio Express-News*, February 22, 2013.

196. "We would strongly recommend": U.S. Senate, 96–97.

197. The landing of the *Clotilda*: NPS Acting Chief Historian to Chief of the NPS Legislative Division, February 18, 1983, National Historic Landmark Program regional files, NPS.

197. The site of the first Pacific Coast cannery: Afro-American Bicentennial Corporation, 63.

197. Judging from the subcommittee chairman's response: Ibid., 105.

197. Grier went on to voice: Ibid., 105.

198. Grier went on to voice: U.S. Senate, 97.

198. The area they nominated: *MR*, October 20, 1985.

198. It also had an even smaller price tag: *MR*, March 26, 1984.

198. But this bill, too, was met with opposition: *MR*, May 20.

198. In January 1984, Governor George Wallace: *MR*, January 12.

199. Smith was given an honorary degree: *MR*, February 6.

199. The festival's gospel concert: *MR*, February 13.

199. Likely the proudest moment: *MR*, February 18.

199. He went so far as to change his party affiliation: *MR*, January 29.

199. In April 1984, the federal government: *MR*, April 19.

199. The city was on the verge of bankruptcy: *MR*, June 30.

199. Smith was up for reelection: *MR*, June 8.

199. He faced five challengers: *MR*, July 6.

199. Come election day: *MR*, July 11.

199. On August 1, Smith eked out: *MR*, August 17.

199. In 1984, design plans were released: *MR*, July 11, 1984, May 1, 1985, and August 29, 1986.

199. A crew placed 216 pounds: *MR*, March 1, 1985; *Azalea City News & Review*, March 7, 1985.

200. "The heart of Africatown": *MR*, January 24, 1988.

200. "Altogether, it was on track": U.S. Department of Transportation, Federal Highway administration, and State of Alabama Highway Department, "Final Environmental Impact Statement," I-210 Connector from I-10 to I-65, February 10, 1984, IV-11, container SG022054, ADAH.

200. Also in 1985, Hauser Realty: *MR*, April 5, 1985.

200. A group of residents: Ibid.

201. A writer for a weekly newspaper: *Azalea City News & Review*, April 11, 1985.

201. Officials at city hall and IP: Ibid.

201. A fifth house in the corridor: Neil Norman, "Report on Archaeological Survey and Testing at Peter Lee House Site and Lewis Quarter," Undated, MHDC, 6–14.

201. Along with roughly thirty others: *MR*, May 1.

202. "You get the feeling of being boxed in": *Inner City News*, May 25.

202. On May 14, the Mobile city commission: *MR*, May 15.

202. Two months later, in mid-July: *MR*, July 16.

202. In the spring session of 1985: *MR*, May 7.

202. Spokesmen for Scott Paper and International Paper: *MR*, May 10.

203. "I do not understand": *MR*, May 8.

203. Figures admitted that he hoped: *MR*, May 22.

203. The *Register* reported: Ibid.

203. In mid-August, Figures met: *MR*, August 21, 1985.

203. The summer edition: "Africatown, USA—A Direct Threat to Alabama's Best Business Area," *Scott Government Relations Newsletter*, Alabama, July 31, 1985, MHDC.

203. The paper companies later told a reporter: *MR*, September 11.

203. The bill passed: *MR*, September 21.

203. On September 26, Governor Wallace: *MR*, September 27.

203. "Africatown U.S.A. is finally on the map": *MR*, October 20.

204. That year's festival opened: *MR*, February 24, 1986.

204. Later that week, Prichard welcomed: *MR*, February 28.

204. On February 26, during a ceremony: *MR*, January 9.

204. Also there to witness it: *MR*, February 20.

204. The following day, Benin's minister: *MR*, February 27.

204. Acquaintances don't know exactly: Ephraim, Ludgood, Norwood, and Wheat interviews.

205. Norwood was persuaded: Norwood interview.

205. The election was on August 23: *MR*, September 4, 1988.

206. In a newspaper interview: Ibid.

206. Smith refused to endorse Norwood: *MR*, September 15.

206. In the weeks after the hairdresser's victor: *MR*, November 25.

206. The 1989 festival: *MR*, March 16, 1989.

206. Eventually, plans for the development: Ephriam and Norwood interviews.

206. Old city directories give a picture: R. L. Polk & Co., 1983 city directory, 41, 99.

206. But there were other businesses: Taylor interview.

206. Letters from 1985: Jim Wilson to Anna Keeby, December 13, 1985, and Wilson to Helen R. Jackson, May 13, 1986, MHDC.

207. By June 1986, state officials: State of Alabama Highway Department to Jackson, June 26, 1986, MHDC.

207. In the end: Ted Keeby interview.

207. Years later, an archaeologist: Norman, "Report on Mapping," 14.

207. The bridge was finished: *MR*, April 6, 1991.

207. It stood 350 feet above the river: Ibid., May 1, 1988.

207. the governor's wife had "christened" it: Emma J. Broussard, "Dedicating the Cochrane Bridge: A Day of Triumph for Mobile's Elite," *Alabama Review* 63, no. 2 (2010): 110–43.

207. "Here in Africatown": *MR*, April 6.

207. On a humid Sunday afternoon: *MR*, April 8, 1991.

207. Two days after the ceremony: *MR*, April 9, 1991.

207. Figures introduced a bill: "Act Number 1991–82." Legislative Acts, Alabama Secretary of State, accessed October 22, 2021, https://arc-sos.state.al .us/cgi/actdetail.mbr/detail?year=1991&act=%20%2082&page=subject.

207. Demolition of the neighborhood continued: *MR*, July 28, 1991.

207. And that spring, another project: *MR*, April 29, 1992.

208. The proposed highway would be paving over: Womack, Mae Jones, and Taylor interviews.

208. As for John Smith: Afra, Daryl, and Yuri Smith interviews; Wheat interview.

208. "In 2006, he died" with "Seven weeks before the election."

208. He was only fifty-nine: Wheat interview.

208. His principal request: Ibid.

209. On a chilly December morning in 1996: Krivor and Tuttle interviews.

209. Finding the *Clotilda*: *MPR*, January 25, 1998.

209. Sometimes he lay awake: Ibid.

209. In 1993, Friend got a leg up: Robert Meaher to Jacob Laurence, April 27, 2011, HMM.

209. In 1994, the Maritime Museum of Mobile: Jack Friend to Robert Meaher, October 5, 1994, HMM.

210. The trio made long passes: Michael Krivor, Panamerican Maritime, LLC, "Summary of Investigations: The Search for the Slave Ship *Clotilda*," December 1998, HMM, 1.

210. By the time they were finished: Ibid.

210. Krivor and Tuttle's firm: Ibid., 4.

210. They had a diver search: Krivor and Andrew D.W. Lydecker, Panamerican Consultants, Inc., "Additional Investigations for the Slave Ship *Clotilda*:

Report of Findings," September 2003, 13. Copy in possession of Stephen James.

211. In November 1994, Augustine Meaher III: AMIII to AMJR, November 21, 1994, HMM.

211. The deck and at least one side: Delgado said this description from R. V. Williams syncs up with what he and other archaeologists found when they studied the wreckage in 2018.

211. But another letter in the same archive: Robert Meaher to Jacob Laurence, April 27, 2011.

212. In a 1998 interview: *MPR*, January 25, 1998.

212. In the wake of its release: Sam Dingman and Vera Carothers, "The Clotilda Legacy: Part 2, The Stronghold," Family Ghosts, December 10, 2019 (podcast), https://spokemedia.io/wp-content/uploads/2019/09/Part-2_-The -Stronghold.pdf.

212. Augustine Meaher Jr. died in 2001: *MPR*, April 7, 2001, and October 5, 2007; last will and testament of Augustine Meaher Jr., MCPC. Robert Meaher also inherited the land their grandfather had left to their aunts, according to MCPC records, so their father left him a smaller inheritance in order to keep the ownership shares proportionate.

CHAPTER 14: GOING BACK TO CHURCH

213. In 2000, three days before Christmas: *MPR*, December 23, 2000.

213. To some of the workers: *MPR*, December 22.

213. It didn't help: AP, October 25.

213. IP had laid off thousands: *MPR*, August 19, 1999, and January 22, 2000.

213. At eleven A.M., Walter Brunson: Ibid., December 23, 2000.

214. Mobile was roughly on par: *MR*, November 12, 1971. As of 1971, Mobile had the highest photochemical oxidant count in the state but was second to Birmingham in particulate pollution.

214. There was no monitoring post: *MP*, August 6, 1971.

214. In 1972, the state: AP, January 4, 1972.

214. The rules did take effect: *MR*, September 27, 1972, January 26, 1973, December 14, 1973, and October 19, 1979.

214. in 1988, when the Environmental Protection Agency compiled: *MA*, June 9, 1989. The *Mobile Register*'s headline on the same day, incidentally, read, "Paper Industries Attack Report on Cancer Risks," and focused on the companies' PR statements challenging the evidence.

214. During the first several years: *MA*, June 9, 1989; *Anniston Star*, August 11, 1989; States News Service, April 29, 1990; EPA Toxics Release Inventory, 1988 data, available at https://enviro.epa.gov/triexplorer/tri_release .chemical.

214. TRI data released in 1992: *MR,* October 1, 1992.

215. hung a huge Confederate battle flag: Nicholls, "Politics and Civil Rights," 268–69.

215. He fined the company: *MR,* July 21, 1979. The plant's annual payroll at the time was $48 million (*MR,* October 19, 1979).

215. And in 1990, the EPA: AP, May 18, 1990.

215. The state warned Alabamians: *Alabama Journal,* May 29, 1991.

215. The story, as Bullard tells it: Bullard, *Dumping in Dixie,* xiv–xv. See also Dorceta E. Taylor's *Toxic Communities: Environmental Racism, Industrial Pollution, and Residential Mobility* (New York: New York University Press, 2014).

215. "These industries have generally followed": Bullard, xv.

215. As Bullard notes, Black workers: Ibid., 9–10.

216. The constitution also prevented counties: Flynt, "A Tragic Century," 43.

216. As of 1920, property taxes: Ibid., 37.

216. The cost is borne by other residents: Institute on Taxation and Economic Policy, "Who Pays? A Distributional Analysis of the Tax Systems in All 50 States," 6th ed., October 2018, 33. Available at https://itep.sfo2 .digitaloceanspaces.com/whopays-ITEP-2018.pdf.

216. But the tax system is also one of the reasons: The Environmental Council of the States, "Status of State Environmental Agency Budgets (EAB), 2013–2015," 18. Report available at https://www.ecos.org/wp-content /uploads/2017/03/Budget-Report-FINAL-3_15_17-Final-4.pdf.

216. ADEM, as a result, has a poor record: Admittedly, numerous other states collect less tax revenue per capita than Alabama and have tax systems that are even more regressive. It should also be noted that the state constitution is not the only cause for the state's budget woes—but it has certainly played a role.

217. Several national surveys: Flynt, "A Tragic Century," 45.

217. Their mother died of a brain tumor: Ballard and Taylor interviews.

218. A study released in 2014: Michael Goodman, Joshua S. Naiman, Dina Goodman, and Judy S. LaKind, "Cancer Clusters in the USA: What Do the Last Twenty Years of State and Federal Investigations Tell Us?" *Critical Reviews in Toxicology* 42, no. 6 (July 2012): 474–90.

218. Even with the most famous: George Johnson, "Debunking the Debunker's Debunker," *Discover Magazine,* July 19, 2013.

219. The challenges of nailing down Africatown's cancer rate: For more on the limits of epidemiology in this area, and the broader relationship between political economy and scientific research, see Phil Brown's illuminating books *No Safe Place: Toxic Waste, Leukemia, and Community Action* (Berkeley and Los Angeles: University of California Press, 1990) and *Toxic Exposures: Contested Illnesses and the Environmental Health Movement* (New York: Columbia University Press, 2007).

219. In 2017, a suit was filed: Complaint, *Samuel Adams, et al. v. International Paper Company, et al.*, Circuit Court of Mobile, February 15, 2017.

219. Stewart's firm had soil and water testing done: *Lagniappe*, March 3, 2021.

219. It seems the new bridge: Norman, "Report on Mapping," 5–6.

219. The city parks department calculated: Dan Otto to John Bell, August 14, 1997, MHDC.

219. In August 1997, E. Ashton Hill: Hill to John Bell, August 25, 1997, MHDC.

220. The result of failing: Norman, "Report on Mapping," 4–9.

220. Robert Battles, a community organizer: Meeting flyers and agenda, MHDC files; *MPR*, February 28, 1997; Battles interview.

220. These would be battered: *MPR*, November 25, 2007.

220. "an afternoon tea": *MPR*, February 13, 1997.

220. "Far from being a hoax": Diouf, 249.

221. Diouf, whose book on the shipmates: *MPR*, November 26, 2010.

221. Henry Williams died in September 2008: Ibid., September 17, 2008.

223. Among the newcomers: These were UNIVAR USA Chemicals, Metals USA, Mobile Service Center, Harcros Chemicals, Eagle Chemical, Kemira, Baldwin Transfer Co., and Hosea O. Weaver. See Polk 2008 city directory.

223. The company was asking: Mobile City Planning Commission, "Zoning Amendment, & Subdivision Staff Report," ZON2008–00061 & SUB 2008–00013, February 7, 2008; Mobile City Planning Commission, meeting minutes, March 6, 2008, 8–9.

224. That February, William Carroll: *MPR*, February 28, 2008; Carroll interview.

224. The residents also presented Carroll: Mobile City Planning Commission, meeting minutes, March 6, 2008, 8.

224. When Craig had an opportunity: *MPR*, February 28, 2008.

224. Before the meeting was over: Ibid.; Mobile City Planning Commission, meeting minutes, March 6, 2008, 8. A second meeting was scheduled in Plateau for March 13, 2008, and the planning commission expected to take up the application again in April. However, meeting minutes show the application was dropped after the March 13 meeting.

CHAPTER 15: ONE MOBILE

229. It was the 135th site: "The National Register of Historic Places" (Microsoft Excel spreadsheet), NPS, https://www.nps.gov/subjects/nationalregister/database-research.htm.

229. Commission staffers, whose backgrounds: Devereaux Bemis to Robert Battles, June 13, 2007, MHDC.

230. In the spring of 2012: Bemis to Yorktown Baptist Church, May 15, 2012; Bemis to Union Missionary Baptist Church, May 15, 2012; Bemis to First Hopewell Baptist Church, May 15 2012; MHDC press release, May 2012; "Public Meeting Agenda," May 23, 2012, MHDC.

230. The parts of Africatown: Ramsey Sprague has made this calculation, based on an extensive review of property records.

230. Lewis Quarters does have archaeological resources: Bemis and Wilson interviews.

230. "up to and including destruction": "National Register of Historic Places: How to List a Property," NPS, https://www.nps.gov/subjects/nationalregister/how-to-list-a-property.htm.

230. As of 2012, crude was selling: Tim McMahon, "Historical Crude Oil Prices (Table)," https://inflationdata.com/articles/inflation-adjusted-prices/historical-crude-oil-prices-table/.

231. as deep as half a mile underground: The Orinoco Belt tar sands in Venezuela, in particular, go as deep as one thousand meters underground. See "Why Venezuela is Alberta's Biggest Competitor," *Oil Sands Magazine,* https://www.oilsandsmagazine.com/news/2016/2/15/why-venezuela-is-albertas-biggest-competitor.

231. in some cases upward of $50: Dinara Millington, "Canadian Oil Sands Supply Costs and Development Projects (2016–2036)," Canadian Energy Research Institute, February 2017, https://web.archive.org/web/20170624204959/http://resources.ceri.ca/PDF/Pubs/Studies/Study_163_Executive_Summary.pdf., ix. This figure comes from 2017, after technology had advanced from 2012. It also reflects a conversion from Canadian currency ($70.08, as cited in Millington) to USD.

231. A top priority was the building: *WP,* June 22, 2012.

231. Once it was finished: *NYT,* July 5, 2013.

231. "essentially game over": Jim Hansen, "Silence Is Deadly," June 3, 2011, http://www.columbia.edu/~jeh1/mailings/2011/20110603_SilenceIsDeadly.pdf.

231. In the summer of 2011, environmentalists: The Hill, February 13, 2013; "Invitation," Tar Sands Action, http://tarsandsaction.org/invitation/.

231. Between 2010 and 2012: Anthony Swift, "Tar Sands Pipeline Risks—Examining the Facts," National Resources Defense Council, March 30, 2013.

231. And in 2010, a tar-sands pipeline: *NYT,* July 10, 2012.

231. Following the demonstrations in 2011: Reuters, August 31, 2011.

231. That November, the Obama administration: *NYT,* November 10, 2011.

232. "Oil will get to market": *WP,* March 2, 2013.

232. Freight railways connect the city: J. Wilburn and Associates, "2013 Alabama Rail Plan," Alabama Department of Transportation, Bureau of Transportation Planning and Modal Programs, June 2014, 2.1–2.7.

232. In late 2012, two companies: *MPR*, November 28, 2012.

232. The tar sands would have to pass: Reuters, November 5, 2012.

232. There were also plans to start harvesting: AP, February 22, 2014; Al.com; May 2, 2014; Al Jazeera America, February 16, 2015.

232. The governors of Mississippi and Alabama: *Quad-Cities Daily*, July 28, 2013.

233. a seventy-two-year-old local activist: "David Underhill: A Remembering," Sierra Club, Alabama Chapter, December 28, 2019, https://www.sierraclub.org/alabama/blog/2019/12/david-underhill-remembering.

233. He had settled in Mobile permanently: Ibid.; Adams-Davis interview.

233. Underhill was also concerned: "Our Water System," Mobile Area Water and Sewer System, https://www.mawss.com/education-and-outreach/our-water-system/.

233. eight miles outside the city limits: Jarrod J. White, "Application for Certificate of Industrial Development," docket no. 31734, October 18, 2011, PSC.

233. Between 2004 and 2007: Consent Decree," *United States of America v. Plains All American Pipeline, L.P.; Plains Pipeline, L.P.; Plains Marketing GP Inc.; and Plains Marketing, L.P.,* Civil Action (number not listed), United States District Court for the Southern District of Texas, September 2013, 1.

233. In 2012, a Plains pipe spilled: "Plains Midstream Charged in Red Deer River Pipeline Spill," Canadian Press, June 2, 2014.

233. at least 12,000 gallons of crude: WDAM, February 9, 2013.

233. "releases of hydrocarbon products": Plains All American Pipeline, L.P., "Annual Report Pursuant to Section 13 or 15(d) of the Securities Exchange Act of 1934," United States Securities and Exchange Commission, 2012, 42, 58. There were also dangers associated with moving oil on railcars. In March 2013, for instance, fourteen train cars full of oil fell off a railroad in Minnesota, spilling thirty thousand gallons of oil. (See Reuters, March 28, 2013.)

233. Plains said it planned: *MPR,* July 17, 2013; White interview.

233. Plains already did a big business: "Report to Stakeholders and Communities," Plains Midstream Canada, 2014, http://www.plainsmidstream.com/sites/default/files/8597%20PM_CSR_FINAL.PDF, 3.

234. Chevron had sought to expand: The Pascagoula refinery handles oil from Central and South America (https://pascagoula.chevron.com/our-businesses/crude-oil-transportation-and-storage). For an example of Chevron trying to add tar sands capacity to an existing plant, see Susie Cagle, "A Year After

a Refinery Explosion, Richmond, Calif., Is Fighting Back," Grist, August 6, 2013, https://grist.org/climate-energy/a-year-after-a-refinery-explosion -richmond-cali-is-fighting-back/.

234. "This had been going on for a year": By the time Underhill started investigating, Plains had already coasted through the permitting process. There had been a hearing before the Alabama Public Service Commission, but it had occurred in Montgomery, two and a half hours from Mobile, at ten A.M. on a Monday, and was announced only via tiny ads in the *Press-Register*'s legals section. The ads made no mention of the pipeline's route. The only person who had showed up to testify was a Plains worker. Two months afterward, the application had been approved, giving Plains the right to use any piece of property along the route. (See "Application for Certificate of Industrial Development for a Pipeline Right of Way," November 19, 2010, hearing, PSC.)

235. "Our drinking water supply": Glynn Wilson, "Citizens Fight Canadian Tar Sands Crude Pipeline Along Gulf Coast" (video), July 10, 2013, https: //www.youtube.com/watch?v=nDeBX_yMXXg.

235. Sam Jones, Mobile's mayor: Ibid.

235. only about 140 miles: The geographic coordinates of the Deepwater Horizon spill were 28°44′ 12.0″N 88°23′ 14.0″W. See Marcia K. McNutt et al., "Review of Flow Rate Estimates of the *Deepwater Horizon* Oil Spill," *Proceedings of the National Academy of Sciences* 109, no. 50 (December 2012).

235. But Womack was haunted: Womack interview.

235. Nearly fifty people who lived nearby: Lerner, *Struggle*, 32.

235. When Womack took his turn: Wilson.

236. All evening, a young man: Ibid.

236. "My name is Ramsey Sprague": Ibid.

236. This opens up a way for corporations: In the run-up to her 2020 reelection campaign, for instance, the PSC president, Twinkle Cavanaugh, received $85,000 from Drummond Company, the state's largest coal company, alone. The other two commissioners, in their 2018 reelection races, received $45,000 and $25,000 from Drummond, respectively. More recently, in 2020, the PSC approved the expansion of an Alabama Power coal plant that Drummond serves as a supplier, blocking only one part of the application—a plan to expand Alabama Power's solar capability. The agency has also allowed Alabama Power to charge one of the highest fees in the country to customers who keep solar panels on their roofs.

The PSC's failure to engage the public in the pipeline decision is also typical of how it operates. During the 2020 pandemic, the advocacy organization Energy Alabama had to fight strenuously to get the PSC to broadcast its meetings on the internet. "If the public knew what they are doing on a daily basis, they would be incensed," said Daniel Tait, Energy Alabama's research and communications manager. "It's easier to keep people out than it is to answer tough questions."

    Sources: U.S. Department of Energy, U.S. Energy Information Administration, Annual Environmental Information, Schedule 8, Part A, Annual Byproduct Disposition, 2020 Final Data; *MPR*, June 17, 2020, and September 1, 2020; Tait interview.

236. In the case of Plains's application: *MPR*, July 2, 2013.

237. The only agency: Ibid. July 5.

237. At the end of July, they recruited: Ibid., July 24.

238. There were also two Plains pipelines: White interview; "The Beginning of Big Creek Lake," Mobile Area Water and Sewer System, https://www.mawss .com/about-big-creek-lake.

238. A safety report commissioned: KBR, "Review of Proposed Plains Southcap, LLC Crude Oil Pipeline in the Big Creek Lake Watershed," prepared for Mobile Area Water and Sewer System, August 9, 2013, 11.

238. Erosion in the creek: Ibid., 12.

238. A nearby car accident: Ibid., 17–18.

238. Plains was having an easier time: White interview.

238. Out of roughly 115 properties: *Lagniappe*, July 10.

238. construction was already 70 percent finished: *MPR*, July 24.

238. In early August, a local company: Ibid., August 30.

239. The plans also included: Mobile City Planning Commission, "Planned Unit Development & Planning Approval Staff Report," ZON2013–01599 & ZON2013–01597, August 8, 2013.

239. The CEO of American Tank and Vessel: *MPR*, December 13.

239. By the end of the summer, this battle: Adams-Davis, Ballard, Bolton, Dodd, Mae Jones, Sprague, and Womack interviews.

239. Despite the recent setbacks, the mood: *MPR*, September 3, 2013.

239. Stimpson had never held public office: *MR*, September 6, 1989.

239. and had chaired the local chamber: *MPR*, January 21, 2009.

240. The family's history in Mobile: Stimpson and Price, *Stimpson Family*, 45.

240. Stimpson raised about $1.5 million: *MPR*, August 25, 2013.

240. Come election day, he won: Ibid., August 11.

240. But exit polls showed: Ibid., August 30.

240. wanted to "reserve judgment": Ibid., August 14.

240. He had close ties: Ibid., September 4, 1996.

240. he'd been the senator's state finance chair: University of Mobile, May 9, 2016, news release.

240. Stimpson had also chaired the board: *MPR*, September 8, 2012. For examples of the Alabama Policy Institute's positions on environmental issues, see Gary Palmer, "Access to Energy Reserves Could Change a Lot of Things," Au-

gust 12, https://alabamapolicy.org/2012/08/17/access-to-energy-reserves-could
-change-a-lot-of-things/, and Katherine Green Robinson, "The Left's Energy
Policies Generate Energy Poverty," October 21, 2016, https://alabamapolicy
.org/2016/10/21/the-lefts-energy-policies-generate-energy-poverty/.

240. "He just approaches things": *MPR*, September 8, 2012.

241. In September, activist Ramsey Sprague: Ballard, Bettis, Bolton, Dodd,
Mae Jones, Sprague, and Joe Womack interviews.

241. Sprague is a Louisiana native: Sprague interview.

241. He was arrested at a pipeline conference: "Anti-Keystone XL Protester
Disrupts TransCanada Speech for Several Minutes," Democracy Now, February 1, 2013.

CHAPTER 16: HOUSTON-EAST, CHARLESTON-WEST

242. He was marching with a couple of dozen others: *MPR*, December 13,
2013.

242. national day of tar sands protests: May Boeve, "Draw the Line on on Keystone XL," 350.org, https://350.org/draw-line-next-step-stop-keystone-xl/.

242. At first fifty to seventy-five people: Sprague and Womack interviews.

242. TV crews were there to film them: MEJAC, "MEJACoalition Draw the
Line March Coverage CBS WKRG 5 in Mobile, AL," video, https://www
.youtube.com/watch?v=UDX5ckN-f94.

242. "I know you've committed": Ibid.

242. "This is not right": MEJAC, "WPMI NBC 15 Mobile Coverage of
MEJAC Draw the Line March," video, https://www.youtube.com/watch?v
=mhCAmoTZ7mw.

242. Just a few days before the protest: White, "Evidentiary Submission in
Support of Application of Plains Mobile Pipeline Inc. for Certificate of
Industrial Development Regarding a New Pipeline in Mobile County, Ala-
bama," Exhibit B, docket no. 32082, PSC, October 24, 2013, 1.

243. Part of the land that it ran through: "IN RE: Plains Mobile Pipeline, Inc.
Docket #32082," October 30, 2013, hearing, 66, PSC.

243. Now Plains was asking permission: White, "Application for Certificate of
Industrial Development," September 26, 2013, PSC; "IN RE: Plains Mobile
Pipeline, Inc. Docket no. 32082," October 30, 2013, hearing, PSC; White
interview.

243. For its part, the company said: *MPR*, October 30, 2013.

243. In a rare decision: *MPR*, October 28; PSC records.

243. The organization Mobile Baykeeper: Callaway interview.

244. Bolton was dazed: Bolton interview.

244. She stood up and reminded the judge: "IN RE: Plains Mobile Pipeline,
Inc. Docket #32082," October 30, 2013, hearing, 2–20, PSC.

245. The bulldozers came four months later: Sheila Hagler, "Pipeline Con-
struction Next to Historic Mobile County Training School and Plateau
Community," video, February 11, 2014, https://www.youtube.com/watch?v
=KzQ25NFhYKg.

245. Before the bulldozers moved: *MPR*, February 12, 2014; Ballard, Mae
Jones, and Joe Womack interviews.

245. When Sprague heard the news: Callaway, White, and Sprague interviews.

246. On the day of the meeting: Carnell Davis, "Martha Peek-Mobile Co Pub
School Bd Supt. Addresses MCTS Oil Pipe Line," video, February 22, 2014,
https://www.youtube.com/watch?v=fFRL-AooN2U.

246. The company had taken that option in 1981: Ibid.

246. the year before Peek became superintendent: *MPR*, March 30, 2012.

246. "In those days, environmental issues": Davis, "Martha Peek"; *MPR*, February 16, 2014.

247. Peek offered to take questions: Ibid., February 25, 2014.

247. Another person asked whether school administrators: David Underhill,
"The Mis-Education of Mobile on an Oil Pipeline Through Africatown," New
American Journal, February 24, 2014, https://www.newamericanjournal
.net/2014/02/the-mis-education-of-mobile-on-an-oil-pipeline-through
-africatown/.

247. "All I can do is apologize": Davis, "Martha Peek."

247. Around the same time, in early 2014: *MPR*, February 11, 2014.

247. Instead the utility settled: *MPR*, November 20, 2013.

248. "For the same token": *MPR*, December 11, 2013.

248. "inherently safe industry": *MPR*, December 20, 2013.

248. But the council pushed ahead: *MPR*, January 1, 2014.

248. The group's proposal: City of Mobile, Alabama, "Ad Hoc Committee
Report," final draft, March 12, 2014.

248. On July 17, he replaced the majority: *MPR*, July 18, 2014.

249. At first it went down gradually: Spot Prices for Crude Oil and Petroleum Products," U.S. Energy Information Administration, https://www.eia
.gov/dnav/pet/hist/LeafHandler.ashx?n=PET&s=RWTC&f=M.

249. This was all a matter of supply and demand: Dave Mead and Porscha
Stiger, "The 2014 Plunge in Import Petroleum Prices: What Happened?"
U.S. Bureau of Labor Statistics, *Beyond the Numbers* 4, no. 9 (May 2015).

249. oil infrastructure projects worth a total of $200 billion: Reuters, June 17,
2015.

249. Plans for the new tank farms around Africatown: "Petroleum & Other
Liquids," U.S. Energy Information Administration, https://www.eia
.gov/dnav/pet/hist/LeafHandler.ashx?n=PET&s=ESM_EPC0_RAIL
_ZAMN-ZAMN_MBBL&f=M.

249. Early that year, Arc Terminals: Mobile City Planning Commission, meeting minutes, June 4, 2015, 1–4, and June 18, 2015, 22–25; Mobile Planning Commission, "Planned Unit Development & Planning Approval Staff Report," ZON2015–01289 & ZON2015–01288, June 18, 2015.

249. But on August 11, when the matter came up: *MPR*, August 12, 2015.

250. the most "business and family friendly": *MPR*, February 15, 2016.

250. The chamber hired two consultants: Mobile Area Chamber of Commerce, "One-Tenth of U.S. Energy Refined on Gulf Coast," *The Business View*, November 2014, 7.

250. "the availability of affordable": Ibid.

250. It opened with a letter: "No Petro-Chemical Storage Tanks on Our West Bank: A Compendium of Citizen Concerns," May 28, 2015, 4–6.

250. Bernard Eichold, a health officer: Ibid., 32.

250. Wladimir Wertelecki, a pediatrician: Ibid., 37–38.

250. "a growing vibrant downtown": Ibid., 51.

251. The last letter in the packet: Ibid., 62.

251. The Alabama NAACP was hosting: MEJAC, October 12, 2015, news release.

251. "Having the facts is never enough!": PURE (Project Urban Renewable Energy), "PURE Building Sustainable Communities One Block at a Time," https://vimeo.com/299767945 (site inactive May 3, 2022).

252. That weekend, Womack took Bullard: Robert Bullard, Twitter post, October 23, 2015, 9:31 P.M., https://twitter.com/DrBobBullard/status /657670693081911298?s=20.

252. Unlike the Sierra Club: In this case, Baykeeper had worked with the Southern Environmental Law Center early on to file a lawsuit against the Army Corps of Engineers, saying Plains's permit to put a pipeline through the watershed ought to be revoked. The suit would not be successful.

252. As Sprague wrote on MEJAC's website: Ramsey Sprague, "Planning Commission Betrays Communities Seeking Environmental Justice with Weak Ordinance," MEJAC Archive Website, November 29, 2015, https: //mejac.wordpress.com/2015/11/29/weakzoningordinance/.

253. there was no requirement for tank companies: City of Mobile, Alabama, "Ad Hoc Committee Report," final draft, March 12, 2014, 5.

253. said nothing about companies' responsibilities: City of Mobile, Alabama, "An Ordinance to Amend Chapter 64, Mobile City Code, as Amended, to Provide Supplementary Regulation of the Location and Construction of New Above Ground Oil Storage Tanks" (November 2015 draft); Sprague, "Planning Commission Betrays Communities Seeking Environmental Justice with Weak Ordinance," MEJAC archive website, November 29, 2015, https://mejac .wordpress.com/2015/11/29/weakzoningordinance/.

253. The tank companies and their allies: *MPR,* November 18, 2015.

253. At the council meeting on March 29: City of Mobile, Alabama, "Live City Council meeting," video, March 29, 2016, https://www.youtube.com /watch?v=JHjLIuIMXvQ.

253. the ordinance passed: Ibid.

253. Brenda Bolton had similar worries: Bolton correspondence.

CHAPTER 17: RECONSTRUCTION

255. On a frosty morning in January 2018: Ben Raines, "Wreck Found by Reporter May Be Last American Slave Ship, Archaeologists Say," video and article, *MPR,* January 23, 2018, https://www.youtube.com/watch?v=_C8 -WINcGPg.

255. Raines took the men to a muddy bank: Ibid.

255. Two days later: Bratten interview.

255. "You can definitely say maybe": Raines, "Wreck Found by Reporter."

256. For months, the two men: Conlin, Flen, Hathorn, Smith-Incer, and Womack interviews.

256. And his leadership committee: Armstead, Flen, and Womack interviews; Womack, "Africatown Dedicates New Freedom Bell," Bridge the Gulf, September 17, 2017, https://bridgethegulfproject.org/blog/2017/africatown -dedicates-new-freedom-bell.

256. The discussions about launching: Flen, Smith-Incer, and Womack interviews.

257. Following the news of Raines's discovery: Conlin, Delgado, Flen, Hathorn, and Sadiki interviews.

257. By then, the AHC: Bratten, Delgado, and Hathorn interviews.

257. It turned out the timbers were too large: Hathorn and Delgado, "'Finding' Clotilda: Now What Happens?" *Alabama Heritage* 142 (fall 2021): 10–23.

258. Throughout the early months of 2018: Delgado, "Archaeological Investigations," 47–48; Delgado interview.

258. In the meantime, Raines resumed searching: *Lagniappe,* December 31, 2019.

259. That summer, they scanned the channel: Delgado, "Archaeological Investigations," iii.

259. "We started at the top": *MPR,* May 24, 2019.

259. When Delgado dove down: Delgado, "Archaeological Investigations," 89–91; Delgado interview.

259. "If every Gulf schooner": Delgado interview.

260. It turned out only eight schooners: Delgado and Hathorn interviews.

261. From the start, there was talk: Bourne, "With slave ship Clotilda found, work of healing a community begins," *NG,* May 31, 2019. Vivian Davis Fig-

ures was the wife of Michael Figures, the state senator who fought for the creation of the AfricaTown, U.S.A. State Park in the 1980s. Michael Figures was an immensely gifted politician; had he lived longer, there's a chance he could have become Alabama's first Black governor (an office many people thought he was angling for). But he died in 1996, at age forty-eight, of a brain hemorrhage. After his death, Vivian Davis Figures, who was a Mobile city councilwoman, ran for his old seat and won. She has won reelection numerous times since then.

261. But some archaeologists had doubts: *MA,* October 16, 2020.

261. One alternative, suggested by *National Geographic*: Joel K. Bourne Jr., "Last American Slave Ship Is Discovered in Alabama," *NG,* May 22, 2019.

262. The exact site of the wreck: Alabama Political Reporter, April 15, 2020.

262. Afterward the state set aside: AHC, July 16, 2020 news release.

262. In 2018, local and state officials: *MPR,* December 4, 2020.

262. The design contract: Ibid., May 7, 2021.

262. In 2020, Merceria Ludgood: Ludgood's story is interwoven with the careers of other figures who appear in this book. She managed Michael Figures's first campaign in 1978, while she was still in law school, and John Smith's campaign in 1980. She and Figures were later partners in their own firm. After Sam Jones was elected as Mobile's first Black mayor, Ludgood ran for his old seat on the county commission and won.

262. She announced plans: *MPR,* March 10, 2020.

262. would have a "meditative garden": *MPR,* June 18, 2021.

262. In 2020, Senator Doug Jones: *MPR,* September 4, 2020.

262. Other organizations across the country: AHC, August 15, 2019, news release.

262. David Padgett, a geography professor: Fiskio, Flen, Kane, and Padgett interviews.

263. For the first Spirit of Our Ancestors festival: *MPR,* February 8, 2019.

263. *National Geographic* covered the event: Bourne, "Their Ancestors Survived Slavery. Can Their Descendants Save the Town They Built?" *NG,* February 15, 2019.

263. Also there was Michael Foster: Foster and Patterson interviews.

263. The foundation accumulated grant money: Flen interview.

264. Gus Meaher, the oldest son: *U.S., Public Records Index, 1950–1993,* vol. 2, via Ancestry.com; Alabama Votes database, Alabama Secretary of State.

264. He attended University Military School: UMS-Wright, "Augustine 'Gus' Meaher, III: Alumnus of the Year," *The Crest* (summer 2015), 25.

264. They have six children: Maureen King, "Family Reunion," *Tulane Magazine,* summer 2011, 39.

264. Robert Meaher, the youngest brother: *U.S., Public Records Index, 1950–1993*, vol. 1, via Ancestry.com; Alabama votes Database, Alabama Secretary of State.

264. He left Mobile when he was young: "Alumni Support," Darlington School, https://www.darlingtonschool.org/media/Docs/Alumni%20class%20breakdown.pdf.

264. Robert Meaher sold his share: "Statutory Warranty Deed," book 5079, 69, MCPC.

265. In his 2015 book: Sledge, *Mobile River*, 3.

266. His will, which he devised in 2006: "Last Will and Testament of Joseph Lyons Meaher," June 22, 2006, MCPC.

266. After Joe Meaher's death in March 2020: *MPR*, March 17, 2020.

266. In 2012, the last time a full appraisal: "Valuation of One Class B United Limited Liability Company Membership Interest In Chippewa Lakes, LLC," Exhibit 81 (Document 274), *Margaret Lou Meaher, et al. v. Joseph L. Meaher & Associations, Inc., et al.*, Civil Action No. 02-cv-2017–903284, Circuit Court of Mobile County, Alabama.

266. A 1981 lawsuit confirms: Eric Embry and Supreme Court of Alabama, *Meaher v. Getty Oil Co.*, 450 So. 2d 443, 1984.

266. It's clear that in at least one: Shackelford, 6–12.

267. The Meahers also own: Property records, Mobile County Revenue Commission.

267. For years, the brothers' holdings company: "Augustine Meaher, III—Examination by Mr. Burns" (Document 174), *Margaret Lou Meaher, et al. v. Joseph L. Meaher & Associates, Inc., et al.*

267. In 2015, the brothers agreed: "Verified Complaint," December 13, 2017, and "Footnotes" (Document 150), *Margaret Lou Meaher, et al. v. Joseph L. Meaher & Associates, Inc., et al.*

267. Chippewa Lakes was low on cash: "Plaintiff's Narrative and Brief in Response to Defendants' Motion to Dismiss, Alternatively Defendants' Motion for Summary Judgment" (Document 242), *Margaret Lou Meaher, et al. v. Joseph L. Meaher & Associates, Inc., et al.*

267. She and her sister, Helen: "Affidavit of Joseph L. Meaher in Support of Summary Judgment on Standing" (Document 176), October 24, 2018, *Margaret Lou Meaher, et al. v. Joseph L. Meaher & Associates, Inc., et al.*

267. The lawsuit carried on: "Joint Motion to Substitute J. Heath Eckert, Personal Representative of Estate of Joseph L. Meaher, as Party Defendant/Counterclaim-Plaintiff" (Document 381), October 20, 2020, *Margaret Lou Meaher, et al. v. Joseph L. Meaher & Associates, Inc., et al.*

267. Gus Meaher told the website: SFGate, February 28, 2018.

267. And Robert Meaher gave brief comments: Joel K. Bourne, Jr., Sylviane Diouf, and Chelsea Brasted, "America's Last Slave Ship Stole Them from Home. It Couldn't Steal Their Identities," *NG,* January 16, 2020.

268. "It is my position": Robert Meaher to Jacob Laurence, April 27, 2011, HMM.

268. In all that had been written about Cudjo Lewis: Ibid.

268. The family owned a building: In the fall of 2021, an estimate came in for the cost of the repairs: $800,000, give or take. Given this price tag, officials decided to demolish the building and put up a new one instead.

269. "we could not think of a better way": City of Mobile, Alabama, June 17, 2021, news release.

270. Perhaps the city's most significant achievement: WALA-TV, April 22, 2021, https://www.fox10tv.com/news/mobile_county/300k-epa-grant-to-help-identify-and-revitalize-historic-africatown-sites/article_601a0ac0-a3e3-11eb-a7a1-13fc9aff6065.html.

270. And a project to add Lewis Quarters: Bemis and Wilson interviews.

271. The city could achieve this: Cochran interview.

271. During the drafting process: Sprague, "Report: Changes Are Necessary for the Proposed City of Mobile UDC Zoning Code Rewrite," MEJAC Archive Website, January 19, 2021, https://mejac.wordpress.com/2021/01/19/final_udc_comments/.

271. In the near-final draft: City of Mobile, Alabama, Chapter 64 Unified Development Code, Draft Version 4, December 2020, Article II, Sec. 64–11–1, Africatown Overlay. Available at https://mapformobile.org/wp/wp-content/uploads/2020/12/11-Africatown-Overlay_UDCv4.pdf.

271. compared to a thirty-one-page section: City of Mobile, Alabama, Chapter 64 Unified Development Code, Draft Version 4, December 2020, Article 13, Sec. 64–13–1, Spring Hill Overlay. Available at https://mapformobile.org/wp/wp-content/uploads/2020/12/13-Springhill-Overlay_UDCv4_rev.pdf.

271. When the planning commission: City of Mobile, Alabama, "Planning Commission Meeting," video, February 25, 2021, https://www.youtube.com/watch?v=2uRafkDEb2c.

271. In the weeks after this hearing: City of Mobile, Alabama, Chapter 64 Unified Development Code, Draft Version 5, December 2020, Article 13, Sec. 64–11–1, Africatown Overlay. Available at https://mapformobile.org/wp/wp-content/uploads/2021/03/11-Africatown-Overlay_UDCv4_March_2021.pdf.

272. In the fall, the code was rejected: WKRG News 5, October 19, 2021.

272. Early on, under Stimpson's leadership: *MPR,* August 1, 2015.

272. Stimpson also spun the city history museum: *MPR,* June 13, 2015.

272. "It's like having stage four cancer": WPMI NBC 15, March 3, 2021.

272. As of mid-2019: *Lagniappe,* May 15, 2019.

272. In the 2020 and 2021 fiscal years: City of Mobile, Alabama, annual budget, fiscal year 2020, general fund, 20; annual budget, fiscal year 2021, general fund, 20.

273. Since the 1990s, the Alabama Department of Transportation: AP, January 1, 2015.

273. Traffic congestion on the existing bridge: *MPR,* February 24, 2019.

273. In 2020, the state was moving ahead: Ibid.

273. It was clear that if this happened: South Alabama Regional Planning Commission, "Draft Amendment to the Envision 2045 Long Range Transportation Plan," April 22, 2020, 14–15.

273. This would in turn create more noise: Maria Cecilia Pinto de Moura, "Historic Black Community Put at Risk by Truck Bridge," The Equation, August 31, 2021, https://blog.ucsusa.org/cecilia-moura/historic-black-community-put-at-risk-by-truck-bridge/).

273. In the spring of 2019: *MPR,* May 4, 2019.

273. The plan was ultimately canceled: *MPR,* August 28, 2019.

A NOTE ON SOURCES

281. Hurston was not skilled at shorthand: Boyd, *Wrapped in Rainbows,* 107.

282. Yoruba is a tonal language: Diouf, 246.

INDEX

Abache (later Clara) (*Clotilda* shipmate), 80, 142, 143

Abile (*Clotilda* shipmate). *See* Lewis, Celia (Abile)

abolitionism, 28, 89, 92

Abomey (city), 41

Adams, Angela, 213

Adams, Clifton, 176

Adams, Nelson, 176

Adams-Davis, Carol, 237, 245

Adoke, 48, 53

Africa: Benin, 13, 81, 170, 199, 204, 208–9; Libéria, 89, 199; Nigeria, 13, 51, 199; West Africa, 11–16, 194, 199, 204; Yorubaland, 13–16, 20, 51. *See also* Dahomey

African Americans. *See* Black people

African Town (original settlement), 2; churches in, 100, 112, 113, 141; communal ethos, 113; education, 100–101, 112, 114; language, 114; laws and leadership structure, 101; name, 101; origins, 98–101; press articles about, 109–12; self-sufficiency, 113; sharing resources in, 113; social life, 113–14, 141. *See also* Magazine Point neighborhood; Plateau neighborhood

Africatown (current area), 2, 3; boundaries, 183–84; building sold by Meaher family to community for food pantry, 268–69; business district, 190–91, 206; celebration after *Clotilda* announcement (May 2019), 261, 274; construction plans threatening, 189–91, 199–201, 206–8, 223–25, 273–74; future of, 263, 274–75; and heritage tourism developments, 188–89, 193–94, 220, 261–63, 271, 275; as historic site/living monument, 3–4, 7, 181, 183, 188–89, 191, 192–94,
229–30; home values in, 191; income levels in, 191; industrialization of, 4–6, 7, 189, 223, more; international attention to, 198–99, 204, 208, 256, 257, 258, 274–75; Lewis Quarters neighborhood, 2–3, 100, 168, 184, 223, 230, 270; literacy in, 191; name, 181; pollution, 3, 5–6, 173–75, 189, 214–15, 217–19, 250–51; proposed parks, 194–98, 204–8; redevelopment, 269–73; welcome center, 220, 262; white awareness of, 237–38. *See also* Magazine Point neighborhood; Old Plateau Cemetery; Plateau neighborhood

AfricaTown Folk Festivals, 194, 198–99, 204, 206, 220

Africatown Heritage House, 262, 270

Africatown Heritage Preservation Foundation, 263

AfricaTown U.S.A. National Historical Park and District, 194, 195–98, 202–4, 206, 257

Afro-American Bicentennial Corporation (ABC), 188

agriculture: Africatown gardens, 113, 124, 151–52, 174; cotton, 24, 25, 28, 29, 102; plantations, 24, 25, 67, 80; sharecropping, 102, 120, 121, 158; West African crops, 13–14

air pollution, 173–74

Alabama: convict-leasing system in, 116–17, 118; freedpeople in, 101–2; local governments in, 122, 216; politics, 119–20; pollution, 175, 214–15, 216–17; and Reconstruction, 94; state constitution, 96, 107, 120–24, 216–17; voting rights, 120. *See also* Mobile, Alabama; Prichard, Alabama

Alabama Department of Environmental Management (ADEM), 216–17

Alabama Department of Transportation, 273–74
Alabama Historical Commission (AHC), 184,
192, 220, 230, 257, 258, 261, 262
Alabama Policy Institute, 123, 240
Alabama Public Service Commission (PSC),
236–37, 243–44
Alabama State University, 184–85
Alberta, Canada, 230–31
Alexander, Allen, 106
Alexander, Peyton, 128
Allen, Clara Eva "Mama Eva" (descendant of
Pollee Allen), 112–14, 141, 142, 194, 202
Allen, Pollee (Kuppollee) (*Clotilda* shipmate):
citizenship, 99; death, 143; descendants,
168–69, 172; descriptions, 142, 143; desire
to return home to Africa, 142; garden, 113;
house built by, 100; marriage, 97; name, 80;
occupations, 52, 97; and religion, 52, 100;
and Roche book, 142; voting, 103, 105, 107
Allen, Robert, 265
Allen, Rose (*Clotilda* shipmate), 97, 100
alligators, 98, 182, 210
Alsobrook, David, 129, 137
Amazons (women warriors of Dahomey), 17,
18, 40
American Colonization Society (ACS), 89
American Folklore Society, 145
American Slavers and the Federal Law, 1837–1862
(Howard), 169
American Tank and Vessel, 238–39
Amistad (film), 212
Anderson, William Strudwick, 131
anthropology, 145–47, 148, 149, 150, 152–54
anti-semitism, 78
archaeology: and Africatown cemetery, 220; and
Africatown nomination to NRHP, 229–30;
identification of *Clotilda* wreck, 2, 209–12,
258–61; search for *Clotilda* wreck, 255–57
architecture, 190, 196–97, 229
Arc Terminals, 249
Armstead, Cleophas, 180
the arts, 14, 183, 194, 272
ash, 3, 174, 217
Azalea City News & Review (newspaper), 201

babies, 80–81
Bacot, John (descendant of Pollee Allen), 172,
173, 174
Baker, Benjamin, 157, 161–62, 176, 179
Ballard, Ruth, 217, 241, 243, 244, 245, 246
Baquaqua, Mahommah, 11, 45, 54–55, 58, 59
Barracoon (Hurston): draft of, 154–56; interviews
for, 146–47, 149–52, 154; publication of,
6–7, 257–58
barracoons, 45, 50–54
baseball, 171–72
Battles, Robert, 220
Bay Bridge Road, 190–91, 200, 207–8
bell, ship's, 184–86

Bemis, Devereaux, 229–30
Benin, 13, 81, 170, 199, 204, 208–9. *See also*
Dahomey
Benson, James, 185, 186
Bermuda, 37
Big Creek Lake, 233, 238
Big Zion A.M.E. Church, 156
bill, federal senate (Heflin/Smith), 194–98
bill, state legislature (1991), 207
bill, state senate (Figures), 198, 202–3
Birmingham News (newspaper), 135, 163
Birmingham Reporter (Black newspaper), 140
The Birth of a Nation (film, 1915), 127
Black Codes, 94, 95, 96
Black history, 188, 192; tourism to Black history
sites, 7, 188–89, 193–94, 220, 261–63, 271,
275
Black newspapers, 140, 156, 183, 202
Black people, aposa environmental racism;
citizenship of, 94, 96, 99. *See also Clotilda*
shipmates; enslaved people; freedpeople;
freedpeople
Block, Harry, 154
blockade runners, 78–79
blueways, 5, 256–57, 262, 270
Blumenthal, Walter Hart, 157
Boas, Franz, 145, 146, 147, 150
Bolton, Brenda, 244, 247, 248, 253–54
Boyd, Terry, 179
BP (oil company), 235, 262
branding of captives, 54
Bratten, John, 255
British Royal Navy, 32, 37, 56
Brookley Air Force Base, 177, 189
Brown, Annie, 170–71, 223
Brown, Isaiah (1907-?), 170, 176, 177
Brown, William (1880-?), 170
Browne, Samuel Barnett, 118
Brunson, Walter, 213–14
Buchanan, James, 27
Buford, Thomas, property of, 100
Bullard, Robert, 215–16, 251–52
Burns, Peter, 250
Burton, Richard, 19, 40, 41, 42–43, 44, 48, 49

Cahaba Gazette (newspaper), 22
Callaway, Casi, 234, 243–44, 252, 253
Cana, Dahomey, 41
Canada, 231, 232
cancer, 5, 214–15, 217–19, 221, 235
cannibalism, fears of, 11, 60
Cape Verde islands, 38
capitalism, 43–44
Carroll, William, 224
Cavanaugh, Twinkle, 243
cemeteries. *See* Old Plateau Cemetery
Centers for Disease Control, 187
chamber of commerce, of Mobile, 127–28, 156,
160–61, 248, 250
Chevron oil refineries, 232, 233–34

Chickasabogue Creek, 174
Chickasaw Creek, 33, 175, 215
Childers, James Saxon, 163
children: in Africatown, 3, 4, 168–69, 171, 174, 175, 178–79; and Black Codes, 94; capture of, 158; Cudjo's, 97–98, 100, 101, 114, 115; Cudjo's grandchildren, 114, 141, 151–52; education in African Town, 100–101, 112, 114; rituals at birth of, 80–81; in Yorubaland, 11–12, 13. *See also* descendants of *Clotilda* shipmates; Mobile County Training School (MCTS)
Chippewa Lakes, 267, 269
Christianity, 99–100; Cudjo's conversion to, 163, 268
churches: in African Town (original settlement), 100, 112, 113, 141; Big Zion A.M.E. Church, 156; Stone Street Baptist Church, 100, 163; Union Missionary Baptist Church (formerly Old Landmark Baptist Church), 100, 138, 141, 163–64, 169, 221; Yorktown Missionary Baptist Church, 112, 167, 200, 218, 221–22, 269
Citizens' Committee, 176
citizenship, of Black people, 94, 96, 99
Civil Rights Act (1866), 96
Civil Rights Act (1875), 107
Civil War (1860–1864), 74–76; and blockade runners, 78–79; and *Clotilda* shipmates, 72–74, 75, 76, 78; and Mobile, 74–75, 77–78, 82, 83–84; runup to, 70–71
The Clansman (Dixon), 127
Clark, Bill, 198, 208
Clarke, Richard, 130, 131
class. *See* poor whites
Cleveland, Suzanne, 265
climate change, 231
clothing, 12, 19, 29, 52, 73, 141, 163
Clotilda (ship): academic historians on, 169; accident in Mobile Bay, 31–32; bell from, 184–86; built by Foster, 30–31; conditions on, 57–60; crew mutinies, 38, 62; destruction of, 64; identification of wreckage, 1, 2, 209–12, 255–57, 258–61; identities of captives on, 52; return to America, 55–56, 58–65, 69; voyage to Dahomey, 32–33, 36–39. *See also Clotilda* shipmates
Clotilda shipmates, 1–2; in barracoons, 52–54; citizenship of, 99; during Civil War, 72–74, 75, 76, 78; conditions on *Clotilda*, 57–60; desire to return home to Africa, 88–89, 90, 110, 111, 139, 142; education for children of, 100–101; first days in America, 66–67, 68–69, 80; as freedpeople, 88–92, 97–101, 104–5; houses built by, 190; identities of, 52; land purchases by, 100; leadership structure of, 101; monument to, 169–70; press on, 109–12, 157–60; relations with American-born freedpeople, 98–99, 111, 115; religion/spirituality of, 80–82, 99–100; Roche book

about, 142–43; stories about, 167–68. *See also* African Town (original settlement); *Clotilda* shipmates, names of; descendants of *Clotilda* shipmates

Clotilda shipmates, names of: Abache/Clara Turner, 80, 142, 143; Abile/Celia Lewis (*See* Lewis, Celia); Annie Keeby, 97, 100; Arzuma/Zuma, 51, 80, 142; Billy Smith, 159; Gracie, 158; Gumpa/Peter Lee (*See* Lee, Peter); Jaba/J.B./Jabez Shade, 52, 100, 101; Josephine Lee, 81, 97; Kanko/Lottie Dennison, 51–52, 80, 82–83, 97, 141, 142, 143; Kossola/Cudjo Lewis (*See* Lewis, Cudjo); Kuppollee/Pollee Allen (*See* Allen, Pollee); Maggie Lewis, 97, 100; Matilda McCrear, 157–59, 160; Oluale/Charlie Lewis (*See* Lewis, Charlie); Omolabi/Katie Cooper, 80, 142, 143; Osia/Ossa Keeby (*See* Keeby, Ossa); Polly Shade, 100; Redoshi/Sally Smith, 159–60; Rose Allen, 97, 100; Sallie Walker, 158; Shamba Wigfall, 142
Cochrane Bridge (later Cochrane-Africatown USA Bridge), 160, 192; and I-10 bridge project, 273–74; state replacement of/highway project, 190–91, 199–200, 202, 206–7
College Woods neighborhood, 198
Columbus, Christopher, 37
Conlin, Dave, 257
construction plans threatening Africatown, 189–91, 199–201, 206–8, 223–25, 273–74
convict-leasing system, 116–17, 118
Cooper, A. J., 193
Cooper, Katie (Omolabi) (*Clotilda* shipmate), 80, 142, 143
Copeland, William, 33
cotton, 24, 25, 28, 29, 102
Craig, Arealia, 200–201, 224
Craighead, Erwin, 125–26, 127, 128
Crawford, Vernon, 177
Creagh, Memorable Walker, 158
Creek, Ely, 108
criminal cases: in Africa Town, 101; and Cudjo Jr., 115–18; investigations regarding *Clotilda* voyage, 65–66, 67–68, 69–70, 71; and lynchings, 134–35; in Yorubaland, 14
Cuba, 18, 31, 88–89
Cudjo Lewis v. The Louisville and Nashville Railroad Company (1903), 130–32
Cumming, Kate, 75, 84
Czar (ship), 63, 70

Dabney, John, 63, 71; plantation of, 63, 66, 67, 69
Dahomey, 17–20; and beheadings, 17, 40, 41, 42–43; economy of, 17–18; festivals in, 42–43; foreign conquest of, 111–12; human sacrifice in, 17, 18, 19, 42, 43; leadership, 18–19; military, 17, 19–20, 39–40, 44; and transatlantic slave trade, 17–18, 25, 43–45. *See also* Ouidah (Whydah)

Daniel, C. L., 200
Davis, Jefferson, 28
Davis, Joycelyn (descendant of Charlie Lewis), 2–3, 217, 263
Davis, Martha West (descendant of Cudjo), 151, 190, 194
Davis, Ron, 176, 183
death. *See* funerals/death rituals
DeFlow, Joseph, 33
Delaney, Caldwell, 185–86
Delgado, James, 2, 257, 258, 259–61
Democratic Party: in Alabama, 1890s–1900s, 119–23; and election of 1874, 103–4, 105, 106, 107; and KKK, 103; and Reconstruction, 94, 96–97, 103–4; and southern secession, 70–71
Dennison, James, 66, 68, 82–83, 97, 141
Dennison, Kanko (Lottie) (*Clotilda* shipmate), 51–52, 80, 82–83, 97, 141, 142, 143
Dennison, Mable (descendant of Kanko), 141, 194
descendants of *Clotilda* shipmates: and AfricaTown Folk Festival, 194; association for, 2, 201; and cancer epidemic, 217; and *Clotilda* announcement, 2–3, 262–63; homes of, 201–2, 206–7; learning family history, 168–69; and new projects in Africatown, 262–63; and tourism plans, 220. *See also* descendants of *Clotilda* shipmates, names of
descendants of *Clotilda* shipmates, names of: Cassandra Lewis Wallace, 168, 169, 190; Darron Patterson, 167–69, 182, 263; Garry Lumbers, 4, 168, 207, 217, 263; Helen Richardson Jackson, 201–2, 206–7; John Bacot, 172, 173, 174; Johnnie Lewis, 151, 168, 169; Joycelyn Davis, 2–3, 217, 263; Lorna Gail Woods, 168; Mable Dennison, 141, 194; "Mama Eva" Jones, 112–14, 141, 142, 194, 202; Martha West Davis, 151, 190, 194; Mary Lumbers, 151, 194
De Souza, Isidore, 204
dialect, material written in, 154, 155
Diouf, Sylviane: on American Colonization Society, 89; on Cudjo's origins, 13, 41; on deaths of Cudjo's children, 130, 134; *Dreams of Africa in Alabama*, 13, 220–21; and female survivors of *Clotilda*, 157; on hairstyles, 54–55; on manner of wearing garments, 73; on ritual practices, 81–82; and Williams as source, 220–21; on women in barracoons, 51, 52
disease. *See* health/illness
Dixon, Thomas W., 127
Dodd, Thayer, 237–38, 247
Dorsett, Mose, 136
Dostal, Christopher, 261
Douglas, Stephen A., 70–71
Dreams of Africa in Alabama: The Slave Ship Clotilda and the Story of the Last Africans Brought to America (Diouf), 13, 220–21

Dred Scott case (1857), 26, 27
Drummond, Barbara, 206
Dumping in Dixie (Bullard), 215
Duncan, John, 48–49, 50, 54
DuPont Chemicals, 222
Durkin, Hannah, 157
Dust Tracks on a Road (Hurston), 147

Echo (ship), 31
Eckert, J. Heath, 266, 267
Eclipse (ship), 67
economic depression of 1873, 103
economic systems: of Dahomey, 17–18; of Mobile, 29; and white southerners, 102, 119–21
education: in African Town, 100–101, 112, 114; in Alabama, 107; college, 180; Plateau schools, 137–38, 139–40, 161–62; during Reconstruction, 101–2. *See also* Mobile County Training School (MCTS)
Eichold, Bernard, 250
elections: Alabama, 1890s–1900s, 119, 120–23; mayoral elections, Mobile, 229, 239–40; mayoral elections, Prichard, 193, 199, 205–6; national, 1874, 103–7
electoral districts, 127–28
emancipation, 6, 84, 87–89, 92
enslaved people: escape attempts, 82–83; identities of captives in barracoons, 51–52; Noah (formerly enslaved man), 62, 69, 73, 74, 80–81, 110–11; working for Mobile's defense, 75–76; working on Meahers' ships, 76–77. *See also Clotilda* shipmates; Lewis, Cudjo; slave trade
environmental activism, and oil pipelines, 231, 234–36, 237–39, 241, 242–49, 250–54
environmental justice, 239, 251–52, 270–71
Environmental Protection Agency, 214, 215, 270
environmental racism, 5–6, 161, 215–17, 236
Equiano, Olaudah, 59
Europeans/white men: and development of African slave trade, 17, 18, 43–44; as mythical creatures, 11–12; and Ouidah, 46–47; West African knowledge of, 11–12

Falconbridge, Alexander, 57, 58, 60
Farragut, David, 82
Fetter's Southern Magazine (periodical), 111
Figures, Michael, 192, 193, 198, 202, 203, 204–5, 207
Figures, Vivian Davis, 261
fishing, 52, 171, 174, 175, 215
A Fistful of Shells (Green), 17
Flen, Anderson, 179, 186, 187–88, 256, 257, 260–61, 263, 275
Florida, 216
Flynt, Wayne, 122, 217
folktales, 144–46
Foner, Eric, 92

food, 60, 77–78, 113, 141
food pantries, 269
Forbes, Frederick, 40
Forsyth, John, 25
"forty acres and a mule" program, 92–93, 94, 95, 102
Foster, Martha Adalaide Vanderslice, 29, 70, 142
Foster, Michael (descendant of Bill Foster), 263
Foster, William "Bill": building *Clotilda*, 30–31; captives purchased by, 69; and *Clotilda*'s accident in Mobile Bay, 31–32; and *Clotilda* shipmates as freedpeople, 90; descendant's apology, 263; family, 29–30; marriage, 70; memoir of, 36, 37, 38, 55, 62, 64, 108; prosecution of, 69, 70, 71; return from Dahomey, 58, 59, 60, 61–64; time in Dahomey, 47–50, 53–54, 55–56; and voyage to Dahomey, 28–29, 32–33, 36–39, 55–56
Frazier, Garrison, 92
Freedmen's Bureau, 88, 89, 93, 95, 101
freedpeople: in Alabama, 101–2; citizenship of, 99; *Clotilda* shipmates as, 88–92, 97–101, 104–5; *Clotilda* shipmates' relations with American-born freedpeople, 98–99, 111, 115; and election of 1874, 103–7; in Mobile, 87–88
Free George (Black free man at Meaher plantation), 80, 99
The Freeman (Black newspaper), 140
Friend, Jack, 209–11, 220
funerals/death rituals: in African Town, 114; and cancer epidemic, 218; of *Clotilda* shipmates on Meahers' plantations, 81–82; Cudjo's, 163–64; in Yorubaland, 15, 163

Garner, John, 244
Garrison, William Lloyd, 89
Georgia, 82, 83, 92–93, 187, 216
gerrymandering, 127–28
Getty Oil Company, 266
Ghana, 199
Ghezo, King of Dahomey, 18, 25
Gipsy (ship), 79
Glélé, King of Dahomey, 17–20, 35, 39, 40–41, 42, 43, 44
Globe (periodical), 164
Godbold, Cade, 65–66, 67–68, 69
gold, 23, 36
Governing (magazine), 217
government. *See* politics/government
Gracie (*Clotilda* shipmate), 158
Gray Jacket (ship), 26, 79
Green, Toby, 17
Gregory, Dick, 204
Grier, Mary Lou, 196–98
Guinzburg, Harold, 155
Gulf Lumber, 168, 223, 239, 240
Gumpa (*Clotilda* shipmate). *See* Lee, Peter (Gumpa)

Haas-Davis Packing Company, 168
hairstyles, importance of, 54–55
Haley, Alex, 7, 188, 204
Hand, Brevard, 215
Hansen, Jim, 231
Hanson, Merlin, 164
Happy Hill neighborhood, 184, 230
Harlan, Louis, 123
Harlem Renaissance, 144–45, 148–49
Harper's Weekly (periodical), 99, 110
Harris, William, 191
Hartselle Sandstone formation, 232
Hathorn, Stacye, 257, 260
Hauser Realty, 189, 200
Hayes, Valerie, 171, 175
health/illness: in Alabama prisons, 117; cancer, 5, 214–15, 217–19, 221, 235; for captives, 50–51, 57–58; for Europeans in Africa, 49–50; hazards of oil industry, 250–51; hoodoo as treatment, 181–82; Lewis sons' deaths, 133–34; in Mobile's Black communities, 126–27; public health work, 187
Heflin, Howell, 194, 195–96
Hickory Club, 128–29
highway projects/construction, 190–91, 199–200, 206–8, 273–74
Hill, E. Ashton, 219–20
Hines, Richard Jr., 108–9
historical monuments: bell from *Clotilda*, 184–86; bust of Cudjo, 169–70, 185; historical sites as, 3–4, 7
historical sites: as monuments, 3–4; in Ouidah, 54; on Scott Paper property, 190, 194; tourism to Black history sites, 7, 188–89, 193–94, 220, 261–63, 271, 275
historic districts: AfricaTown National Historical Park and District, 194, 195–98, 202–3; National Register of Historic Places, 188, 192, 194, 197, 229–30, 270
Historic Sketches of the South (Roche), 142–43, 146–47, 168, 260
history, local, 183
History Museum of Mobile, 185–86, 268, 272
Hog Bayou, 98, 160, 169, 174, 230
Hollingsworth, James, 63
Holly, W.D.F., 32
Holmes, Oliver Wendell, 123–24
Hope, Charles, 244
housing: homes demolished, 190, 200, 201–2, 206–7, 272; and oil industry, 238, 252–53; repairs to, 270
Howard, Warren S., 169
Howe, George, 108
Hubbard, Edley, 176
Hueda people, 46, 49
Hughes, Langston, 145, 148, 149, 153
human sacrifices, in Dahomey, 17, 18, 42, 43
Hurston, Zora Neale: anthropology fieldwork, 145–47, 149–52, 154; *Barracoon*

Hurston (*continued*)
  manuscript, 6–7, 154–56, 257–58; and
    Cudjo, 162–63; on Cudjo Jr's death, 129,
    130; *Dust Tracks on a Road,* 147; on hoodoo,
    181–82; interviews with Cudjo, 6–7, 146–47,
    149–52, 154; and Mason, 147–49; *Mules and
    Men,* 146, 152; plagiarism of Roche, 146–47,
    150; on Redoshi, 159
Hutchings, Tom, 234–35

I-165 project, 200, 206–7
illiteracy, 120, 121, 191
industry: industrialization of Africatown, 4–6, 7,
    160–61, 168, 189, 223, more
industry/manufacturing, 3, 160–61, aposa more;
    and environmental racism, 5–6, 270–73.
    See also oil industry; paper industry; trade/
    markets
inequities, racial, MORE; and architectural focus
    of Park Service criteria, 197
Inge, Herndon, 266
Inner City News (Mobile Black newspaper), 183,
    202
International Paper (IP): employment at, 170,
    172; factory opened by, 160–61; impact
    on community, 173; opposition to historic
    district status, 202–3; pollution by, 174–75,
    214–15, 219; and rezoning, 201; shutdown
    of Mobile factory, 213–14; tank farm on old
    site of, 238–39, 248
Islam and Muslims, 51

Jaba (*Clotilda* shipmate), 52, 100, 101
Jackson, Helen Richardson (descendant of Ossa
    Keeby), 201–2, 206–7
James, Stephen, 210
J. L. Meaher & Associates, 267
Johnson, A. N., 122
Johnson, Andrew, 93–94, 95, 96
Johnston, Joseph F., 118
Jones, Bella, 129
Jones, Clara Eva Allen "Mama Eva" (descendant
    of Pollee Allen), 112–14, 141, 142, 194,
    202
Jones, Doug, 262
Jones, Mae, 244, 245
Jones, Sam, 229, 235, 239–40
Jones, Thomas Goode, 119
Jones, Will (Plateau man), 129
Jones, William (federal judge), 67–68, 69
Journal of Negro History (periodical), 146

Kanko (*Clotilda* shipmate), 51–52, 80, 82–83, 97,
    141, 142, 143
Keeby, Annie (*Clotilda* shipmate), 97, 100
Keeby, Joyful, 138
Keeby, Ossa (Osia) (*Clotilda* shipmate):
    citizenship, 99; death, 143; descendants, 201;
    garden, 113; getting on *Clotilda,* 55; houses
    built by, 100, 201; marriage, 97; name, 52;

occupations, 52, 97, 101; and Roche book,
    142; in Washington book, 139
Keep Mobile Growing, 252
Keils, Elias, 106
Kelly Hills neighborhood, 184
Keystone pipeline, 231–32, 236, 241
Kimberly-Clark, 213, 223
Knox, John B., 120, 122
Kolb, Reuben, 119
Kossola (*Clotilda* shipmate). *See* Lewis, Cudjo
Krivor, Michael, 209, 210
Ku Klux Klan, 103
Kuppollee (*Clotilda* shipmate). *See* Allen, Pollee
    (Kuppollee)

land: as communal property, 13–14, 20, 171;
    "forty acres and a mule" program, 92–93,
    94, 95, 102; and oil industry, 238, 246–47;
    owned by Meaher family, 22, 67, 69, 72,
    168, 169, 178, 216, 230, 243, 259, 266–67,
    268–69; purchased by *Clotilda* shipmates,
    100; and Reconstruction, 92–93, 95, 96,
    102; redevelopment in Africatown, 270;
    sharecropping, 102, 120, 121, 158; zoning
    of, 189–90, 200–202, 216, 223–25, 271.
    See also historical sites
language, 47, 51, 73, 112, 114, 154, 155
Law, Robin, 41, 50, 54
law enforcement: in African Town, 101; and
    Clotilda voyage, 32, 37–38, 59, 61; and
    Cudjo Jr., 115, 118, 129; and Lewis brothers,
    115, 128–29; in Yorubaland, 14
Lee, Josephine (*Clotilda* shipmate), 81, 97
Lee, Peter (Gumpa) (*Clotilda* shipmate): children,
    81; citizenship, 99; death, 131; house built
    by, 201, 207; interviews with, 111–12; as
    leader, 90, 101, 111; marriage, 97; name, 80;
    purchased by Foster, 53
legal proceedings: bills on AfricaTown historic
    district, 194–98, 202–3; hearing on PSC
    and Plains pipeline, 244–45; and lynchings,
    134–35; regarding *Clotilda's* arrival, 65–66,
    67–68, 69–70, 71; on renaming Cochrane
    Bridge, 207; zoning of property, 189–90,
    200–202, 216, 223–25, 271
Legal Services Corporation of Alabama, 191
Lewis, Aleck Iyadjemi (1867–1908), 97–98, 114,
    115, 128, 133, 137
Lewis, Angeline (1901–?) (descendant of Cudjo),
    114, 151, 168
Lewis, Cassandra (descendant of Cudjo), 168,
    169, 190
Lewis, Celia (Abile) (*Clotilda* shipmate) (?–
    1908): children, 97–98, 100, 101, 114, 115;
    death, 137; in garden with Cudjo, 124;
    grandchildren, 114; land purchase, 100;
    marriage, 97–98; name, 80; on religion, 99;
    on sea voyage, 60; and sons' deaths, 129–30,
    132–34
Lewis, Celia Ebeossi (?–1893), 101, 114

Lewis, Charlie (Oluale) (*Clotilda* shipmate): citizenship, 99; descendants, 2, 168, 263; land purchase, 100; marriage, 97; name, 80; and Roche book, 142; voting, 103, 105, 107

Lewis, Cudjo (Kossola) (*Clotilda* shipmate): and Abile's death, 137; after arriving in Mobile Bay delta, 66–67, 68–69; bust of, 169–70, 185; capture of, 34–35, 39–42, 44–45; and Charlotte Mason, 149, 152, 153, 156, 162; children, 97–98, 100, 101, 114, 115; citizenship, 99; during Civil War, 76, 78, 84; and *Clotilda* shipmates as freedpeople after war, 88, 89, 90–91; death, 163–64; descendants, 4, 168; early life in West Africa, 11–16; on Foster's character, 60; grandchildren, 114, 141; house built by, 100, 190, 207; and Hurston, 146–47, 149–52, 162–63; influence on Henry Williams, 182; at Jim Meaher's plantation, 73; land purchase, 100; marriage, 97–98; name, 80; in *The New Negro*, 144–45; occupations, 97, 141; old age, 150–52, 156–57, 162–63; in Ouidah barracoon, 50–53; press reports of, 110, 111, 156–57; religion, 141, 163, 268; and Roche, 142, 163; and sons' deaths, 129–30, 132–34, 137; train accident, 124, 130–32; voting, 103, 105, 107; voyage on *Clotilda*, 55, 56, 59–60; as widower, 141–42

Lewis, Cudjo Jr. Fëichitan, 101, 115–18, 128, 129–30

Lewis, David Adeniah (?-1905), 101, 115, 124, 128, 130, 131, 132–33

Lewis, Emmett (1897–1921) (descendant of Cudjo), 114, 151

Lewis, James Ahnonotoe (1870–1905), 100, 115, 128, 133–34

Lewis, Johnnie (1920-?) (descendant of Cudjo), 151, 168, 169

Lewis, Louisa (Thomas), 115

Lewis, Maggie (*Clotilda* shipmate), 97, 100

Lewis, Mary Woods (1875-?), 114, 137, 163

Lewis, Motley (1895-?) (descendant of Cudjo), 114, 141, 170

Lewis, Pollee Dahoo (?-1905), 101, 115, 128, 133

Lewis, Zanna (1892-?) (descendant of Cudjo), 114

Lewis Bros. Grocery Dealers, 128

Lewis Quarters neighborhood, 2–3, 100, 168, 184, 223, 230, 270

Liberia, 89, 199

Lincoln, Abraham, 71, 92, 93

Lipscomb, Oscar, 204

literacy, 120, 121, 191

The Literary Digest (periodical), 157

lobbyists, 122, 127–28, 203, 217

Locke, Alain, 144, 148, 152–53, 154–55

Louisiana, 120

Louisville and Nashville Railroad Company, 124

Lowe, Lella, 271

Lowe, Robert, 121

Ludder, David, 216

Ludgood, Merceria, 193, 205, 208, 262, 269, 274–75

Lumbers, Garry (descendant of Cudjo), 4, 168, 207, 217, 263

Lumbers, Mary (descendant of Cudjo), 151, 194

lumberyards, 3; Gulf Lumber, 168, 223, 239, 240; Meaher's, 22, 72, 89

lynchings, 6, 134–37

Lyons, Jimmy, 248

Magazine Point neighborhood, 184; annexed by Mobile, 177; conditions in, 128; growth of, 126; industry in, 160; nomination to NRHP, 230; oil tanks in, 242–43; and replacement of Cochrane Bridge, 190–91, 199–200; white fears of, 127

Manzie, Levon, 248, 253

Marine Corps, 187

Maritime Museum of Mobile, 209–10

Mason, Charlotte Osgood, 147–49, 152–53, 154–56, 162

Mason, Rufus Osgood, 148

MAWSS (Mobile Area Water and Sewer System), 237, 238, 247

McCann, William P., 79

McCants, Valena, 161–62, 180

McCrear, Matilda "Tildy" (*Clotilda* shipmate), 157–59, 160

McGray, Henry, 100

McLean, Charles, 118

Meaher, Augustine, 111, 118, 143, 160

Meaher, Augustine III "Gus," 178, 211, 212, 264, 267

Meaher, Augustine Jr. "Gus," 178, 183, 209, 211, 212

Meaher, Burns: in business with T. Meaher, 22, 23; and *Clotilda*'s arrival, 63; court summons for, 71; enslaved people owned by, 68, 69, 72–73, 83; property of, 67, 69

Meaher, Helen, 267, 269

Meaher, Helen Van Nimwegen, 143

Meaher, James (Tim's son), 143

Meaher, James "Jim" (Tim's brother), 21, 22, 69, 72, 73, 76, 78, 80

Meaher, Joe, 178, 212, 240, 264, 265–66, 267

Meaher, Margaret Lyons, 178, 212

Meaher, Mary, 73, 74

Meaher, Mary Lou, 264

Meaher, Meg, 267

Meaher, Robert, 178, 209–10, 211–12, 264, 267–68

Meaher, Timothy, 1, 21–23; as blockade runner, 79; and *Clotilda* voyage, 32–33, 61–64, 67, 68–69, 71, 76–77; contemporary description, 22; and election of 1874, 104, 105; end of life, 108, 109; and freedpeople, 88, 90–91; interview, 108–9; move to Alabama, 21–22; property, 22, 72; support of slave trade, 26, 27; wreck of *Orline St. John*, 23

Meaher family, 7; and freedpeople after war, 88, 89; property owned by, 168, 169, 178, 216, 230, 243, 259, 266–67, 268–69; reticence about Africatown and *Clotilda,* 267–69
Meaher's Hummock, 22, 72
Meaher State Park, 169
media: and interest in Black history, 188; racism in, 127. *See also* press
MEJAC (Mobile Environmental Justice Action Coalition), 241, 242–44, 245–46, 251, 252, 270–71
Middle Passage, 57–60
military, 186–87
mining, 116, 117, 232
Mississippi, 120, 216, 232, 233
Mississippi State University, 262
Mobile, Alabama: Black political machine in, 205, 229; city commission, 128, 177, 189–90, 202; city council, 128, 237, 248, 249, 253, 272; city government, 127–28, 269–73; as "city of perpetual potential," 125–26; city proposals affecting Africatown, 189–91; and Civil War, 74–75, 77–78, 82, 83–84; and cotton, 25; and Cudjo's 90th birthday party, 156–57; culture, 30, 249–50; demographics, 87; development regulations, 270–72; economy, 29; and election of 1874, 105–6; electoral districts, 127–28; freedpeople in, 87–88; growth of, 29, 125–26, 176–77; history, 29, 273; history museum, 185–86, 268, 272; income levels, 171, 191; infrastructure, 126; Jim Crow, 126–27; loss of prominence, 125–26; and lynchings, 134–37; mayoral elections, 229, 239–40; and oil industry, 232–40, 247–48; and paper industry, 160–61; pollution, 214–15; and Progressivism, 125–28; and Reconstruction, 94; segregation, 126–27; and slave trade, 24–25; suburbs, 126–27; white flight from, 177
Mobile Area Water and Sewer System (MAWSS), 237, 238, 247
Mobile Bay, 2, 31–32, 61, 209–10, 258
Mobile Baykeeper (environmental organization), 234, 243–44, 252, 253
Mobile County Training School (MCTS), 176; bell at, 169, 174, 184–86, 256; establishment of, 140; growth of, 161–62; and new projects in Africatown, 263; and oil pipelines, 243, 245, 246–47; Womack at, 179–80
Mobile Daily Advertiser (newspaper), 31, 75
Mobile Daily Herald (newspaper), 127
Mobile Daily Item (newspaper), 115, 134
Mobile Daily Register (newspaper), 23, 25, 107, 136, 161
Mobile Daily Tribune (newspaper), 104, 105, 106
Mobile Environmental Justice Action Coalition (MEJAC), 241, 242–44, 245–46, 251, 252, 270–71
Mobile Evening News (newspaper), 72
Mobile General Hospital, 171

Mobile Historic Development Commission, 229
Mobile Mercury (newspaper), 69, 169
Mobile Press, 122
Mobile Press (newspaper), 183
Mobile Press-Forum (Black newspaper), 156
Mobile Press-Register (newspaper): on AfricaTown Folk Festivals, 220; and discovery of *Clotilda* wreck, 255–56; Figures column on AfricaTown U.S.A., 203; and IP plant closing, 213; on Mobile mayoral election, 240; and Prichard mayoral election, 206; on Williams, 183
Mobile Register (newspaper), 164; on Africatown as historic district, 193; on Africatown U.S.A., 203; on *Clotilda* voyage, 65–66; on crime, 134; on Hickory Club and law enforcement, 129; merger with *Mobile Press,* 183; and Mobile's status, 125–26; on renaming Cochrane Bridge, 207; and T. Meaher interview, 108
Mobile River, 2, 33, 171, 182, 209, 238
The Mobile River (Sledge), 265–66
Mobile Weekly Advertiser (newspaper), 21
Mohr, Charles, 126–27
Montgomery Advertiser (newspaper), 104, 143, 159
Moore, Robert, 182
MS Industries, 232
Mules and Men (Hurston), 146, 152
Munroe, Kirk, 110

NAACP, 251
names, 80
The Nation (periodical), 97, 107
National Association of Black Scuba Divers, 262
National Geographic (magazine), 261, 263, 267–68
National Geographic Society, 1, 2
National Historic Landmarks, 197
National Memorial for Peace and Justice, 4
National Park Service, 188, 195–98, 256–57
National Register of Historic Places, 188, 192, 194, 197, 229–30, 270
Native Americans, 23, 148, 236, 241
navigation, 36
Nettles, Jane, 162
The New Negro: An Interpretation (Locke), 144–45
New Orleans Daily Picayune (newspaper), 109
New Orleans Times-Democrat (newspaper), 112
newspapers. *See* press
New York Evening Post (newspaper), 157
New York Times (newspaper), 27, 109, 139
Nicaragua, 26
Nigeria, 13, 51, 199
Noah (formerly enslaved man), 62, 69, 73, 74, 80–81, 110–11
No Man's Land neighborhood, 179, 223

Norman, Neil, 220
North Carolina, 120
Norwood, Jesse, 205

Obama administration, 231–32
Oberlin College, 262
oil industry, 230–41; Keystone pipeline, 231–32, 236, 241; and Meaher land, 266; Mobile local activism against, 234–38, 239, 241, 242–49, 250–54; Plains pipeline, 233–34, 236–37, 238, 242–43, 246–47; and shipment/stockpiling in Mobile, 232, 249–50; spills, 231, 233, 235, 238; tank farms, 189, 232, 235, 238–39, 247–48, 250, 252–53, 267, 270–71, 272–73; tar sands, 231, 232, 233–34
Old Landmark Baptist Church (later Union Missionary Baptist Church), 100
Old Plateau Cemetery: Africatown welcome center near, 220, 262; burial of shipmates in, 114, 137, 164; and highway construction, 208; historic importance, 169, 183, 229; maintenance, 219–20
Oluale (*Clotilda* shipmate). *See* Lewis, Charlie (Oluale)
Omolabi (later Katie) (*Clotilda* shipmate), 80, 142, 143
Orline St. John (ship), 23
Oro (Yoruba deity), 15–16
Ossa (*Clotilda* shipmate). *See* Keeby, Ossa (Osia)
Ouidah (Whydah) (port city, Dahomey), 46–48; and *Clotilda* voyage, 36, 47–50, 52–54; conditions in barracoons, 50–52; culture, 47; importance of port, 46–47; landmarks, 54; layout, 47–48; market, 48–49; purchase of captives, 52–54; religious sites, 49; sister city with Prichard, 199, 204, 208–9; and slave trade, 17, 25, 36, 46
oysters, 78, 175

Padgett, David, 262
palm oil, 14, 18, 46
Panamerican Consultants, 209–10
paper industry: employment in, 170, 172–73, 213–14; industrialization in Africatown, 160–61, 168; opposition to Africatown park, 202–3; pollution by, 3, 161, 173–75, 214–15, 235; shutdown of Mobile factories, 213–14. *See also* International Paper; Scott Paper
Parker, Jabez J., 118
parks: AfricaTown U.S.A., 194–98, 204–8; Meaher State Park, 169; National Park Service, 188, 195–98, 256–57
Patterson, Darron (descendant of Pollee Allen), 167–69, 182, 263
Peek, Martha, 246–47
People's Party, 119
Pittsburgh Dispatch (newspaper), 109
Plains All American oil company and pipeline, 233–34, 236–37, 238, 242–43, 246–47

Plant, Deborah, 263
Plateau neighborhood, 184; annexed by Mobile, 176–77; beginnings of, 100, 111; blighting, 4; Citizens' Committee, 176; and Cochrane Bridge replacement, 190–91, 199–200; communal ethos, 171; conditions, 128; fires, 139–40; income levels, 171, 191; industry, 160, 168; Lewis family in, 128; lynchings, 134–37; municipal services, 171, 176, 177–78; nomination to NRHP, 230; and paper mills, 172–75; population, 126; rezoning of residential property, 189–90, 200–202; schools, 137–38, 139–40; violence, 115, 128. *See also* Africatown
Plateau Normal and Industrial Institute, 138
political activism: H. Williams, 181, 191–92, 222; J. Womack's activism against oil developments, 234–35, 237, 239, 242, 243, 245, 246, 247, 251
politicians, sexual liaisons of, 187–88
politics/government: Alabama state constitution, 96, 107, 120–24, 216–17; bill for renaming Cochrane Bridge, 207; bills for AfricaTown Historical Park, 194–98, 202–3; electoral districts, 127–28; and environmental racism, 216–17; mayoral elections, Mobile, 229, 239–40; mayoral elections, Prichard, 193, 199, 205–6; Mobile city government, 127–28, 269–73; and pipeline project, 236–37
poll taxes, 106, 107, 120, 121
pollution, by oil industry, 250–51
pollution, by paper industry in Africatown, 3, 173–75, 189; and cancer clusters, 5, 217–19; and environmental racism, 5–6, 161; monitoring of, 214–15; and opposition to historic district status, 202–3
poor whites: and Alabama constitution, 122–23; and land redistribution proposals, 96; and voting rights, 107, 120, 121, 123
Populist Party, 119, 120
Porter, Charles, 183, 185, 221
Portuguese, 11, 37–38, 47
Powe, Samuel, 129, 130
Powers, John F., 134–35
Praia, Santiago (Cape Verde islands), 38
Pratt Mines, 117
press: on African Town settlement, 109–12; on Africatown, 201, 258; Black newspapers, 140, 156, 183, 202; on *Clotilda's* identification, 256, 257, 260–61, 274–75; on *Clotilda's* voyage, 64–65, 69; on Cudjo, 110, 111, 156–57, 164; illegal slave expeditions in, 26–27; interview with T. Meaher about story of *Clotilda*, 108–9; and Meaher descendants, 212; on other *Clotilda* survivors, 157–60; racism in, 127. *See also* *Mobile Press-Register*; *Mobile Register*; specific newspapers

Prichard, Alabama, 208; and AfricaTown
     attraction, 193–94, 198–99; AfricaTown
     Folk Festival, 194, 198–99, 204; and
     annexation of Plateau, 177; and international
     trade with West Africa, 193–94, 199, 204,
     208; mayoral elections, 193, 199, 204–6; and
     Smith, 192; white flight from, 193
prisons, 116–17
Progressive League, 170, 192
Progressivism, 125
property. See housing; land
property taxes, 105, 107, 216
publishers, 154–55

Quigley, Ann, 87

race: and activism against oil pipeline, 237–38;
     and paper mill workers, 172
racial violence: and election of 1874, 103;
     lynchings, 134–37
racism: Black Codes, 94, 95, 96; and
     constitutional convention of 1901, 119–22;
     and election of 1874, 103–4; environmental
     racism, 5–6, 161, 215–17, 236; stoked by
     segregation, 126–27; white supremacy,
     119–22. See also white southerners
Radin, Paul, 153
railroads, 116, 124, 130–32, 232, 239, 242
Raines, Ben, 255–56, 258–59
Randolph, Deborah, 206
Randolph, John, 176
Reagan administration, 195, 199
Rebecca (ship), 108
Reconstruction (1864–1874), 92–97, 101–3, 107
Redoshi (Clotilda shipmate), 159–60
religion: in African Town, 100, 112, 113;
     and battle rituals in Dahomey, 42–43;
     of Clotilda shipmates, 80–81, 99–100;
     Cudjo's conversion to Christianity, 163,
     268; funerals/death rituals, 15, 81–82, 114,
     163–64, 218; hoodoo, 181–82; in Ouidah,
     49, 54–55; in Yorubaland, 15–16. See also
     churches
reparations, 183, 269–70
Republican Party: and election of 1874, 103, 104,
     106, 107; and Reconstruction, 93, 94–95,
     96–97; Union League, 102, 104
Requier, A. J., 69, 70, 71
Rhodes, Eugene, 170
Risher, Malcolm, 208
Robertson, James "Fats," 171
Robertson, Natalie, 13, 51, 221, 263
Robinson, Cornelius, 134–35
Robinson, Edward M., 115–16, 117–18
Roche, Emma Langdon, 260; on Clotilda
     voyage, 55, 64, 66, 74; and Cudjo's old age,
     163; Hurston uses material from, 146–47;
     interviews by, 142–43
Roger B. Taney (ship), 21, 26, 63–64, 70, 71
Romeyn, Henry, 56, 111–12

Roots (book and miniseries), 188
Rountree, David, 236–37
Russell, William Howard, 22, 23, 76–77, 78

Sanford, Thaddeus, 65–66, 67–68, 69–70
sawmills, 89, 160, 168, 197
Schuler, Jacob, 158
Scott, Mary McNeil, 69, 110–11
Scott Government Relations Newsletter (bulletin),
     203
Scott Paper: employment at, 172–73; factory
     opened by, 168, 172; historic site on property
     of, 190, 194; impact on neighborhood, 173;
     and Meaher land, 266; opposition to historic
     district status, 202–3; pollution by, 175,
     214–15; shutdown of Mobile factory, 213
Scribner's (magazine), 108
secession, 28, 71, 74–75
segregation, 107, 126–27, 237
Selma Sentinel (newspaper), 22
Selma Times-Journal (newspaper), 158
Serda, John, 250
Sessions, Jeff, 240
sex workers, 187
Shade, Jaba (Jabbar, Jaybee, J.B., or Jabez)
     (Clotilda shipmate), 52, 100, 101
Shade, Polly (Clotilda shipmate), 100
sharecropping system, 102, 120, 121, 158
Shell Chemicals, 187, 222
Sherman, William Tecumseh, 82, 83, 92–93
shipbuilding, 23, 30–31, 72
shipmates. See Clotilda shipmates
Sierra Club, 233, 234–35
Simonton, John M., 33
Skertchly, J. Alfred, 19
slave raids, 19–20, 34–35, 159
The Slave Ship Clotilda and the Making of
     AfricaTown, USA (Robertson), 221
slave ships, 27, 31, 57–58, 60, 108. See also Clotilda
     (ship)
slave trade: Clotilda's involvement in, 31–33; and
     cotton production, 24, 25; and Dahomey,
     17–18, 25, 43–44; illegal expeditions in
     press, 26–27; and Ouidah, 46, 48–49, 52–54;
     price of enslaved people, 24–25; U.S. ban
     on importation of Africans, 24, 25; West
     African knowledge of, 11–12
Sledge, John, 78, 209, 265–66
Sloss Iron and Steel Company, 118
Small, James, 33
Smith, Billy (Clotilda shipmate), 159
Smith, James M., 33
Smith, John Henry, 191–94, 195–96, 198–99,
     204–6, 208–9
Smith, Lethe/Lethia/Letia, 159
Smith, Sally (Redoshi) (Clotilda shipmate),
     159–60
Smith, Washington, 159
Smith, Yuri, 205
Smithsonian Institution, 256, 262

South Carolina, 120
Southern Commercial Convention, 25
Southern Courier (civil rights newspaper), 178, 233
Southern Republic (ship), 26, 76, 77
Spirit of Our Ancestors festivals, 263
Sprague, Ramsey, 235–36, 241, 245–46, 252, 270–71
Spring Hill neighborhood, 106, 186, 271
Stanfield, James Field, 59
Stevens, Thaddeus, 94–95, 96
Stewart, Donald, 219
Stimpson, Sandy, 239–40, 248–49, 250, 269, 270, 271, 272
St. Louis Globe-Democrat (newspaper), 109
Stone Street Baptist Church (Mobile), 100, 163
The Story of the Negro (Washington), 139
strip-mining, 232
Sullivan, Bill, 172
Susan (ship), 26

tank farms: and city council, 247–48, 253; environmentalists negotiate with industry over regulations, 252–53; and industrialization of Africatown, 189; on land leased from Meaher family, 267; MEJAC requests phasing out of, 270–71, 272–73; planned in Mobile, 232, 238–39; and possible disasters, 235; reports on, 250
"T'appin (Terrapin)" (Lewis), 144–45
tar sands, 231, 232, 233–34
taxes: and Alabama constitution, 107, 122, 216; in Dahomey, 18, 46–47; and freedpeople during Reconstruction, 94; and municipal services in Plateau, 177; poll taxes, 106, 107, 120, 121; property taxes, 105, 107, 216
Taylor, Washington, 217
Tennessee Coal and Iron Company, 117
Ten Percent Plan, 92
Texas, 216, 241
textile industry, 28
Thirteenth Amendment, 95
Thomas, Gilbert, 115, 118
Thomas, Louisa, 115
Thompson, Will, 134–35
350.org, 242
Threemile Creek, 22, 100, 113, 175, 256
Tombigbee River, 83, 159
tourism to Black history sites, 7, 188–89, 193–94, 220, 261–63, 271, 275
Toxics Release Inventory, 214–15
trade/markets: and American industry, 28; international trade in Prichard, 193–94, 199, 204; in Mobile during Civil War, 77–78; in Ouidah, 48–49; in Yorubaland, 12. *See also* economic systems; industry/manufacturing; slave trade
trucking, 222, 223–25, 274
Turner, Clara (Abache) (*Clotilda* shipmate), 80, 142, 143

Tuttle, Michael, 209, 210, 211
Twelvemile Island, 63, 83, 258

Underhill, David, 233, 234, 235, 237, 241, 245, 247, 252
Union League, 102, 104
Union Missionary Baptist Church (formerly Old Landmark Baptist Church), 100, 138, 141, 163–64, 169, 221
unions, 172–73, 213
United Confederate Veterans, 109
U.S. Department of Housing and Urban Development, 177
U.S. Navy, 79
USS *Pickering* (ship), 37

Vanderbilt University, 262
Vanderslice, Jacob, 29
Vanderslice, Martha Adalaide, 29, 70, 142
Van Nimwegen, Helen, 143
Vietnam War, 186–87
Viking Press, 155
voter fraud: accusations of, 105; by white southerners, 119, 120, 123
voting rights: in Alabama, 107, 120, 121, 123, 189–90, 216; and poll taxes, 106, 107, 120, 121; and Reconstruction, 93, 95–96. *See also* elections
Voting Rights Act (1965), 189–90, 275

Walker, Charlie, 217
Walker, LeRoy Pope, 107
Walker, Sallie (*Clotilda* shipmate), 158
Walker, William, 26
Wallace, Cassandra Lewis (1964-) (descendant of Cudjo), 168, 169, 190
Wallace, George, 6, 173, 198, 203
Wanderer (ship), 27, 28
warfare, 15–16, 17, 43–44, 186–87. *See also* Civil War
Washington, Booker T., 123, 137–39, 140
water and sewers, 126, 176–78; MAWSS (Mobile Area Water and Sewer System), 237, 238, 247
water pollution, 174–75, 215
waterways: blueway project, 5, 256–57, 262, 270; Chickasaw Creek, 33, 175, 215; danger of contamination from oil pipelines, 231–32, 233, 235, 238; Mobile River, 2, 33, 171, 182, 209, 238; Threemile Creek, 22, 100, 113, 175, 256; Tombigbee River, 83, 159
Watson, Tom, 119
Watt, James, 195
Welch, James, 33
Wertelecki, Wladimir, 250
West Africa: Cudjo's early life in, 11–16; and international trade in Prichard, 194, 199, 204; knowledge of enslavement in, 11–12. *See also* Dahomey
West African Herald, 19

West Africa Squadron of British Royal Navy, 37

Wheat, Barbara, 181, 189, 192, 193, 205, 208, 209

White, Jarrod, 243, 244, 246, 252, 272

white flight, 177, 193

white people. *See* Europeans/white men; white southerners

white southerners: and activism against oil pipeline, 237–38; and Civil War, 74–75, 88; at Cudjo's funeral, 164; and Cudjo's old age, 156–57, 163; and economic system, 102, 119–21; and Mobile's history, 273; and nostalgia for Confederacy, 109; opinion of freedpeople, 111; poor whites, 96, 107, 120, 121, 122–23; and Reconstruction, 92, 94; and segregation, 127; support of slavery by, 25, 27; white supremacy, 93–94, 119–22. *See also* Mobile, Alabama; racism

white supremacy, 93–94, 119–22. *See also* racism

white terrorist groups, 103

Whitley, Isaiah J., 137–39, 140

Whydah. *See* Ouidah

Wigfall, Shamba (*Clotilda* shipmate), 142

Williams, Christopher, 218, 219

Williams, Edward, 181–82

Williams, Henry, 181–84; and Africatown U.S.A., 203–4; and bust of Cudjo, 169–70; calling for heritage tourism, 188–89, 193–94, 208; and cemetery, 219–20; and Cochrane Bridge replacement, 200, 207; death, 221; and Diouf's book, 220–21; family, 181–82; and MCTS bell, 184–86; political activism, 181, 191–92, 222; teaching local history, 167–68, 169, 183; workshop, 183, 189, 192

Williams, R. V., 211–12

Wilson, Augusta Evans, 100

Wilson, Lorenzo, 100

Wilson, Margie Moberg, 199, 205, 206

Wilson, Shaun, 270

Womack, Annie Brown, 170–71, 223

Womack, Jesse (1948-), 170, 175, 186, 215, 245

Womack, Joe (1950-): and activism against oil developments, 234–35, 237, 239, 242, 243, 245, 246, 247, 251; on Africatown's future, 275; and Africatown's history, 2, 98, 167, 251; and Africatown's nomination to NRHP, 230; on bridge plans, 274; career, 186–87, 221, 222–23; childhood, 171–72, 176, 178–80; and *Clotilda* search, 256; education, 179–80, 186; family, 170–71, 217; giving tours of Africatown, 4–5, 251–52, 258; on MCTS bell, 184, 186; reengagement with Africatown, 221–22; speaking at DC event, 1, 3–4; and zoning, 223–25

Womack, Joe Sr., 170–71, 173

Womack, Portland, 217

women: in barracoons, 51, 52; and beginning of African Town, 88, 90; bread riot in Mobile, 77–78; female survivors of *Clotilda*, 157–60; female warriors of Dahomey, 17, 18, 40; violence against enslaved women, 74; in Yorubaland, 12, 14, 16

Woods, Lorna Gail (descendant of Charlie Lewis), 168

Woods, Martha, 114

Woods, Mary (1875-?), 114, 137, 163

Woods, Sandy, 114

Woodson, Carter G., 145, 146

Woodward, C. Vann, 109, 125

World's Fair (1893), 111

Wynn, Octavia, 158–59

Yorktown Missionary Baptist Church (Africatown), 112, 167, 200, 218, 221–22, 269

Yorubaland, 13–16, 20, 51

Yoruba language, 51, 114

zoning of property, 189–90, 200–202, 216, 223–25, 271

Zuma (Arzuma) (*Clotilda* shipmate), 51, 80, 142